Praise for *Inner Views*

"The shrewd, showboating, disarming, obsessive, funny, cranky, thoughtful, childlike, powerful characters who people these conversations rank among the most elusive specimens of American Hero. Now, David Breskin turns the camera on them, and demonstrates that the best way to make a big picture is to pay attention to the details."
—Mark Rowland, *American Film*

"An impressive book of in-depth interviews with eight of the arguably most influential contemporary American filmmakers. . . . Detailed and provoking in his questioning, Breskin brings the usually faceless figures behind the camera to life." —*Film Threat*

"Breskin's interrogations are elegant, thorough, and dogged."
—Katherine Dieckmann, *Voice Literary Supplement*

"David Breskin's collection demonstrates a skill in getting helmers to open up as few feature writers have. In *Inner Views* he presents transcripts of his conversations and there's not a bad one in the bunch. Although it is the directors who are center stage here, Breskin's technique is nothing short of amazing as he transforms himself from interview to interview, trying to get each subject to go beyond his normal canned answers. . . . *Inner Views* provides some of the best dialogue available between two covers in some time. Indeed, in some cases, they might have been better off if they had skipped the movie and filmed the interview instead." —*Variety*

2-17-98
for fiona
always ± again

INNER VIEWS
Filmmakers in Conversation
EXPANDED EDITION

David Breskin

[signature]

DA CAPO PRESS • NEW YORK

Library of Congress Cataloging-in-Publication-Data

Breskin, David.
    Inner views: filmmakers in conversation / David Breskin.—Expanded ed., 1st
Da Capo Press ed.
        p.   cm.
    "Portions of these interviews first appeared in Rolling Stone magazine between
September 1990 and September 1992"—Verso t.p.
    Includes filmographies.
    Contents: Francis Ford Coppola—David Lynch—Oliver Stone—Spike
Lee—David Cronenberg—Robert Altman—Tim Burton—Clint Eastwood.
    ISBN 0-306-80801-3 (alk. paper)
    1. Motion picture producers and directors—North America—Interviews. I.
Title.
PN1998.2.B74   1997
791.43′0233′0922—dc21   97-20013
                                                                                          CIP

First Da Capo Press edition 1997

This Da Capo Press paperback edition of *Inner Views* is an unabridged
republication of the edition published in Winchester, Massachusetts in 1992,
with the addition of a new preface, dedication, acknowledgments, and an
interview with Clint Eastwood; the filmographies have also been updated.
It is reprinted by arrangement with the author.

Portions of these interviews first appeared in *Rolling Stone* magazine between
September 1990 and September 1992.

Published by Da Capo Press, Inc.
A Subsidiary of Plenum Publishing Corporation
233 Spring Street, New York, NY 10013-1578

for Trixie, different in every frame

Preface to the Da Capo Edition

The eight directors spraying their fire and hiding in dark corners on these pages did not give these interviews to further film scholarship or to enlighten future biographers, or even to contribute to this book. They gave them to promote their then-current films in a popular national magazine. But sometimes the right thing happens for the wrong reason; and I took the opportunity to explore with them broader and deeper issues related to their lives and work, which in only a tertiary mode might be thought of as having a "publicity" value. Accordingly, I must thank them for not having excused themselves from the room as soon as they knew I had enough material to suit their purposes. The ground rules for the discussions were simple: four hours, two sessions, bare minimum. (The Clint Eastwood interview was conducted too late for inclusion in the first edition of this book.)

But why these men and not others? And why all *men*? First of all, the brief was to interview directors who work within—and perhaps push against—the bounds of commercial narrative cinema, and who each have produced a substantial body of distinct work: directors who might be thought of as auteurs within the system loosely conceived as "Hollywood." Secondly, the scheduling of interviews was pegged to up-coming releases, and such other commercial and non-commercial trivia as: Was there space in the magazine? Was the film in question antici-pated as "major" as opposed to "minor?" Could the director sit still and sincerely participate in a protracted interview? Did the director demand the cover of the magazine? Given that this was hardly a science, we didn't end up with a bad bunch. Martin Scorsese and Woody Allen, to name the two directors most conspicuous by their absence, may very well have been included if these interviews had been conducted over a slightly different period. Indeed, by the end of the series, Hollywood publicists were calling, explaining why *their* director clients should be included. They were not. But there are other directors who might naturally attain pride of place in a parallel or future collection: The Coen Brothers, Jane Campion, Quentin Tarantino, to name just three who have become more prominent since these interviews were conducted.

As to the question of sex: there's no gender bias implicit in the selection of these eight men other than that which already exists in the world of commercial cinema. The simple and quite complicated fact is that Hollywood is still a Boys Club, and that there was not at the time (still isn't) a female director with a distinctive and deep enough body of work to meet the demands of inclusion. Peggy Marshall, Barbra Streisand, Kathryn Bigelow, and Nora Ephron have done and continue to do mainstream Hollywood films with varying degrees of success, but none of them can be thought of as auteurs—with the possible exception of Streisand, and then, only comically. That there is no female director in Hollywood (or New York) occupying a position equivalent to that which Lina Wertmuller occupied in European cinema in the 1970s is sad but true. With more women now sitting in positions of power in Hollywood—executives at studios, female stars with production companies—one can hope that this will soon change. (Among young directors, Jodie Foster and Jane Campion certainly show signs of arrival.) Given this situation, and given the fraternal nature of the entire system—beginning with the semiotic certainty of the "male gaze" and ending with the cashed check for work done—I thought it only fair to inquire of these eight men as to their filmic relationship to women: their sexual politics of female representation.

Since these interviews were completed, each of the directors has gone on to do other work. The results—how could they be otherwise?—are decidedly mixed. Coppola followed the sumptuous bacchanalia of *Bram Stoker's Dracula* with the sophomoric jumble of *Jack*. David Lynch barely survived the abject failure (both commercial and aesthetic) of *Twin Peaks: Fire Walk With Me*, only to surface five years later with the even creepier, more postmodern *Lost Highway*, a movie which consistently denies and defeats expectations of narrative coherence, and does so under the umbrella of the most beautiful lighting, framing, editing, art directing, and music imaginable. (The movie feels like a war wound in a silk dress.) Meanwhile, Oliver Stone, as is his wont, has been marking territory: he makes movies the way lions patrol the Serengeti. The *cause célèbre* conspiracy conflation of *JFK* gave way to his final nail in the Vietnam coffin, *Heaven & Earth*, which gave way to the speedfreak over-the-top "satire" of *Natural Born Killers*, which gave way to the impeachably heavy-handed *Nixon*, in which he nonetheless and true-to-form coaxed compelling performances from all his major players. Spike Lee retreated from the grand designs and very real achievement of *Malcolm X* into a kind of stylistically calcified marginalia: *Crooklyn, Clockers, Girl 6, Get on the Bus*.

David Cronenberg went terribly wrong with *M. Butterfly*—a film about sexual identity that figured to be right up his warped alley—but which he somehow managed to make simultaneously dull *and* icky. *Crash*, to the disapproval of distributor Ted Turner and moral guardians everywhere, marked a ferocious return to form and content. Robert Altman followed the bubbly success of *The Player* with the relentlessly superficial *Ready to Wear* (making a superficial film about fashion displays the imitative fallacy in all its glory), and then mucked up jazz in *Kansas City*. Tim Burton, veering further towards the shoulder of the road and the eroding cliff (out where he likes it), made the wonderfully sly *Ed Wood*, in living black-and-white, and then cooked up his own Ed Wood movie on a filet mignon budget, *Mars Attacks!*, the darkest (and most self-destructive?) spoof to come down the superhighway of Hollywood filmmaking in years. (If you "read" the Martians as studio executives, the picture is much funnier than otherwise.) Lastly, Clint Eastwood has churned out three pieces since his Oscar-winning landmark, *Unforgiven*: the quietly downbeat *A Perfect World*, the absolutely forgettable *Absolute Power*, and the gooey romance of *The Bridges of Madison County*, where he attempts to take the best-selling novel equivalent of a corny pop song and *redeem* it—as do the jazz artists he loves so much—simply through sophistication of performance and depth of interpretation. He almost succeeds. Unfortunately, as fellow pianist Joe Zawinul once said, "You can't polish a turd."

In any event, interviews can be read backward with a biographical bias, and they can be read forward as promises or predictors of future triumph and failure. Either way, as compendiums of character, as vehicles for revelation and disguise, they provide a historical record: something more than publicity and propaganda in an age which valorizes both, and something resembling the plain but not-so-simple truths of how these artists view themselves and their work, the world and their odd place in it.

—DAVID BRESKIN
San Francisco
March 1997

Acknowledgments

Many thanks to Yuval Taylor, my editor at Da Capo, for hustling this book back into the dark of print. Also thanks to Edward Dimendberg, film editor at University of California Press, for giving me the Glengarry lead; Mark Fox, of BlackDog, for clarity in Bulls' colors; Hiroshi Sugimoto for visual inspiration; movie partners Steven James and Caroline Herter for the stubs; Don and Barbara, who lugged me then let me go; The House of Rosemary, Sophia and Ro for the el ay hospitality; Daisy, for being the world's greatest flying spanoodle; and the one and only Isabel, for Sunday nights at the Lumiere and the Kabuki and steamy Indian action-musical matinees in Kashmir.

CONTENTS

1
FRANCIS COPPOLA

FRANCIS COPPOLA FILMOGRAPHY

1961	Tonight for Sure
1962	Bellboy & the Playgirls
1963	Dementia 13
1967	You're a Big Boy Now
1968	Finian's Rainbow
1969	The Rain People
1972	The Godfather
1974	The Conversation
1974	The Godfather, Part II
1979	Apocalypse Now
1982	One from the Heart
1983	The Outsiders
1983	Rumble Fish
1984	The Cotton Club
1986	Captain Eo (short)
1986	Peggy Sue Got Married
1987	Gardens of Stone
1988	Tucker, the Man and His Dream
1989	Life Without Zoe (episode of New York Stories)
1990	The Godfather, Part III
1992	Bram Stoker's Dracula
1996	Jack

for television
| 1985 | Rip Van Winkle (Faerie Tale Theater) |

as screenwriter only
1966	This Property Is Condemned
1966	Is Paris Burning?
1967	Reflections in a Golden Eye
1970	Patton
1974	The Great Gatsby

as producer only
| 1971 | THX 1138 |
| 1973 | American Graffiti |

Francis Coppola

Throughout the 1970s, Francis Ford Coppola was the heir apparent to Orson Welles. He wrote like a devilish angel. He directed marvelously complicated, challenging pictures. He became an impresario and produced interesting work for others. He had *control*—control of opera and theatre and radio and publishing; control of sound stages and vineyards and distributors and high-tech gizmos he could only fantasize about as a child; and control of his own studio, Zoetrope. Even in his days as an undergrad phenomenon in the drama department of Hofstra University and then at the film school of UCLA, Coppola had been impulsive and inspired, a magnetic personality.

He started by making little sex films (called "nudies" at the time) just to get work, to get film in the can, but his first real opportunity came from Roger Corman, for whom he would write and direct a trashy formula horror film, *Dementia 13*. Already, a Coppola trademark was apparent: the picture reeked of family dynamics—specifically, fraternal tension. Four films very much of the 1960s followed: a zany coming-of-age story, *You're a Big Boy Now*, which Coppola wrote, produced, and directed at age twenty-seven; an awkward attempt at a musical, *Finian's Rainbow;* and a provocative, improvisational road picture, *The Rain People*, which found Coppola working with George Lucas, James Caan, and Robert Duvall for the first time. His screenplay for *Patton*, announcing his obsession with power and his finely tuned perceptions of it, won an Oscar the following year. Clearly, Coppola was emerging as a force.

But nothing could have prepared his audience for the work that followed. *The Godfather, The Conversation, The Godfather, Part II,* and at least the first three-fourths of *Apocalypse Now* represented the highest level of cinema art. Storytelling that was classic and yet inventive, subject matter that was broadly important and yet passionately personal, a dazzling command of craft that worked in service of great performances instead of swallowing them—these were the touchstones of Coppola's 1970s work. At its best, it had the power of myth and the depth of great literature: it was rich. And so, once the box office receipts for the *Godfather*s had been counted, was he.

3

But his agonizing, protracted experience making *Apocalypse Now* in the Philippine jungle left him emotionally and artistically rudderless. Somehow, he emerged from that jungle and that film as part Citizen Kane, part Colonel Kurtz, and in no shape to oversee the running of a studio whose assets teetered precariously upon the success of a little love story musical which Coppola had perversely turned into an audacious formal and technological experiment. *One from the Heart* felt like one from the lab, and laid an egg of such gigantic proportions that Coppola would spend most of the 1980s scrambling it, just to regain his footing. He worked on small projects, some of which *(Rumble Fish* and *Rip Van Winkle)* were interesting as stylistic flights of fancy, and some of which *(The Outsiders)* were simply dull. And he worked as a director-for-hire: on modest successes, like *Peggy Sue Got Married,* and on expensive wrecks, like *The Cotton Club.* Even his return to personal subject matter – the family – in his *Life Without Zoe* proved a well-deserved embarrassment.

By the end of the 1980s, Coppola seemed an irrelevancy: serious people didn't care enough about his movies to argue about them, or even see them. Indeed, in that decade of disappointment and disaster, Francis Coppola lost his studio and his audience and his fortune; lost his artistic instincts and his confidence; and lost, above all, a son. His oldest boy, Gio, was killed in a boating accident just as Coppola began shooting *Gardens of Stone,* a film set in a cemetery. But one thing Coppola never lost was his desire to make art.

Unfortunately, given his position as a rusted boy wonder, he had to make more than art: he had to make commerce. *The Godfather, Part III* represented his bid for both financial and artistic redemption, his ticket to the third act of his own life. With the film released on Christmas Day of 1990 to the riotous orgy of opinion that *Godfather* movies have always provoked (the first two pictures, now acknowledged as masterworks, in fact opened to widely mixed notices), Coppola found himself with an uncomfortably sharp stone in his shoe. The casting and performance of his daughter Sofia, in one of the film's key roles, had provoked a barrage of criticism. That Coppola would risk so much on family – for family – says everything about a man for whom the border between life and art long ago collapsed.

I talked with him about such matters in November of 1990, just a month and a half before the release of *Godfather III,* in the penthouse office/bedroom of the building he owns in San Francisco. Coppola was gracious and soft-spoken, and, at first, defensive. Eventually, over the course of five hours in two days, he breached his own battlements and revealed some kinds of emotional truths, making the interview, if not definitive, at least one from the heart.

SESSION ONE

In Godfather II, *consigliere Tom Hagen, upon finding the dead prostitute, says, "The girl has no family. It's as if she didn't exist." And he repeats it, like a mantra. It's one sign of the centrality of family in your work—that family is how you do exist—so I'd like you to start by talking about yours.*

Well, I was born in 1939 and raised in a second-generation Italian American family, so my infant memories of World War II and that era were the first things to consider. Also, because my father was a musician, we traveled a lot. It was my father's gypsy nature not to stay in any one place too long. We were always moving—we thought in regard to his career, but really it was his nature.

Our moving every year and the many schools I went to because of it tended to let me encapsulate time differently. Because when I was five there was one set of friends and impressions, and that was very, very radically changed each time we moved. In some way it allowed me to remember things in a much more vivid way than kids who are just raised in one neighborhood. I went to twenty-five different schools before college. Each one was a little episode of my life—ages four, and five, and six, and seven—like a separate movie with a separate cast of characters. My childhood, and my memories of my childhood, have always remained very vital to me and very accessible. I may have only been in a particular neighborhood for six months, but I still remember what the pretty girl's name was and what the bad boy's name was. Those memories are more vivid for me than for other people, who are always amazed that I can remember this stuff.

We were a family of five. An older brother five years older [Augie] and a younger sister six years younger [Talia Shire]. My mother [Italia] was an extremely good-looking woman and my father [Carmine] was very handsome, and in a glamorous profession—I saw him dress in a tuxedo. My initial memories of them were very idealized and very full of love. My brother was very nice to me, and we had all sorts of uncles and aunts in that sort of second-generation Italian family.

My first impression of family was that it was very much like a fairy tale. And we were taught that Italians had great culture: that Meucci invented the telephone, and Fermi the first nuclear reactor, and Verdi, and so on. And my father was the solo flute player for Toscanini. So there was always an element of glamor and romance to my family, and to this day, if I do gravitate to them or they are the wellspring of my fondness, it's because from when I was a little kid, they were.

Yet there was a lot of tension there as well. Your father dominated the scene, and there was always the risk that he was failing or would fail. He was dissatisfied as an artist even if he was at a fairly high level.

He was at a high level as an instrumentalist, but in those days it wasn't like today, where a virtuoso flute player is on records and is a celebrity. He always had ambitions to write music and write songs, to do Broadway, to conduct opera. He longed for recognition in areas other than playing the flute. So he weaned himself off of that nice comfortable career as a symphonic instrumentalist and started to branch off into other areas. One was movies. In fact, when I was born he had just gotten back from Hollywood. He'd been there a couple of years and had tried to get started as a film scorer, making connections. There was a phone call from some musician friends—he heard that he was being fired off of his job—and so rather than deal with people thinking that he might have gotten fired, he left Hollywood and drove across the country to Detroit, and that's why I was born there. So that was the flavor of the kind of family it was.

Was his level of frustration, what he perceived as his failure, painful for you?

Oh yeah. Yeah. Literally, when we said our prayers, at the end we said, " . . . and give Daddy his break." Even before I knew what "his break" was. I thought it was the brake of the car! The way they saw things, getting your break was political—it was who you knew. Even to this day, I take great exception to this attitude. I always felt it was your talent and your willingness to keep working: if no one will hire you to do a play, then go do the play yourself anyway. A glancing difference between my father and me is that I feel talent can be realized by hard work and imaginative application. It's not politics, it's not who you know.

It's sort of ironic that he got his big break scoring your movies—he did know you.

[Laughs.] I know. We were very involved in my father's talent. That was the focus of our family. If I went to school and said my father was a soloist for Toscanini, people thought I was special, even though I was new in the neighborhood.

He, during a very black period, threatened to put his hands into the lawn mower in your back yard.

No. He, during a period, had an accident. He was mowing the lawn and was stupidly adjusting the mower and cut off the tips of his fingers. We took him immediately for plastic surgery, which he needed to keep playing the flute. I, later, always thought what a Freudian thing that was: that a man who *hated* the instrument, who thought the instrument had held him back, who resented it, had done that.

You idolized your older brother, Augie [Nicolas Cage's father]. He was older than you, better looking, smarter, more successful socially—but wasn't it hard not to resent him for that?

But he was always so kind to me. And so affectionate. And so generous. He didn't have to take me to the movies, and introduce me to his friends. He was such a good older brother. Rather than be competitive with him, I just wanted to be like him. So my impression of my brother was always very golden. If anything, I was more concerned that one day I would have to look out for him. I didn't want the bad kids to beat him up, so there was anxiety on that level.

There's a real sense of fraternal dynamics in your work—in even your first film, Dementia 13, *through the* Godfathers, *to the Tulsa films—The Outsiders and* Rumble Fish. *By the time of* Rumble Fish, *dedicated to "Augie, brother and best teacher," there's a sense that the younger brother has to make his own mark, and throw off the influence of the older.*

Well, you know, I'm sure that I cannot give a clear picture of it. I can only tell you from my feeling. If my father wrote some music and people insulted it, it would really *hurt* me. If anything happened to my brother—he was always full of great schemes, he was like an Errol Flynn guy—my feeling was always not to get past him but to protect him, and to be like him.

I had a dream when I was a little kid. It was so vivid that I never forgot it. The bad kids were putting my brother in a big manhole, and I was running to all the houses to get the phone. They were going to cover him.

He was like a hero to me. And when I got a little older, more adolescent, he was so kind: he would tell me about life, about sex—which my family pretended didn't exist; if you asked a question, you'd get hit—or he would tell me about books, or how to dress and be attractive to girls. And he would share his dreams with me, his crazy inventions. And I was trying to copy him. He would encourage me. He liked the fact that I was good at drama because I was sort of the black sheep of the family—they didn't know what kind of profession I would go into. They would say I wasn't college material. He would always stick up for me.

Augie has said that you've often regretted your successes, because they were meant for him.

Without a doubt.

So that must have given a really bittersweet twist to the successes you've had.

Definitely bittersweet. Augie's always on the verge of some incredible success. I think he got trapped in the academic world, getting the Ph.D. It was a practical thing. He was the first one to get one in our family, but like for many people the academic world was a ticket to nowhere. I was lucky to get into drama, and when you do it for so many years you become expert at it.

Yeah, but Francis, a lot of people get into drama and don't do what you did—

But he had all the same ingredients that I did. A lot of feeling, strong feelings, a lot of imagination and ideas. Willingness to work hard. He has all that. He just hasn't found his niche—yet. But *he* was the prototype, the one who first looked towards creative literature, philosophy. Things I would have had no way to know, I knew because I had an older brother.

You did something odd when you were fourteen, when you were working at Western Union that summer. You knew how much your father wanted "his break" from Hollywood, how much success meant to him, and yet you sent him a fraudulent telegram from Paramount Pictures telling him he'd been selected to score some big movie.

It's a true story. I delivered the telegram. And it was only after doing it and seeing how happy he was that we were going to go back to California, that I began to sweat, and realized, "My God, how am I going to tell him?" And I told him and he was very disappointed. I thought I could just give him his break. Kids are sensitive to what's wrong with their parents. And I wanted my father to get that telegram, and I wanted my family to get that telegram, so that he would be happy and we would be happy.

But you knew it wasn't real—

That's the madness of it. It's sick.

Wasn't the madness really anger under the surface of the wish? Anger that your dad and his "talent" were always the focus of attention and that you were not considered as talented as him or Augie?

I never had a big competitive thing. I just wanted to be accepted by them. I never had those kind of needs to be a famous person. I don't think there was any anger connected to it, because for me, my ambition was more to have a year's subscription to *Popular Mechanics*. I wanted to be a scientist or an inventor.

We're going to cut to the record, Francis. When you were nine, you wrote your mother a note that said, "Dear Mommy, I want to be rich and famous. I'm so discouraged. I don't think it will come true."

She has that note. I think I was older, and already pursuing the drama and show-business world. I always felt I had a lot of gifts, but that my gifts were somehow not easily showable. I always felt I had a lot of stuff in my heart, but that I didn't have the skills or the obvious talents of kids who can play an instrument, tap dance, or draw. I always felt like I had a little vein of gold, and that if I could follow it further down I'd find a deposit of it. But I was not good at anything, except science. I always felt I put in a lot of perspiration, rather than had a God-given gift.

But I feel you can have a person with a God-given gift and a person that works hard, and in the end the person that works hard can make the more profound art. I love the fact that in art, you can see a turkey actor and five years later you see him and think, "God, what happened?"

Life happened.

Yeah. And I've seen that happen. The most talented guy in high school is inevitably the failure at the reunion. And there are reasons for this.

You had polio and were paralyzed for a year when you were ten, and described yourself as "a lonely ugly duckling, sad and sick and thinking." How much of that kid do you still carry around, or did you carry in your formative artistic years?

Well, I would say that my childhood years are very vividly what I'm like now. And what happened after that didn't make much of a difference. Polio, and the fact that I was the new kid in school every year, and that my name was Francis, which was a girl's name. And I was very skinny, and looked like Ichabod, gangly. And I had a very big lower lip—which was the bane of my life, my lower lip. Of everything, the thing most profound to me is the shape of my lower lip. Everything that happened came from this condition.

And in 1949 I was struck with polio, taken out of school, and didn't see another kid except my sister. Sitting in that room paralyzed, watching television, listening to the radio, playing with my puppets, cultivating a kind of make-believe private life, augmented by technology. I became obsessed with remote control. Obviously, if you're paralyzed, how to turn the channel of the TV is very important.

Do you ever think now, sitting off the set in the Silverfish [Coppola's high-tech Airstream trailer, from which he monitors the shooting], that the idea of "remote" and the idea of "control" have been realized in a quite substantial, quite personal way?

There's no doubt that it goes back to that year I spent in bed, looking at a monitor, listening to radio. I spent a lot of time with my puppets; I became quite a puppeteer. I'm sure that my taste for this kind of work, and also the position of the director—and how *I* am the director sometimes, being this person doing it all by remote control—probably comes from something I was comfortable with as a kid.

You also had fantasies about listening in to other people's conversations elsewhere in the house.

Not so much a fantasy. We did bug the bathroom one time. That was all from my idea of Captain Video, high atop a mountain, fighting for Good, using Modern Technology! I was very susceptible to those stories. I wanted to be Captain Video. I wanted to have a TV studio. And not long after I recovered from polio I went down to our basement and I built out of wood the sound booms and the television cameras and a window, where you could "play" television. I was crazy about television.

I always lived in my fantasy life. I felt like an outsider at school. I'd get tremendous crushes on girls that I didn't ever get to talk to. You would see her, but you wouldn't have the wherewithal to meet her. So I lived a tremendous fantasy life, all my life. And I still do. [Pause.] I spend most of my time by myself. And I do the same kinds of things I used to do: I play with the technology, I edit, I make believe, I write and read. The same things I did in the garage.

Was there a Rosebud in your youth—something unrecoverable? A feeling that you've never been able to aquire again?

I would really say that the five-year-old Francis, who was the *best* Francis that there ever was, is still here, intact, whenever I choose to be comfortable with that. I do still approach things with that enthusiasm. And in a man, the line between enthusiasm and megalomania is very blurry. Is that person just enthusiastic about what he's doing, or . . . ? During the *Apocalypse Now* period, I was identified as a megalomaniac.

But I think that I was able to retain a young kid's point of view with an older man's experience and, hopefully, emotional togetherness. But very much I can be that little kid I remember. If all kids could start that way, they would make better people.

You've talked about the advantages of being successful early in life, but I get the feeling you never sat too easy in the saddle of your own success.

Well, it doesn't ever seem that when you make films that are real famous, or that become part of the culture, you really think of them so possessively as "my film." You're well aware of what collaboration it took, and how many people put how much into those pictures. I don't believe truly that I'm a person who's so interested in my own aggrandizement. I want to be *part* of something exciting. I do feel I'm an element in this creation, and that I'm playing a part of it. But when you do something really beautiful, it does reflect what's already there. I feel like we're more the custodians of this art form. Some guy wakes up in the middle of the night and he hears a tune. Did he *make* that tune, or was he made to be sensitive enough to hear it?

My proudest thing, if people were really going to butter me up—if they said I was a person who was *imaginative*, I'd like that. Because I feel I am. If they say I had ideas, I'd like that. Or that I like to work with kids. But to say that you're so good at something—fumbling through it, obviously, I don't see it that way. I always chastise my father: What is this ego thing of yours? You're just part of this whole thing. Why are you so obsessed when someone says, "Oh, I love that music"? Sure, it's nice to be connected with something that's successful, but why is it such a cause célèbre? He's always been that way.

But earlier in your career—you were a very ambitious, very driven man—you felt like the greatest thing around if people liked a picture, and an abject failure if they didn't.

Very much so. Over the years, I've had people like my stuff and not like my stuff. More not like my stuff, in truth. In its time, when my stuff comes out, even *The Godfather*, and certainly *Godfather II*, and certainly *Apocalypse Now*, in their time, *inevitably* they're not received very well. I think it's because they're a little different. My impression is I'm always sweating an uphill thing, trying to convince the powers that be (if there are powers that be) to kind of come in my direction.

So, in terms of my ego, at age fifty-one, as someone who's been around a long time, I'm aware that people regard me as a venerable old grandpa, and I *like* that. Like Leonard Bernstein. He wasn't stuck-up about his abilities. I've had such a backward and forward controversial reception, and very often related to other stuff than what I was actually doing. And I really have taken myself off the market in terms of ever really being gratified, in the way I saw, let's say, Peter Bogdanovich gratified once when I went to see the L.A. screening of *The Last Picture Show*. I remember that very vividly. Boy, that audience saw that picture, and that audience was *with* that picture in such a fabulous way that when it was over, everybody in that theatre, including myself, stood up and gave him a standing ovation. It was thrilling to be there. But I've never experienced anything like that. Except once, when I did a college play, the cast gave me an ovation like that. But never again since. And I sort of have reconciled that that will never happen to me, except maybe when I'm eighty years old and they trudge me out to give me some humanitarian award. In other words, I have taken myself "off the hook" on a number of issues that young people fantasize about. And that's one of them.

Was your son Gio's death a part of taking yourself off the hook, in a way?

Well, sure, but I'm not sure I even totally understand that event, because I've never been able to look at it in front of my eyes. I always look at it this way. [Looks out of the corners of his eyes.] And as the years go by, I realize I don't want to look at it.

After that, I realized that no matter what happened, I had *lost*. That no matter what happened, it would always be incomplete. The next day, I could have all my fondest dreams come true: someone could give me Paramount Pictures to organize the way I would do it, and develop talent and technology, and have my dream of dream of dream of dreams, and even if I did get it, I lost already. There's no way that I could ever have a complete experience, because there will always be that part of me missing. It makes you react to things with more of a shrug. If you told me that people saw *Godfather III* and they thought it was the greatest thing since chopped liver, and for the first time in ten years I can go out and buy a car without figuring out how I'm going to pay for it, I would be happy, I would be happy, but in the end it would make me sad.

Right now, listening to you, you seem like a very different man from the one who said, just before going into the jungle to film Apocalypse Now, *"I know more about every aspect of filmmaking than any other filmmaker in the world, and that's not a boast."*

Yeah. But I still might say that, though, only because the areas I'm in are so diverse. But that's not to say I'm the best filmmaker in the world, or know more about filmmaking, but in terms of *every aspect* of filmmaking—from orchestration to foreign deals, to running your own company, to understanding how electronic editing really works—yeah, I have an extremely broad and comprehensive view of this profession I'm in. The accident of my makeup: that I come from theatre, that I was a boy scientist, that my father was a musician, and I had some business and political smarts, may make that statement very true—although it may sound like that of a megalomaniac.

If Godfather III *is a great success, would it make you sad?*

No. It's just that anything that makes me happy is always followed by a footnote of being sad. Because what I really wish could happen is already gone. I could lose Hollywood General Studios, where I had so many dreams, and I could buy it back in two years—probably will—but somehow I haven't quite figured out how I could restore these other parts of my life. You can see a picture of my two kids, Roman and Sofia, taken after that accident happened, and it's a picture of *three* kids. Because you can see on their faces the one that's missing. But all human beings run into tragedy. You're going to run into it, if you already haven't, and I'm going to run into it again. We're all going to lose people we love. It's a little harder when it's your child, more than your uncle or your grandpa, your wife or your husband. I try to understand: that's what makes us human beings. Would you rather be a rock? Would you rather not have those feelings? That's why tragedy is such an exalted art form.

Once the trauma wears off, you never experience the world again in quite the same way.

Aeschylus said something really beautiful, something like, "This thing pours on your heart, drop by drop, until in awful grace of God comes wisdom." In a way, you can't experience things in a bigger, deeper way, until you understand or have some tragedy.

I was always a magical kid. All I had to do was say a Hail Mary and it would come true. That story Fredo tells in *Godfather II* – every time you say Hail Mary you catch a fish – that was me! I once caught twenty-two fish because I said twenty-two Hail Marys. And then all of a sudden you say the Hail Mary and it doesn't work, in the most profound sense you could imagine. It just makes you realize that being a human being is not to have everything go the way a child wants it to go.

In a sense, losing a kid like that, that particular kid, the relationship we had, it will just be my story. [Pauses, teary.] I always was shocked that Odysseus comes back and his son, Telemachus, rejoins him, and I didn't know that in the next chapters Telemachus is killed. Oh! You never told me that! It gives it another slant. It's your stripes for being a human being. You have to welcome it, understand it in the bigger sense of things. And of course, I have two great kids, and we all share the vitality of that boy, and in some funny way he still figures into things; he's still around in a magical way. He was a magical kid. We got him for so many years. And for the twenty-two years he lived he had a complete life; someone could live eighty years and not do what he did. It's not like I'm a *broken* guy. But in a way, there's always going to be that arm missing. It'll never come back, I guess.

If it takes the edge of the successes, perhaps it also might take the edge off the failures you'll no doubt encounter – they might not be as devastating from now on.

I'm less interested in successes or failures, quite frankly, at all. The thing about the failures: I still have that new-kid-school thing, I hate to be embarrassed. It's very embarrassing to be taken to task all the time in the newspapers, and all your neighbors see it and they don't want to bring it up. I never have been such a megalomaniac that it is not very easy to hurt my feelings. And sometimes they are hurt by the dumbest things that are not important. Like a promise was made to someone, and that person thinks I broke the promise – and that person is of no importance whatsoever! – but it'll bother me for a week that that person feels I broke the promise. The capacity to have my feelings hurt, to feel unfairly characterized, or dealt with, those things can really get me depressed. But to consider that I'm not the greatest filmmaker in the world, well, I never particularly expected to be, nor do I care. I don't have to be the big guy all the time. I have had my share of that, anyway.

You told your British biographer that you were "embarrassed by the duality of your failure and your success." What's to be embarrassed about?

Well, you have someone telling you how great you are, and you accept that, and then you barely walk out of the room and you have someone telling you what a jerk you are. If they wouldn't tell me that I'm so great, and they wouldn't tell me that I'm so terrible, it would be easier to navigate. I never know what's coming from whatever quarter. I never know when someone's going to embarrass me and make me feel just awful. It's embarrassing when someone calls me a genius. What is that? I would like it if it meant I was a unique person, one of a kind, but I don't particularly want to be that.

Is this one of the reasons you've threatened to leave Hollywood filmmaking? From your second feature on, in 1967, you've been threatening to go make cheap little "amateur" movies on your own.

My happiest thing is to be cozy. Just to have a little place, to have my own thing, a little shop. It could be opulent, but it would always be cozy. And I would like my career to be cozy. I envy people like Woody Allen, who has found a way to function: he writes a script every year, he makes a movie every year, and people find it interesting.

That seems to have been your ideal about the time you were making The Rain People *in the late sixties.*

I wanted that. And if anything, I got off on the other tack, because like my father I was flexible. I could be an arranger, I could conduct an opera. If you think about my movies, every one is a different style entirely. And some are big, mammoth productions and some are little, intimate things. Some are comedies. I'm sort of a professional director. But I'm also a writer who would like to use his writing to explore personal feelings and subjects that interest me. I'm tempted to go off and do different things, rather than staying there like Woody and just knocking out my personal script. I've always been uncomfortable about that, and in fact I didn't do what I really wanted to do. My flexibility worked against the coziness I was trying to find.

There was financial need, too! When you took the first Godfather *film, you said, "I don't want to do this hunk of trash, I want to do art films."*

Totally! Yeah, I wanted to do little Antonioni films, little Fellini films, and get my own theatre company and do experimental writing. All cozy and off to the side. I never planned on being part of the big stuff. I never imagined it.

When you were at the top, after the second Godfather *movie, you announced that your biggest fear was that your talent wasn't commensurate with your success.*

I have a certain personality. I have a certain talent. Do I have as much talent as Roman Polanski? No. But maybe my talent isn't just "talent," but also application, broadness of point of view. Talent is like electricity, it's a hard thing to talk about.

Weren't there times, at the height of your success, when you wondered, "Is this me?" It happened in such a hurry.

I was the first one! It wasn't like Hollywood was filled with young people. There had been Orson Welles, the boy wonder, who was an example for everyone. But generally, the motion picture industry was closed—men in their fifties who had worked in the studio system. So for me, not only was I one of the first young people in a generation that had fallen in love with film, but I also was one of the first young people to become rich overnight. And my attitude towards money was, you know, I wasn't in London with models, gambling, I was buying cameras and I was buying radio stations and I was starting magazines. I was ahead of my time in a way. I was interested in the communication age. What was my dream here, in San Francisco, twenty years ago? I bought this building, a radio station, a theatre, a magazine, a film company. Of course, I was seeing one day where there'd be a production that could be written for the theatre, broadcast simultaneously on radio, that would become the basis of a screenplay, that would be in the magazine, and then become a film. I was already thinking about the kind of communications company that these guys are supposedly thinking about now, except I was doing it. And I was greeted with general resistance: who is this megalomaniac and what is he doing?

Well, it didn't help that you'd compared yourself to Napoleon when you talked about power.

Yeah, but you can compare yourself to Hitler—

Which you also did!

I know. The fact is you learn from these people. When I talk about the fact that Napoleon was a person who understood that artillery was power in his time, and communications is power in our time, it's because I was the kind of person that read all those stories of Napoleon, Caesar—those people. I tried to learn. It didn't mean that I'm Napoleon, or that I'm Hitler by any means, but we do use the people who are the prime movers in the culture to inspire us. People confused the enthusiasm and the sincerity of what I was doing with megalomania. God, how many filmmakers who have made money have put any of that money into their love? George Lucas, that's it. And why George Lucas? Because he is my younger brother in a way, and so George did a lot of things that we cooked up together. I don't see any of these other fortunes going into anything other than hard securities.

What is money to me and what is position? What would I do if I had the power-of-powers in the film industry in terms of money and influence? You *know* what I would do. I would try to use it to create a situation where this artistic activity could go on, and young people and technology would be constantly advancing. Now it's people saying: let's make movies that have incredible chase scenes, that have violence, let's make *Die Hard*. That's not coming out of young men and women involved in something *alive*. That's not alive.

Were you comfortable with all the money when you made it?

Well, I had it and then I spent it. I spent it the next day on the things that I loved.

But sometimes people who aren't comfortable with money find ways to get rid of it. They give it away, lose it all on some speculative venture, gamble. You were criticized heavily by your film school peers for "selling out," becoming instantly successful in mainstream Hollywood—and maybe it was hard not to internalize that criticism.

I think it has to do with these things that are so important to people: talent, attractiveness, beauty. So many people, especially younger people, go through private hells over these things. There wouldn't be the industry in cosmetics if it wasn't so. The truth of the matter is, I learned around thirty-seven, forty years old, around *Apocalypse Now*, the answer to the question: Was I talented? The answer came to me in one moment, and the answer was: No, I wasn't talented in the way I defined talent. I didn't have the God-given ability to sit down and write a beautifully written story or just draw a gorgeous picture. That kind of talent, Mozart's talent, I didn't have. But that's not the only kind of talent there is! That's easy, apparent talent. That's Roman Polanski's talent.

But there's another kind of talent which you don't even know that you have. A lot of the things a filmmaker does—don't have the girl do that there, let's have the violin do this—he doesn't even think he's doing anything, but in fact he is asserting his personality, even though it's not in that flashy kind of way that defines talent.

Wasn't that a comedown for you, though? From very early on, you had identified with the talent of great philosphers and writers, the people Augie had introduced you to, the James Joyces and the Thomas Manns—and you wanted to be an original writer in that way. You said, "I am a writer who directs."

That's what I still want.

But what you're saying is that during Apocalypse Now *you found out that that wasn't exactly the case. That maybe your strengths were more adaptive, more interpretive—*

I didn't say adaptive, and maybe not interpretive. But that the concept of talent, the flow of imagination, meant maybe not being able to draw the perfect picture in one stroke, but to draw it fifty times, and finally say, that is right! That's also talent, but of a different kind. It comes in the form of instinct, hard work, perspiration. I realized, after so many years of worrying that I didn't have any talent, that I *did* have talent, it's just that talent itself is different than I thought it was. It's related to your very instincts, your very personality. There is nothing that I touched that I didn't in some way imbue with my style. So, of course I felt bad at not living up to my own expectations, or feeling like I didn't have the kind of gifts I saw others have. But then others don't have the kind of gifts I have.

It's like attractiveness. So many people are told that if they don't look like some kind of prototype in a magazine, they're not attractive. But then they realize that they really are attractive, because they're *them*. It was that kind of a realization.

Did that realization solve the crisis of confidence you were having?

I think from that moment on . . . when I was in the middle of *Apocalypse,* biggest problem I'd ever had—it came to me one afternoon. Yes, I was talented. Just as I was attractive. But I didn't fit my own profile of what talented and attractive was.

What triggered this?

Some of the turning points that were going on at that time. I was very crestfallen that during *Apocalypse Now* America didn't see me as "Francis Coppola, the American director, on an expedition for *America.*" I wanted to be thought of as American, and that America would be proud that, if I had $30 million of my own money, I would fearlessly invest it in a movie that had serious themes. And I was so destroyed when I saw the perception of me in the press as a wild man, ridiculing what I was doing. In those days, if a movie cost $30 million, much ado was made of it. But there were a lot of movies that cost that much—the film industry had changed. And I was just crushed that they ridiculed *Apocalypse* because it seemed to be an out-of-control financial boondoggle, and yet for *Superman,* which cost much more than *Apocalypse* and was about nothing, there was respect.

I realized that being really respected in this culture is not about being courageous and having imaginative ideas, but it's about being financially successful. I mean, the real decision on *Godfather III,* about how good that movie really is, will be made on the basis of how much money it makes. It's sad.

We're living in an age where box-office grosses are printed in the daily papers.

Why is that? Because people are more comfortable with sports. They want a score. A batting average. It will be announced soon that I'm taking steroids.

It tells you to go to the number-one-grossing movie because more other people are.

And don't go to the number-six-grossing movie, which really has value. It's such a disservice, this new attitude of scores, of grosses, in the paper. Even the obsession with how much a movie costs. When you start to make a movie, really, ninety-nine percent of what people want to talk to you about is how much it costs.

Why do you feel people were rooting for you to fail with Apocalypse Now?

Because I had had a big success with *The Godfather,* and then I tempted fate and had another success with *Godfather II.* That's enough. That's *enough.* Look at David Lynch. Here's this guy, a real artist, totally on his own wavelength, and already I read articles sniping at the guy, just because he's been successful. We should be proud of David Lynch! I'm proud of him.

Some people felt that you came back from Apocalypse Now *thinking for the first time in your life that you were a genius, and that you haven't been the same ever since.*

How can someone think that? Never in my life have I even wandered on the threshold of thinking of myself in those terms. When I came back from *Apocalypse* I was really depressed. And rather than thinking that I was a genius, I was thinking that I was in trouble, and that the film wasn't working and I wasn't sure how I was going to make it work. It was a time in my life I was having a little bit of marital problems and that made me really depressed.

Was it painful to you that your marital problems became as public as they did? That your wife, Eleanor, published her journal?

More I would have to say that it was all a state of confusion for me. I was very frightened: I had taken all the money I had, $30 million, and had it all riding on this mad project. Two, I realized that I was starting to be portrayed as a megalomaniac surrounded by "yes men," when in fact that's never been what this company has been. Never. This portrait of me as this Hollywood executive gone mad à la *The Bad and the Beautiful* is so easy to say: I had my own studio and things were moving fast. You have to remember that we were in terrible shape financially. Even *One from the Heart* was just to get one more deal going in case we lost all our money on *Apocalypse.* So it was frenetic. We had such lofty ambitions. So people chose to see me as this guy going mad, but I don't think it was ever like that.

To be fair though, you yourself said that during Apocalypse *you had turned a bit into Kurtz, although you said you were a "nice Kurtz."*

Yeah, but by being Kurtz, I started to get the idea that life was made up of a million things that are most important to you, which are usually around the corner. What's going to happen to the film? What do they think of me

in the United States? No one likes to be ridiculed. But what's *really* important to you is whether you've got the glass you like, the toothbrush you like,
do you have a window to look out of where you like what you see. So I became like Kurtz because I became very cozy in this little place, and began
to be more obsessed with the details of life that touched me. So I would send
home and say I'd like a certain kind of glass sent over—

*And air conditioners and steaks, and it led to Eleanor saying you were setting
up your own little Vietnam over there.*

No, that isn't the case. It wasn't steaks and air conditioners, but it was a good
hi-fi preamplifier. My feeling was that if I had to be in this jungle situation,
it would be nice to have the glass that I like. People are always quick to fill
in the blanks when you're acting supposedly irrationally, but if you really
think about it—if I were to take you with me and say, "Here's my little house,
and here's where I want the loudspeakers and here's where I'm doing my
cooking"—you'd say, "Well, the guy is just making himself cozy." It was
more that we had become really famous, and we were putting our own
money into a movie that no one could really figure out, and everybody
wanted to be involved with me.

What saved your marriage?

I think bottom line is that a man like me operates with a kind of lodestone
of loyalty and commitment to his family that in the end is not easily disrupted. In the end, you do what you feel is right and what you feel is right
comes from your upbringing, your family. In the end, I realized you could
change wives every ten years and be in the same situation. And that it's better
to just have one wife. That marriage is best in the long term.

But you certainly risked losing that many times?

Well, not many times. I became involved with someone who was extremely
worthwhile. The people that I went out with were not like chorus girls. They
were like real human beings who also had a lot of value, and in the end, even
to be thrust into such an exotic life—I'm in the jungle filming, I'm famous,
I'm this kid from Long Island, I'm rich, I'm not rich—there was a state of
confusion. I always gravitated to warm personal relationships in my collaborators and my friends. It's true, there was a little empowerment, of me saying, "In the end, I gotta do what I gotta do, and I shouldn't be bound by
everybody else's opinion of what I should do." I wasn't sticking pins into
animals. I was reading, and listening to music and talking about the future
and becoming interested in electronics. Everything I was doing was good!
There was nothing decadent or wasteful. Even the romantic involvement
wasn't a weird one; it was more like a relationship with a schoolmate who
shared my ideas in a way that empowered me. Mostly, I throw out ideas and

people dismiss them. So to have someone say, "Gee, that's interesting!" is a very powerful thing.

My problem was that my wife always was very conventional in her thinking, like everybody else. A lot of things that I do at first are not popular, and I am hungry for some approval or encouragement. In fact, my story in regard to the country, basically, is that I'd like a little encouragement. It's true you can tear me down. All living things need some sustenance. Rather than being called a genius, which is another way of calling me nothing—because no one knows what one is, anyway—I'd rather be encouraged for what I am doing good. I do try to put a lot of myself into things, I experiment, I don't give people one formula project after another, which other directors do. All I want is a little encouragement. I don't want to be adored. It would only embarrass me. Sure, you can break my spirit. Sure, I can lose my confidence.

One from the Heart *was supposed to be your way of channeling your romantic angst—you said, "Everyone knows love kills"—and putting it into a creative project.*

I was interested in something on the subject of love more as I had personally experienced it. I was working on a very different project. But the little fable-like story of *One from the Heart*, written by Armyan Bernstein, echoed my themes, simple as they are: the man, the woman, the other man, the other woman. Elective affinities. It's very simple. My mind then was just sure that the motion picture industry was going to turn into a worldwide electronic communications industry, that television was going to be international, that satellites were going to make any part of the world as viable as any other part of the world, that advanced editing and forms of high-definition television were going to allow filmmakers to cook up what they had in their heads cheaper and easier, and there was going to be a great golden age of communication. And I wanted to be in on that. And I wanted that studio!

But this story for that ideal?

Listen, the way I think, if you said to me now, "Hey, Hollywood General Studios is available, and if you can be on the stages in three months with a big picture, the rent for working there can be the down payment for buying the studio, and we got this script—I don't know what it is but it's sort of about something you're interested in," I might very well do it. Or I did then!

My idea was to get the studio and equip it and then do *Tucker* on those stages. And my problem was that *One from the Heart*, rather than just staying as this little love story, got turned into fuel for this whole other thing. And my associates are all insane. The art department went insane. They weren't supposed to build all of Las Vegas. The photographer went insane. One of the good things about me is I give everybody else the same empowerment that I have. And I have a lot of talented, crazy people working for me. And

I was always interested to know more about the Hollywood musical, and was it possible to have a musical without people singing but where the songs sang for them, and there was enough *right* about the decision that I just blindly made it, and figured, like I normally do, I'd just swim as hard as I can to get out of it. Sometimes I pull it off, sometimes I don't. But *One from the Heart* suffered from the perception of me as some wild, egomaniac Donald Trump type of guy, and once they think about you that way, it's just so many months before you're brought down.

True enough, but once people sit in a theatre and watch the film, if it works magic on them, they forget about budgets and news stories.

Don't you think that the way something is presented to an audience affects them? I'm not going to argue about *One from the Heart:* to some people it was magical, to many others it wasn't. But it was a controversy before it was finished. People were looking at early prints. In the end, how many people who were sure *One from the Heart* was this embarrassing failure had really even seen it?

Looking back, don't you wish you had made it a more personal movie? After it was over, you said you didn't really care about the characters and you didn't really care about the story. And that showed.

I think it was a mistake that I got into the project for the reasons I did, and that it was somebody else's script. If it had been more personal it probably would have been more realistic. But was it a disgrace? I don't think so. I thought it was an interesting and an imaginative experiment. But it's a little bit like a cigarette lighter. If it doesn't light, it doesn't light. But that doesn't mean it won't light.

One from the Heart left its mark. Things looked like it after it was over. Television looked like it. It did things that no one had done. Kurosawa made a little innocuous love story and people hated it as well. I just wanted to do something sweet and innocent. Would *Singin' in the Rain* have been better if it was personal? Did you really get under those characters' skin? *One from the Heart* didn't get much of a chance. It was doomed from the moment I started it. And so has my career been since after *Apocalypse Now,* because of the way people perceive me. It's enough. But it's not enough to stop me from what I'm doing. I think if *One from the Heart* had done well [commercially], people would have respected it. I think it was a much better movie than some giant, successful movies. You want to talk about Kim Basinger in *Batman*? You want to talk about that role, that film, that story? But they hired the guys who did *Batman* to run Sony! It wasn't if the film was any good or not.

When you make twenty films in your career you're bound to make some that don't glance off the public right.

Which of your films are closest to your heart?

I tend to like the ones I wrote, like *The Conversation,* and the ones that weren't such a hassle. I like *Tucker.* It was another kind of show, another kind of device. I happen to believe movies can be different from one another. How can you compare *Tucker* to *Rumble Fish* to *The Godfather* to *Apocalypse?* Four totally different filmmakers made them. I like to think that the punishment suits the crime: I like to ask myself if the stuff I make the movie out of can be what it's about.

But if you want to make movies that are what they're about, how does that figure with One from the Heart? *What it was about was love, really, but what it was was an amazing formal and stylistic technological experiment.*

But even that's interesting. To tackle the theme of love and avoid it completely. If I were a painter you'd think that was pretty interesting.

Okay, a structured absence. But for a film audience watching a narrative movie, they don't just want the style, they want the sentiment.

Well, was *Love Story* about love? What are we talking about here? Those kind of movies aren't about it either. *One from the Heart.* I paid for *One from the Heart,* millions of dollars, ten years of my life. My idea was good: to do a film in that formal way, to use music and images in that way; the idea was worthwhile. It was more worthwhile than ninety percent of the movies that come out. But had that film not devastated me, *Tucker* would have been a very different movie. It was just an experiment for *Tucker,* really.

As it turned out, Tucker *turned into very much an autobiographical movie.*

Superficially, not really.

You didn't think in telling his story—the ways he succeeded and the ways he failed—you were telling your own?

I knew that, superficially. I was interested in Tucker years before, and all those stories about guys who thought they could do something, and tried and failed, or succeeded. That's the kind of story I like. Sure it's true there's some of me in Tucker, and some of me in *Godfather III* and some of me in Kurtz. What else is new? I'm the guy making it, and I'm going to make it out of my own body and out of my family and out of my children, and make it out of the stuff I feel strongly about. And if I didn't, I'd be a formula filmmaker, which I'm not.

Tucker's story was a tragic story, and yet you presented it with a strangely optimistic spin.

Because I want young people to know that if they have good ideas, they shouldn't have to think they'll be beaten out of them. As culture evolves, more and more, people with creativity and ideas are going to be important in the world. In America's case, our creative people are our number-one asset. If we turn our back on that, we're in trouble. This person, the Tucker kind of person, is going to be very important to the future of the country.

Speaking of love stories, the absence of sex on screen in your films, given how out in front you've been in other ways, has been remarkable.

It's an interesting subject. I've thought about it a lot myself. I have a theory about it. When I was young, I directed a couple of nudie films. My attitude is that when you're trying to portray erotic situations, it's almost a real advantage to sort of not care and be very blasé about it. It's like going out with girls when you're very young. If you radiate a certain feeling of shyness, or "respect for the girl" as my mother taught me, the girl gets that vibration and she behaves with you in that way. Whereas she might be going out with your friend, who doesn't treat her in that way, and be doing *everything*.

My feeling is in those situations on the set I tend to be very shy, and very protective of both my own feelings and the actors' feelings, and feel very inhibited about trying to pursue the erotic. My point is that it may be that those for whom that area of life is not so overwhelming in their own lives are a lot better in bringing it out on film. But people who have a lot of it going on in their own lives, or it's tempestuous, or it has great power for them, may just prefer to avoid it.

So the more important it is in your own life—

—The less able you are to deal with it in film. Let me give you an example. If you go on a set, and you say to the girl, "Okay, now, I really like you in this moment, take your shirt off," she can sense your discomfort about it, and you give to the actor a certain inhibition because you yourself value that. People who really *love* love are private about it. People say, "We're liberated, and we're so sexy!" Well, if it meant so much to them, maybe they wouldn't be so able to just throw it out there. So, in a way, the director who can shout, "Okay, honey get your shirt off! Get her boobs out!" may make the actor comfortable, 'cause it's no big deal. And I have the feeling that those few times I attempted to do love scenes in movies, I have not really been able to put on the screen my own attitudes about eroticism. I have never felt comfortable. Somehow I was never able to set the environment, even for myself. If I was ever able to do that, it could be that I might be able to make a real contribution to erotic film.

What do you think is the source of the discomfort?

I think at a very early age I was told by my parents not to think bad thoughts, and that deviants thought them; they were shameful. I never made advances in high school because I thought I was showing respect to the girl.

As far as your own sexual identity goes, you've said you're very "feminine, almost effeminate."

Not effeminate, but feminine. Yes. I'm a feminine person, I really am.

And yet the point of view in your films is very masculine.

I don't know the answer to those questions. It would be interesting if I would really try to deal with a subject that dealt with masculine and feminine, and sex, and romance. I think maybe I could do something very beautiful if I could find something comfortable—something I had written, and could be encouraged not to be shy about it. That's a new frontier for me. I'm a man fifty-one years old who always saw his life in terms of romance and, certainly, the feminine ideal of women. I have many more personal feelings about that than I do about gangsters and violence. I am not the slightest bit interested in gangsters or violence. I am interested in power. But I'm interested in legitimate, constructive, Faustian power. Building cities, and new systems that bring people together in some joyous way. I'm not interested in power to be Ming the Merciless.

Well, one could be interested in power and make a movie about relationships.

I could make a movie about relationships. I might *really* be able to make a movie about relationships. I haven't done it. I have more to do.

You're fairly chauvinistic: family, children, the man at work, the woman at home. Those are the things you still value.

Oh yeah. But I tried when I was very young, I made *The Rain People* thirty years ago, even before women's liberation. It was my own original idea, of wanting a woman heroine—a woman who loved her husband but didn't want to be married. That was pretty remarkable for a twenty-four-year-old guy. But even that film, I didn't hit it off very well with Shirley Knight [who played Natalie, the lead]. Whereas I wanted the character to be a well of feeling, I found her very masculine, very abrasive.

It's interesting, because while you send your heroine out on the road, her destination is always to get back to her husband.

Well, that may be the destination. Also I was the first one to hire a woman to be the head of a studio, Lucy Fisher. My teacher was a woman, Dorothy Arzner. We had several woman directors' programs when there weren't any. So while it's true I have the family/children/wife, maybe I'm trying to keep my hands on all the good things. Just like I'm so interested in technology and the future, and yet I'm so traditional about books and old-fashioned things.

People are always most interesting in their contradictions.

Characters certainly are. [Coppola tries to turn on a light in the darkening room, but it doesn't work.]

See, technology, Francis! It's not gonna save us!

[Laughs.] It's not reliable. But neither is anything else.

The women who leave the family in your films, they pay a price for it, a great deal of guilt and anguish in the face of leaving, and they return. Natalie does in The Rain People, *Franny [Teri Garr] returns in* One from the Heart, *Peggy Sue [Kathleen Turner] returns even when she has a chance to do it over again, a different way, in* Peggy Sue Got Married, *and even in* Gardens of Stone, *a very independent woman played by Angelica Huston improbably commits to a man who's just about to leave her to go off to Vietnam. Even the few strong woman characters you have, always return to their men.*

It would be interesting to see how I treated subject matter I wrote myself—not about gangsters or about war; I got sort of waylaid on *The Godfather,* so I spent six or eight years of my life on it, rather than the two I thought. I was interested in directing *Agnes of God,* I guess because of the whole Catholic thing. I'm a very emotional person. I'm very moved all the time, by things I witness. I would like to make some films that are more emotionally the way I feel. Sometimes I hear a piece of music, like a piece of Spanish music, and it rends my heart. I would love to make a film like that. I didn't care much for the *Peggy Sue* project or *Gardens of Stone,* but in that one I was struck by the honor and sweetness of the army, that appealed to me, I was moved by it, maybe because I went to military school. These were projects I was doing to try to get through the debt payments I had. I never did anything, even *Peggy Sue,* that I disrespected. I always try to find something, one concept about it I can latch onto, and in *Peggy Sue* it was "Our Town." A lot of it is the deal of the deck.

I would like to do a project dealing with eroticism, dealing with women, that deals with the subject of a woman's femininity. I would feel very pleased to study it, learn about it, do the research on it. That's the secret: film directors choose their projects by what they want to learn about. I would love to be able to explore how to put my feelings on the screen about love and romance.

You have a big project called Elective Affinities.

No one's going to hire me to go do that now. They're going to hire me to do something like *Bonfire of the Vanities,* not these cockamamy movies I have in my head. But if I am able to be wealthy and powerful, through the success of other work, then I'm going to get the chance.

What about doing these movies the way you've always talked about wanting to do movies—really small-time, like an "amateur"?

With the facilities here, what we can do with post-production, all electronically, and what we have in Napa, it is possible for me to operate more as a, quote, "amateur." Maybe what's going to happen is that I'm going to do a big picture, then a little picture, a big picture, then a little picture. Maybe that's my destiny.

When you went to Tulsa to do The Outsiders *and* Rumble Fish *you were really down on the world of adults.*

I'm always like that. I get along well with kids, and adults I find much more arch in the way they organize their opinions and their relationships. Most adults worth knowing still have a lot of kid in them. I really believe children are born wonderful and good and full of everything we admire and it's only in this period of education that we knock them to hell, and we do it generation after generation. To the extent adults keep this point of view, they're wonderful.

Now, your own kids are no longer kids, but young adults. If Sofia was a kid when Godfather III *started, she's certainly not anymore.*

No, she's retained it. She had a big finger pointed at her, and she was tough enough. I wouldn't have subjected her to it otherwise. What you must have figured out by now is that I made a casting choice. She was right for the part and no one else on the horizon was. That character has to do something very specific. I was thrilled to have gotten Winona Ryder [his original choice for the role]. I went way out of my way to accommodate her, 'cause she was coming late to the picture. And so when she couldn't do it, I had nowhere else to turn, and I reached out for my daughter, more as I always do with members of my family, because I knew I could count on her.

Paramount has never known anything about these *Godfather* pictures, and they were much more curious about what star could they put with Andy Garcia, and they were ready to just fly Madonna in there. It's got to be Diane Keaton's daughter! It's got to look like Al Pacino! If you've seen the stills, she looks like their daughter. It was *casting*. If she had not been my daughter, but had been the babysitter that I had seen on the set, I might have done the same thing, if I had felt that the girl had enough stuff to come across.

There were some associates close to you who were upset with you for putting your daughter through it.

Look, we make decisions every day that my associates banter and argue about. To be quite honest with you, Tom Cruise didn't get a bigger part in *The Outsiders* because Fred Roos [Coppola's long-time producer] wanted Rob Lowe. And we made a trade-off there. What went on in this movie is no different. A lot of times I put people in movies who I have a gut reaction about, who other people don't see. Al Pacino in the first *Godfather* movie is the biggest example. There wasn't a chorus of approval.

I know you had to fight hard for him. You had to fight hard for Brando!

I could give you fifteen examples. I didn't want Talia to play Connie, because I thought she was too good-looking. I thought the sister should be like the homely Italian girl – that's the way I understood the character – and my sister is really pretty in my eyes.

With Sofia, all these Paramount guys were hovering around, and they didn't have the right to make the decision, to question me, but they did – on the angle that it was for my own good, and that they wanted to be sure I knew what I was doing to my family. It was bullshit – they wanted to have a famous chick in there with Andy! It got very weird. I said, "Look guys, get off my set. Get out of here. You had nothing to do with the first two *Godfather* pictures, don't bug me now." And Sofia cried. I talked to her that night and said, "What do you think, Sofie? Do you have the guts to try this, 'cause I think you're right for the part, and if I don't cast you I don't know who I'm going to cast. I'd rather cast you – and we'll do it together and nurse our way through it – than have them send some thirty-five-year-old actress because they want to put her on the cover of a movie with Andy Garcia." And she said she'd do it. She had the guts to do it. The thing about Sofia is she's real, she's authentic.

[Pause.] You know, I was never sponsored by anyone. If I had been, I might have been able to do things in a more methodical, orderly way. Usually, we're using our resources to their limits. We're borrowing $10,000 and I have to use that $10,000 as if it were $50,000. We're independent. It's probably foolish that I haven't tried to become more ensconced with some business interest. But I've never been portrayed as anything but a guy on a tightrope, which is an interesting story, but it's not the whole story. I've been on a tightrope for twenty-five years. I have not been able to find a place to be a comfortable part of the American film industry.

But being a part of that system was something you had never been comfortable about.

But I want to be part of America!

Okay, you want to be part of America, but as far as "the system" goes, you were on the phone to Warner Bros. when you were out on the road in the sixties making The Rain People *telling them that the system was going to fall under its own weight. Yes, you didn't have that sponsorship, but in large part because you never trusted that sponsorship.*

Uh-huh, and I don't! I was a kid of the television era. I know all of the history. I was raised in show business. I thought day and night about it. Whatever happiness I've had, I've been given by show business. But to see people come along who are Johnny-Come-Latelies, and to see them enslave it, and mislead it, and who aren't interested in it—it makes you feel like that. It's not that I don't love the system, it's that I *do* love the system. And it seems like it would be so easy to have it be right. It's a frustration I can't get my hands on.

Not that it was so great under the old studio system, but parts of it were. Those studio gates are always closed, and I don't understand it. A little studio like Zoetrope, if we had been allowed to survive, would have come to our equilibrium. In fact, it's a better company today—more fertile, productive, and better run—than it ever was. But it takes a while to learn those lessons.

Don't you think part of the reason sponsorship has been hard to find is that in the heady days in the beginning of Zoetrope, both in the late sixties in San Francisco and then in the late seventies in Los Angeles, you were pretty combative about what you said Zoetrope's place would be in the industry? People resented you for it.

There's no question that they resented me.

You said in the late sixties that within a few years you'd be "bigger and more important than any two Hollywood studios combined," and when you finally got your Hollywood lot ten years later, you said it was going to be the survival of the fittest and that "the long-established studios will be brought down." Maybe this made it kind of pleasant for the powers that be to taste your failures.

Yeah, my failures . . . as long as they don't tell me there's some spot on my X-ray and I have to stop. I think I'll always be cooking up ideas and having those passionate feelings. Whether I try it again, or am in the position to try it again, or whether I would try it again, if I get to live another ten years I'll do ten years of interesting things. I never made it a secret that I wanted to run things along the lines that I tried. Whether I was too rash about what I said . . .

We did have a high school apprenticeship program, we did develop technology, we did give women opportunities, we were doing what we said we were going to do. Even in this crippled time in the last ten years, we've been doing these things.

Do you see renewed expansion of Zoetrope along the lines you had imagined? It's been a one-director studio for a while now.

Yes, in terms of famous directors, we haven't had the clout to attract others. I'm clearly a little different at fifty than I was at thirty. I think a lot more about the country than I do about the Hollywood system. It's all one subject, of course. Running up against the Hollywood system is like running up against the State Department.

Do you want to make movies for the rest of your life? After Tucker *you hinted that you wanted to try sculpting.*

I just didn't want to make movies anymore then, that was such a heartbreak. I don't know. I'd like to be an inventor. I like to get excited about projects. Like the old days of theatre in college: it was the only place on the campus where you could go at night, work, and pretty girls would be there, and you could stay up late, you could go to the opening. In the modern world, this building is full of electricity. Where else can young people go? They are pretty much closed out of everything. I like generations interacting, like a family. Old people's destination is their own death.

You still have as much faith in technology as you've had in the past?

Oh yeah.

It's somewhat paradoxical, given that the first movie you produced, George Lucas's THX 1138 *warned—very strongly—of the dangers of technology, and in some ways your most personal and greatest film,* The Conversation, *does the same: warns that technology is very much a double-edged sword.*

Without a doubt. Someone once said to the great Goethe, after drinking too much, "You poison yourself." And he said, "Too much of anything is poison. If you drink too much water, or eat too much bread, it can be poison. However, a little bit of poison, in moderation, makes you feel good." What I get out of that is that technology, this incredible stuff we're dealing with, requires balanced human beings to embrace it and function with it in a positive way. If we produce human beings who at a young age are taught to be out of balance, then you give them technology—and all other stimulants—of course they're not going to know how to deal with it. Because they're not healthy themselves. We're going through a transition in the family itself. So many kids are from broken homes and live away from their family . . .

The way in which you've talked about technology is so grand. You said, at the Oscars ten years ago, that all this new stuff was "going to make the Industrial Revolution seem like an audition in a small-town theatre." That's a great line, but it hasn't.

Well, I was trying to talk to them as show business people!

Your attitude reminds me of the modernist architects in the early twentieth century, who felt that because building technology was changing, people would be changed. Because we'd remove ornament, people wouldn't lie; and because we'd have glass walls, people would have to tell the truth—there would be no room for hiding. That the technology would actually change people's souls. Well, that didn't happen. And it seems like you have the same kind of born-again faith in technology, that it will in some way free us.

Don't forget I'm a theatre director, a film director. You need technology in world communications because technology makes it possible. The other part of the formula is, you need a constant stream of artists that have developed. Even the home video cassette. You will see—mark my words!—a tremendous amount of talent come from the fact that everyone has the technology, cheap. The whole film industry is going to be astonished that in six years some little fourteen-year-old fat girl in her garage in Akron is going to emerge as Mozart! Because of the technology that's spread around now. Some lonely little kid is gonna do their own thing, and do something beautiful of gargantuan proportions. I believe in this. Even in that Oscars speech, I was trying to make it clear that it's technology united with the human spirit, and not to be afraid of it. It can be the servant of the artistic community.

But that's all it is, and it's a dumb servant. Synthesizers certainly haven't made music any better.

Artists just work with the technology they have. If there's only eggs, you have to use yellow paint. Matthew Brady's photographs are not inferior because he didn't have a Nikon. All I'm saying is that you have to use the technology that's there.

You've predicted that soon film production will go twenty times faster. How so?

I believe this. Look at modern movie production, in New York, with Bobby De Niro and Harrison Ford: they get a shot for twenty minutes, then they go back into the trailer for two hours. Now, if you could figure out a way for all those creative people to not sit in their trailers for four-and-a-half hours a day, if there was a way they could go in and just do their thing, it would go incredibly faster. And the actor would prefer to be acting for six or seven hours, like a musician. But the stop-start part of mechanical filmmaking drives everybody crazy.

But what's going to change it?

Well, I always believe that modern filmmaking will be a synthesis of film techniques: cinema style (especially as it relates to editing), and live television, sound-on-sound modern recording, and videotape production and theatre. And that the best of those mediums, due to the extraordinary revolution in things related to technology, would make a sort of new medium possible. And together it would give the film artist such incredible control and flexibility. Because sometimes now making modern movies is like trying to climb Everest. Everything is so hard.

Here you are climbing Everest again with Godfather III. *Yet at the end of 1987 you were still saying you had no interest in gangsters—*

I don't!

—And you would not do Godfather III *because you'd just have to tell the story again, which you were loath to do. By the end of 1988, you were in. What changed your mind?*

[Pause.] I do everything by my feelings. If my feelings are hurt, I'll do something stupid, to try to get some relief from that. I'm a person, probably a manic-depressive person: I'm either very enthusiastic or I really get sad, and I regret, or I feel badly. I showed *Apocalypse Now,* unfinished, because my feelings were hurt because everyone was bugging me that I didn't have it finished. I pulled *One from the Heart* from theatres because I was so hurt by what happened with the picture—that it was reviewed before it was done, and everything else—so I pulled the picture back to lock it up in a safe so that no one would ever see it, and that someday, years from now, if anyone wants to see it, I'll show it to them. (But I didn't know it had already been sold for videocassette!) Everything I do is because of my feelings.

What changed your feelings about doing Godfather III *after resisting for so long?*

Over the years, I had heard about them doing scripts, with different people being involved. And I was shocked that they would do that without consulting with me. And they said they didn't because I'd told them I wasn't interested—which was true. But, still, the real reason they did that was because it was the cheaper, easier way for them to control it. So for sixteen years I heard of developing things, and they never once came to me and said, "You can do anything you want to do." They always said, "Will you do this script?" and it was always some stupid script. I was the one that made the first film, and I made the second one just out of the top of my head. I was sort of hurt that they never came and said, "Francis, we offer you *Godfather III,* do it any way you want."

So, finally, when they came to me and said *that,* I realized that if I could pull it off, I could once again have an audience. All movies have a style. And I think if *Tucker* had been a little more conventional, and emphasized more naturalistic acting, it would have been more successful. So I didn't know who my audience was. The kind of film I liked wasn't the kind of film the audience at large did. And I really felt that if they gave me carte blanche to do *Godfather III,* I knew the public really liked that style of film, and I might have an opportunity to do something artistic, as I did with *Godfather II,* where I worked an old screenplay idea of mine about telling of a father and son at the same age. So, in a sense, *Godfather II* was just an opportunity to do that.

Here they were, offering me once again the opportunity to have an audience. All I needed was a concept to be interested in, so I wouldn't think it was just drivel. And then I started to think about all that had happened to me—now that I'm older— all those thoughts that a man has: God, I've made mistakes. Will my children love me? Am I leaving anything, really? And I realized I could approach Michael Corleone more as that kind of man. That he could be older, that he could be a kind of King Lear.

And then I began to read about the Banco Ambrosiano scandal and the Vatican scandal. I felt I had a fertile story context that wasn't just going to be about Venezuelan drug lords and machine guns. And so with those two things I started to find myself speculating about it, and so when they really said to me, "Would you do it?" I had an angle. I didn't have an angle before that. That's all you need. Something that gives your heart permission to pursue it.

In doing this, were you in some way saying it was okay for you to return to the field of classical storytelling, and that you were accepting that you were very, very good at it?

I return to the field of classical storytelling in a story that should be told that way. I'm not eschewing certain types of movies. It's just the tyranny where *all* the movies are the same that really bugs me. The fact that, as Godard said, you could cut the main titles off the ten most acclaimed directors in America and all the movies would be in the same style. Whereas if you go to the East Village and take the ten most acclaimed artists, they'd all be different. I don't understand why our art form has to be enslaved. It's big enough, it's broad enough that it can afford to have a little variety and variation.

Well, it has something to do with the intersection between commerce and culture.

Oh, it's economics, without a doubt. Those studios, at the time when I wanted a studio and I was conspiring to see if I could get Fox—those studios were selling for $300 million. Now they're selling for $6 and $8 billion. Let's be honest: it's a profitable business! And the studios are run by people who are, generally, not geniuses. And they make a lot of money. It's more profitable, with more upside than there's ever been. And now it's going to be the whole world. It *is* the whole world! What was the question you were asking me?

We were discussing why all those ten movies look the same. What kind of "programming" is being done?

It has to do—yes!—with some type of slavery. I know that. Some enslavement. My only point about the fact that these movie companies are worth so much is: among those great profits, isn't there a *little* bit to develop talent and allow for a little variety, to do lower-budget films? Isn't there a little bit for R & D that can go back into the film industry? There isn't anything. They don't put anything back into it.

SESSION TWO

Are you still happiest when you're writing? Is that still your greatest joy?

I just enjoy imagining things. Daydreaming. Daydreaming is nice, before it's checked. An idea can give birth to another idea before it's prematurely killed. I found in dealing with people, with society, that you barely get an idea out into the room before there are four or five reasons why it should be killed. Sometimes good reasons, sometimes not. Nonetheless, if you kill off an idea too early then you never get to places you would have gotten to. I like very much the imagination process. As I've gotten older, I've found I can do it much better alone.

When you write, do you turn off the censor completely—the critical mind—on the first pass through?

According to my biases, I have it off. And it's only when I'm educated by someone else to why something is a stupid idea that I can see that. I just feel that everyone is too soon to say "No."

Despite what you learned in the middle of Apocalypse Now, *do you still feel like a writer first and a director second?*

Well, like an inventor, a creator, an instigator of ideas.

One of the things you're known for is a more improvisatory style during the actual production of a film—

Yeah, I call it collaboration. All projects are a combination of structure and improvisation. There's the comment that a script by me is like a newspaper—you get a new one every day. On *Godfather III* maybe the script was a newspaper because the news was coming in every day: Robert Duvall will not be in the picture; we don't have enough money to do the funeral scene; Winona Ryder won't be there for this or that scene. So I kept trying to make changes so that the script would hold water. I don't think if I was directing "Streetcar Named Desire" that there'd be a new script every day, unless Blanche maybe will not be there for the nervous-breakdown scene.

But even on Apocalypse, *while you were making it, you were wrestling with what you wanted it to be more than probably most directors would allow.*

33

We started out making it from an existing project, and I was trying to find my own personal take on it. We had a John Milius screenplay that had a lot of great elements but hadn't gone through the final gestation process, even with that writer. The last quarter of it was unresolved. The way that script usually ended was: Kurtz [Marlon Brando] and Willard [Martin Sheen] meet up and the next thing Willard knows, he's side-by-side with Kurtz, fighting in the trenches. It wasn't appropriate anymore for what we had done.

Again, there's a big difference when you're dealing with an existing piece of literature, a play or a novel, because that piece has already gone through an improvisatory period. Kazan, Brando, out-of-town tryouts evolved "Streetcar Named Desire." Any performing art goes through that process where everyone contributes. When we make something like *Godfather III*, we're not just trying to make a movie, given the serious nature of this drama; we're trying to make a little piece of literature, and do it on demand. So of course, unlike an existing novel, it's going to go through all sorts of rewrites.

Let's talk about your decision to make this "little piece of literature." The end of Godfather II *feels like as much of an ending as one can imagine: Michael Corleone may have become one of the most powerful men in the country, but he's, as you once said, a corpse. And not only is he a corpse, but all the thematic strains that you've worked through both movies have been resolved—the immigrant saga, the story of American business and the entrepreneur, the sociopolitical tableau, the family saga—all have been beautifully resolved. Now here we are sixteen years later, and you're going to breathe life back into that corpse and make him walk. Did it ever strike you that this was something you shouldn't be doing, that there were great risks involved?*

I didn't see it from the point of view of risks so much, but I did see it from the point of view that I made *Godfather II* to end the thing. For many reasons, I wanted to end it. It's not an episodic adventure along the lines of Indiana Jones. I couldn't just start a new adventure. I'd have to do it with the human being, Michael Corleone, and he was effectively Richard Nixon. And I didn't know how to do it, and I didn't know you could do it. That was maybe part of the reason I didn't want to tackle it again.

But when I finally accepted the job, I thought I had one last card to play, which is Michael's dialogue with himself about his morality. Was he a good man or a bad man? If he was a good man, how does he feel about how he stained himself? If he was a bad man, how does he feel about his hypocrisy, in relation to his children? With younger people, you want to portray yourself as a good person because you want them to believe in good. So, just in itself, that was interesting to me. And then I began to think I could do it like a Shakespearean play. So I thought if I work on it, if I stay up enough nights on it, maybe I'll be able to get a handle on it. And that's why I attempted to do it. And if I am able to bring Michael Corleone to life, and he's a man in the third act of his life, then it will have been a success.

You said yesterday one of the reasons you hadn't done it sooner was that your feelings were hurt they hadn't come to you and said, "Francis, it's your ball, go play with it." But you had announced any number of times and in any number of ways that you had no interest.

That's true. And I didn't want to do the second one, either. First of all, understand that the things I say—a lot of times, and maybe you can see this in my talking to you—as I discover things in talking, I get excited about them. And I may say, "And I tell you without any doubt!" because I myself am in the moment of discovery. I'm an emotional person. I speak and I say things without thoughtful consideration. And nine times out of ten there's truth in what I say, because it does come from intuition.

Let's go back to your period as a director-for-hire: The Cotton Club, Peggy Sue Got Married, Gardens of Stone. *Was that a dark period for you?*

Well, I knew that I was in trouble. That was a period where I was fighting to keep my home. And a lot of things in my life were falling apart. And my response to trouble is to work hard. That's my conditioned response. I was digging myself out of a hole. I enjoyed making *Rumble Fish* very much, being able to make a stylistic flight of fancy. *Peggy Sue* was very easy. *Tucker* was pleasant, being with George Lucas again. But clearly, I felt there would be a point in my life where I was going to go with a very low-budget, amateur-type, hi-8 production or I would find myself in the industry where they would allow me to do what I had done on *Apocalypse,* where I take a big subject my own way.

Your heart wasn't really in those movies.

I wouldn't say that—

You did.

Well, I said a lot of things. I didn't like *Peggy Sue,* I didn't like the script. But it's like, with a girl, and she isn't really "the one," but after you get to know her you find something about her that you like. I can't say I dislike any of my films, at all. Every one of them has something endearing, or interesting, or sweet, or that I was able to enjoy.

Did you ever feel in those years like Natalie in The Rain People, *who says, "I used to wake up and it was my day . . . and now it belongs to you"? Did you feel then that your day belonged to the accountants and the studios and the lawyers?*

I've felt that throughout my career. I felt that on *Godfather III.* I thought there were unreasonable demands being made on me, as far as time went.

I thought that if I could have made it over a slightly longer period of time I could have finished the script before we were cast. I feel like that little bit of rush turned a difficult job into an even more difficult job. Every day and every night I have to be worried about something? Would it really have been a less good work if it came out six months later? What's the difference? Paramount waited for sixteen years—they couldn't get it together—why do I have to do it in sixteen months? [Pause.] At the same time, I also know that pressure can bring out good things that wouldn't come if you didn't have your back up against the wall.

Did you make any aesthetic choices on the films between Rumble Fish *and* Godfather III *that you've come to regret?*

I can't say that.

One of the things you said before making Life Without Zoe *was that "this is going to be as bad as the horse's head."*

What I was expressing was that I have a feeling there's tremendous biases and prejudices out there, especially about something on a little rich kid. I knew that a little rich kid who sips a martini with her father, who likes to go shopping, was going to be considered improper and wrong. It was prejudice. A little kid like that had a good heart—she kept her promises—so what that she sips strawberry daiquiris? Well, obviously, that stuff was all based on my kid. I always thought my kids, when push comes to shove, are always real loyal, true blue, honest, won't let down a friend. That's much more important than whether she loves Chanel clothes. Sometimes she can't afford Chanel clothes. I was trying to do something that I knew was not in the popular culture to accept. That's what I meant by my comment. There are people who aren't interested in their children, who have nothing to do with their children—right away they have all these strict, condemning ideas. And I, who am with my kids, and live with them and play with them and drink with them and live with them: I know more about children than they do because I really do it. That's what I meant. People are very quick to condemn, but they don't always have the right to do it.

I'll speak for myself: I wasn't offended by the world of rich kids being depicted—it's an interesting world—but I was troubled by the kind of un-ironic celebration of status, wealth, and materialism.

Well, what happened was, it was a longer play put into that format. Disney pretty much liked the "Eloise at the Plaza" thing, and through each cut, all the darker stuff, about the little girl's relationship with her father, was just cut out. If you wanted to see the real version, I have it. But you can't talk about that. The original screenplay had a lot of dark parts about it. And in the attempt to make it delightful and charming, they were eliminated.

It leaves an awkward feeling. You have a scene with a homeless man—who's in a box, never seen—that feels gratuitous. Because this little rich girl gives him a bunch of Hershey Kisses, he says, "She's why I love New York!"

It's not that she gave him Hershey Kisses, but that she *promised* that she would and she kept her promise. All throughout the story she kept her promises. She was always trying to do good things for people. At that point, not that I didn't care, but I knew a certain kind of people in New York were not going to like it. I feel there's more to it. That particular project was also very personal, and I have a lot of insights that nobody cared to get. And I accept it. I don't mean to say that all of my films people should like. *One from the Heart, Life Without Zoe* are the acknowledged failures according to the people that declare failures. But I know, having made the film, that there is something there. I know that I am especially not popular with New York writers.

Just take all my work and clip the *New York Times*. There is a certain mentality. It's very predictable. It was stupid of me to do that film. I really only did because I wanted my daughter to design the costumes, just like I only did *One from the Heart* because I wanted to have my studio. I sometimes do things like that. If you could read the whole screenplay or see my cut, before Disney cut it, you might think there was something there, but the way it was received was extremely insulting. So I'm sorry you saw it, but I like the version I have in my house that I can show people ten years from now.

Also, we had other problems. We had Dominica Scorsese [Martin Scorsese's daughter] playing the part, who was much more like my daughter, but we had to replace her with a second girl. The whole thing didn't happen the way it was supposed to.

Yesterday you said you're not interested in gangsters or violence. Of course, after The Godfather *you vowed you were never going to make another violent movie—*

I said that? You heard me say it? You read it in some article?

They're all lying, Francis. Every journalist you've ever talked to has put words in your mouth!

No, but thirty-five percent are. That's why I think journalists ought to let you read what they write before it's published. You'd have an opportunity, not to change what they say, but to point out a mistake they've made. But they have a fit about that.

Let's follow this lead. There was a period, maybe vendetta is too strong a word, where you and the press were definitely not getting along.

The press didn't like *me*. What did I do?

Well, you didn't like them either. You told Gay Talese in Esquire *magazine that a rampant press was the scourge of the country.*

Well, a lot of people feel that.

Let's consult the record, accurately, on this. You said, I quote, "The press is a millstone around the country's neck. It is not a force for honesty, ethics or truth. It is a bullshit racket." And Talese said, "Yeah, but the press brought down Nixon." And you said, "I think that having Nixon in power would be better than a rampant press."

I believe that. I'm very worried, because, first, the press is a business. The press has a board of directors that runs like the one that runs Paramount, or any other company. And they're very sensitive to what's good for their business and what's bad for their business. So that's a factor. The press likes to represent itself like a public service, but we know that it's not. Secondly, there's about a sixty-five-percent chance that what goes on is represented correctly. Consequently, when I read about the Middle East or Iraq I really wonder about that thirty-five percent. There's more to the story. And a third thing: very often journalists already have their story, or photographers already have their picture, and the encounter is more to get you to fit into the position they have. Plus, there is another kind of psychology at work, in that the press is not a thing, it is a lot of individuals, and certain kinds of individuals: they're smart, they're ambitious, they're usually from a certain kind of social strata. They're the children of taxicab drivers, people who now are in the position, if they're with the *New York Times*, to call up Carl Icahn and he'll answer their call. So there are a lot of factors that make the press extremely complex and a very powerful entitity.

It's the power of the press that interests you. It's power that really interests you, period, and your greatest work fundamentally concerns its use and abuse.

I think all people share an interest in power, because all people are subject to it. Anybody who's ever had someone park in front of their house wishes they had the power to say, "You can't park in front of my house." Children are very sensitive to power; men and women are very sensitive to power. Living in the world, your power relative to the other forces is a concern. But I don't think I'm obsessed with it. I'm also interested in other broad things: beauty, imagination.

What have you learned about power through your exercise of it?

I learned: don't scare the natives. Don't let them be afraid that your power will be bad for things. I think after World War II there was a movement in philosophy to shun the charismatic individual. In fact, to go the other way, to think more about generality and plurality.

History from the bottom up.

Yeah. And beware the unusual individual. So I do feel we, as a culture, have turned from being attracted to that type of individual to being distrustful of it. There will be another period where there are charismatic political leaders, until there's another Mussolini and everyone's hurt. But there is a distrust for people like me in this period. So therefore a person like me should try to be a little more prudent. Go slow. Don't frighten anyone. My exuberance is mistaken for megalomania.

What else have I learned about power? The value of partnership, and the value of being vested with the previous power. To really make it in our world you need to have a godfather. You need to have an old . . . what they call an alter cocker, or godfather. That Lew Wasserman should like you. That Herb Allen, that Charlie Allen, Sr., should take an interest in you. That there are kingmakers. Like Mexican politics. There is no way around it. Unless you strike lightning in the bottle, like Steven Jobs. Even a man like Ted Turner—it was only because he was so *right* about media that he survived.

Everybody knows that power in America is economic. And that five percent of the population controls some incredible percent of the wealth, and that the real political power of the country is vested in other forms not immediately apparent.

How do you feel about being a part of that five percent?

Well, since I'm always on the verge of total extermination, I don't think of myself as a wealthy, powerful person. I feel sort of like the guy in "The Fugitive" on television. I had the happy accident that my home turned out to be a very valuable asset. Since that got put on the line in every transaction I made, the issue was, was I going to lose my house? And I was always running, out of that anxiety. I've really wished sometimes that I just had a little regular house somewhere. [Coppola has residences in New York, Los Angeles, San Francisco, and Belize, in addition to his estate in Napa.] The smart move for me after *One from the Heart* would have been to go bankrupt. But I didn't want to lose my home and the rights to my movies.

But even the businessman who's making $100,000 a year is in that top five percent of the American pyramid, and by world standards, he's in the top fraction of the top one percent—

Without a doubt, without a doubt. But if he's really sweating that he's going to lose his house and they're going to take away his job, it's hard to portray him as being in power. Because he's gotten himself into a position of being more vulnerable than my friend who lives in a sixty-five-dollar room and just lives his life.

There's all kinds of power, too. I would more like to be, now, this kindly old guy where somebody might once in a while ask me my opinion and value what I say. That's a kind of power that I think I would like, because that's a soft power. Let's face it, as the great people die that we have in our culture, people my age are being promoted into being the kindly grey eminences.

And people might like the fact that I don't have axes to grind and might want my opinions. And that's the kind of power I want a lot more. No one's frightened of it, and everyone loves that kind of person.

Let's go back to what we were speaking about yesterday, the duality of your failure and your success. I'm interested in your feelings about being successful, when you were. I'm going to bring up some things I guess there's a sixty-five-percent chance you said. After The Godfather, *you said that you were as rich and successful as you'd ever want to be, and because of that, all your motives would have to change. What had your motives been before that?*

I wanted to have a niche for myself. I wanted to be considered an interesting filmmaker who wrote his own stuff. And all I wanted was a million dollars to invest, to know the rent was paid, and not have to use my family's money to buy cameras and stuff. And then when I got more than that, it opened me up to another threshold. That's just the way it is with wealth and power. You always want just *that,* but each time you're on a new threshold, there's always another flight of stairs to go up.

And then after Godfather II, *you said some things that reflected back on your family experience. You said you had finally lived out all your "hopeless childhood fantasies." You also said, "I've got my name in the paper, I've got a big house, but those are my parents' dreams." That you hadn't yet made a movie from your own heart.*

It's true. Coming from the family I did, I wanted the approval of my father and my mother a lot, and so consequently their dreams, that generation of dreams, was pretty conventional. Be rich and famous, have a mansion, drive a Cadillac. You're at a party and you're talking to a girl and she's impressed to know you. All those things I did have. But what I started to realize is that I like very much to be cozy and secure and in a small place. If you see my house in L.A., or my Volkswagen I go camping in—this penthouse is very opulent because it's the vision of Dean Tavoularis [Coppola's production designer], but it's still a little tiny bedroom—you see that I really prefer to be secure, in comfortable, cozy quarters, to be by myself, to explore my different interests, working on an invention or working on a script. That's my real nature. And I don't need to have so much of the other stuff. Although for anyone, it's a kick to be put into a big suite in the hotel in Paris. Maybe you wouldn't want to live there.

Let's talk about your filmmaking technique. First off, your desire for extensive rehearsal.

I always get what they give me, which is two weeks. I always ask for three. That's a theatrical thing. A play has six, seven weeks. I think more spatially, less linear. So I need to see the whole thing in order to be motivated to go on. I'm not a good one-two-three-four-five personality. I want all of it at once, to bring it up, like the way a Polaroid comes out, and that's very different.

I add scenes in rehearsals—not in the shooting script—to give the actors "memories." One thing I often do is have a scene where two characters meet for the first time, even though in the story they've already known each other for a while. I find that giving the cast sensual memories always helps them. As artists, as they're playing a scene, just the fact that they share a memory—it becomes like a little emotional deposit in their bank account that enables them to better know each other.

You really like long takes, to let a scene build, rather than to chop it up into smaller pieces.

Well, when you have really talented actors, and they have been properly prepared and properly rehearsed, you never know when something you couldn't have planned, or couldn't have caused, might happen. You keep adding stimuli to invite that kind of accident. When I was a young director, as soon as something weird would happen, I would say "Cut." But later I would look at the film and see some incredible thing happen and some schmuck says "Cut." And I realized it was me! The mere fact that it felt wrong when you were watching just meant that something had *happened*. And that's ultimately what you're trying to capture.

Are there other things you do differently now as a director?

Oh, I've changed a lot. I've become more more knowledgeable about how to guide certain situations and deal with certain problems. I've been in some pretty tough spots on movies over the years—hopeless situations—and I've seen how it's worked out.

How do you make "the part play the person," rather than the person play the part?

Through rehearsal and these little deposits in the actors' bank accounts, certain memories you give them through improv and sense memory and stuff, and letting the actors spend time together in that rehearsal period without being pressured or having to perform, allowing new relationships to be formed. It's a little bit like cell culture. You're using life, but you're encouraging it to grow and evolve according to a plan. Like if an actor is going to hit an actress in a scene and she flinches—because in the improv he really did hit her. Stuff that is too delicate to do totally mechanically. You have to use your impulses. Working with actors is such sensitive stuff.

Do you still think Gordon Willis "hates and misuses actors"?

Yeah. I don't know. He's such a genius and such a complicated guy and there's such wisdom in him. But he sure is mean to them and he sure is intolerant of them and in some ways he's in competition with them. Like many great artists, he is the actor.

Was the Godfather III *shoot a struggle with him?*

Well, it's a struggle only because of the time constraints, and the fact that with Gordy you're going to get five or six spectacular shots a day, but you are not going to get twelve. And that means you very often have to forgo a shot that might have been very useful for many reasons. You're getting six great images, but just six. Not eight or twelve. Sometimes I envy directors who have more shots to work with. But on the other hand, one of Gordon's points is that a certain purity of image—where the camera doesn't fool around, go under the glass table, be in stupid places—has a certain kind of classic, what Gordon would call *structure,* on the long pull that clicks in and gives it a certain beauty.

I like to suit the style to the subject matter. Gordon and I sat in a room before we made *The Godfather* and decided that the camera would never move, the camera would never use a long lens, and stuff like that. To suit the recipe of that piece. If you give me a subject, I'll find a style I think is appropriate. My movies are as eclectic stylistically as anyone's. And in the future the things I'm thinking of are very different from one another.

Give me an idea about your long-discussed big project, Megalopolis.

It's very ambitious. It's a dramatic piece about society and the city of the future. I've always had a lot of opinions about that but I've never had a dramatic piece I could put into that. It's based on republican Rome and contemporary America: debt was the plague of both societies, both have a patrician class, but are republics. And I've tried to imagine the Catiline conspiracy as happening in contemporary New York, and I've evolved an original screenplay based on that.

I'll be able to work on the scale of *Megalopolis* if *Godfather III* is successful, and my hunch is that it's going to be very successful, certainly like the other *Godfather* films. And I think the news will be that the big studios will want me to do another big event movie in the next few years. I know that certain Hollywood entrepreneurs think I'm good for that. I've already been offered. I can feel that they think I'm acceptable to big actors, that big actors like to work with me.

What's the strongest personal connection you have to each of the Godfather *films?*

The first one, the connection was that they didn't like any of my ideas, that I was going to be fired every day, but that I kept doing it the way I thought it should be done. The second one: that I had made something too big and diffuse and I wasn't sure I could make the point I wanted to. The third one was more, how far to go with the tragedy and the operatic aspect. That the family had become myth, become opera, and how could I do that without it becoming too big?

Do you see your life as a tragedy?

No, not at all. I have a great family. I have a wonderful career. Even if I was to be, with this, disgraced as I was in the past, I'm a very flexible kind of artist. There are a million options that I have. I could direct a soap opera and probably enjoy it. I could write. I could do something technical. I love comedy. There's no project I couldn't direct. I love people. I live in a great place. I live in a great country.

But everybody's life is tragic. That's why we read the Greeks. Human life is tragic. Everybody's life. And in that sense my life is a tragedy, but only in that sense.

How would you describe your own Achilles heel? Can you do it without giving yourself a back-handed compliment such as "I'm too generous with my time"?

I get terribly embarrassed. *Terribly* embarrassed. Very self-conscious. It was my lip, it was my eye-glasses, it was my weight. I'm very easily embarrassed. It's that new-kid-in-class syndrome; I get very, very embarrassed in certain situations.

It's easy for artists to be embarrassed by work they've done in the past, but I've heard that you are going to go back to all your work and review it.

And I'd like to do that, but I haven't yet. By the time a movie is ready to come out, I'm so sick of it, and so polarized by it, that I've never been around when any of my films have opened. But then three or four years later I'll go into a theatre and see it on the screen. I saw *Apocalypse* that way, also *Godfather II.* So I can see it as a member of the audience. And I would like one day to start with my first movie, *Dementia 13,* and look at them all, and use that as a helpful way to proceed in the future.

Did you really enjoy shooting Dementia 13 *more than any of the others?*

No, the ones I enjoyed the most were *Rumble Fish*—there was a great sense of freedom there. *Tucker* was not unpleasant, because it went smoothly. *Peggy Sue* was pretty pleasant, because I was close to home. I would say those three were the easiest. I have a hard time with production because I get very scared every day. I get very scared that I'm not going to know how to do it. One of the things you learn real fast making movies is that *everyone* has an opinion and none of them tally. And I'm very self-conscious about being there, in front of everyone, and having to make a decision. I find it uncomfortable, scary.

Remember this? "I've been in the custody of my parents for twenty years and they've taught me nothing but self-doubt, frustration, and perpetual guilt."

That's from *You're a Big Boy Now*. Of course, I derived that from my life.

But yesterday you gave me such a rosy picture—

But talk to anyone about their parents. If they're happy people they'll talk about their parents in positive terms; if they're unhappy people, negative. My parents have that typical Italian previous-generation thing that makes you doubt yourself and lose your confidence, and feel guilty about being alive. It's true that many of my complexes and embarrassments about myself, my insecurity about what I look like, come from that. My wife maintains that I've stayed overweight to "fit in" with that idea. Because if I lost the weight I'd be attractive and I'm not prepared to do that.

You're still in a sense conforming to their idea of you as a kid.

It's very powerful stuff you get when you're a kid. I used to go into school with my glasses off and face covered, I was so embarrassed about my lower lip. Everybody has one thing about them that their mother . . . she wanted me to get a lip job. Now people get lip jobs to make their lips fat. She wanted to me to get a lip job to make my lip skinny.

Really? When you were how old?

All through, when I was thirteen, fourteen, fifteen. She was very good looking, my mother. It's what I meant when I said I was an ugly duckling. I didn't have anything going for me as a kid. Except that I was affectionate. "Augie's the bright one, Tally's the beautiful one, Francie's the affectionate one." And it was true.

Natalie's line in The Rain People *seems autobiographical for you: "Ask my mother, she'll tell you I'm incompetent."*

Everyone's parents always seem to underline the bad. Is it the fear that they have? I'm sure we even do it to our kids. I'm always on Sofia for her diction and her speech. Parents' expectations for their kids are so taken to heart. Everyone's walking around with that stuff.

There's a moment at the very end of The Cotton Club *when this guy who's been sleeping at his nightclub table wakes up and, seeing everyone else clapping, begins to clap. This is rich, because it can be interpreted two different ways: either Francis is making a self-deprecating comment about the whole film—here's a guy who's just slept through it—or he's making a sardonic comment about the audience: that it's asleep, and has been asleep for his last few pictures, and will only like a film (clap) if they see those around them liking it (clapping).*

My boy Gio shot that. It was second unit. And I just liked that. And I did catch that it had those ramifications. But it wasn't something that I did, it was something that my son did.

One last question about Apocalypse. *Eleanor, in her book, mentions almost in passing an ending that you briefly played with, where the air strike gets called in on Willard himself, after he kills Kurtz. Where Willard himself gets fucked over. When I read that, I thought, yeah, that's the real heart of darkness, that's a fabulous resolution and—*

Why didn't I do it? I wanted the ending to be not-horrible. That it would show some improvement, that Willard, now having killed their god, throws down his weapons—and I had all the people throw away their rifles—and he takes this child, Sam Bottoms, and takes him, takes him home. After all that work on that movie I wanted to say something hopeful, a bit. Because I felt that. Throw down your weapon. If you're a god, they're going to imitate you. And if you're a good god, they'll be good. I knew that I didn't want the ending just to show everybody just screwing everybody.

There was a period when you said you wanted to leave the ending vague, because you wanted your own life to answer the question of whether Willard stays at the Kurtz compound, in the heart of madness, or comes back down the river. So I guess I'm curious as to whether you feel you've come back down the river?

I feel I have, really. I still get . . . I . . . I'm a depressive person. A manic-depressive person.

Have you been diagnosed as such by doctors?

Yeah.

Have you ever tried to take medication?

I did for a while, a few years. But I didn't like it, it made me nauseous all the time, and I felt I ought to be able to arrive at some sort of stability more through my mind. Although they say it's chemical. But I didn't like the thought that I was going to be on this medication, and I just stopped. They said, "You'll be depressed," so I said, "Well, I'll be depressed." They said, "Just don't shoot yourself."

My wife just gave me this William Styron book on depression [*Darkness Visible*]. She said I should read that because I sound like him. I can get depressed. I can get sad. I wonder: "What am I doing? Am I doing what I want to be doing? Everything is so hard. Nobody likes me. I've done so much good and yet I'm fifty years old and I'm in exactly the same situation as when I was twenty-five. I've got this little company that's always on the verge of bankruptcy." I can get pretty depressed.

Then on the other hand I can say: "I have the most wonderful children. My mother and father are still alive. My father is working and excited. And all my family gets along now. No one's mad at anybody. It looks like I'll have some kind of financial peace now. And I have a beautiful company and all these nice young people."

And I can see it, the two ways. But mood is not a question of anything logical, it's kind of chemical.

Have you ever been afraid that medication would take the edge off the creativity?

Although they say it doesn't, you wonder about that. I'm a person of such enthusiastic fits, I may stay up all night to do something. You wonder about that. When I was taking it . . .

How long ago was that?

I haven't taken it for about maybe three years. But I took it after *Apocalypse* for about four years. This was lithium. I always maintained that if I could get the elements of my life into a little more reasonable harmony . . . actor availability drove me crazy on *Godfather III*, because you never knew what you were shooting, and I just lost this big lawsuit, and I was going to go bankrupt, at one point I didn't know where to turn. I couldn't leave Sicily. There was a whole new rash of articles that brought up all my problems. They say "TROUBLED." My name is synonomous with trouble, though I have a lot less than many people. My point is that I wouldn't have so many depressed times if I didn't have so many problems. But then my wife says that's not true.

That you would create them.

Yeah. So I'm hoping now, if I get a breather . . . I'm in pretty good shape physically. I'm very strong. I've never, ever been sick. Even in *Apocalypse*, the so-called nervous breakdown phase was more, I think, related to the fact that I was doing all these things that I hadn't done before. I was smoking cigarettes. I never smoked cigarettes. I was smoking grass. I had never smoked grass.

There was talk you had a bad cocaine habit.

Never. I never was a cocaine type. The only drug I really experienced was grass. I had cocaine three times in my life and it wasn't good for me. I don't understand its appeal. I'd tell you if I did. The only drug I ever used was grass. And all of it recently, during [and since] *Apocalypse*.

And I was in, you know, like, love triangles, beyond my thing, and I almost—and I was tired, and Marty Sheen had just had a heart attack, and it was my own money, and I didn't feel good about my relationship with my wife. I didn't feel my wife understood me. I felt she was meddling, and lining up with the people that I . . .

What I learned was that when you are really overwhelmed with problems, it's easy to faint on the floor, or have an epileptic fit.

You used to do that to get what you wanted, didn't you? Back at UCLA film school, or trying to convince studio executives to cast Brando in The Godfather?

I am an epileptic, and these fits are real. I never did it to get something. But at a moment of weakness, it's always a voluntary option—I think even to a real epileptic. But the difference is, it's an easy step to do it, but a very hard step to get back. And that was an interesting thing I learned.

I was exhausted. The cigarettes, more than anything, were making me weird. The personal relationships were changing. Up until the *Apocalypse* period, I'd been pretty innocent: the romances I'd had were pretty conventional, schoolboy kind of romances. No drugs whatsoever, no smoking, moderate drinking. My love life was extremely conventional. Mainly all I did is work. And on *Apocalypse*, being freed in that way—you know, I saw these sexy Italian guys smoking on a boat [Vittorio Storaro's camera crew], so I started smoking, unfiltered cigarettes. And started smoking grass. It was like in Vietnam: it was there and everybody was doing it. And I had a couple of romances that were sort of the-most-beautiful-girl-you-ever-saw kind of things, which all of us, when we're young, have that fantasy. All that stuff was happening to me, and I could fly a helicopter and I lived in a volcano and my life was becoming like a story. And then, like all good things, it was too much. And when Marty had the heart attack . . . also, the grass affected me a little bit: I was much more able to say how I felt. I also started getting very paranoid. I wrote a memo to my company. I felt my own staff was jockeying for political position, and trying to bring my wife into it. And I wanted to organize things more clearly, and I wrote this memo to set things straight—and they published it. And everyone made fun of me, and I was very embarrassed. And that's when I got the idea that it wasn't fair what the press was doing. That I was doing all this stuff, and everyone back home was just laughing at me. And that's paranoia. And it increased because of the trouble I was in. I was scared, too. I was scared! I didn't know what was going to happen.

That so-called breakdown episode, I remember that night. It was over a girl, basically. And what I noticed was, the next morning, I couldn't quite *get back*. I didn't have the energy. I didn't want to do anything. I would go for four or five days and look through the camera but Vittorio knew that I was lobotomized. Like everybody, I take personal things really strong. Some little misunderstanding with a woman, or my wife, or another woman—there were two women involved, and I was devastated by the implications of that. I didn't want to lose my family. I didn't want to lose my children. A lot of men can do that. But I was just not the kind of person who could go and wipe out my family like that and do a second family or something. I'm just not that kind of person. I never will do that. I just can't. I can talk very comfortably about the great strengths of my wife. And of course, as you can gather by now, I really consider my wife like a regular person. So she has the same kind of doubts about me as you might, or the so-called "they" at large.

So now I'm very much at peace. We've been married so long and she's so much my friend and stuff, that I don't need her to be everything to me. I can provide the other in my own mind. A lot of young men go through things like that. Like for a long time, I didn't want to be alone. If I was going to go to L.A., I would rather go be with some girl or woman. And after *Apocalypse*, I spent two weeks in some little Japanese inn that was half the size of my bedroom. It was the first time where, not knowing anyone in Japan, there wasn't the option of calling any girl. I just stayed by myself. When I go to L.A. now, I just stay by myself: I'll cook, or I'll watch television. I don't have any need for company.

But a lot of people, like my nephew Nicolas Cage, he's always gotta have friends or girls around. He can't just be comfortable by himself. Like when I stay in the city, when I don't go out to the country, like last night after you left, I just worked on my computer, and went and had a little dinner, and went home, listened to public radio, and fell asleep. So different from what my behavior had been like.

Male artists often use the power or presence of a female to get them going, to help them create.

There is something to say—whether it's real or just conditioning—for the idea that a girl can be a muse. Especially a girl who has confidence in you. See, I never felt that my wife had any confidence in me.

But there was one particular woman—one of the women in question—who just thought I was really . . . like the girl who has a crush on her professor. And her confidence in me made me feel confident. And when I didn't have that, I didn't feel confident anymore. Confidence is a very important thing. When everyone is saying, "You're going to fail," you're likely to fail.

And that's why a girl, and the particular woman at the time of *Apocalypse*, always made me feel like a million dollars, in terms of "I was talented and I could do it." And then when all that got disrupted, I was floating around. And there is the question of loss of confidence, in a ballplayer, in an artist. If enough people are telling you you're a failure enough of the time . . . I've seen people, very, very talented people, sort of lose it. And never get it back. You can seem pretty forlorn. Even though you seem famous to people.

I have wept over the impossible question of dual loyalties. You feel loyal to your wife and your family, but you feel loyal to another person whom you have singled out for mutual confidence. This person was a writer, too. And she was a good person and she was always on my side. That's probably the most destructive thing I've ever been through.

But also, as I look back, I don't think I was so much in love and I don't think that was so much the issue. I thought after *Apocalypse Now* that I just didn't know where I was. The loss of this girl, who was always the one to make me feel really good—but I didn't know what to do with the movie and how to finish it. She was a great, wonderful girl; she's actually quite successful today. Do you know who she is? I enjoy that she's happy and I see her once in a while and I have no residue of feeling about what I might have lost. I'm very happy I made the decision I did. I think it was all really about the project and needing that kind of muse to get myself together.

I kind of diddle around all the time, and some of the diddles become a project. But I don't attach so much importance to it all. I attach more importance to how my kids are. It's more like an older person's point of view.

Values shift as you age.

You're not as hungry for stuff as you were. I'm not as hungry for that kind of woman—that kind of succubus. They're just real creatures. But as a younger man I always idealized them so much.

Early on, all your fantasies about being an artist involved beautiful women hanging around.

That was my big thing. That was all I wanted. That's why I got into theatre. Women, girls were presented to me at a young age as extremely wonderful, goddess-like creatures.

Wasn't part of that because you looked up to Augie the way you did, and he was very good with girls—

He was very popular. And oddly enough, even as the Ugly Duckling against the wall, girls have always loved me. I'm very affectionate. And the way I am with them they've always liked, so I've always been very successful with women, though I haven't portrayed myself that way. Women have always liked me, all my life. But I was always real shy. And I've always been surrounded. It's so funny the way we perceive ourselves so different than what in fact is real. I have this great life, if you think about it.

If someone feels that they're a loser in some way, or it's been beaten into them that they're a loser, then even if they win big, they'll still feel like a loser. And the contradiction between winning and still feeling like a loser is a very—

What you do is then you sabotage it; as I said, my wife feels that I am fat to fulfill my idea that I'm unattractive. So that you go around doing everything you do to sabotage yourself, and then you say, "See!" But you've done it.

[Pause.] It could all work out really nicely. I still have my company, and I like the company now more than I have. It seems to run more evenly, logically. I like this role of the grey eminence. People *want* to come see me, talk to me. The young director working on something wants my opinion. I like that. The grandfather.

Well, when you become a grandfather . . . you see what my grand-daughter looks like? [Coppola walks across the room to show me a photo of Gio's daughter, born after his death.] This is Gia. [He then points to a photo of Sofia, removes it from the wall and holds it in his hand.] That's what I wanted for Michael's daughter. I wanted the part of the daughter to represent the part of Michael that was still pure. Any man, any person, no matter who—Saddam Hussein, whoever the villain of the day is—there is a part of him that is sweet and kind, and it's when they lose that, they lose all. [He looks down at the photo of Sofia.] The real truth was, the girl was like *this*.

2
DAVID LYNCH

DAVID LYNCH FILMOGRAPHY

1967   Six Men Getting Sick (short loop)
1968   The Alphabet (short)
1970   The Grandmother (short)
1974   The Amputee (short)
1977   Eraserhead
1980   The Elephant Man
1984   Dune
1986   Blue Velvet
1990   Wild at Heart
1992   Twin Peaks: Fire Walk with Me
1997   Lost Highway

for television

1989   The Cowboy and the Frenchman (short)
1990–91   Twin Peaks (pilot and selected episodes)
1991–92   On the Air (pilot)
1992   Hotel Room (two episodes)

David Lynch

David Lynch was born in Missoula, Montana, in 1946. His father worked in the woods for the government; his mother worked at home, raising David and his brother and sister. The family made stops in Spokane, Washington, and Sandpoint and Boise, Idaho, before settling in Alexandria, Virginia, where Lynch unhappily went to high school. (He ran for class treasurer; his slogan, "Save with Dave." He lost.)

After attending both the Corcoran School of Art in Washington, D.C., and the School of the Museum of Fine Arts in Boston, and after an aborted trip to Europe to study with a painter whose work he greatly disliked, Lynch wandered through a series of sad jobs, marked only by his talent for being fired. Mired in extended adolescence, he retreated to art school, this time to the Pennsylvania Academy of Fine Arts in Philadelphia. There he began by studying painting, but ended four years later by making his first live-action movie, *The Grandmother,* in which a distraught, bed-wetting boy, abused by his parents, secretly grows a benevolent grandma from a seed.

In 1970, Lynch enrolled at the American Film Institute in Los Angeles as a fellow in the Center for Advanced Film Studies. His first advanced film, *Eraserhead,* wasn't released until 1977, because he'd spent a lot of time painting, delivering the *Wall Street Journal,* collecting garbage, building sheds, dissecting animals, getting divorced, smoking cigarettes, slurping shakes, and sitting in a chair, silently, thinking. *Eraserhead,* a blackly comic, pleasurably disgusting meditation on bringing up baby—a virtual feast of anxiety!—became a midnight movie hit. His next film, *The Elephant Man,* was refined and subtle, if not sentimental, by comparison. A tone poem on Victorian England, a place, to Lynch, where the beast *was* the beauty, it won eight Oscar nominations and commercial legitimacy for its director. This he quickly bastardized on *Dune,* his only commercial and critical bomb. Lynch tried to thread its gigantic narrative through the eye of his trancelike moods and methods, and failed, quite spectacularly.

Blue Velvet was a return to form, scale, and intuition. A wickedly funny, overripe orchestration of all of Lynch's obsessions, set in small-town USA,

Blue Velvet was arguably the most original and powerful American movie of the 1980s. Remembered and discussed mostly for having put the vile back in violence, it moved Lynch to the forefront of American directors.

His next film, *Wild at Heart,* went even further with the kind of surreal psychosexual slapstick that's become his "name brand." Despite the Palme d'Or prize it won at Cannes, it wasn't the masterpiece *Blue Velvet* was—its weirdness felt applied and artificial, and it came perilously close to self-parody. Still, *Wild at Heart* was still a curious and engaging film—a hokey, jokey joy ride through the bottomlands of Lynch's own imagination.

Between those two films, Lynch and a partner, Mark Frost, unleashed "Twin Peaks." A whimsical subversion—but not destruction—of all TV's codes, it served up that strange slice of American pie where distortion meets recognition, producing a kitschy sugar high, Lynch à la mode. Accompanied by a feeding frenzy of media attention, the first season of "Twin Peaks" in the spring of 1990 was brilliant: nine hours of dancing dwarves and echoing owls and an aura unlike anything in the history of American television. But the second season proved flaccid and banal, and the show was soon canceled. Lynch, frustrated, sought the last word, which in this case would be the first word. A cinematic prequel, *Twin Peaks: Fire Walk with Me* would be his continued attempt to explore the improbabilities of this mythic town, free from the restrictions of commercial television.

In addition to screenwriting and directing, David Lynch has also written naive song lyrics, produced pop albums and the non-symphonic "Industrial Symphony No. 1," and for years drawn the cartoon "The Angriest Dog in the World" for the *L.A. Reader.* He takes pictures, paints, makes perfume commercials, and is preparing a coffee-table book of his collected visual work, which will reflect, in part, his interest in dental hygiene.

Our two conversations occurred in late June and early July of 1990, between the first and second seasons of "Twin Peaks." The initial session took place at the midtown Manhattan apartment/studio of his music maven, Angelo Badalamenti, who was at work in the adjoining room; the subsequent, in a booth at the Studio Coffee Shop in Hollywood, an anti-trendy diner much favored by Lynch.

Lynch was prompt, courteous, and completely uncomfortable with the process of analysis and verbalization demanded by an in-depth interview. His aw-shucks Americanisms and anti-intellectual bias—the Jimmy-Stewart-from-Mars persona—is delectably odd: funny, comfy, yet coolly distanced and distancing. I felt he'd thought about everything I asked him: he just didn't want to lug all his bags up out of the basement.

SESSION ONE

When you've talked about your childhood, you've said it's filled with beatific memories but also with traumatic horror. Could you elaborate on this a bit?

Well, it's hard to elaborate, but I kept coming to Brooklyn to visit my grandparents, and that was part of the horror. *Part* of the horror. In a large city I realized there was a large amount of fear, because so many people were living close together. You could feel it in the air. I think people in the city obviously get used to it, but to come into it from the Northwest it kind of hits you like a train. Like a subway.

In fact, going into the subway, I felt I was really going down into hell. As I went down the steps, going deeper into it, I realized it was almost as difficult to back up and get out of it as to go forward and go through with this ride. It was the total fear of the unknown—the wind from the those trains, the sounds, the smells, and the different light and mood—that was really special in a traumatic way.

Then there were traumas in Boise, Idaho, too, but they were much more *natural*, I would say. There was more light around the place, and not so much fear in the air.

You oppose the blue skies, picket fences, and cherry trees of your youth with the red ants crawling out of the cherry tree—

That was in Spokane, Washington, where we had a cherry tree in the backyard, and it was a real old one. There was this pitch oozing out of it—but really, *really* oozing out of it—and then ants just, like, *alive* on the tree. That was something I would stare at for hours. Like watching TV.

It was a pretty normal scene at home. You say your parents didn't smoke or drink and never argued, but that you were ashamed of them for that. You wanted them to carry on. You wanted a strangeness that wasn't there.

Yeah, it was like in the fifties: there were a lot of advertisements in magazines where you see a well-dressed woman bringing a pie out of an oven, and a certain smile on her face, or a couple smiling, walking together up to their house, with a picket fence. Those smiles were pretty much all I saw.

But you didn't believe them.

Well, they're strange smiles. They're the smiles of the way the world should be or could be. They really made me dream like crazy. And I like that whole side of it a lot. But I longed for some sort of . . . not a catastrophe, but something out of the ordinary to happen. Something so that everyone will feel sorry for you, and you'll be like a victim. You know, if there was a tremendous accident and you were left alone. It's kind of like a nice dream. But things kept on going, normally, forward.

Did you secretly wish to be orphaned?

Well, I wished to be, not orphaned, but I wanted to be special and set aside. Maybe it's an excuse for not having to do anything else. You're instantly important. You've kind of got it made in a certain way. I was thinking about things like that. I was sort of embarrassed that my parents were so normal.

More abnormal things were going on in your friends' households?

Oh yeah! Yeah.

So you pursued a kind of danger on your own to bring this into your own life?

I didn't get into too many dangerous things. And I don't talk about a lot of dangerous things. People are going to do what they do anyway, but it's not so good to sell the idea—because you don't need to do a lot of dangerous things to be creating. Just to introduce a thought of certain things is not so good.

You wanted your parents to argue, but you've said elsewhere that you didn't like tension or conflict, that you were always trying to smooth things over.

Yeah, I did that. It goes back to feeling this bad thing in the air. I'd see my friends who just moments earlier were getting along, and then it would all fall apart. And I'd try to make it go back and be smooth. Just so we could all have fun.

The "smile" that you talked about, in the ads, were you feeling something akin to this smile inside, or were you feeling very different?

No, I had a tremendous smile. I have pictures of me underneath the Christmas tree with a smile that is like total and pure happiness. I sort of had a happiness.

But at the same time there was something about it you didn't trust.

You know, that's another thing: there are too many possibilities for something to go wrong—so you could always worry about that. And there are many things that are hidden and seeming like many, many secrets; and you don't know for sure whether you are just being paranoid or if there really are some secrets. You know little by little, by studying science, that certain things are hidden – there are things you can't see. They've run experiments; they know there are things like atoms, and a lot of things that you can't see. And your mind can begin to create many things to worry about. And then, once you're exposed to fearful things, and you see that really and truly many, many, many things are wrong, and so many people are participating in strange and horrible things, you begin to worry that the peaceful, happy life could vanish or be threatened.

What were the things you thought were hurtful or worrisome?

Just every sort of negative thing you feel in the air was bringing the situation down.

Let's try to be concrete. You're the master of the specific, come on –

[Laughs.] Yeah, right! Like in Philadelphia a family is going to this christening. I happened to be upstairs at home painting the third floor black. And my wife at the time, Peggy, was taking my daughter, Jennifer, who was one, out in this perambulator. It was like the Cadillac of perambulators, that we got at Goodwill for about a buck, but it was unbelievable. It had springs – it had a ride like a giant Cadillac. Anyway, Peggy was taking this down the steps. And a large family was going to a christening of this small baby. And a gang came swooping down on the other side of the street, and attacked the family. And in the family there was a teenage son who tried to defend the whole bunch, and they beat him down, and they shot him in the back of the head. Those kind of things will spoil the atmosphere – permanently – and bring it way down.

Is art your only defense against things like that?

There is no defense. Your horror of horrors is that all of us are so much out of control, and if you start thinking about it you can worry about that for a long time.

But you've managed to survive things like that.

Well, you go along. But you realize that basically you're pretty lucky to be able to just go along.

You've said that as a kid you felt "a force, a sort of wild pain and decay, accompanying everything." What did that pain feel like?

I don't know what I was talking about there, but whenever you finish something, it starts decaying. Instantly. Just like New York City. The idea of New York City is a great one: you can have business and residential things all together, and people all together, and really fine restaurants and theatre, movies, and great architecture! Buildings that look so great and were built so well. They're functional, but also sculpture. But then time goes by and the bridges – they're rotting so bad! The roads, the buildings are falling apart.

New ones are going up but they're not built the same way. This thing about decay and nothing remaining constant is another thing to worry about.

Our bodies are like that, too.

They sure are. They grow, and then they start reversing themselves. And strange things happen. You say, "That won't ever happen to me. No way!" But then one day you look in the mirror and it's happening.

What have you seen happening in the mirror that was traumatic for you?

Well, right above my ears there's these kind of silver, fish-scale silver hairs.

And when you first saw them?

I couldn't really believe it.

That wasn't the first time you had a sense of your mortality?

Uh, no.

That "wild pain" you talked about—what makes it wild?

Because it's not able to be controlled. See, a small world like a painting or a film gives you the illusion that you're more or less under control. Or that you're *in* control, rather. So I guess the smaller the world, the more safe you feel, and in control.

So you build a world.

You build it, yeah. I love going into another world, and film provides that opportunity—*Eraserhead* way more than any other film, because I really did live in that world.

You lived on the set.

I lived on the set, and in my mind I lived in that world. And the set helped a lot; the lighting, the mood of it helped. And since it took so much time I really sank into it. But now films go so fast: you move into a set, you check and make sure the mood is correct, and the next moment you're shooting it. And moments later it's being bulldozed. So it's captured on film, but it's real fun to live in it for a while, too.

You don't feel you're getting to inhabit your own films the same way you used to?

No. It's not as long and as satisfying.

This kind of worry you talk about—what's the nature of it? Why not accept the decay?

Well, you have to sort of learn to accept things. But I don't like it. Nobody likes to accept things. You fight decay by painting those bridges. The Golden Gate Bridge in San Francisco, they don't ever stop painting it. You've got to do something to maintain things. And the more you let it slip, the harder it is to bring it back to the original condition. And a lot of things, when they get older, if they have been maintained, get another degree of quality. Nature goes to work on them a little bit, but they have been maintained, and so they are called antiques and you can get a lot of money for them.

A patina of rust can be beautiful.

A patina. Exactly. Absolutely.

Would anyone who looked at you on your fifteenth birthday, this little worried Eagle Scout, in uniform, down by the White House seating VIPs for JFK's inauguration parade—would anyone have thought you were unusual or had some different ideas?

No. I was like a regular person. There wasn't much happening upstairs. I didn't really *think*, at all, not that I can remember, until I was about nineteen.

What triggered that?

I don't know. I think Philadelphia.

When things started happening upstairs, was it always in terms of images?

And sounds, but I didn't really know about that part, until later on. Always, since I was little, I was drawing. And then I got into painting. But there wasn't any thought behind the drawings.

Your parents were supportive of your early work?

Oh, very supportive. My mother probably saved me: she refused to give me coloring books. Which is pretty interesting, because there was lots of pressure to color—and once you have that coloring book the whole idea is to stay between the lines. Not having that restriction . . . and paper! My father worked for the government, and he'd bring home lots and lots of graph paper, and one side was old news and the other was blank. So I had lots of paper, and I was able to draw whatever I wanted all the time. My father also helped pay rent on a painting studio when I was in high school, and helped pay for my first film.

Yet you were rebelling like crazy at the time.

Yes, I was.

From about age fourteen to about age thirty?

Yes, and my theory is that most people rebel that long these days, because not counting accidents or strange diseases, we're built to live longer. And so all the stages consequently last longer. And so you're going to find people living at home, going through these strange rebellions. And maybe they'll be sixty before they realize they're an adult, and get serious about things.

What were you rebelling against?

I never really thought about it. They call it rebellion. I just didn't want anything to do with anything except painting, and living the Art Life. Nothing else was fun.

You didn't want them to know about what you were doing, did you?

I was doing many things that I figured they would not enjoy knowing about. So I was forced to live a secret life.

Now, there's a kind of power in having a secret.

There's a horror in secrets, too.

What's the horror?

You know, trying to keep it secret.

What's a secret? A secret is something you absolutely have to tell someone!

Well, yeah. There's that problem too.

Did the fact that they didn't know what you were up to—living this very nocturnal Art Life—help you start to feel like your own person?

Yeah. I felt like my own person before that, but I didn't think about things in the same way. I mean, I was smoking cigarettes; that was before any kind of drug things. I don't know if I would have gotten into drugs, but I was absolutely born to smoke. I loved to watch my Grandfather Lynch smoke cigarettes. I could hardly wait. I loved the taste of tobacco. Being addicted to it was one thing, but I really and truly loved every part of smoking: the texture of the smoke, all the business, the lighters and matches. The taste of it, particularly.

What was sex like as a teenager? Scary?

Umm, what kind of an interview are we doing, David? [Laughs.] I tell you what: sex was like a dream. It was like a world that was so mysterious to me that I really couldn't believe that there was this fantastic texture to life that I was getting to *do*. It was so fantastic, and I could see a world opening—this sexual dream. It was another great indication that life was really great and worth living. And it kept on going, because I see that the vast realm of sex has all these different levels, from lust and fearful, violent sex to the real spiritual thing at the other end. It's the key to some fantastic mystery of life.

But there's a sense in your films that the flesh is not to be trusted.

Well, I think until a person has reached a certain degree of evolution there's no such thing as trust.

What stage of evolution would that be?

[Pause.] If you were to believe in evolution, you would see that there are different levels of human growth. Degrees of awareness or consciousness. You could see a person being totally aware and totally conscious at the end of this evolutionary trail. And dealing with a full deck. And if you are able to deal with a full deck, I think then you'd be pretty trustworthy.

How many cards are in yours?

I don't have any idea, but it's not fifty-two.

The Europe experience, very briefly—

And it was a brief experience—

Austria was too clean—

Austria was way too clean. I didn't know why I was waking up there so early, but looking back I know why. It was early enough in the trip for me to be getting jet-lagged. But I was so young it didn't slow me down, I just woke up early, which is completely unusual for me. I attributed it to the clean air in Austria. At that time, part of the Art Life for me—since I grew up in a place so clean, with forests and all—was about American city life, so I didn't really take to Salzburg. I was glad I went, but once that fell apart the whole trip unraveled. But the Orient Express was an incredible journey.

The Art Life means: stay up late, smoke cigarettes, don't get married, don't have children, stay dedicated to seeing beneath the surface, drink coffee. And yet you got married, not once but twice, and had two children.

[Pause.] These things happen.

Happen to you, or you make them happen?

Well, it's a two-way street. Nothing happens to you. It takes two to tango, and this is what happened to me.

How was it, living inside those contradictions?

It was kind of tough. But again, absolutely good and meant to be. Sometimes a jolt of electricity at a certain point of your life is helpful. It forces you a little bit more awake. It makes something happen inside you. I didn't really understand what was happening, but because I had these new responsibilities, I think it really helped—it overlapped into the work. I was just starting to make films, and it made me focus in and take things more seriously. I might have been drifting around for a lot longer had these things not happened.

Eraserhead seems to be, on one level, the work of a man completely unprepared for, and terrified by, fatherhood.

Eraserhead is an abstract film. It's hopefully not just about one thing. But that's definitely in there. [Smiles slyly.]

Going to the morgue in Philadelphia was another turning point.

Well, Philadelphia itself was the turning point. Seeing a lot of different things. The morgue was kind of a clinical thing. It was very powerful, but it wasn't a twisted thing to me. It was more like seeing my neighbor's dog. That was another image I'll never forget. Their dog, they fed so much, it looked literally like a water balloon with little legs. The legs kind of stuck out. Almost couldn't walk, this dog. Had a little bitty head. It was like a Mexican Chihuahua with a watermelon in the middle. And there were lots of little bowls of candies in the room, and these things stuck with me a lot.

Was the dog your first link to surrealism or were Dali and Buñuel?

I never saw, I still haven't seen a lot of Buñuel and I saw *An Andalusian Dog* a lot later. I don't even know that much about surrealism—I guess it's just my take on what's floating by. I wasn't exposed to too many sophisticated things.

What was the spiritual crisis you underwent during the filming of Eraserhead?

The spiritual crisis was that I thought I had every reason to be completely happy. I was making a film I wanted to make. I had the greatest crew and friends working. The list of things that I thought were going to do it for me were all checked off. I was sitting right where I thought I should be completely happy. And I wasn't happy. So I really wondered about that. It made me think about the idea of happiness, and what it might be.

Did you want it, badly?

Oh yeah, you betcha!

Is it still paramount?

Well, it's another word for lots of things. It's another word for: fifty-two cards.

That unhappiness led to Transcendental Meditation?

That's right. That's what it did.

And did that at least start shuffling the deck?

Yeah, it did. I don't really talk about meditation. A lot of people are against it. It's just something I like and I've been doing it since 1973.

It seems like your background as a painter led to a film style focused on texture and the single image—it demands real examination of the frame. Was that something conscious for you when you moved from the canvas to film?

No. I forget the word . . . oh, composition. This thing of composition is so abstract. It's so powerful, where you place things and the relationships. But you don't work with any kind of intellectual thing. You just act and react. It's all intuition. It must obey rules, but these rules are not in any book. The basic rules of composition are a joke.

Really sophisticated composition works like really sophisticated pieces of music: you can't believe what you're seeing. You could spend years looking at one great work and still find new things in it that are so perfect. Like great symphonies. You can't believe that that chord flows into that, and then *that* swoops in. It's too great. Too thrilling. And how they come to be is a mystery.

So you don't find particularly compelling parallels between your painting and filmmaking?

No. They obey some of the same rules, that's all. And these rules are found in nature. Like the duck. You could pick any animal, but let's take the duck. The duck is real good for many things—like textures, proportions, shapes. How a duck is made and where the different things are on a duck can give you a clue to a more or less perfect composition for a painting. If you could interpret a duck, if you could work with the rules of a duck, you could get something close to a well-composed painting that had neat things happening.

Your famous first Botched Commission, where in art school you worked for two months shooting and came out with one long blur because the camera was broken—you point to this as something that led you on into film, but isn't that twenty-twenty hindsight?

It felt funny. It was a very weird thing. It took two months to shoot two minutes and twenty-five seconds. I remember holding the film up to the light to see frames, and I saw no frames. I was not depressed, I was curious to know what was happening. There was no depression. I remember someone asking, "Aren't you upset?" I said, "No." The hindsight part came in later. If that had come out and I had sent that to the American Film Institute, it wouldn't have been good enough to get me the grant I got later. And of course that grant I *had* to have, if I was going to get into film. So fate was smiling on me.

The feeling you had after a subsequent film didn't turn out right wasn't quite as uplifting. Dune.

But I learned a lot of stuff on *Dune*. I started selling out on *Dune*. Looking back, it's no one's fault but my own. I probably shouldn't have done that picture, but I saw tons and tons of possibilities for things I loved, and this was the structure to do them in. There was so much room to create a world. But I got strong indications from Raffaella and Dino De Laurentiis of what kind of film they expected, and I knew I didn't have final cut. And little by little by little—and this is the danger, because it doesn't happen in chunks, it happens in the tiniest little shavings, little sandings—little by little every decision was always made with them in mind and their sort of film. Things I felt

I could get away with within their framework. So it was destined to be a failure, to me.

Well, the failure of Dune *saved you from having to do* Dune II *and* Dune III.

Yes, that's a plus. Though I was really getting into *Dune II*. I wrote about half the script, maybe more, and I was really getting excited about it. It was much tighter, a better story.

Did you feel like a failure?

Yeah. I was made to feel like one, and I felt like one too. There were times before, like on *The Elephant Man*, I went through some things that I thought would be the end of me, but *Dune* was pretty bad. Even in post-production, I started feeling the writing on the wall.

What did you think would be the end of you on The Elephant Man?

I was supposed to build the Elephant Man's makeup. And again, I worked for two months, maybe more, two months in England, and what I built was a complete and total disaster. It was a disaster because I wasn't prepared to build things for a human. And I didn't know how certain things worked. Though parts of what I did were interesting, it was a disaster. For four days I had nightmares at night, but when I woke up, being awake was worse than the nightmares. Mel Brooks [the film's producer] came over to England and found a guy to do it in the time we had. Mel's good attitude pulled me out of the torment of being a complete failure.

Had you ever felt like that before, during those years doing all those lame jobs, before and after school?

No. There I felt like, not like a failure, but very frustrated. There are an awful lot of people who feel this way, and I felt this way for a long time. In order to do a painting, you've got to have canvas, stretchers, paint, brushes, turpentine. You have to have a place to paint. You have to have time to paint. And you have to have a certain mental freedom, to think about the painting. And if you have a job or any kind of other responsibilities or an apartment where you're going to be sued for getting paint here or there? There are so many obstacles to getting set up to paint. That initial outlay of cash to just get set up. It's almost too much to overcome. It's staggering to get set up to do anything. If you are going to do photography, just to get a darkroom—there are so many things that can stop you. It's pretty frustrating. I felt frustrated during all those times, because I never could get set up to work.

Let's shift gears. I'd like to talk about some elements that seem to be present in all your films, despite the differences between them. First, you have an obsession with obsession.

Yeah, I got that.

Now, during Blue Velvet, *when you were filming the scenes of Frank [Dennis Hopper] abusing and raping Dorothy [Isabella Rossellini], apparently you were beside yourself with laughter. You thought this was sort of funny on some level?*

I'm sure pretty near every psychiatrist could tell me right now why I was laughing, but I don't know. It was hysterically funny to me. Frank was completely obsessed. He was like a dog in a chocolate store. He could not help himself. He was completely *into* it. But I was laughing and I am a human being; there must be some logical reason why. It has something to do with the fact that it was so horrible and so frightening and so intense and violent that there was also this layer of humor.

I don't know what it is, but it's there, and it has to do with this degree of obsession, where people cannot help themselves. In New York, especially, you see it on the street all the time. And because you see it on the street, you know it's happening in their apartments too. But the poor people on the street don't have any place to go do it privately. These kind of things strike me as humorous sometimes.

Are you obsessive?

Yeah, I'm sure I am. Habits are obsessive things. Having things a certain way. This is sometimes humorous.

That can come from feeling out of control, using habits as centering devices—

Oh, absolutely. I must be completely out of control.

Because you are such a creature of habit?

Yeah. I like to try to control my local environment as much as I can. And it's impossible to do it.

Do you really feel out of control?

Yeah. There are certain times when it's an illusion that you have some sort of control. It's a gift just to get just a little bit of that feeling. There are so many things that can come in and pull the rug out from under you so fast.

Is there a freedom in understanding you don't have any control? Then you don't worry about it so much.

Well, yeah. But you still strive for it as much as possible. It's not control for control's sake; it's to get something a certain way. Making something a certain way is really, really hard because there are so many forces at work to undermine what you're doing. And to stay one jump ahead of it, or even two or three jumps behind it instead of ten or twenty jumps behind it, is sort of fun. It's sort of what it's about.

Is it scary to feel out of control?

Yes. Very scary. And there's nothing you can do about it.

What's the worst that can happen?

I'm sure that's the kind of thing a psychiatrist might ask you: "What's the worst thing that could happen, David?" [Laughs.] And then if you could face that, you could face anything. The worst thing that could happen is that . . . [Long pause.] I don't know. There's also the fear of the unknown – who knows what could happen? In the case of a film, the worse thing that could happen is something like *Dune*. Where the film is halfway there and halfway not.

Let's look at something else that seems central to your work: the presence of cruelty and physical and mental abuse.

[Angelo Badalamenti comes in, asking if anyone wants coffee.] Angelo, you've said the magic word! Light! With sugar! . . . Cruelty, uh-huh.

Where does it come from?

Beats me.

I'm not denying it's out there on Thirty-fourth Street, but it's very much there, specifically, in your vision of the world.

It could be a lot of different things. It could be partly what I feel is out there. Partly the stories that attract me. That tension. See, I see films more and more as separate from whatever kind of reality there is anywhere else. And that they are more like fairy tales or dreams. They are not, to me, political or, like, any kind of commentary or any kind of teaching device. They're just *things*. It's another world to go into, if you choose to. But they should obey certain rules. The same as a painting. And these rules are abstract and found in nature.

And one of them is Contrast. It can't just be a flat, straight line of pure happiness. People fall asleep. So there are conflicts and life-and-death struggles. I like murder mysteries. They get me completely, because they are mysteries and deal with life and death. So I'm hooked right away. The letdown is if the story is too simplistic or it's not structured properly so it doesn't have a lot of satisfaction. But initially, if you say "mystery" and "murder," that always gets me, and if you throw in the word "hotel" or "factory" I get even more involved.

So you don't know where this predilection for cruelty comes from?

No. I was not tortured as a child. And I didn't ever see anybody get tortured. So either it's a coincidence that this is all through there or the reason lies beyond, somewhere else.

Okay, let's look at one aspect of "Contrast." In your work, there's a constant dichotomy between Good and Evil, between Light and Darkness, and Innocence and Knowledge, where Knowledge is aligned with guilt, danger, horror—Knowledge as a kind of sickness.

Uh-huh. Knowing the wrong thing, like the man who knew too much, is sometimes a real drag.

I guess what I'm wondering is whether, outside the constructed world of the films, you see the world as having these very strong dichotomies between Good and Evil, as opposed to a kind of complex, integrated—

No, I know it's complex. Everybody's got many threads of both running through them. But I think in a film white gets a little whiter, and black gets a little bit blacker, for the sake of the story. That's part of the beauty of it, that contrast, the power of it. Maybe it would be very beautiful to have a character that had an equal mixture of both, where the forces were fighting equally. But maybe they would just stand still.

You mentioned life and death. It's compelling that all your movies have a birth scene—or some kind of abstracted birth scene—and also death scenes, scenes of murder or murderous intent. Finally, in Wild at Heart *the birth scene* is *a death scene—an abortion. How we start and how we finish seems the biggest subject on the table for you?*

Absolutely. [Pause.]

Is it on your hard disk?

I guess so. [Laughs.] It must be. You know, it's in interviews that you can sometimes see some sense to it. Most of the time the thinking exists on a more abstract area. You don't even worry about what things you've done before, or if these things are out there or are they just in here, is it out of proportion, or whatever. You're just going along and catching this fantastic train that leads to a new world and another story.

What I'm saying is that the trains run to all kinds of destinations and through all sorts of scenery—

But might be going all to one place. [Laughs.]

No, not at all: but wherever they're going, they're still in Lynchville! Even in The Alphabet, *your first four-minute animated film, the capital letter A gives bloody birth to little a's. The Grandmother has an excruciating birth,* Eraserhead *has any number of disturbing births,* The Elephant Man *and so on—what gets you about it?*

For a long time, and I suppose, still, the idea of birth was a mysterious and fantastic thing, involving, again, like sex, just pure meat and blood and hair. And then at the same time, this feeling of life and the spiritual thing. There are too many things going on there not to be fascinated by it. [The coffee arrives.] Angelo, bless your heart, I sure am gonna dig this!

Did you attend the birth of either of your children?

Both. For Jennifer, in those days, at the hospital in Philadelphia, they wouldn't let fathers in there. And so I was real proud of myself, because I could convince the doctor that I could handle it. I did, because he kept taking blood from my wife Peggy, and I figured more of it than he needed to take, just to see if I would pass out or something. And when he saw that I was able to handle that, he said okay, I could come in. So I scrubbed up and put on the green shoes and the outfit. I went in and, like twenty-five billion people, witnessed this thing. And it's not so much what you see as an abstraction you feel. It's the weirdest thing. It's real weird.

All of a sudden there's someone else in the room.

There's a *lot* in the room, it feels like! Things you can't see. It's pretty powerful.

Could you make a film without birthing or dying?

Sure, you could do it. But it's putting the cart before the horse. Some people get on a kick. They say, let's make a film about *this*. And then they create a whole story to support this idea. It's backwards. Later on, you maybe find out what the film is about. I'm not saying it's good, it's just more natural for me. And they don't all happen at once: they happen in fragments. Even a book, you're reading in fragments, one chapter after another. You're carried forward by these things and a world is starting to go in your mind. But for me, the world of the mind, it's fuzzy. It's not complete. It has holes in it. It can't be shared so well. When you make it specific and concrete and have so many elements swimming together, it becomes so powerful and shareable.

Now, let me bring up a touchy subject. The position of women in your films. For Blue Velvet *you took some abuse about—*

Because people have an idea that Dorothy was Everywoman, instead of just being Dorothy. That's where the problem starts. If it's just Dorothy, and it's her story—which it is to me—then everything is fine. If Dorothy is Everywoman, it doesn't make any sense. It doesn't add up. It's completely false, and they'd be right to be upset.

Ideas are the weirdest things. They're out floating, and you catch them, and you can build them into something. Like a table. It's right there floating. And then it appears in your mind: suddenly you've caught it, it bubbles up, shows itself to you, and you can go in your shop and put it together. And that's how these things go.

Let's try to talk more concretely about women in your films—the "disease" that Dorothy has. There's a kind of physical threat that hangs over women in "Twin

Peaks" and Wild at Heart *and* Blue Velvet. *And there's a certain amount of female complicity in it. Even in "Twin Peaks," Ronette Pulaski, who's beaten to within an inch of her life, rates four red hearts in the department store manager's secret book of call girls, and we know Laura Palmer, who's brutally murdered, is not Snow White. Are you ever afraid that you sidle up close to a sort of "blaming the victim"?*

I know what you're talking about. Again, it goes to Ronette Pulaski not being Ronette Pulaski as Everywoman, but just Ronette Pulaski. Everyone can picture in their mind a situation where the girl—for one reason or another—went along with the situation. And everyone can picture in their mind where the girl said, "I'm not into this one little bit!" and got *out*. And then there's a borderline, where it's right on the edge for a person: where it's interesting, but it's sickening, or it's frightening or it's too much, or almost, or not quite. There's every different combo in this world. When you start talking about "women" versus "a woman," then you're getting into this area of generalizations, and you can't win. There is no generalization. There's a billion different stories and possibilities . . .

In the naked city—

You betcha!

Now let's talk about these women. Both Dorothy in Blue Velvet *and Laura in "Twin Peaks" have the "disease." Laura gets off on a man almost killing her, because it makes sex great. What's the "disease" to you? Can you be more up front about it?*

Um, no.

Come on, David.

No, because just the word "disease" used in that way . . . it's so beautiful just to leave it abstract. Once it becomes specific, it's no longer true to a lot of people, where if it's abstract there could be some truth to it for everybody.

But come on, we know there's a kind of masochism at work here—

But even *that* can be so complicated that even to start talking about it wouldn't do it justice. It would always make it be less than it really is, because it's so *unbelievably* complicated. And if it wasn't complicated, people could be fixed and made perfect so easily. It just is so complicated.

One critic pointed out that in Blue Velvet *women were either abused or useful to men, and that the only choices women had were those put before them by men.*

That's this person's take on it. How would what he said have anything to do with Sandy [Laura Dern]? She wasn't totally manipulated by anybody, you know, any man. She did tons of stuff on her own. She liked certain things. She didn't like certain things. She made decisions on her own. She acted and reacted with her own apparatus. She gets Jeffrey into the situation on her own. On her own. But instead of *her* going over to that woman's house, she is able to catch the interest in Jeffrey and fire it up, so that he does the dirty work. Meanwhile, Aunt Barbara and they are at home, all they can do is watch it on TV, they don't even want to go out of their house. They'll see it in the safety of their living room. But they're interested in it. It's all about an interest in things that are hidden and mysterious. Sandy is very smart and very together. What he said was kind of a general thing, and when you put it against what's really there it doesn't make a whole lot of sense. [Lynch assumes, wrongly, that the critic is a man.]

How about Lula, though, in Wild at Heart? *Lula [again, Laura Dern] in the movie is certainly a step back as compared to Lula in the book in terms of her assertiveness, her aggressiveness, her control over the world around her. In the book, Lula tells Sailor where to get off, orders him when to drive. She finds him dancing with another woman at a club and throws a bottle at him, which hits him, and lets him know how pissed she is at him; whereas in the movie there's a club scene where Sailor [Nicolas Cage] sort of "rescues" her, and defends his territory when another man tries to dance with her. Couldn't one say that Lula is made a less modern woman through the way you've channeled the book?*

[Long pause. Irritated] Well, I don't know about modern women. Except that Lula is . . . it just so happens that both those other scenes were shot, and because of time and one thing after another, they didn't get in. It may not be that she throws a bottle at him, but there are still lots of indications that she would be very pissed off at Sailor if he ever did something like that. You can tell that from the way she just is. The thing that got me about Sailor and Lula is their relationship: they're so really good to each other and in love and they treat each other with respect, in my opinion. I don't know about a modern man or a modern woman, but that's a modern romance. Because Sailor can be cool and masculine, but still have tenderness toward Lula and treat her as an equal. Never talk down to her. He just talks to her. And the same with Lula to him. One of the reasons I love this relationship and this book is them being equals.

But in the book she's sensitive to the fact that he might be talking down to her. She doesn't like being called "Peanut" all the time. She says, "I don't know that I completely enjoy you callin' me Peanut so much . . . puts me so far down on the food chain."

Oh, I don't even remember that. No, she *loves* to be called Peanut.

It's in the book. Now, there's an Oedipal thing happening in your films. You either have a kind of mystical reunion with the lost mother or you have—

Well, that's *The Elephant Man*. That's specific to that story. For the Elephant

Man, his fondest memory was of his mother. His whole life was built trying to live up to something he imagined her wanting for him. So that when he died it needed to be that way: with the mother. It felt right. What other films?

— You have, in Blue Velvet, *and elsewhere, a kind of "sex with mom" thing going on.*

How's that?

Frank is like an infant, calls Dorothy "Mommy" and says at one point, "Baby wants to fuck!"

He's either daddy or he's baby.

And in Wild at Heart, *Lula's mom [Diane Ladd] comes on to her boyfriend, Sailor—*

And that happens in *Eraserhead,* too!

Right, Mary's mom comes on to Henry [Jack Nance]. And now, on "Twin Peaks," we get to see Benjamin Horne confronting his daughter Audrey in a whorehouse bedroom. There is a pattern here.

Well, yeah, the trouble is if you do more than one of anything, then people start comparing. A lot of times it leads you into strange conclusions that have no bearing on reality or the way it came about. It could just be a coincidence that each story . . . some of them I didn't write, I didn't think up, even though I was involved in the script. Ideas come along. How much is something inside me? I think the inside-you part dictates a lot, but then the idea part coming in from outside is a big part of it, too. I don't know. There's a lot of things that human beings do that are completely fascinating, and at the same time you think they are somewhat strange.

That seems to be the way we're built.

That's exactly right. And those are the things that are so interesting to work with in films. If things are real normal, you might as well just stay home— they're strange enough there. In film, things get heightened. You see things a little bit more and feel things a little bit more.

You seem kind of defensive about this.

Because I don't know if it's true that there are these similarities.

Well, let me bring up one more for observation. There's a sense, at the ends of your films, in the redemptive power of fantasy, of the imagination itself. There's a, not childish, but maybe childlike sense that you want to see or imagine something brand new, that the possibilities of your imagination are what save you.

Yeah. It's tough, again, to talk about some general thing, but I guess—for myself—I believe in this force of evolution. Being in darkness and confusion is really interesting to me, but behind it you can rise out of that and see things the way they really are. That there is some sort of truth to the whole thing, if you could just get to that point where you could see it, and live it, and feel it and all that. I think it's a long, long way off. In the meantime, there's suffering and darkness and confusion and absurdities, and it's people kind of going in circles. It's *fantastic*. It's like a strange carnival: it's a lot of fun, but it's a lot of pain.

Is it all darkness and confusion?

Everything is relative. I'd say this world is maybe not the brightest place one could hope to be.

One of the confusions seems to be over whether art has to mean anything. Let me quote you: "Why do people want art to make sense when they accept the fact that life doesn't make sense?" First off, I don't think people accept the fact that life doesn't make sense. I think it makes people terribly uncomfortable. Religion and myth were invented against that, to try to make some sense out of life. Don't you think that's where art comes from too?

Maybe some of it does. But for me, I'm of the Western Union school. If you want to send a message, go to Western Union. It's even a problem with responsibility. You have to be free to think up things. They come along, these ideas, and they hook themselves together, and the unifying thing is the euphoria they give you, or the repulsion they give you (and you throw those ideas away). If they're all stringing themselves happily together and they're forming a story that's carrying you forward, the first way you can kill that is to start worrying about what other people are going to think. Then you start worrying about what your immediate friends or family are going to think—that can kill it right there. The next thing to worry about is the general public. It's so abstract, you kill it instantly. Then you have to worry about the future people, and you can't even imagine what they're going to be like, so you'd have to figure they're not going to like it. You have to just trust yourself. If you have any sort of moral thing or boundaries you won't cross over, that's going to shape your story. Then, if you're given permission and the money to make this into a film, you say, this is just the way it is. Please walk out of the theatre if it's upsetting you. If you don't like it, fine. I'm real sorry you had to see even a frame of it. People have to be able to create these things.

But that's not to say they don't mean anything?

No, but if you start worrying right away about the meaning of everything, chances are your poor intellect is only going to glean a little portion of it. If it stays abstract, if it's in an area where it feels truthful, and it hooks in the right way, and it thrills you as it moves to the next idea, and it seems to move and make some sort of intuitive sense, that is a real good guideline.

There's a certain kind of logic and truth and right workings that you have to trust. That's the only thing you have to go by. Fifteen trillion decisions go through this same process: it's either kicked out or taken, or turned this way or that way. That's how it goes along.

So you don't resist the idea that your films mean something?

Not a bit. But they mean different things to different people.

Let's hope so.

Yeah. But even so, some mean more or less the same things to a large number of people. It's okay. Just as long as there's not *one* message, spoon-fed. That's what films by committee end up being and it's a real bummer to me. *No message* is hard to do, because people will read into anything. You can't do a no-message film, it's impossible.

So to say that art doesn't need to make sense because life doesn't make sense—

Life is very, very complicated and so films should be allowed to be too. That's more like the way it is.

Is there an element in this filtering process—the fifteen trillion decisions—where there's a line, or boundary, that you'd like to cross, your intuition tells you to cross, but which you pull back from because it would be too much for people to take?

Yes. And that happened on *Wild at Heart*. When you make a film, it's like a soup. And so much is evaporated out before you get it in the bowl, and probably some is lost off the spoon, and some is stuck in your tooth that you spit out later on: it's only important finally what gets in your stomach, what gets on the screen. And so this process of making the film doesn't stop until someone sits down in the theatre. Like they say, the projectionist has final cut. They can chop off certain things, rearrange the reels. So you keep on checking what you're doing with the intuition thing, or, like in *Wild at Heart*, if vast numbers of people get up out of the audience and leave the theatre, you've got a decision to make.

They're straining the soup.

They just don't like the soup.

You had two test screenings of Wild at Heart *where you had an elephant-stampede out of the theatre—during a scene that involved masturbation, gun-play, and bottles—*

It didn't even involve that. Yes, that's the scene, but it didn't really involve those things that way. The scene is almost there in its entirety now. But it really taught me something: an audience can really be with you, but if you rub it in their face too much—which I didn't think I was doing—they say,

"That's enough!" and out they go. And you can't blame them. I thought it was more powerful that way, but it reached a point where it was too much.

We lopped off the end of the scene, and that brought it back into the good zone. The scene is necessary. At one point I took it out entirely, and without that scene, there was no life-or-death threat, and it was very important to underlie the rest of the film.

What do you think causes such discomfort for people watching certain images?

I don't know. There again, an experienced doctor could tell us. All I know is, it went one step too far, and it snapped their involvement in the story. They rose up out of the story, then they rose up out of their seats, and they eventually got out of the theatre. And the ones that stayed never got back into the film after that. I can't really blame them.

Is there anything you can't watch yourself, other than for reasons of boredom?

Oh, sure. Sure. I don't know what they are, but there are a lot of things all of us don't want to see.

What won't you look at? What have you turned away from or turned off because you couldn't handle it?

[Long pause.] Umm, let's see. [Long pause.] I can't remember. I can't remember.

Have you seen the footage from the concentration camps?

Well, that would be hard to watch and hard to not watch. A lot of people could not watch it. The stuff that human beings do to one another is sometimes impossible to understand or believe, but they still do. So you want to watch to get a hint of how far we'll go as human beings. It's just unbelievable. So you could question your motives for watching and question your motives for not watching. It's a complicated thing.

Were you surprised that it took an external stimulus, a test audience, to tell you to take that scene out of Wild at Heart?

Yeah, I was. That's when I started changing my ideas about these test screenings. There's something about several hundred people sitting in a room. It's not what they write on their cards at the end of the screening, it's the feeling you have sitting in the room with them. It doesn't matter who they are. There's a certain thing we'll all do if three hundred people are together. It's important to see your film with that *presence*. You can learn so much. If there was a machine that could give you that feeling of them being around you . . . but there isn't. It needs to be those souls sitting right next to you. You feel things completely differently. It's unbelievable. It's so frightening but it's so important. The reason people don't like it is because it's so hard to endure. So they say, "I don't dig test screenings. I don't believe in them." Well, I believe in them, but I don't dig them. I really believe in them now.

So even though on an important level you don't care what the audience thinks, you want to communicate, don't you? You're not just making these things for yourself.

No, you don't make them for yourself, but you don't make them for . . . uh, it's, well, I don't understand how it works. You can *think* that you're making them for yourself, but when you sit with the three hundred people you realize that if you were really making it for yourself you would have done this a little differently. I don't understand exactly how it works, but they tell you certain things by being there. Certain things you tricked yourself into thinking were working you see honestly and truly are not working when you have three hundred people there. So it's really a way of checking yourself, by having them there.

SESSION TWO

Let's talk about some of your work that hasn't been produced, starting with the oldest project, Gardenback.

Gardenback is a good example. It should have been a short film. Very abstract. It's the script I submitted along with *The Grandmother* to the Center for Advanced Film Studies. No one really understood what I was trying to do with it. I don't blame them.

You described it as "an abstract film about adultery."

And it was, but they made me say that. Finally, Frank Daniel asked me, "Is this film about adultery?" I guess it is, but it's about other things, too. A guy who was making low-budget horror films told me he'd give me $50,000 to do it if I'd turn it into a feature. He didn't understand it either. But it had a monster in it—which is all that he cared about. He *thought* it was a monster. Fifty thousand dollars was like someone now giving me five million. But it had to be expanded to be a feature . . .

And that killed it?

That killed it for sure. Because it became less and less abstract and more and more "normal" in a boring way.

Have you been able to steal from the corpse?

Maybe a little bit. It crept into paintings and lots of things. I was fascinated with gardens: people standing in gardens in paintings, form in a garden, at night. I really loved that. Then I became really frustrated, but all that was good because it led to *Eraserhead*.

Your most celebrated unmade work is Ronnie Rocket. *Is it dead in the water, completely?*

No, no, no, no, never, not in a million years. It's hard to say I'm going to make *Ronnie Rocket* next. I don't know if it'll ever be made. It's definitely not dead. I've talked about it so much and scripts of it are around—I'm waiting for the next step to happen to do it, if there is a next step. I'm waiting for a time where I don't really care what happens, except that the film is finished. I do care, now, enough so that a film like *Ronnie Rocket* is frightening, because it's not a commercial picture. It's an American smokestack industrial thing—it has to do with coal and oil and electricity. It might be a picture that I would love, but I don't know if too many other people are going to dig it. It's very abstract.

There's not an arrow of narrative?

Well, I think it's pretty straight ahead. I think it's kind of plain. But it is kind of absurd. It's not like a regular picture. And I want to have time to go into that world and live in it for a while, and that costs money. I don't really want to have a normal eleven-week shooting schedule on *Ronnie Rocket*. I'd rather go with a smaller crew, and build the sets and live in them for a while and let it build up that patina that we were talking about.

Is there anybody out there who would afford you that opportunity?

There are some people, kind of coming around, that have *so* much money that they don't really care, necessarily, about making a profit. They wouldn't mind getting their money back.

Would you junk narrative if you could? Would that be the first thing to go if you could work outside commercial Hollywood cinema?

No way. What are you calling narrative? The story?

Yes, the linear "A leads to B leads to C . . . "

Well, not necessarily. Sometimes it really works and you need it. Sometimes the linear thing isn't really so hot. It doesn't take you underneath the surface and allow for surprise or thrill. But I really believe in a story. How it's told is the key to the whole thing.

After Blue Velvet, *there were a couple of other projects you were interested in. What about* Red Dragon, *the novel Thomas Harris wrote before* Silence of the Lambs?

I was involved in that a little bit, until I got sick of it. I was going into a world that was going to be, for me, real, real violent. And completely degenerate. One of those things: No Redeeming Qualities.

So that movie couldn't even get into your country club?

The way I was thinking of it, I didn't want to let it into my country club. It was made. It was called *Manhunter*.

Your first project with Mark Frost, which never got onto its feet, was Goddess. *What can you tell me about that?*

That's when Mark and I first met. I always, like ten trillion other people, liked Marilyn Monroe, and was fascinated by her life. So when this came along I was interested, but, you know, what's the drill? I got into it carefully.

They were going to put a writer on it. CAA [Creative Artists Agency] loves to package people together. So they packaged me with Mark. I met with him and liked him, and we had a plan. We met with Anthony Summers, who wrote the book. The more we went along the more it was sort of like UFOs. You're fascinated by them, but you can't really prove if they exist. Even if you see pictures, or stories, or people are hypnotized, you never really know. Same thing with Marilyn Monroe and the Kennedys and all this. I can't figure out even now what's real and what's a story. It got into the realm of a bio pic and the Kennedys thing and away from this movie actress that was *falling*. I got cold on it. And when we put in the script who we thought did her in, the studio bailed out real quick.

For political reasons?

Yeah.

Who did you finger?

Never mind. Never mind. [Laughs.]

Was your attraction to Monroe another example of what Wendy Robie said was your attraction to "broken beauty"?

I don't know what it is. It's a sadness in the beauty. It's like mystery and beauty and sadness.

One Saliva Bubble. *Steve Martin, Martin Short. Kansas. A ray from a military satellite. And then what happens?*

And then all kind of wacko hell breaks loose. And out-and-out wacko dumb comedy. Cliches one end to the other.

Your version of It's a Mad, Mad, Mad, Mad World?

Well, sort of. It makes me laugh. Mark and I were laughing like crazy when we wrote it. I thought of this idea on an airplane. Steve Martin and I had met and we were interested in this one particular project way back when. We had both read a book, I've forgotten what it was. He loved it, and he still loves it. The only problem is, every time I get ready to commit to it, I think the problem for me is that there's not enough meat to it. I feel like a lot of people could do it.

Where did the title come from?

It came from a funny accident that caused the satellite to go off.

What about The Lemurians?

The Lemurians was a thing Mark and I were going to do as a TV show. Based on the continent of Lemuria, which was fictitiously thought of as a very evil continent. It was sunk way before Atlantis even rose—sunk because they were so evil. Jacques Cousteau inadvertently moved a rock, very early in his travels—part of it was "Jacques, Jacques, had to move that rock." A lot of poems in it. Part of the lore surrounds the leaking of Lemurian essence from the bottom of the Pacific Ocean. Anyway, the essence is leaking, and becomes a threat to all goodness in the world. It's a comedy!

NBC said, "Thank you very much—"

"—It's real nice seeing you fellas." The problem with *The Lemurians* is it's a complicated show.

There are detectives tracking extraterrestrials, right?

Yes, and all sorts of things. It's so complicated that we don't have time to introduce another TV show right now. It would mean cutting your concentration down to where it's impossible . . .

Too thin a pancake gets—

I'm a real thin pancake! I'm right on the edge.

What about The Cowboy and the Frenchman?

I really want to release that. I was in Paris with Isabella. And we were taken to a restaurant by this Frenchman. The restaurant was really, really good!

Almost as good as this one!

Yeah, when are we gonna get some food? I'm getting so hungry. It's 4 p.m. for you. You must be just going insane! So this guy said he was interested in doing this thing—the French newspaper *Figaro* was going to have six directors do short films commenting on the French, for their two-hundred-year anniversary. And I was going to be the American director. So I said, "I'm flattered that you asked me, but I don't have an idea about it right now. And I'm busy. But if I get an idea in the next two weeks, I'll call." It was a real small thing.

That night I got an idea. I called him. He said, "That's great, two cliches in one!" I said, "You got it!" So I made it. It was supposed to be four minutes long. Mine turned out to be twenty-one minutes long. I didn't really go over budget, just over time—because I was having so much fun. It was Harry Dean Stanton, Jack Nance, Tracy Walter, Michael Horse, and the Frenchman, Pierre. We had strange music and horses. We were on a little farm outside of town.

It's an absurd comedy. A Frenchman was in New York City and some very kind people gave him some pills in Central Park. Then he took them, and the next thing he knows is he ends up at a ranch in the West and Harry Dean Stanton is the foreman and Jack and Tracy are the sidekicks. And they don't know what he is, until they start going through his valise. Finally, they figure out that he's a Frenchman. And it goes from there.

That piece is very dreamlike. Do you use your own dreams in your work?

No. One time. Well, twice. There was a scene in *Eraserhead* that was cut out. And in *Blue Velvet* I'd been having a lot of trouble solving the ending—not the "ending" ending but near the end. One day I went over to Universal Studios, I forget why I was over there, and I had my script with me, and I was trying to finish it, and I was sitting in a chair, there was a receptionist, and I started writing, and as I was writing I remembered I'd had a dream the night before, and it suddenly became clear. The dream was the scene in Dorothy's living room. And in the dream I saw Jeffrey reach into the man in the yellow suit's pocket. Two things came from the dream: the police radio and the pistol in the yellow man's jacket. Then I went back in and wrote the scene where they're driving to Ben's and he says, "Hide the police radio," so Frank would know that Jeffrey knew he had it. So anyway, those things came from the dreams. That's the only time it's happened like that.

What about your acting debut in Zelly and Me *in 1988? It seemed like such an odd choice for you—because the movie itself was so precious and sticky-sweet, and everything your work is not. I couldn't understand the choice, except that Isabella was the star.*

It was all Isabella. I consequently met Tina [Rathborne, writer and director] and liked her a lot. I don't think Tina set out to make the movie as sweet as it was. It was her first feature film, one thing happened after another. Mainly I did it because I had a fascination to see if I could do it. Mainly to overcome this fear of acting, which is phenomenally fearful.

You mean you didn't do it so you could expose your manly chest?

I was afraid I would cause a lot of guys to feel very bad about themselves. I'm sorry.

Are you still making any kits? [Lynch used to dismember small animals to make "kits," like organic hobby-shop models.]

I have a strong, strong desire to make kits. I did a duck kit and chicken kit during *Dune*. I did a fish kit. I didn't do anything during *Blue Velvet*. I haven't done anything lately. My duck kit didn't turn out well. The photograph was very blurred, you couldn't read the writing. I wanted to do a mouse kit. I have a photo which may go into a book of a children's fish kit—which is much more simple than the adult fish kit.

The period after Blue Velvet, *when you were all tied up in the bankruptcy of your producer, Dino De Laurentiis, was that a—*

Trying time?

Yes, sir.

Yeah, it was. I almost was going to make *One Saliva Bubble* then. We had all our scouts, had it cast, was right there ready to go. Dino kept delaying it, delaying it, delaying it. It became obvious it wasn't going to happen: there wasn't any money. Shortly thereafter his company went bankrupt. We saw the writing on the wall.

Was there a period where you were kept from working?

No, but if I had wanted to make *Ronnie Rocket* then, I wouldn't have been able to do it, because I found out that Dino owned it. And *Up at the Lake* and *One Saliva Bubble.* Not only did he own it, but he had made money on it. And so when I finally got it back, I found out that if anybody makes any of those projects they will have to pay, out of first profits, a bunch of money to DDL that Dino has already taken.

How has Dino made money on them?

He paid himself a salary.

That's nice. How was your parting with him?

Very amiable. Dino does his thing. You can't fault the guy. He's just one or two steps ahead of everybody in a certain way, and by the time you learn the game, you've already been hurt bad. [Laughs.]

Let's go to "Twin Peaks." You've been to the Philadelphia Museum of Art, haven't you?

I used to live right next door.

That's what I figured! But in an interrogation, David, sometimes one has to ask even the obvious questions. Do you know a piece by Marcel Duchamp, dated 1946–66, so it would have been finished just before you got to Philly?

No.

Well, the piece is called Given 1) The Waterfall 2) The Illuminating Gas. *It's a dark, empty room. Along one wall are dark wood boards, nailed up. In the boards, at eye level, are two peepholes, and through them you can see a constructed scene. And in the scene is a naked, sort of dead woman, lying on her back, and off to the right pulses this amazing waterfall. Except for the fact that it's not a lake, it feels like the beginning spark—*

—Of "Twin Peaks." I'll be darned!

With TV being the modern peephole, exposing the darkness, in a paradoxical way. I just thought you might have seen it?

Maybe so. Maybe so. But the waterfall was not in the script. We didn't know there was a waterfall up there. And the girl would have been naked, but it was on television—you can't do that.

She seemed naked, but we couldn't see—

Underneath the plastic. But everyone is naked underneath their clothes. [Laughs.]

How did you feel watching the pilot, at your New York City hotel room?

Actually, it was pretty depressing. I was amazed by the poor quality of the image and the sound. There's a gigantic, huge loss of quality. If we could know the way it should be, and experience that, it's a whole different thing.

So you were depressed?

Yeah, but the commercials didn't depress me. I liked them. The commercials, I thought, were sort of thrilling. It was live. It was all around the country. It was kind of nice.

But before "Twin Peaks" ever aired you called commercials "big, violent interruptions" that you thought were pretty absurd, that the system didn't work—

Well, I still think they're absurd.

But by the end of the first year of the series you were watching to see who were the advertisers, and you were glad they were big companies; you'd changed and become more of a participant in the world of commercials.

Yeah, I . . . I . . . that's true. I'm joining in the absurdity. [Laughs.]

Did that change your attitude about making them, or was it a check someone decided to write you?

No. I've only done one legitimate commercial.

For heroin, right?

For Opium. [Laughs.] Now I'm doing one for another company, but we're not going to mention it [Calvin Klein's Obsession].

It's going to be tough to keep under the rug. Are you doing it for essentially financial reasons, or you like the challenge, or you've always secretly in your heart wanted to sell products?

Let's see. It's sort of, it's—obviously, it's got to be partly the money. But, these commercials. I liked the idea of them. And I like to—I've got kind of a thing now about keeping busy. It's sort of getting a little bit absurd.

Ultra-frantic creativity?

Yeah, something like that. I hope I'm not biting off too much. The Opium spot aired a long time ago. I like it, it's kind of pretty.

Back to "Twin Peaks." There's a sense that there's a lack of respect for certain characters on the show. There's a thin line between laughing at a character and making fun of them—

Who are we making fun of?

Maybe Nadine with her eye patch, or Leland in his grief, or Johnny in the head-

dress banging his head up against the dollhouse. These are things I found spectacularly funny, but there's a part of me that isn't comfortable with my own laughter in some cases. Do you feel there's a danger here?

There's danger around every corner. I think . . . it's, uh . . . it depends. If Johnny had a disease or something that you were making fun of, that would be one thing. He could just have an emotional problem and could come out of it. He could be pretending this whole thing, too. It sort of depends on how you see it. It's not meant in my mind to be offensive or to make fun of anybody, really. But at the same time, because he's the way he is, there's a humor side you can't avoid. A lot of times, someone who's in bad shape can do something funny — you laugh. At the same time, there can be a lot of compassion underneath that laugh. And yet it's the way the world is. It's so screwy — we're all kind of in this thing together, and there's got to be some room for a realistic attitude towards things. You can't just — TV and all these things would be reduced down to Tarzan movies, and we'd have nothing more.

Have you heard of the "Moment of Shit"?

[Very interested.] No, I haven't heard that.

The "Moment of Shit" is what TV writers call it when everything comes together, and you have that edifying moment, when you are supposed to get the Message, and the Morality comes across—

We have a lot of moments like that. [Laughs.]

The nice thing about "Twin Peaks" is that it turns the fan on all that. Now, is it true that, filming Eraserhead *in 1972, you looked at Catherine Coulson putting on her glasses and said, "I see a log in your arms. One day I'll do a series and you'll be the Log Lady"? It seems wildly impossible.*

It's sort of true. What happened was, Cath and I did another piece called *The Amputee*. It's about four or seven minutes long. I'd like to show it to you. She's a very interesting actress. Through *Eraserhead* she got into the other side of the camera and became a camera assistant, and she's been doing that ever since, until the Log Lady.

I had an idea for a show I wanted to call "I'll Test My Log with Every Branch of Knowledge." And that is true. And I wanted her to be a woman who lived with a son or a daughter, single, because her husband was killed in a fire. Her fireplace is completely boarded up, his pipes are there, his sock hat, stuff like this. And she takes the log to various experts in various fields of science or whatever. Like, if she goes to the dentist, the log would get put into the chair. With a little bib put on it. The dentist would X-ray the log, even to find out where its teeth were. Or he'd say to the little kid, "Let's say the log had a cavity. First I'd give it novocaine." And go through all the steps.

So, through the log, through this kind of absurdity, you would learn, you'd be gaining so much knowledge through the show. A lot of times they wouldn't even go to the scientists. They'd stop off at a diner, and there'd be stories there. This was my big show.

So when it came time for shooting the "Twin Peaks" pilot, I called Catherine. And she got herself up to Seattle on her own, stayed at a friend's house, and came in and did this thing. Flicked the lights at the town meeting. "Who's that?" "We call her the Log Lady." And that was pretty much it. Except it was just one of those things that just stuck, so consequently, it became more than that.

Let's talk about the psycho-killer. In Blue Velvet, *"Twin Peaks," and* Wild at Heart, *you have characters who are very attractive, in an almost magnetic way, who are psychotic killers. What's the pull for you in using these characters?*

I think it's the scariest thing to know someone, or suspect someone, that has a very intelligent mind—really nothing is wrong with them in any way—but who is possessed by evil, and who has dedicated themselves to doing evil. This is so unbelievable, so hard to figure.

You think it's just an act of volition for these people? That they just "decide" to do evil because they're in the mood for it?

No, I think it's a complicated thing. I think there is some disturbance, electrical or chemical, and some people might believe it is even beyond that. Some disturbance where they're smiling at you, but something you see in their eyes gives you the willies. And your smile back to them doesn't change their mind. The meals that you buy them, the schools they go to: none of that makes one bit of difference to these people. They do what they do, regardless.

The public obviously has a great appetite for characters like this, not only in film and TV, but on the news as well, as if they free us from the bounds of our own civility. There's a kind of wild freedom in what they do that's attractive.

I don't think it's that at all. We don't want to do these things. We're fascinated only because—I've never exactly figured out what the fascination is, but I think we want to understand it so we can conquer it. First of all, we want to really see it, so we can see if it's true. And then, we want to learn about it enough that we can do something about it. It's just too, too . . . there's something that captures our interest, but it's not a sickness, I don't think.

It was ten years for you between Eraserhead *and* Blue Velvet, *and I'm interested in why, after such a long stretch between original pieces, you would turn after* Blue Velvet *to essentially someone else's story,* Wild at Heart.

Well, it's hard to figure, you know. [Long pause.] A lot of my stories from that time were owned by Dino. And when you've been thinking about something in your mind, it was just forming up so nicely, certain things I was thinking about, and Dino, or anybody, takes that—and you can't do that. Your mind refuses to—you want *those* ideas, and in order to go to the next step in your own work you have to do the ones that are there. I couldn't finish *Eraserhead*, but I couldn't start anything else until it was done. So I was really in a frustrating place. This last go around, after *Blue Velvet*, the ideas that were really my own were locked off from me, and when I read Barry Gifford's book it was just what the doctor ordered. So many different things in the air pointed toward this way to go. Sometimes you go and you get nothing but red lights, and you can fight it for a while, but pretty soon it's like you drive a block and stop, drive a block and stop. This one just got green lights like crazy.

Obviously, a film and a book are always going to be different animals—make different noises and eat different things—but you really radically changed this book. There are whole plot development and feeling differences in the movie. How did you come to these things?

When I read the book, they came to me. Barry said, "I don't care what you do with this—there will be Barry Gifford's *Wild at Heart* and David Lynch's *Wild at Heart*. Go with it. Go for it." So it became a point of departure for a lot of things. But Sailor and Lula, what I really loved about the book, stayed always through it.

Did you know at the beginning that the Wizard of Oz *thing was going to be so blatant?*

No, that kind of crept in at different times. The last piece that came in was the character Jack Nance plays, talking about, "My dog barks some. You may even picture Toto from *The Wizard of Oz.*"

You make an interesting aesthetic choice to make it so front and center, as opposed to subtle or subliminal. Was that a difficult decision?

No. Sailor and Lula just have this fascination with *The Wizard of Oz*. It's just part of them, like it's part of so many people.

Do you share this fascination?

Oh yeah. Yeah.

Is that where Dorothy in Blue Velvet *got her name?*

I think so.

Also in Blue Velvet: *Frank Booth and the Lincoln Apartments—Booth and Lincoln—I thought was not coincidental.*

No, there are all sorts of things like that.

Another of the changes involves Lula. In the book, she's raped, but in the movie it's much more violent, more traumatic. Why did you change this?

Because I didn't really believe the book. [Laughs.] I wanted Bobby Peru [Willem Dafoe] to go to work on both Sailor and Lula. And I wanted what he did to Lula to tie into what she'd been through before. It also pointed out that Lula plays tricks on herself, like we all do—she blocks out many parts of reality so that she can still continue to be Lula.

I thinks that's called denial. Denial is a river in Eygpt.

Yeah, denial. Thanks, doctor. [Laughs.]

How would you describe Wild at Heart? *You can't say, as you have, "a road picture, a love story, a psychological drama, and a violent comedy."*

Well, I wouldn't be able to describe it then. [Long pause.] I don't have a one-sentence thing that captures it.

You described Blue Velvet *as a moral picture—*

I did?

Yes. You said that Jeffrey learns about the world and that he helps Dorothy in the process. Would you make the same claim about Wild at Heart?

Well, like I always say, we're all coming at things from different angles. And I think that Sailor and Lula are trying to live *properly*. They're struggling in darkness and confusion, like everybody else. It's hard to say. I don't know for sure. The idea that there's room for love in a really cool world, that to me is really interesting.

At the end of the picture, the Good Witch in a bubble tells us, "Don't turn away from love, don't turn away from love, don't turn away from love." Might one accuse David Lynch of going to Western Union to send a message?

No. That's the Good Witch talking.

But you resolve the story and the movie in a way that seems to pull back from what's happened—

In a way. But not . . . see, I didn't buy the ending in the book. In the first script, the ending was true to the book [Sailor and Lula go their separate ways]. But emotionally, it wasn't ringing true at all! I couldn't think of a reason when Samuel Goldwyn asked me, "Why is he leaving?" He hated the ending. If it had been honest, I could have given him an answer. But I said, "I hate the ending, too." I think they've learned a lot more, and grown more, even through fantasy, this way. The other way was a real . . . defeat.

Does the happy ending make you happy?

Well, the thing is . . . yeah, of course it does. And it rings true, to me, also. I think that Sailor and Lula are so fantastic a couple—I really like them a lot.

So you don't feel that, when push came to shove, you ducked on the harsh realities of love with—

With the happy ending? No. It was even the reverse of that. Even Siskel and Ebert were talking about it—that commercially, a negative ending isn't so good. So, I almost wanted to do a miserable ending just to show that I wasn't trying to be commercial. And that's wrong—doubly wrong. And so, like I said, it's got to feel honest, and if it does, that's what you have to do.

Blue Velvet *has a happy ending—with a twist.*

There's the same . . . there's a resolution in both films. Both of them have happy endings.

They both rely in the end on the power of imagination and fantasy to conjure up something: the robin, although the robin may come with an insect in its mouth, or your own good witch, making fantasy real. What happens, though, when you run out of fantasy?

Things get kind of boring.

In your first student film, that ten-second animated loop, heads catch on fire and then they throw up. In Wild at Heart *fire is the controlling image and vomit is a recurrent motif—*

[Laughs.] I can't get away from it!

There are not many movies in which you get to see both a mother and her daughter throw up!

Yeah, it's a real thrill. That alone is worth the price of a ticket.

And the flies on the vomit—

That's my favorite shot! When the door opens—they take off, they lift up as Sailor comes in.

That's your favorite shot in the film?

It's one of several favorites. I do like it.

But it's interesting that these motifs are there even in your earliest work.

Yeah, a lot of things. There are a lot of things in *The Alphabet* that keep coming back. And *The Grandmother,* too. Maybe you do keep doing the same thing over and over.

In the past, you've argued for Life as the inspiration for your work, as opposed to Art, which puts you—almost strangely—in the modernist, not postmodernist, camp. But in our last session, you said you're increasingly feeling the separation of film from life. Is there a change here?

No. To me, stepping into a film was always going way far away from regular life. Way far away.

But does your inspiration remain life its own self?

Oh yeah. Because the closer to the source of an idea you can get, the more power there is.

You've said that you never want to be too busy, because if you're too busy then you can't dive down and catch the big fish. Well, now you are crazy busy!

Yeah, and I'm not getting any big fish. Right now, I'm in a speed boat, and I'm dragging everything I can to catch what won't slow me down—it's the fish near the surface. I'm going to have to cut the gas off and throw the line in, and let it roll out all the way.

Years ago, you said your films both reveal and hide your fears. Do you still think it's true?

Yeah. Oh yeah. When you go with intuition or subconscious or whatever, you can't really filter that stuff out. You kind of have to let it come out and happen, without interrupting it. Once you start intellectualizing too much, or talking to the doctor about it, you might say, "Oh my god, man, that's very bad, I don't want people to think that!" so you'd start filtering, chopping off that little conduit. So it's better not to know so much, in a way, about what things mean or how they might be interpreted, or you'll be too afraid to let it keep happening.

But how do the films hide *your fears?*

Well, they hide them, because when they bob up, they may already be hidden. They don't come up and tell you so realistically. They're more like a dream thing. It might be one or two steps removed from a sentence describing your illness. So they're more like symbolic things that could be open for interpretation. Just like you talk about a piece of decaying meat. If you happened upon it in a certain setting, you could almost hear people oohing and aahing about its beauty. Until they realized what it was. Then they would not find it beautiful anymore. As soon as it had a name to it.

Sometimes there's no beauty in anything with a name attached. Isn't that feeling what kept you out of psychoanalysis?

Well, no, I went once. People have—at least I have—habit patterns, and I wanted to look into one particular one.

It was disturbing?

It was disturbing to me and other people.

Self-destructive?

No. It was . . . yeah. In a way, yeah. So I decided I would go see this psychiatrist, who was recommended by a friend. I liked this person and we sat down in his office and talked for a little bit, and it was kind of interesting. I realized that so many times you want someone to talk to who isn't judging you. And that's kind of cool about it. I could see it would be very good for getting ideas. Just to pay someone to listen to you. But even more than listen, someone who is fascinated from a technical aspect—so they kind of egg you on. It was interesting, and then I asked him about whether it could affect creativity—and he said, "Maybe." And that was it.

Affect it doesn't necessarily mean ruin it. Maybe change it?

Anything that would improve it, fine. But I think I asked him if it could affect it negatively, or interrupt it, that wouldn't be too good. I could see how if you disturb the nest too much you're liable to . . . you don't know what could happen.

You might not want to know so much.

I want to go about it in a different way.

Your own method of exploration?

Yeah.

Were you afraid that psychology barks up the tree you've so happily climbed?

What it does is destroy the mystery, this kind of magical quality. It can be reduced down to certain neuroses or certain things, and since it's now named and defined, it's lost its mystery and the potential for a vast, infinite experience.

And do you still have the same disturbing habit pattern?

Oh yeah!

Would you like to share it with the class?

[Laughs.] It wouldn't make any difference.

You used to have this kind of fear that dominated you, the fear of being restricted.

Yeah. Yeah, I guess I did.

How did you get over that?

I'm not over that. I think that's why I love money so much. I think that the freeing power of money is a very healing sort of thing. Because all we want to do is to be able to do what we want to do. And if we can do that, we get the sense of freedom.

One of my frustrations, one of the limiting things, was the lack of money. And I still don't have enough to do all the things I want to do yet. But at least I have more than I had then. In terms of painting, I don't have a studio, a place to paint, but I have enough money to get good canvases made, and enough paint. I really like to paint thick.

Camus, in one of his last books, proposes that to solve the existential problems of life you need money, because money is freedom.

Yeah, up to a certain point, it sure is. It won't help you if you've got a bad disease. And it won't help you if you desperately want to go to Mars.

There was a period in which you were actually afraid to go out of your house.

Luckily, school came about. But I had a touch of that disease where you are afraid to go out.

And what makes you the angriest dog in the world?

Well, I had tremendous anger. And I think when I began meditating, one of the first things that left was a great chunk of that. I don't know how it went away, it just evaporated.

What was the anger like? Where did it come from?

I don't know where it came from. It was directed at those near and dear. So I made life kind of miserable for people around me, at certain times. It was really a bummer. Even though I knew I was doing it, there wasn't much I could do about it when the thing came over me. So, anger—the memory of the anger—is what does "The Angriest Dog." Not the actual anger anymore. It's sort of a bitter attitude toward life. I don't know where my anger came from and I don't know where it went, either.

You've said both that you have to be happy to create and that you have to create to be happy. There's a serious chicken-and-egg problem here.

Yeah, it's like, creating things maybe makes you more happy, but if you're really, really miserable, you don't feel like creating stuff. But if you're kind of into it, it's a certain kind of happiness: happy gluing one piece of wood to another. You kind of like the wood, and the sun is just right, and the glue, you've got enough of it. Some little bit of wire. And you know what the wood does and you know what the glue does, and the wire, and your imagination is seeing the whole thing. And a little bit of action and reaction. It's a fantastic thing, and it can make you more happy—the doing of it. In the beginning, you're in the mood to do it, which is a certain kind of happiness.

Are you more attached to process or to achievement?

To me, the process has got to be enjoyable. You can't just think about the end result. Otherwise, I think eventually you'd have to stop. I don't see how you could wake up—if you hated the process so much. You'd soon be out of the business. You sort of have to love the trip.

A number of years ago, you said your life was split between innocence and naiveté, and sickness and horror. Do you still feel that polarity?

Yeah. I think my father . . . he's in his seventies, but I see him as real innocent, and a little bit naive in the same way I am. I think it's good, up to a point, until you become a fool. Europeans are so much more sophisticated, generally speaking. There's an innocent, naive thing still swimming around here.

What are you innocent of?

Well . . . [Long pause.] Maybe it's not so much innocent as unsophisticated. More easily shocked, or at least not afraid of showing shock at something. Certain things I still can't believe are happening.

That in Africa a few years back Bokassa threw his rivals into pits of crocodiles? Or that he dined on the flesh of his victims? That still shocks you?

You bet!

What's horrific and sick, on the other hand, about your life?

No, you don't want to know all that. [Laughs.]

I do, David, I do.

There are many things that swim together.

Besides semen.

[Laughs.] There are all kind of things going on.

That are horrific and sick?

Yeah. You know, just ideas. Mainly it's all on the idea level. I think that's the last frontier.

Anything disturb you these days?

Oh yeah, a lot of things disturb me. I'll tell you what's disturbing me now. It's something in the air again. The decay I feel is spreading faster than the building.

Well, the very air around us is decaying.

Well, yeah, everything is falling faster than we can clean it or build it or make it right. So that side of nature is winning. And it's our own nature. It's not really our fault in a lot of cases, 'cause we didn't understand what we were doing, like to the ozone. But when you visit New York City every now and again, you notice each time it's fallen further. It's not maintaining, it's falling. And that's an indicator of something happening in a lot of other places, but it's harder to see.

What about politically? You've indicated that you don't think of your films as political, but the two most famous men of the 1980s who called their women "Mommy" were Frank Booth and Ronald Reagan.

[Surprised.] Really?

You know he called Nancy "Mommy."

I didn't know that. I'll be darned.

You met him twice at the White House.

I sure did. I know there are a lot of very intelligent, wonderful people that would be upset at me, but I really like Ronald Reagan. There's something about Reagan I liked from the very beginning. I can see why people didn't like him, and when he was governor I wasn't feeling the same way. I think I saw him make one speech one time and I must have been moving into some right-wing frame of mind, or something. It was something in the air again. I mostly liked that he carried a wind of old Hollywood, of a cowboy and a brush-clearer. And I thought that, for a while, he was like a real unifying thing for the country. Maybe not for the intellectuals, but for a lot of the other people. Maybe for a lot of the intellectuals too.

Anyway, there's no winning in politics. It's something I don't even know a little bit about. Zip!

But you voted.

But all you have to do is pick up a pencil. Not even a pencil.

Well, most Americans stampede away from the polls. I think there's never been a democracy in the world where a lower percentage of eligible voters vote.

Yeah.

So you vote because you feel very patriotic, like a real American?

Yeah. But the way you say that is like— [Laughs.] Do you vote?

Yeah. I feel very patriotic. I can't imagine living anywhere else.

The thing is, America is suffering such a . . . everybody's got a . . . maybe it's changing a little bit now, it's coming back a hair. But for a while we were all so down on ourselves, it was not one bit cool—just the word "patriotic." Because we'd done a lot of things in the name of that that were so, so bad. Anyway, it's a losing game and it has nothing to do with the films I'm making.

You think not?

Not one bit.

But don't you think the things that led you to vote for Reagan—not necessarily intellectualized, but the feelings you have inside—involve the decisions you make aesthetically, and what you choose to show, and how you portray x, y, or z?

[Long pause.] You could say so, but not really. But so many things start from an idea. It seems very foreign to me. I know it's important, but it doesn't seem so important to me.

Knowing your work, I wouldn't have imagined that you voted. I could imagine you might be interested in the weird personalities of politics, or the power itself, but not that you would necessarily cast a ballot.

No, I did. There was quite a period when I didn't. Maybe I didn't realize it was voting day.

What were these White House events like?

The first time I went there was for a state dinner. I forget who all was up there, I think it was for the president of Argentina. You go to the White House, you meet the president, and then you have dinner. It's kind of incredible.

How did you get invited?

I don't know how I got invited. The first time, *Dune* was going to open at the Kennedy Center. The next time Isabella got invited, and she took me.

Do you think politics is serious business?

See, you *know* I don't like talking about this.

Well, David, if I was just trying to be your friend I wouldn't make you.

[Laughs, pauses.] I guess it's very serious, you know.

The implications are. If you're writing a story and you open one door, the characters walk through that door and there may be no getting back to open a different door, and each door leads to two more doors and you need to make decisions. Elections and politics are just like that, don't you think?

See, you should just take a certain number of pages and write out what you feel, and that would just be fine with me.

Well, I want to know what you feel.

I'll tell you what. I'll tell you what's really sick. See, I just—I'm involved with something over here, and I know nothing about this business of politics. It's totally absurd for me to comment on it. I don't know anything about it.

Well, you had your vote, Citizen Lynch, which you exercised.

And that's about it.

I feel your discomfort here, but I feel that people who know your work were very surprised—because your work seems to shred so many mythologies, and to penetrate under the surface—that you would make a political decision based on what seemed like very superficial things: that you liked the guy's haircut, that he's happy, you liked that sense of a brush-clearer, an old Hollywood actor. And I think that itself disturbed people, or confused people. You are in the public realm, for good or bad.

That's why I say it's a no-win situation. All those things that are aside from the film are not one bit important. There's nothing I can say about it.

But there are even times in talking about the films when you say there's nothing you can say.

Yeah. Uh, the words . . . unfortunately that's what this is all about.

I actually thought of giving you a sketch pad so that if you couldn't answer a question you could sketch me out an answer.

I could draw you one, yeah.

Let's go back to something we talked about last time: secrets. You put a line in Wild at Heart *for Sailor that was not in the book: "We all got a secret side, baby." It's a repeated motif in your work. I said there's a certain power in a secret, and you said there's a horror in it, too. Can you address yourself to both sides of that equation?*

Well, it's like common sense.

How's that, Doctor Lynch?

We talked about the man who knew too much. There are so many different kind of secrets. Part of the thing about secrets is that they have a certain kind of mystery to me. A dark secret. Just the words "dark secret" are so beautiful. Again, for the same reason I don't want to go back to Spokane, Washington. I don't want to see something so clearly that it would destroy an imaginary picture. And I'm real thankful for secrets and mysteries, because they provide a pull to learn the secret and learn the mystery, and you can float out there. And I hope, in a way, I don't ever get the total answer, unless the answer accompanies a tremendous rush of bliss. I *love* the process of going into a mystery.

You're secretive yourself, wouldn't you say?

That's a possibility, yeah.

Jack Nance says you're the most secretive guy he's ever known.

Well, I'm probably speaking much too much with you. [Uneasy laugh.]

There were some pieces written in the mid-eighties that made mention of the fact that you didn't have any visitors. Your response wasn't that you didn't like the way your house was, or, "I have a small house, I can't have visitors," or, "I'm never in town"—any of which would have been perfectly fine excuses—

What was my response?

Your response was, "I'm doing things that I don't want people to see."

At the time, I probably was. I'm not always doing these things in my house. [Laughs.]

See, but you didn't tell anyone what you were doing.

No.

So you created *a secret.*

Well. I suppose I did. In an answer to a question, I created a secret.

I'm just wondering if part of your attraction to secrets is that there's a kind of power, a kind of control in secrets. I think one reason secrets are so important to teenagers is that for them the world is completely out of control.

I don't know. Secrets then were totally traumatic to me, because I was doing so many things that I thought could change my world in a negative way. I was living in a fearful state. Secrets and mysteries provide sort of a beautiful little corridor where you can float out and many, many wonderful things can happen in there.

Now it's come time to deny the rumor or admit to all America that you've a woman's uterus in a bottle somewhere.

What have you heard about this?

We know you're interested in body parts. We heard that a woman producer was having a hysterectomy and you asked her to save the tissue.

It wasn't that way at all! This woman was having this operation, and *asked* the doctor to save this for me, as something she felt that I would want to have. A gift.

Sort of like a valentine.

Yeah. It's like, there's many things I have in my house, right? But some things—like the Log Lady—have stuck with certain people as very interesting things. So I guess that could be one of them.

3

OLIVER STONE

OLIVER STONE FILMOGRAPHY

1974   Seizure
1981   The Hand
1986   Salvador
1986   Platoon
1987   Wall Street
1988   Talk Radio
1989   Born on the Fourth of July
1991   The Doors
1991   JFK
1993   Heaven & Earth
1994   Natural Born Killers
1995   Nixon

as screenwriter only
1978   Midnight Express
1982   Conan the Barbarian
1983   Scarface
1985   Year of the Dragon
1986   8 Million Ways to Die
1996   Evita

as producer only
1990   Blue Steel
1990   Reversal of Fortune
1991   Iron Maze
1992   Zebrahead
1992   South Central
1996   The People vs. Larry Flynt

Oliver Stone

Born in 1946, the only child of a Jewish stockbroker father and French Catholic mother, Oliver Stone was raised in the East Coast tradition of button-down conservatism. Since then he's spent much of his life in antagonistic conversation with that background: as teacher, seaman, soldier, freak, failed novelist, decorated director and screenwriter, gangster of Hollywood. Stone dedicated both *Salvador* and *Wall Street* to his father, who died in 1985, but his mother is very much alive, and was hanging Christmas stockings when we met in December of 1990 at the Santa Monica home he shares with his second wife, Elizabeth, and their seven-year-old son, Sean.

Stone's work tends to be loud and angry and fast, full of jagged politics and big emotions. Screen his movies in succession and you're left feeling you've survived a cinematic bar fight – a bit dented about the head and heart by the velvet fist of his vision. From his pumped-up screenplays for *Midnight Express, Scarface,* and *Year of the Dragon* to the populist revisionism of *Platoon, Born on the Fourth of July,* and *JFK,* Stone's films again and again show the solitary man's fight for possession of his soul in a world which seeks to steal it, corrupt it, and destroy it. He's a true modernist; a brutish man with the mind of an artist but the soul of a boxer. He wears his heart on your sleeve.

Alan Parker's *Midnight Express,* a xenophobic, scary tale of an American dope-smuggling boy trapped in the dark recesses of a Turkish jail, won Stone his first Oscar, and his first real acceptance. His first major directing opportunity, *The Hand,* starring Michael Caine, was a psychological horror film about repression, projection, and evil. It left Stone crushed, pondering the question: does the sound of one hand clapping in a theatre make a noise? He recovered with a screenplay for Brian DePalma's *Scarface,* brayingly displayed the elements that would become trademarks in Stone's own pictures: overdrawn characters, heated action, controversial politics, a flaming arrow of narrative.

Then *Salvador,* his scrappy, leftist take on civil war in Central America, nudged open the door which *Platoon,* after years of waiting, marched through. *Platoon* was not just a movie, but a personal exorcism for Stone, and for many Americans an opportunity to finally mourn a lost war—a kind of filmic national catharsis. It won Stone great fame, and his first Best Director Oscar. He won again for the second piece of his Vietnam trilogy, *Born on the Fourth of July*, an epic of emotional fireworks on the domestic front. For all his heavy-handedness, Stone is hardly a one-dimensional director. Even in his weaker pictures—such as *Wall Street*, his moralistic bromide on 1980s materialism, or *The Doors*, his exuberantly romantic but hollow portrayal of one of his great heroes, Jim Morrison—Stone has the surprising ability to coax absolutely superior performances out of his actors.

For our first session, we talked between his appointments while driving around Los Angeles in his black Mustang convertible and in a barren office at his editing studio, where he was hurrying *The Doors* to completion. We spent our second session, in January of 1991, on the patio and in the living room of his home. Stone spoke quietly, in a kind of portentous half-whisper. He complained, repeatedly and good-naturedly, about how much time this was taking—as if four hours of reflection made for a painful wedge in his busy schedule. He seized the upper hand on the patio by suggesting I sit on a chaise longue that, to me, looked and felt wet. I protested. He waved off my complaint and sat himself on a dry one. When I did sit, I was instantly soaked, and though he did allow me the benefit of a towel, it was little help. So I went through the interview feeling as uncomfortable as many feel watching his films. Say what you will; the man is a master of tactics.

A chronological footnote: at the time of our conversations, the controversy over the historical veracity of *The Doors* was already beginning to brew. This proved simply the orchestra tuning up in the pit compared to the onslaught of discord attacking *JFK*, which was in pre-production at the time. At the end of our drive around town, I had asked him when was the last time he'd been down to city hall to have his poetic license renewed. He just laughed. And then he laughed some more.

SESSION ONE

Let's start at the beginning, really the beginning. What's your first memory?

[Pause. Big, exaggerated laugh.] Oh boy. Beautiful women in trees in a jungle. I had erotic dreams when I was three, four. And they've always stayed with me, throughout my life. Many erotic dreams.

Did you have any understanding of them? Did you report them to anyone?

No, no, I never talked about them. Not even to my mother. [Laughs.]

Were the women blondes?

Yeah, primarily blondes, but there were colored women and a lot of Oriental women, some striking brunettes. Even some redheads. I would say it got liberal. My fantasy is like that Fellini film, what was it, *City of Women?* I don't think it was one of his more successful films, but I loved the idea of having a walled city [laughs] and being the only male in the whole city.

And you were a three-year-old waking up with a "woody" to these dreams?

Oh yeah, my pecker used to get hard. It was great. I think that eros is the most underrated force in the universe. I think eros carries us through the darkest hours. The deepest, darkest tunnels of the mind are the places you hide in, like Viet Cong warriors did. And the bombs are being dropped by B-52s. The VC used to build caves—I've been down them and seen the maps. There'd be a first layer, then a second layer underneath, like an onion skin. Sometimes these things would go down seven or eight layers deep, and there'd be an R and R facility down in the bottom, like a golf course or something, hospitals, schools, video clubs down there. [Laughs.] Often I'd retreat to this place in my head, where there'd be some kind of sanctuary. And eros was the driving force. Eros, and its correspondent, love.

What did you do with this stuff as a kid?

Oh man, it's secret stuff. It's like Viet Cong tunnels, I told you. I wouldn't reveal more than that, but it's certainly a driving thread to my life. Simone de Beauvoir said, "Sex is the sixth continent." It's the place you can go for free. Everybody can do it. I like that idea. It's a democratic impulse. I think

101

sex is the driving force, the resistance to totalitarianism in our age. The totalitarian spirit is everywhere—in orthodoxy, in politics, in emotions, in TV. Controls, I think, are the keynote of our age. The way people have always fought back through the ages—the medieval ages, the poor people, the worst times of history—has always been through sexual freedom. Sexual impulse. It's going on now with censorship and repression all over the world—in China, in Arabia, what they do to women. We're fighting this on a global front. It's just not the US. The American story is minor; the feminists are a minor thing.

Yeah. Sure. [Pause.] Okay—

[Sighs.] I see you got bored.

No, I'm not bored at all.

Yeah, you shifted the subject. I was trying to tell you that . . . I think, well, I think I said what I said. [Quietly] The sixth continent.

Some of my earliest, fondest, most nostalgic memories were France in the 1950 to 1954 era. My mom took me to France and left me there for the summer with my grandparents in a country house, and I grew up in the French style in the summers, playing around the countryside, riding bikes, hanging out with French kids, in the Algerian war days, the Vietnam days. We'd play soldiers and stuff, and I'd hear about Indochina—little did I know I'd end up in Vietnam. I remember loving my grandfather. He would tell me World War I stories. He was gassed in World War I, he was a French infantryman. And I remember my American grandfather. He was an old, old man, walking around the East River Drive in New York City. And I remember New York in the late forties and early fifties. I remember the overcoats and the hats and the ties and the cold. I remember going down to Wall Street and being knocked out by all the buildings that were so high, with little windows and no light.

Your dad gets described as distant and negative—

Not at all, not at all. My dad was very loving. Very loving man. That's a partial description of him: he was sarcastic and distant at times, but he was very loving—he was so proud of me, he admired me, I was the only child. He just didn't want me to get spoiled by my mom. He would take a little harder tack with me. He wanted to enforce discipline, he wanted me to learn discipline very early. He said, "Every day you got to do something you don't want to do." [Laughs.] And he made me write by giving me money. He'd encourage me to write a theme a week.

For your allowance?

Yeah, so I could buy comics. And he always would give me math problems to do. He was a very good writer, very intelligent. He had a warm heart, but he had difficulty—as all men, as a lot of men did of that era, the Depression era—he had difficulty *expressing* his feelings. He thought it was unseemly.

What did he fear from self-expression?

He was sort of a secret playwright. He had written three or four plays which he kept in the drawer; they weren't good enough to be produced. And he was an unpublished poet. But he thought it wasn't something you do for a living. Also, he thought a man should not be seeking visual distinction. His clothes should be anonymous, the man should be anonymous—short-haired, wear a tie. You see, I suppose I was wildly indulgent to my father.

He accused you of "showing off."

Well, no, at first I was very conformist in my youth. I wore a tie and a jacket, I wouldn't go out of the house. It was very difficult to live in New York because it was very conformist. But dad would be sarcastic and sometimes he would hurt people's feelings, including my own. You had to understand how to take that kind of humor. He was a loving father.

He was "there" for you?

He was there for me.

I'm thinking of the scene in Wall Street *with Bud Fox [Charlie Sheen] and his father [Martin Sheen], where they're arguing in the elevator and then on the street, and Bud says, "You've never been there for me." I wondered how much of that was autobiographical?*

I probably felt that at times from my dad, because it would be very rare for him to give me any kind of compliment. I was a bum to him, especially after Vietnam, because I was dope-smoking and talking black talk and in jail and had no college education and was writing these kooky screenplays. So he thought I was becoming like his brother Joe, who he said never did anything his whole life.

Your dad was successful with his investment newsletter, wasn't he?

Successful intellectually. And he was respected. But financially, he never became a millionaire. Close. When he died, he left my mother with some money, and I think I got $19,000, after a whole lifetime of making money for others.

You'd think that if a guy is going to be such a Republican he should do better than that.

[Laughs.] I can't fault him. He was worried about money, but he was never ultimately that interested in it. He never had the knack for making it. He was more interested in ideas. Every investment he'd make would go south. He opened a factory in Connecticut to make machetes for Guatemala.

[Jokingly.] Probably some of the same machetes used by the death squads you were dealing with in Salvador!

That's a stretch. He went out of business before the death squads. And then all his stock deals! Everything he'd buy for others would do well, but whatever he'd buy for himself—generally he would get hurt.

I guess that runs in the family. You had a bad experience with stocks just after you filmed Wall Street.

Every investment I've made on Wall Street has gone south. Never again. I'm stopping it. I don't like it. It's all easy money. I don't treat it seriously.

You should have listened to Lou [fatherlike Hal Holbrook] in Wall Street.

What did he say? What was the line?

He said, "There's no sure thing. Things take time."

[Laughs hard.] He was like my dad, too.

You should have taken your screenplay's advice! But of course, Lou was not as interesting or magnetic as Gordon Gekko [Michael Douglas]. There's probably more of you in Gekko, isn't there?

Gekko's another character. It's not my dad. Gekko is a character out of my mom. Sort of flashy, flashy. My mom is more outward, external, physical, in the world—not as abstracted as my dad. She never made enemies, she made friends. Dad would make enemies with his tongue. Mom was a charming woman. To me, she's a bit like a piece of Auntie Mame and a piece of Evita. Just larger than life. Big parties. Loved to travel, loved to tell tall tales. She'd invent anything. She was the best friend of anybody who would come into her mind that moment. She had a tremendous ability for fantasy.

Did you ever feel like a bum at home, before Vietnam?

Oh, I always felt like an outsider at school.

Why?

Just a quality of one's character. It's an existence, it's an anguish that you have.

Do you think that was nature or nurture?

I think it's nurture. I think it comes from being an only child. I think it comes from not having access to easy conversation, or easy living with a sibling—which makes you less important in a way—and I think you get more self-conscious as an only child. I was very self-conscious when I was young. I'd walk down the street and I would feel that people were condemning me, judging me, looking at me.

Back between nine and twelve years old, you did a lot of writing . . .

I wrote themes every week. In Paris, I wrote a Balzackian, romantic novel about the French Revolution. I was very influenced by Balzac and Dickens. It was more a romantic image of writing. I didn't get very far. It just seemed that writing was a possible retreat from reality that was acceptable, in the sense that the world of the imagination was a sanctuary from real life. As were movies. I loved being in the dark, and seeing movies. It's an escape. My mom was very much into that.

You played hooky with her

I'd play hooky with her, she'd take me to the movies a lot. A lot. On Wednesdays they'd change the movies; they'd have double features every week. And we'd go and see double and even triple features some days. It was great. I'd go to the movies with my father, too, and we'd see Kubrick films and David Lean films, and he was always very impressive in his analysis. He'd walk out and inevitably—no matter what movie we'd seen—he'd say, "We could have done it better, Huckleberry." And then he'd tell me what was wrong. He'd analyze the plot for loopholes, and of course, movies always have loopholes. Why didn't so-and-so do such and such? It was quite an education.

We saw *Paths of Glory* together, *Strange Love*. I think Kubrick was my favorite in that time, when I was between fourteen and sixteen. And then David Lean, *Lawrence of Arabia*. *One-Eyed Jacks* I remember seeing and loving. And Fellini made a big impression. I remember seeing *La Dolce Vita* in '59 or '60 and that just blew me away. It seemed to be doing things in black-and-white that American films were not doing. That you could just take an ordinary person, an ordinary life, and re-examine that life in mythic terms. I think it was seven days and seven nights that he crosses the city. I loved the theme of that movie.

What kind of reality were you seeking to escape?

Oh, I think the reality of school. Rigid law, orthodoxy, oppression to some degree. I think school was rough. I went to a very strict boarding school, all boys. Had to go to chapel every morning. Four to five hours of homework every day. Five classes. Discipline. The teachers were good. The smell of locker rooms. The dank food. How can I describe the food? It was totally Dickensian.

Perfect for someone named Oliver. Apparently you had the shock of your life when you found out your parents were getting divorced.

Put it this way: the first shock of my life.

The first shock. But the first shock is really the shock, in a way.

Well, I had another shock. I had a couple of medical shocks, but I don't want to discuss that.

Why not?

I just don't. My medical records, my tax records, I don't think that's really
. . . I had a couple of medical things that happened, I had a few operations
that really were hard. Doctors sometimes don't tell you stuff for about ten
or fifteen years because they don't think you're old enough to hear it—so
sometimes you get some pretty good shocks. But aside from that I think my
parents' divorce was major for me.

I had thought they were very contented and that I was rich, and that we
had it made. And, basically, my father said that they were unhappy and that
they were betraying each other, that she was screwing around and he was
screwing around, and that he was broke, in debt. He didn't have money, he
owed money: that whole concept of debt, I just didn't understand it until that
point. And my mother, according to him, was profligate in her expenses, and
spent everything.

And she had a lover, she took several lovers. It was shocking. It was an
interesting time. It was sort of the onset of the sexual liberation of the sixties,
and couples from the fifties were starting to play around on each other. It
was amazing. My father had been with other women since the forties, and
my mother had had other lovers.

You didn't know anything about this?

No, no. It was all delivered to me on a weekend in boarding school, and by
phone. Nobody even came to tell me. It was delivered to me by the headmaster and that was really hard to take. My father had talked to him and he
thought it was his obligation to tell me. My mother didn't even want to come
and see me; she was hiding in Europe. And you can imagine the way the
headmaster tells you these things: "Buck up, young man, this is not the end
of the world." It was hard.

If you had to put it into a literary hindsight, I would say it was very close
to *Catcher in the Rye*. A very depressing novel, but emotionally right on. I
felt like shit, like nothing. Everything was metallic. All the surfaces were
metallic. All the people, all the adults were dangerous, not to be trusted. The
world was a very empty place to me.

I think that set up, basically, a period for me, from sixteen on, until thirty.
I was going through a sort of adolescent thing, especially from sixteen to
twenty-two, a sort of revolution in my life. Everything was thrown topsy-
turvy. Basically, I ended up in the merchant marine, in Vietnam, going
through a lot of changes. All the old rules were thrown out.

*What was that feeling like at sixteen? You talk about feeling "sheltered and spe-
cial" before that. Maybe in juxtaposition it was even worse, maybe all of a sudden
you weren't so special?*

I went to Yale, so I was doing very well, but emotionally I could just not engage myself for four more years. I had to get out of this world. I didn't believe it. I didn't believe anybody at Yale. I didn't believe what they were trying to turn out. It wasn't like I was a genius and knew what I wanted. I just knew what I didn't want. And I had vague glimpses of the world of the Far East from Conrad, *Lord Jim*, and I'd also read Kipling, and *Red Badge of Courage*, and Hemingway, and I was very romantic in my thoughts. And it was through getting out into the world, getting away from all I knew, pushing out into history—Hemingway used that phrase—that I would have nothing more to do with the East Coast, New York City, that world.

Did you feel like a bum when your parents broke up? I would think that for an only child it would be difficult not to internalize that schism.

Oh yeah. Yeah. My father moved into a hotel, where I lived with him. And my mother was moving into another kind of life, a sixties life—drugs, parties. I was really mixed. I felt I had nothing to do with it: I was an outsider. I had to find a new family in a sense. The family was *over*. It just disintegrated. You don't have a brother or a sister, you don't have any second person you can still be family with. Basically, the triangle splits and we're three people in different places, and I'm sixteen and all of a sudden I'm on my own. Dad said to me, "I owe this and this and this, I will put you through college and then you're on your own." To me, it was a new world.

As a loner, I just floated out to the Far East, and to this day I think it was an orphan home for me, and became for me the means by which I began to see the world with a new family, a new light, the light of the Far East. And then the irony of marrying a girl from the Middle East when I came home from the Far East, and then I spent time in the Middle East. I really sort of journeyed, and I wandered. And through a process over a long time, I got my existence back together. And by the age of thirty I started to kind of feel it again: to feel like I used to feel, being home, and having my integrity.

The tall ships came into the New York harbor for the bicentennial and you wrote Platoon.

Yeah, around there. I wanted to go back to where I was when I was sixteen. And: be straight again, be disciplined again, don't let this madness, this adolescent madness, this raging war—these experiences of life were like combat, spitting in my face—don't let this blow your mind out. Because I saw a lot of that in 'Nam. People came back wrecks, carcasses, human burning wreckages of people. And I was almost one. But it took me time. I wrote. I wrote, it seems, for therapy: between twenty-two and thirty, I wrote eleven screenplays. I never stopped writing. It was my only home. Every day to write. No matter how dissolute I got—and I took a lot of fucking drugs, booze, and all that, *bad*—I would get up each day. Like my dad said, you do something every day you don't want to do. I felt an obligation, to hold up my sanity, to write.

After your first period in Vietnam as an English teacher, you wrote a 1400-page novel, A Child's Night Dream. *What was it really about? It began as a suicide note, no?*

Yes, it did. It was a wild sort of Hindu time story, where everything goes back and forth. It started in the present, with a suicide note, and then it went through Asia, the merchant marine, Custer's Last Stand, James Joycean poems without any punctuation, tripping on the tongue. I was very influenced by Joyce and Donleavy, *The Ginger Man*. Just writing to a beat, to a rhythm.

Why was the rejection of it by the New York publishing houses so significant to you? You felt again like a complete bum.

Well, the thesis, after 1400 pages, is that the person saves himself from suicide by the act of writing. But then I played it two ways: I had him also extinguishing himself through the act of writing. He basically self-destructs at the end of the manuscript. And then there was another chapter where he saves himself through the manuscript. So I couldn't decide which way to go. Except at the end I threw away my manuscript, destroyed it. I thought it was over for me. I was so depressed. One guy at Simon & Schuster I owe this to—probably threw it out and said it was a piece of shit. He gave me a horrible letter, said something horrible about it. Just remember that when you're up there at the top you can break a writer's heart. And I thought, I'll never get anything done, with my life, with my writing. I'm sick of being special, I'm sick of the act of writing about "self," and therefore I'm going to be anonymous. I'm going to the bottom of the barrel—what the Charlie Sheen character says in *Platoon*, "I'm going to be anonymous." I'm going to go into the army, and I'm going to be totally anonymous.

How much of that was self-punishment?

A lot. I was ready for death. A lot of my book was about suicide. *River's Edge* has made it popular now, but teenage suicide was not that talked about in the sixties. Nobody dealt with it, except in *Catcher in the Rye* Salinger deals with it at one point. It was like—people would scoff at your pain. It was just before the hippie revolution. It was just before *Time* magazine decided people under twenty-five *matter*. I remember a world where we were never consulted. It was sort of like: "What pain can you have?" My dad was responsible for a lot of that. He'd say, "What experience do you have? How can you write? What pain do you really feel?"

Is that where your anti-psychological bias comes from?

What do you mean?

What you've called your "animus to psychology."

In what connection?

I could go back to The Hand—

Yes, *The Hand.*

Jon Lansdale [Michael Caine] says the new illustrator has "weakened" the cartoon character he draws "by making him look too deeply inside himself."

[Laughs.] Yes, that's right. That's right. That's funny. Oh, God!

So your dad was minimizing your pain, what you felt inside.

Yes, Dad was very anti-psychological. Oh, I see! That you're not supposed to talk about your inner feelings, or show them, or be, quote, "an artist." Showing the public—what is art but prostitution, as what's-his-name said, who's that great French author? The fellow who wrote *Madame Bovary,* Flaubert. Flaubert said, "Art is public prostitution," and he's right. Because the prostitute—*prostituere*—makes public the private. That's what Dad was saying: art is prostitution, because you're making public your private fantasies.

How did your dad take the rejection of your book?

Oh, he was vindicated, you see. Fuck him! I wanted to get out. I hated him.

So going to 'Nam was an actively suicidal choice in many ways.

Oh yeah. I was ready to die, but I didn't want to pull my own trigger. Many a time I stood in the bathroom and looked in the mirror and had the razor out—part of my book was about the eighteen ways the kid tries to kill himself. I went through all the computations of death in my head. I don't know how close I came. I certainly thought about it, and I emotionally identified with it, but I stopped myself. I said, "Look, I'm not going to die this way. If I'm going to die, I'm going to die in combat. I'm either going to make it through or I'm not going to make it through."

Norman Mailer was very important to me at that point. I read all his stuff. I loved *An American Dream.* God, that was a great book. I remember the whole discussion of death and suicide in that. And he'd been in a war, Mailer had. And Hemingway. And I felt like I had to go out there and make it through. And if I don't make it through, it wasn't meant to be.

Would your death have been a way of punishing your parents?

[Pause.] In part. But not wholly. More of punishing myself. I wanted to prove to my father that I was as tough as he was, because he'd been through World War II. And also I wanted to prove that I didn't need him, that I could make my own way in life by being in the army, and going to war. And being in combat, which he never was. He was always a lieutenant colonel, on the financial side of it—he was on Eisenhower's staff, actually. He was very important.

You've said you knew it was a mistake, your being there—like Charlie Sheen's character in Platoon—*from the very beginning, yet after you were wounded and were put back into the rear echelon, you fought to get back to the battle. So there's a contradiction there.*

Yes, there is. When I first got there, I got scared right away. My experience was very similar to *Platoon*. I cut point my first day, and I got shot in my first major firefight. I got wounded in the neck, then I got shot again. So I took two hits and got out of it; they had a policy that they evacuated you to the rear. At that point, I was a veteran in a sense. I knew my way around the jungle better than when I had just got there. And I was in the rear, with a bullshit job guarding barracks, and hating it 'cause I had to spit-polish my boots. I had a fight with the sergeant, and he wanted to court-martial me—Article 15—and I said, "Let's make a deal." They might have extended my time in 'Nam and I wanted to get out, so I said, "Let me go back to the combat zone and you drop the charges."

Because death might be better than a court-martial?

No. No. [Pause.] I missed combat. The truth was, I missed it.

The adrenalin?

Yeah, there was something happening. It got me excited. I was bored shitless in the rear. I don't know, it was weird . . . you really hit on something. I just wanted to see if I could do a better job of it than I had done the first two times. I wasn't too proud of my first stint. You live through a lot of shit, and I was scared out of my pants, and was shot twice. And I guess I wanted to prove to myself that I was a better soldier.

I went back into the First Cav, and I *was* better. I wasn't great, but I was a better soldier. And I got a bronze medal for some combat action. I was more attuned to the jungle, and I got into the jungle, heavy. The smell, the look, the feel. I remember one thing I did, toward the end. I walked up to a deer, on point. Carrying sixty pounds, with a machete. In other words, I was part of the jungle—to come right up on a deer. That's pretty good.

The other thing that happened was I got into grass, heavy. And then I got into music. It was a good tour, the First Cav. Blacks were my best friends, and they brought me in—believe it or not—as a sort of adopted brother. A blood. Like the scenes in *Platoon*, getting high, high, high, down in the hootches. At the base camp, not in the field—we didn't fuck up in the field. And I listened to that music and it really got to me: Smokey Robinson, Marvin Gaye, the Supremes, the Temptations were the hottest.

I'm struck by how, when you failed so badly at creating – creating your book – you turned so fiercely to destroying, going to war. If you couldn't succeed at creation, maybe you could succeed at destruction?

Yeah, a lot of that, that Lee Harvey Oswald thing. I saw that in this country, that's where I learned it. Going to the dark side, you really see the underside of life. Lee Harvey Oswald. I was in that world. I know that world. I know those people. All those guys, such sad cases, going back to small towns, guys that knew weaponry, hanging out in bus stations.

The worst years of our lives . . .

Yeah! I took the bus all the way down through Oregon, California, talking to guys in bus stations and cheap hotels. And trying to get laid, with hookers in Oakland. I met a lot of Lee Harveys. I met a lot of guys who were really screwed up. The drifter mentality in American society is very interesting. But Lee Harvey Oswald is a lot deeper than everybody thinks he is, he wasn't just a drifter; he was something else too.

How much of your drug use was –

[Upset, frustrated.] I'm trying, I'm trying to get to a point. It came out of a thing about destructiveness. Yeah, so when I got back to New York, I got a cheap apartment on Ninth Street and I painted the whole thing red. I was doing acid and stuff. I'd really get angry and I'd have rages that were uncontrollable. Like, the Black Panthers were talking their talk and I'd say, "Come on man, stop talking it, *do it!*" So I went to NYU film school, and there was the big mini-revolt of 1970, and the construction workers on Wall Street beat up some kids, and I thought, let's go all the way. Let's get some guns and let's *do* Nixon and let's take over Washington. Let's not talk revolution, let's go do it. Because guys like me, we knew how to shoot. So let's organize some stuff and go do it.

It was pure destruction, not creation. A revolution has to create something, but you didn't have a better thing to put in place of what you wanted to destroy. You weren't even very politicized at that point. You were only anti. You were contra.

I was *contra*. I was *contra*. I knew something was off in Vietnam, and I knew subconsciously that the government was really shitting us, but I didn't know exactly how. My rage was such that I knew something was wrong. And I thought, let's do the government, let's take it down. What's the big deal? Let's go to Washington with some rockets and some mortars and fucking fight. And we can win it. I just didn't like all the talk, all that hippie bullshit. It made me sick. There was too much talk and not enough do.

I felt a bit like an assassin. I was alone. Like Oswald. A drifter in my own culture. I didn't know where the fuck to go. I couldn't go back to school, I couldn't deal with those people. And the hippies were kind of screwed up –

they were into all that [sarcastically] L-O-V-E, love-and-peace. And I was more into Morrison: "Five to one, one in five, baby, no one here gets out alive!"

Eight, nine days after coming back from 'Nam I'm in the county jail in San Diego for federal smuggling charges, coming back from Mexico with grass, my Vietnamese grass. I'm walking back stoned out of my head. It was really stupid. I'm facing five to twenty years for smuggling. They throw me in this shit hole where they're supposed to have three to five thousand inmates. They had like fifteen thousand *kids* there. And they were all poor, from the underclass—Mexican, black, some Anglos. All in there sleeping on the floor. And I had this vision in the slammer. People were saying, "Where you been, man, this is the war at *home*. Wake up! This is happening right here in America." I had come back with this image of *Best Years of Our Lives*, some shit like that, that I'd be some kind of hero, you know. It wasn't to be. Here was my reception. Welcome back to the USA, Amerika with a capital *K!* The war at home, revolution, anger! Well, that freaked me out.

I got out after about three weeks, and went home to the East Village, and I got robbed. Fucking guy came up to me, stuck a knife right on my fucking stomach, said, "Gimme your money." I got freaked out, very frightened, because I knew either he'd die or I'd die—'cause I knew the meaning of death and he didn't. I was so stunned. I'll never forget it: I looked at him, and he saw my eyes, and I walked away. Just like that, walked away. And he never followed me. He left me alone. But then I got robbed about six times up in that fucking dump. Guys were breaking into my windows and stuff.

America is—what I'm trying to say is, I saw the underside. Never forgot it. Made a severe impression on me, for the rest of my life. I live relatively well now, and I'd like to stay away from it. I have no illusions about it. I'm not in love with it, as a liberal. But I see it and I feel sorry for the root causes of it.

How much of your drug use was self-medicating?

What's "self-medicating"?

A lot of people in a great deal of pain "medicate" themselves with drugs, rather than go to a doctor. A lot of people don't take drugs to "expand their consciousness" so much as to numb themselves out.

I think that's a very good question. That's a tough one, because you cross that line, back and forth, through the years. Because half the time it's expansion of the mind and the other half of the time it sort of creeps into numbing yourself. And I certainly am "guilty" of both. I was doing grass on a daily basis, getting high, really high; doing great acid, in the Village. I would do acid anywhere, in the subway, in restaurants, I didn't stand on religious grounds about it at all. I never picked environments that were particularly soothing. I'd do it for a rush. I had some heavy bad trips. Volatile trips. And I had some great trips. Looking for a woman, man. I was looking for a woman. Peripatetic affairs. Wild affairs. Crazy women, crazy nutty women loose across the city. One-night stands, here, there. I was just burned out—and no love in the world. I had a few friends that would do some drugs, but I didn't have any vets around New York. My vet friends went back to small southern towns and they would write me about unemployment and drug use and alcohol. It was depressing. I didn't have anybody. There was no network to fall back on. I was alone. I lived in a shit hole on Houston Street. I had a broken window, with the snow drifting in in the winter. I'd wake up in the morning and there'd be a pile of snow in my room. [Laughs.] I was writing, though.

Were the drugs fueling your anger or muting your anger?

Both. The alternate expansion and contraction. I'd say acid to expand and grass, eventually, to numb. And music was so important. You can't underestimate that, in the sixties. Listening to Motown, hour after hour, on grass, getting into that mood. And the Doors, Jefferson Airplane, Bob Dylan, the Grateful Dead, Sly and the Family Stone. The Fillmore East.

And then I met this incredible woman named Najwa, who was four years older than me and really psychologically balanced, really strong. She was Lebanese and working for the Moroccans. I married her and she did a lot to integrate me into a more orthodox kind of life. It was too orthodox eventually, and I left again.

So this woman domesticated you, in a way.

Yeah. Returned me to the fold. But ultimately I rebelled again.

Did you have a need to rebel, no matter what it was you were rebelling against?

At that time, yes. I needed to get my freedom back. I felt like my freedom had been terminated, tamed, put in a cage.

Don't you still have to rebel? Isn't it just "in the soup" with you?

I think it is. How do you know?

I don't know—it just seems like that's part of you. If you're not rebelling against a woman, you're going to rebel against how videocassette rights are sold or how Hollywood is structured or how critics "misinterpret" your work. You get angry about everything, but I'd also like to know, what gives you joy?

Optimism. A good feeling around you. Family. Love. Eros. A feeling that the world is a healthy place. I think that optimism is really necessary. I like to be surrounded by gaiety, by friends who laugh, who have a positive attitude towards life. I like to be surrounded by a lot of light bulbs, turn on a lot of lights. I like to have a TV on once in a while. I like to see movies that are good, that make me appreciate the possibilities of life, that engage the mysteries of life. I like good books, fine wine, beautiful women. Intelligent men. *Daring* men. I like ships that sail. I like children. I like toys. Material things. Spiritual things. What do you want, a catalogue? An index?

No.

The book of joy? Joy is a mental state. You have to be healthy to have joy. The doctors are right: life seems to me to be a cycle of pain and of pleasure. It can't all be joy. There is that pain that comes. Aeschylus said, "Suffering that falls, drop by drop, upon the human heart, until it comes to know the infinite wisdom of God." Aeschylus! You ever hear of it? You know the line?

Yeah, Francis quoted it to me.

[Surprised, his thunder stolen.] Did he, really?

Yes, he was talking about his boy, Gio, being killed.

Well then, Aeschylus got it right, so why not quote him.

You've talked about failure and humiliation as a stimulus to learning. I'm interested in this vis-à-vis control. The horse's mouth words are: "It's wrong always to be in control. You'd never learn anything, and learning is more important than being in control. Most of the stuff I've learned in my life has come from humiliation, defeat, or stretching myself and making a fool of myself."

You mean the "Who am I?" scene in *Wall Street?* [Laughs.]

That's the only line the audience actually hooted on—it was a tough New York audience. I'm interested in how you've, as the Buddhists say, taken the poison and made it medicine.

Good question. I think I've told you. Didn't I talk about coming back from 'Nam in that sense, restructuring the personality? Isn't that taking poison? How can I elaborate more?

Well, I'm interested in how it relates to control. Okay? The value, as you stated, of not being in control. Because now you are at a point in your life where you are very much in control.

Oh, I see.

You're sober, you're comfortable, you've got a certain amount of power, and you've matured—

So you're saying, how can I learn anymore? Is that what you're saying?

How are you going to find it if you're in control all the time?

By not being in control all the time.

How do you do that?

You have to pick your spots. You have to be in a position as a writer. As a writer, I go to the field and I meet a whole new set of people, and I listen, and I don't *judge*. I don't prejudge. And I try to be humble, because that's the only way to approach a new subject. As a writer, as a research journalist (not as a controlling director), that's where you learn. So I'm out there a lot, I travel a lot. A lot of my time is spent writing and researching. Also in my home. One can have many fights with a wife, a child, where the child is the king and you're the slave. The child reverses the roles on you.

But I think it is more difficult, I think you're right. It's essential to be honest with yourself as a writer. When you're alone with the page, you can't bullshit yourself that much. If it's no good, it's no good. It doesn't matter who you are, Woody Allen or Francis Coppola. The gods of paper, the gods of movies, are ruthless.

Is it okay to fail now, though, when the stakes are so much higher? It's one thing to fail in that room painted red, taking acid and writing the tenth of eleven screenplays, and to go out on the limb that you're living on; but now with the structure of the deals you're in, and who you are, and what people's expectations are, doesn't that get in the way, a little bit?

[Long pause.] Failure is more severe, harsher, but I like to gamble. I'm quite willing to gamble. Knowing that failure is noble, knowing that I've been there before with failure several times in my life, and I've reconstructed myself from failures, most notably, recently, with *The Hand,* I guess.

That was ten years ago, man.

Talk Radio wasn't received particularly well by the audience. It was ignored. It was a good lesson. That was three years ago. *Wall Street* was hooted at, by snobby people. But that was fine. I learned from that experience, a lot. *Born on the Fourth of July* was castigated by a lot of people, I think for unfair reasons, but so be it. Each time there's a humiliating thing that goes on.

I don't think being at the Academy Awards and seeing all of my team on *Born* fail in winning awards in all categories was a particularly great night. It was kind of difficult for me to accept that. Because I wanted them to win in their categories. When the sound people lost, it really broke me up, because I thought we had a really great sound track. When John Williams lost for music, I just thought there was a lot of politicking going on. And a lot of the people that hated the movie—the intellectual circles—took what they needed from Pat Buchanan and the right-wingers to slam the film. And that hurt!

Come on, so I mean, what are you saying that I don't learn from . . . there's no, the control thing, I mean I get calls every fucking week from the press, with some new scandal or other. I have no control over what they're going to say. What the hell control? What control?

Clive James, the British writer, says, "It is our failures that civilise us. Triumph confirms us in our habits."

[Long pause.] "Corruption is more ruthless than war." Juvenal. Yes? Yes or no?

Corruption is more ruthless than war?

Yeah. No, excuse me, "Luxury is more ruthless than war."

Yes, because we go to war for it, as we're about to in the Gulf for the luxury of cheap gasoline and big cars.

[Defensively.] Did my answer about success and failure, did it convince you? Or are you questioning it still? Do you think I'm complaining about success? I'm being too, uh . . . did you buy what I said? Did you understand what I was trying to say about control?

I think I do understand.

You had no counter-argument.

I'm not arguing with you—

No, but I mean, there's no further point you wanted to make on that.

I felt I did understand what you were saying.

[Relieved.] Okay. Success is good. It nourishes, it replenishes the soul. It makes you feel good about yourself, and there are times when you need to do that. And humility keeps you going. Humility is what makes great films. You mustn't believe too much in yourself; you must believe that you're the vessel for an idea. You must believe that your team is with you. That you're working with great people, on all fronts. I think a film is like a football team going to the Super Bowl. You got to play as a team through the whole thing, through all three acts of the movie: the writing, production, editing, and distribution. That's actually four acts. Let's say three creative acts, and then there's the distribution. You're a football team and you really have to be in sync. You can feel the energy. If one actress isn't in sync, it really screws up the flow of the whole movie.

You write from pain, quite personally, but eventually you're going to run out of it. What happens then? Or will you have a replenishing supply to write from?

We'll see. How can I project that?

A lot of people end up making the same movie again and again.

Nothing wrong with that. If you can make it interesting, and dress it up in new clothes in a new way, what the hell? Madonna recycles herself every six months.

Yeah, but are you seeking to achieve the level of Madonna with your films?

No, but if you can dress up the old story in a new way that interests you and makes it interesting to the public, what's wrong with that?

Nothing's wrong with it, but you seem, to me, to be a guy who wants a new story.

I think I do. I might be disillusioned, I might not be the best judge. I try to write 'em and make 'em. I admire the prolificness of Balzac and John Ford—they just kept doing it. And Hitchcock. They didn't get too much into regret or remorse, looking back. If they missed 'em, they moved on. Don't get tripped up in your self, your own psyche, or in analysis. I do think there's something to be said about getting out there and doing it.

Are you keeping a diary?

Yeah.

Every day?

For years. I've done a massive tome. Either I throw it away at the end of the course, or otherwise I might do something else with it.

Have you saved them, year by year?

Yes, but now it's getting dangerous.

Why?

[Incredulous.] Why? 'Cause it's a written document.

What are you scared of?

Revelations.

Why?

[More incredulous.] Why? Because it's my most private self.

Why do you write it?

To keep a record with myself of what I felt at such and such a time.

You're afraid that if you didn't write it—

—I'd lose track, yes. When I was doing most of the drugs, I stopped writing it for several years, and I noticed when I went back to writing it that I felt that I was doing better work. It's like a balancing act, and I'm evaluating day by day. I was taking the time to evaluate the day before, each day. So that it would not be an unexamined life, in a non-Socratic sense.

What did you write about yesterday?

[Long pause.] Yesterday was mainly about the *Doors* cutting. We made some significant cuts, roughly fifteen minutes from the film in the last few days, so it's been a massive intellectual journey into the bowels of the movie, for me. But I've been doing some work on the side involving the writing of *JFK*. Actually, I'm making some big breakthroughs mentally there, in trimming that script. So I'm trimming a script and trimming a film at the same time. Mostly idea work in the last few days. And it's been about that. And also who I met. I met a bunch of actors and actresses, and I wrote what I thought of them.

As a coda for today, I'd like you to enter a scenario. You're a rebel held hostage by a regressive, right-wing government, and you know where the rebel leader is. You're his right-hand man, you're close to him. But they have you, not him. Now, the government men holding you know that you know where the leader is — the hero of the revolution — and they tell you that they are going to round up local villagers, and take them in front of you and shoot them, one a day, until you tell them where your leader is. What do you do?

I wouldn't hesitate at first. I would sacrifice one villager a day up to a certain point. The leader of course would know that the villagers are being killed. He would have to show his hand. The situation would have to change in a matter of, let's say, thirty days to sixty days. But I would make a modest sacrifice in that direction. Because if Leader X is important on a larger scale than Villager Y — I'm assuming the revolution will be good for the villagers, I'm not assuming the leader is Bob Kerry of Nebraska, I'm assuming he's going to do something significant — then it's worth sacrificing the villagers. And I assume they are going to catch the leader if I tell them. I would wait.

You'd be strong enough to watch people being killed under your nose?

Yes, I would.

What if you had the option of suicide?

The "option" of suicide?

Yes, let's say your captors in some way couldn't keep you from killing yourself. Now, if you're dead, your captors have no leverage, and there's no need for them to kill the villagers. They're only killing them in front of you to try to get you to break down and give them the information they need — to make you talk. So if you die, they live. Would you kill yourself?

I'd have to. I'd have to. If I had that option, I'd kill myself. You must be ready to die for those stakes.

SESSION TWO

Let's go right to the films. The dominant criticism of your work is that it's too loud in some way, that it tries too hard. I know you're aware of it, and I want to know where you think that criticism comes from.

Probably my hearing. I think that in 'Nam I went to the ear doctor [laughs] and I thought that my hearing had been impaired over there from all the artillery, and the bombs. So maybe my mixes are too loud.

You know I'm not speaking literally.

Well, I am. [Laughs.] I think your question has to be dealt with on levels. Anyway, physically, at one point I had my ears checked and the doctor said I had very good hearing. But I feel sometimes that I can't hear people, and he says it's probably a lack of concentration. That I'm not listening.

Obviously, I'm aware of that criticism. And obviously, it's in my interest to practice on myself, refine my thinking, refine my heart, refine all the aspects of myself as I get older. So I try to listen. But one thing I always felt I had, when I was doing all the writing, was a good ear. As a screenplay writer I would go down to Miami and I would listen to people talk, and I feel like after a little time with you I could probably do your rhythm in dialogue. I try to pay attention to details, I try to be a realist, dealing with real things, real people, real events. I think that that sometimes *plays* loud — because it's real.

I think you have to be specific. *Born on the Fourth of July* to me is about a very real thing: certain families that live like this, a blue-collar existence in America. And it came from observations of Massapequa, Long Island, and hanging out with Ron [Kovic], and being in his circle of friends and family. And these people say what's on their mind: they sometimes speak loudly, crudely, wrongly, but I'm putting it down as I hear it. There's nothing wrong with that, because that's part of the vitality of life, it's part of the contrast. But as I get older I want to do more, I'm more and more aware of contrast. Because the older you get, the more and more contrast you get in your life. When you get older, old versus young becomes a lesson. Loud versus soft.

Is that what you asked me, loud? What was the question again?

Not the volume, but that the films in some way try too hard, that you are too much in the audience's face, that you always use the sledgehammer instead of the stiletto. Instead of your response just to that, I'm interested in where you feel this criticism comes from.

Do you agree with it?

Sometimes I do sympathize with the criticism.

Specifically, give me an example.

At the end of Born, *bringing the mother's dream back in, her dream about Ron speaking to a large audience like Kennedy. I feel, and I know other people who felt similarly, that it was hitting us over the head with something that was already in our reading of the film.*

Not everybody is so perceptive. I could argue that it was two-and-a-half hours before, screen time. It was a long film. You'd gone through so many changes. I could argue that people—maybe the majority of the audience—didn't remember. Possibly I go sometimes for the lowest common denominator, in terms of getting the message across, in terms of getting what I want to say across. I think sometimes it's better to be wrong on the side of clarification than of obscurity.

That's the thing my father used to always beat on me for. Because about all my earlier writing, he'd say, "That's too obscure." And all my English teachers would drive me nuts: "This is too obscure. What do you mean?" Something you've broken your heart writing, that's so clear to you, and nobody understands. And I wrote a lot of obscure stuff. The novel was mostly obscure, it was symbolist poetry, it was Rimbaud-like. It's part of that Vietnam thing too—maybe my hearing—and that I just want to be *clear*. It's like you have to be a commander to be a director. You have to be clear, you have to really project yourself, make an effort of projection. Because I come from obscurity and confusion, essentially, and shyness. I was terribly shy in school, always an outsider. Sort of avoided groups and cliques, didn't want to run with any gang. Always wanted to be alone. Reconciled myself to being alone. So I think that maybe part of going the other way is trying to fight all of those earlier tendencies, where I felt like I was totally irrelevant to the human race and that I was totally obscure and confused. 'Cause my childhood was very confused.

Do you ever feel that you compromise subtlety in pursuit of clarity?

Possibly. But subtlety is a technique; I admire subtlety as I would a dance step. And there are some subtle things in my movies that I know are there, and have sort of not been seen, *yet*, but they will be seen eventually through time. And I think the movies will last because there are subtleties that few recognize. But as I say, what is subtlety? It's a technique. You're essentially communicating something, but you're doing it another way; it's less "in your face." It's pulled back. But it's essentially the same form of communication.

And I'm all for learning more technique as I go on. But the technique should never overcome the heart of the matter, and a lot of films I see that are always getting praised for subtlety have nothing to say, to me. And have nothing to do with the life I know around me. They become abstractions. A lot of their subtleties become abstractions, and abstractions, to me, are difficult to respond to, as an audience.

When Born *was screened in Berlin, you were reported to have said you had never seen the audience move so much in their seats at any of your films.*

Yeah, we screened it in East Germany, and it was a very emotional crowd. And they would sigh and gasp and you'd hear them physically moan, and suffer along with the protagonist of the movie—

That's what you want—

They shared, they completely crossed the barrier, they were empathetic in the Greek sense of the word. Totally involved! We were affecting them. It was a wonderful thing to experience, for me. I like that. I like the internationalness of film. It's great just to get into Albania, to Greece, Japan, China. When they see me on the street, I'm a friend of theirs, you know. They come up to me and shake my hand, like they know me. I don't know them, but they know me.

Are you ever afraid that it doesn't happen enough, that film is "just a show"—to quote from the end of Talk Radio? *All these horrible, sad, frightening, deep things are discussed on Barry Champlain's [Eric Bogosian's] radio program, and the kid who's invited to the studio interprets it all in a way that completely surprises and ultimately depresses the host, Barry Champlain/Oliver Stone: that it is "just a show."*

[Laughs.] That's a very—you've been waiting to say that.

So that people walk out—after this catharsis—and they're back to square one again.

[Pause.] I think you got to the heart of it. I have an ambiguous response to it, definitely. There are times I cross the barrier and I meet a total stranger and he knows my world. He's shared my world. And there are other times I feel that everything we do, all our efforts, are for naught. That we're mere abstractions, that we're mere reflections of life. We're like a mirror that passes up to life for two-and-a-half hours, and goes into their subconscious but often it's forgotten. And there are so many other reflections going on right now—music, video, television, all kinds of leisure forms are booming, so movies are even a smaller part of it.

And I see the day where one of two things will happen. Either movies as a form will disappear. They'll become like antique woodworking, like cabinets, seen by a few people and brought into a few homes: very nice but expensive and difficult to come by, a rarefied art form, like opera. Or, I could see it going another way: the movie that gets released in one night on a billion screens, all across the world, and speaks a universal tongue. And will come into our living rooms on a wide screen. I'd like to have the screens curved, with a tremendous new Lucas sound system. Digital picture, digital sound. A great home experience. And more people would see it. That would be great. The future of communication. Then movies would play a central role.

I would go either way. I would still make movies. I think if tomorrow I had a series of failures and people didn't want to see my movies anymore, I would retreat back to a form where I could do as cheap a movie as I could, like *Salvador*, like my NYU films.

To go back to the essence of the question, about the function of film. Rousseau wrote a letter to d'Alembert, about the theatre, in which he argues against the theatre. For example, you go to watch a play, let's say its theme is about some social problem, and it's an effective play, and you weep over the tragedy of this problem as it is displayed for you by these characters. And you feel like you've experienced it, and there's a catharsis. But it's a false one. So the man in New York City attending a play about homelessness weeps in the theatre, but then steps over a homeless person on his way into the cab that takes him home.

Well, I don't agree with Rousseau at all. If you never had that experience in the theatre you'd run the risk of becoming a senseless human being, without any empathy or sympathy or feeling for others. And through the act of empathy you have in the theatre, you are able to remember some of the roots of your consciousness. So when you step out in the street and you see that homeless person, you may not do anything, you may step over, but you're thinking about it, and you're seeing life from where he is, for that moment in time. So you've made one small step. So it works for me, the theatre.

It also works in a negative way, I suppose, with a horror movie. You step out and you see everything in shadows, in darkness. You see vampires and you see werewolves, like my little kid does. Like I used to, and I still do actually. [Laughs.] The act of imagination, the act of seeing beyond yourself, stepping outside your ordinary, small, mundane life, living a larger life through theatre—that can only help you in your everyday life. No matter how mundane your life is, if you can preserve the imagination, it's a wonderful thing. It will make your life so much more joyous, less painful. When I was in my worst periods, driving cabs, horrible times in the army, horrible times in the merchant marine, life was really getting to me and I was starting to feel that I was losing it, it was the retreat to a walled world, an imaginative world, that allowed me escape and freedom.

How would you assess your strengths and weaknesses as a filmmaker?

[Pause.] I don't know. Help me on that. If you want an answer to that . . . that's a real leading question. Say anything. [Joking, with Eastern European accent.] "Well, I can press six hundred pounds. You see this bicep, here." God, I hate that. Do I have to answer that? Can we just come around to that some other time?

Okay, we'll try to double back to it.

You're very noncommittal. You listen. You're like the *Citizen Kane* character, in the back of your head. You don't agree, disagree. You don't interrupt. You don't lead it, you're just sort of like a Rorschach test.

Is that bad?

Well, sometimes, when you ask cold questions like that. It throws me.

Let's talk about how you feel you've "redefined heroism." That was one of your repeated refrains after Born: *that it had taken you a long time, but what you wanted that movie to do was to redefine heroism.*

[Chuckles.] I said that? I never said that.

Many times.

No. A redefinition of heroism? It's not a verb.

"It took us a long time to redefine heroism." That's a direct quote.

Is that what I said? In what context? See, that's the thing, you're taking it out of context.

No, I'm not. Let's talk about it within context.

I don't remember quite the context. Go ahead.

This is another context: "We wanted to show America and Tom [Cruise], and through Tom, Ron [Kovic], being put in a wheelchair, losing their potency. We wanted to show America being forced to redefine its concept of heroism." Here's the other quote, vis-à-vis vets: "It took us years sometimes. We didn't join the protest movement. It took us a long time to redefine heroism."

I suppose we lived—to put it in a black-and-white era—we grew up believing that to go to war, to be courageous in a war situation, was heroic, in a John Wayne sense. And when *we* went over there, it was more like— Marlon Brando goes to war. [Laughs.] You started questioning everything. Nothing was what it seemed to be. Ron went to the end of the road on that matter: he lost his body in what he thought was a courageous action but which he now admits was a foolish action. He came to a reversal of appreciation for what he'd done. He'd charged the enemy *blindly,* without any reason.

*But did he think it was foolish only because he ended up in a wheelchair as a re-
sult, or because—*

Well, at first he did. He cursed himself for his stupidity in the hospital. He
cursed the day he did it. He rued it. He went through a heavy period of self-
loathing and self-abnegation. Many times he wanted to be dead. He went
through hell. Now he's sort of reached a point where he's accepted his destiny, and he's said to me, many times, "I would never have learned the things
I did if I hadn't been in this chair. And now I'm a wiser person. What would
I have become if I had stayed in Massapequa, and never gone to Vietnam?
Would I have been like my father?"

*Didn't the political conversion come from the personal impotence? It was as if
the country had promised you something out of war, out of being a man in a
war—the John Wayne idea—and it didn't deliver it, and now you're angry as hell
at the country for not giving you what had been promised?*

[Pause.] I think in Ron's case there was a lot of that. Because I think Ron
was extremely patriotic in the conventional sense of the word, with a love
of Motherland. And he felt he had a special bond to Motherland, and that
Motherland did not pay him back. I think that was a very strong consideration. The film was criticized in intellectual quarters for not dealing with the
cerebral basis of his emotional shift, but I have difficulty believing in that
basis. I believe that the emotional shift, as you say, was the result of the physical condition. And also of reading books. It's not that he didn't read. He was
conditioned by books by Ghandi and Martin Luther King, which were very
strong influences.

*There's a line of thought which argues that heroism is not changed at all by the
end of that movie, that the focus of it may have changed, but the act remains
the same. He's now in a wheelchair and he's telling his comrades to fall out, to
"take" the convention hall—he's barking orders again. He's very much in the same
place, it's just that there's a different enemy to attack; it's not the Viet Cong, it's
the prowar conservatives.*

Is that real life, or is that drama? Is that real life, to you? Do you believe it?

Do I believe it? Yeah, very much so.

Once a leader, it's hard not to always be a leader.

*I agree with that, yes, but that doesn't redefine heroism in any way. The concept
of individual heroic action—the male animal attempting to change the world in
a traditionally heroic way—is preserved at the end of the film every bit as much
as it's offered in the beginning, with Ron in the diner with his buddies, talking
about going to Vietnam to stop the spread of Communism.*

Well, maybe what I meant by redefinition was taking loss and making it into victory. Most people would regard loss, as in Vietnam, or as in body, as a negative, and it's not. Pancho Villa had a great line: "The defeats are also battles." And my life, too, has been a series of many defeats, many defeats. [Laughs.] From an early age. Divorce. Institutionalization. Insecurities, fears, failures, the army, Vietnam. Huge amount of rejections in scriptwriting, where I developed a strong rejection virus, immunity. Defeats. But I felt I was able to transcend the defeats by learning from them.

Both heroism and cowardice are reactions to fear, are they not, in your eyes?

Yes. What are you trying to get to? There's a quote.

"Cowardice and heroism are the same emotion — fear — expressed differently."

Hmm. Interesting.

It would be interesting to go through all your protagonists to see how you would interpret their heroic actions in terms of what they feared.

Umm.

You don't sound like you want to do that.

[Pause.] It's a lot of work. You'd have to help me.

Instead, let's talk about the position of women in your films. [Stone sighs.] It's like going to the dentist, Oliver! The world of your films is a boys' club, really. True?

No. I'd say the boys have been the protagonists of those movies, yes, but look at the movies. They were about ideas which primarily concerned men: Vietnam, the world of cocaine smuggling, a prison in Turkey, Wall Street, which is a men's club. But in each film there have been more women, you know. I'm not trying to deny their existence.

No, but due to their marginality, it's interesting to see what position they have. Since your films are not exactly overrun by women, the women that do show up are going to "stand for" more, in sort of inverse proportion to their dominance in the film.

Because less is more?

Not necessarily. Look, if you have seven major women characters in a film, each one does not carry as much weight — representationally — as if you have only one.

I see.

So now. The women in your work tend to be prostitutes, bimbos, housewives, stick figures. And if they're developed at all, they tend to be either emotionally cold or sort of along for the ride, as appendages to the male characters.

Well, Kyra Sedgewick in *Born on the Fourth of July* is a girl who marches to her own beat. She leaves Massapequa, Long Island, and goes to college, and she starts to think for herself. She becomes a terribly influential figure in Ron's life. She was the girl he never had a date with, but that he loved, that he wanted to love. He was the yearning romantic, and went back to see her after the war with the illusion that it could all still be good together. He *listens* to her, he hears what she has to say. From his generation, from his town, she questions the war. When he first hears it, it's strong coming out of her lips.

I think you're picking an exception to the corpus.

Well, it's an important exception.

Even she, though, has an edge of coldness, doesn't she? She just leaves Ron at the foot of the steps to the building she's going into on campus. Of course he can't follow—he's just left there, in his wheelchair.

That's right. And then the next day she holds the hand of her boyfriend at the demonstration, which drives him nuts. She just has another life, and she knows it.

I'm not going to be noncommittal now, and I want to you to address the general issue I brought up. You pointed to a female character who goes the other way— and I think we could find a few others—but the dominant feeling one gets from the work when one sits down and screens all your screenplays and movies is—

Ellen Greene. Ellen Greene in *Talk Radio* has an emotional attachment to Barry Champlain, comes back for him, abandons her boyfriend in Chicago, flies down to Dallas to be with him, extends her heart once more, against all her better judgment—and he breaks it again.

Yeah, she's ready to take more of his abuse.

And, number three, Elpedia Carrillo in *Salvador*—she has enough of James Woods, she tells him to go fuck off, she doesn't want him anymore, she screams at him: he's a drunk, he's a louse, he's no good. He realizes he wants her, and he begins to behave in another way. He expresses his devotion, he goes to church with her, he makes a confession with her, for her, and ultimately he risks all to take her out of the country, back to America, because she in some way has graced him, has transcended him, has given him grace. And he knows it. He knows she's the best thing in his life.

Yes, he says, "She and the kids are the only decent thing I've ever fucked and had in my whole life."

Well, that's his mode of expression, but that doesn't change his feeling towards her. His heart has been transformed in some way. He risks taking her out. And then he has his heart broken, doesn't he? At the end, on the bus. And she does too. He risked it and he lost it. He'll never be the same person again. Elpedia was the driving force that changed his heart. These are three examples of women reaching out. And in *The Doors*, Meg Ryan, in a sense, makes Jim more human.

Okay, let's look at the way she's presented in The Doors. *My understanding is that Pam Courson, Morrison's girlfriend, was a lot more independent—less traditional, less monogamous—and displayed a lot more freedom than in the movie, where she is presented almost as the jealous "wife" who's horrified when she sees him with others and who only sleeps with someone else as the "spurned woman," to get back at him.*

Well, that's not what I heard. I heard that she may have had affairs before, but that she really was enamored of the image of a domestic life with Jim. And wanted to make a real home. And prided herself on cooking certain things for him, and giving him a warm domestic environment to his previously solitary life. He continued to live in the motel and could not stand, ultimately, domesticity. She was not screwing everything that came along. She had a crush on certain people, often in response to the way Jim was screwing anything he cared to. It was more of a reaction to that than her being that way from the beginning. That's the impression I got from the witnesses. [Pause.] I'm sorry, but I'm trying to defend my position.

Do you feel you've done a good job with the way you've presented women in your films?

Not in *Wall Street*.

They're really commodities in Wall Street.

Yes, I think that was a failure in the writing. But I admire—I adore women. I've lived with many women in my life. I think women dispense grace.

I tried to make *Evita*, which would have been interesting. That would have been my first woman protagonist. The most hated and loved woman of her time. Meryl Streep would have been great. It would have been a wonderful movie, but it didn't happen for various reasons. And I have another project that I'm working on that has a woman for the main character [*Heaven & Earth*, the third film in Stone's Vietnam trilogy]. I would very much like to make that kind of movie, because it's nice to work with women. I had more women working on *The Doors* than on any other film I've ever done, and I really enjoyed being around them.

You know, beauty is important on the screen. I don't want to belittle it. I realize that. When you see a beautiful face, you respond. We like to see models of our best-looking sides. It's as old as the world. It behooves me to use beautiful faces. I could watch Garbo for many minutes. She just fascinates me. Just her face.

When I asked you what gave you joy, and you gave me a shopping list, at one point you said, "Beautiful women. Intelligent men." There's a dichotomy here.

And even now, when you're talking about having more women, the locus is physical beauty, rapture, and not intelligence or action.

Oh, I have the appetite of an African chief! [Laughs.] No, I–of course there's the other side. But let's say, to a man, a woman who is intelligent and beautiful is very sexy, and he gets excited by her, not only physically, but in all ways–talking to her, dealing with her in business, playing sports with her, every aspect of life becomes a playing field.

At the same time, you know as well as I do that a beautiful woman without a brain in her head can still be exciting to you. I don't know if Marilyn Monroe was smart or dumb; my impression is that she didn't have much of an education. But she turned many men on. Carole Lombard had intelligence and beauty and I find her ravishing, as I do Katharine Hepburn. Greta Garbo is *primal.* Garbo never showed her intelligence, she never had to: you imputed it. I loved Irene Dunne, because her spunkiness was great. I always loved her. She was smart, she was fresh. She talked back. I liked Myrna Loy, because she was bright, more on the refined side, more sophisticated. A little coldish, not animalistic, but that was certainly an East Coast woman to me. I loved Ursula Andress too, because of her animalistic qualities when she was young.

Now, today, actors are like new breeds of flowers: they come up each season. There are many I would like to work with. From Meryl to Glenn Close, Julia Roberts is wonderful, I can't even name them all. Debra Winger is great, she's intelligent, she's fiery; she has both sides. I always had a thing for Jane Fonda, when I was in Vietnam. I still do. I think she's an incredibly vital woman. Working with Meryl was so exciting because she's so bright. She's got a mind like a rapier.

And women think differently than men. All the signals that are given–you have to be a railroad man in this life to figure out all the signals.

Anthropologists have actually studied pick-up behavior in bars, and they've been able to catalogue a series of gestures that a woman will perform if she's interested in the man. There's a whole ritualistic physicalization of desire, I guess, the semiotics of attraction.

I think Carole Lombard was about as perfect as they came.

That'll be the last word on this subject.

Do you feel I was trying to answer it, or do you think I was . . . ?

Yeah, I think you–I think you tried.

I think there are some unresolved things with my mom, that I always had. Because of the divorce. She was a bit of a foreign–how do you say?–a foreign queen. She was like a queen to me when I was a kid. She was sort of living in a fairyland. She'd come and go. She was sometimes distant and sometimes very close. It was like ECUs [extreme close-ups] and long shots. It was consistent, or steady, my relationship with her, and it turned into a messy thing later on in my adolescence, and I think there are still many un-resolved problems with my mom, uh, as there were with my dad. [Pause.] I always married, I married my opposite, I mean, the opposite of my mom, which is interesting, too.

Showing maybe a kind of contrary dependence?

Yeah. A contrary dependence? How do you define that?

If you reject a certain model—and by doing that need to seek the opposite of the model—you are actually just as dependent on the model as if you were slavishly seeking to duplicate it, as in, let's say, the man who seeks to marry his mother. You still may be equally dependent on the mother, only it's a contrary dependence.

I see. Well, I think I have that. [Laughs.]

Speaking of parents, do you think your career would have gone in a different direction if your father had still been alive?

[Long pause.] No. I think it would have been the same. Because he died right before *Salvador* came out. I'm sorry he missed it, because he would have en-joyed being surprised. [Laughs.]

He's certainly the only man in history who's had both a movie about leftist rebels and a movie about Wall Street made for him. Both sides of the dialectic . . .

[Big laugh.] And now I've got to do some things for my mom. She always wants me to do *Gone with the Wind*. "Oliver, why don't you do something romantic? Clark Gable, Claudette Colbert, two people *in love!*"

Well, you've threatened to do a great love story.

That's something to look forward to. That's something to try. When I'm ready. Well, *Born* is a love story: it's about a boy's heart and his feelings for his country. It's sort of a love affair. The best love stories are—how do you say?—unrequited. Ron's unrequited love for America. [Laughs.]

Richard Boyle in Salvador *has some of that too, no? He's hurt by the deceptions of America when he sees her behaving badly. He says, "I believe in America. I believe we stand for something. For a constitution, for human rights, not just for a few people, but for everybody on this planet." Are you at one with Richard Boyle on this?*

It's a nice thought. Without becoming an "ism" I would agree with it.

You really think America has betrayed a kind of grand benevolence?

I don't think benevolence was ever the motivating factor in American politi-cal history. I think it was already a tough place. I think there were always neo-, nascent fascists in America. I think half the people during the American Revolution were pro-British.

It was an economic revolution.

Was it?

The Stamp Act, man. It was about autonomy, but not about universal freedom or human rights.

I haven't studied it, but I think that we all as filmmakers and literati and politicians refer to an idealistic America as we do to an idealistic Greece. [Stone's wife Elizabeth walks out of the house, towards the garage, and tells him she's going skating. Then she kicks a huge blue ball across the lawn at us.] That's a David Lynch image: blue ball coming at you, blonde wife, retriever by a car.

Where's the garden hose?

[Laughs.] Then a gardener walks out behind her with one eye and a scythe in his left hand and starts to fuck my wife right in front of me!

[Returning to the subject.] It's an idealization, but I do believe in those concepts. I do believe in democracy. I believe the people know better. That people have a cognitive function, that they're able to understand. I don't believe in the secrets of governments. My greatest fear in the twentieth century is totalitarianism. Totalitarianism feeds off of war. War gives the state the authority to control its citizens. It becomes the organizing principle of society, the war-making power.

I fear that governments have too much power and are getting stronger. I resent the liberalism that casts the responsibility onto the government, because it always sets up a new set of problems. I think that governments generally do badly with money and with human functions, though there are examples of their doing well. And the Constitution has been usurped. It was usurped in Vietnam when they declared war, when they declared war—

We never declared war!

Excuse me, when Johnson declared unilaterally without Congress. I think the Constitution—I think there was a coup d'état when John Kennedy was killed. So, the ideals of democracy and freedom are ideals we return to like a Frank Capra movie, because we *have* to believe—it's this battle between hope and despair. The end of the world versus the birth of the world.

So you would favor continually remythologizing American history because we need a better "good" to believe in than the one that we have?

Yes. That's a good point. But at the same time, a balance: you show the truth, but you try to show a goodness in the truth, too. It's an argument you have with yourself. It's an argument with yourself, a movie, a screenplay.

[It has gotten cold, and Stone asks that we go inside. We sit in his living room, flanked by two large Julian Schnabel paintings. Stone picks up a little sculpture on the coffee table in front of us.] Sleeping Buddha from Cambodia. It's a national treasure. I took it out.

Bad, bad boy.

Bad.

Let's talk about another major theme in your work: the dominance of death. In all of your films, save Wall Street, *the protagonist kills, or is killed, or barely, barely escapes death. Clearly, in some very fundamental way, it's a moving force in what you do—both obsession and wellspring.*

"Death shall have no dominion." [More dramatically.] "And death shall have no dominion." Who said that?

Beats me, dad.

You don't know? You don't know? God, it was a great poem by Dylan Thomas. You should hear him do the audios of it, he does his own poetry. He was a man wracked with death, as was Jim Morrison. I admire both of them as giant men who lived in the shadow of death. I feel much less enamored of death than they did; or else I'm running from it and not admitting it. I think it's a strong force in my life. I've used it. It's there. I've thought of death, often. At the age of eighteen I went to Vietnam as a form of death. I was ready to accept death. I saw much of it in Vietnam.

I think the Mexicans are so damn right, I have that thing in my office—a corpse, a skeleton. It grins at me: keep death around as a reminder, make it part of your life. Not to mystify it, or make it something horrific, but to live with it on a daily basis is, I suppose, to prepare for it, to get ready for it. And probably when it comes the ideal position is to want it: to be tired of life, to have exhausted the variations you intended to play as a human being. And then to go back to the womb. You want to be nascent again. You want to be quiet. You've had enough. You've seen enough people, you've seen enough colors, you've lived through enough lights and . . . [Sighs.]

Death is a framing experience of life and birth. Everything is seen in that light to me. I'm very aware of it, on a daily basis, driving around. Looking out the windshield, I see violent accidents in my head. 'Cause I saw a lot of that in Vietnam and I see death around me—quickly, obscenely being cut off. Every time I get on a plane I have to deal with the concept of death—I have to redefine it for myself, for everyone, for my child, in terms of him being hurt.

So I guess what I'm telling you is: it is a steady and mundane presence in my life, and no, I haven't come to deal with it completely. But I like Dylan Thomas's line, "And death shall have no dominion." So that when it comes, it will come as a friend and not as a dominant master. It will come as my equal. My spirit will be equal to my death. I will be wanting and willing to die. That would be nice.

You've said you feel it coming on.

What do you mean?

Even on "60 Minutes," you said you feel the approach of death.

Yeah. I was talking in terms of the feeling of it, yes. I didn't mean that it was going to be on Tuesday. The older you become, the more measured your days. You understand . . . you *see* the lengthening shadow.

Is your work against death in some way?

All work is. William Butler Yeats said, "raise your raiments to the sky, raise your colors, raise your raiments to the sky." Parade yourself, parade what you know, parade your human being-ness, have fun, stir some shit up, rattle some cages. "The Soft Parade."

In Jim Morrison, you finally found a protagonist who's as death-obsessed as you are.

No, more obsessed. I think more so. Jim lived it. He loved to walk with it.

"The appeal of cinema lies in the fear of death."

[Laughs.] Is that Jim?

Something he wrote while at UCLA.

The appeal of cinema lies in the fear of death? God, what's the context of that? Is it from his *Lords and New Creatures* poems?

No, I think it was in a paper for a film class.

Well, everything with Jim is death. A bottle of whiskey is death, a woman is death. Death is in every poem. Cinema of course has death in it. So do snakes, fires. [Laughs.]

Well, Roland Barthes argues in Camera Lucida *that the very act of photographing is tied to the idea of mortality—you preserve the image past—*

Yeah, you're aware that the image will never return again.

So that by making the image move, and not be a static impression, you suspend mortality all the more. A denial of, and a pushing past, death in some kind of way.

Well, when each film comes to an end, it always feels like a form of dying. Making that one stamp through time. We all come together as a collective, all these people agreeing to do something, and we share this life experience, and we know we will never do this the same way again. So it's a memory—the moment you shoot it.

Let's focus on you and your protagonists. You very closely identify with your protagonists, I would say as much as any director now working, and I'd like to go through them and have you tell me what's you in them.

There's a soft parade of assholes you've presented us with: Tony Montana in Scarface, *Stanley White in* Year of the Dragon, *Jon Lansdale in* The Hand, *Matt Scudder in* 8 Million Ways to Die, *Richard Boyle in* Salvador, *Barry Champlain in* Talk Radio, *not to mention Gekko in* Wall Street *and Barnes in* Platoon, *who are not protagonists but leading men. And then there are the innocents: Billy Hayes in* Midnight Express, *Conan in* Conan the Barbarian, *Chris Taylor in* Platoon, *Ron Kovic in* Born on the Fourth of July. *And now you've finally come to the innocent asshole: Jim Morrison in* The Doors.

The Holy Fool.

Let's look at these guys, one by one.

[Long pause.] David, help me.

Tony Montana, let's start with him.

Okay, use some adjectives. What are you looking for?

No, I want to know where you identify.

How I identify myself with Tony?

There's a lot of you in these characters, no?

Yes.

Come on, yes.

Tony Montana. Tony Montana. [Pause.] Well, he was an outsider to the system. He came from abroad. He jumped tracks. He was unorthodox. He was a rebel. A nonconformist who at the end of the day wanted to be a conformist. [Laughs.] And bought into the dream of the wife with the blonde hair and the mansion [laughs, looks around at his house] and then started putting security cameras outside his gates to watch the cops watching him. And then he starts to freak out on drugs.

"Me, I want what's coming to me, the world." Ambition too, yes?

[Laughs.] Well, there's a little bit of a gangster in me, there's no question. I like that grandiosity of style. I like the excess. The concept of excess works in a lot of these characters. In Gordon Gekko and Jim Morrison. Jim says, "I believe in excess." In the power of excess. Because through excess I leave, I live, a larger life. I inflate my life, and by inflating my life I live *more* of my life; therefore, I know the world more. I have more experience of the world. I die a more experienced man.

Stanley White.

Stanley White is based on a character I know called Stanley White, an LAPD homicide cop. Stanley's a colorful ex-Vietnam veteran marine, and I spent a lot of time with him in the streets, going around. His view of the world is not like Tony's at all. It's much more narrow and in some degree, vicious. Dog-eat-dog world, very tough, very street-oriented. You would not like to meet Stanley White in a fight. A real scrapper, willing to step outside the law to get the job done.

Are you?

I'm talking about him.

I want to know about you. I don't want glosses on these characters. I want to know particularly what you feel is your connection to the character.

Oh, I see.

What of you lives in that character?

Well, not much. Michael Cimino wanted him to be Polish, so he was more of an ethnic blue-collar than I was. I think I identified with the sense, the *Dirty Harry* sense in the film, of wanting to clean things up, of cops not really doing their job. The Chinese were pouring huge amounts of heroin in—which has been proven, by the way!—but at the time the film got a lot of flak for supposedly making up these stories about the Chinese. He was a wounded animal, Stanley, who didn't have that much understanding for himself. He was looking desperately for love with a woman, but I don't see that much closeness to me.

Okay, Jon Lansdale in The Hand.

Boy, that was a strange movie. At the time I thought he was the farthest thing from me, and I still do, I guess. Of course, you could say that that's me, too. If it is, it's certainly my darker side. Intense jealousy, paranoia about his wife, which I've never felt in my personal life, but maybe I'm denying . . .

See, what's interesting about Lansdale is that everything he denied was true. He was an interesting psychological man, because he repressed everything, as we all do. We all repress something. And everything that he repressed was coming out.

It's all about control, and what you can't control. Very tellingly, the first panel of his cartoon strip that the camera lingers over in the beginning of the film says, "For now that I control you, I must consider how you can best serve me."

[Laughs.] That's right!

Which kind of serves as a metaphor for your relationship with the camera, too.

I never want it to be static, to watch the other. That the self and the other are moving at the same time—that's the way I see the camera moving.

As a participant and not an observer.

Yeah, I always respected the camera as another actor. I hate the type of direction that makes the camera a slave. I always respect the camera. I walk on the set and I see the actor, I see the camera, and I see myself: I see a triangle. So that the camera, although inanimate, is as much a human participant to me as I am. It's an interesting relationship. So often the camera will speak to me on the day, and say, "Not this, that." And it will become clear to me. So I might sit here and for days make notes on what I want to do, as I would with an actor. But when I have the actor and the camera there, they start to talk, and sing, a different kind of song. The camera is different in each scene. The camera has an eerie kind of power. It will often suggest to me a better way of doing it.

So you grant it a kind of autonomy.

Yes. Exactly. Thank you for understanding me. Whereas, I've noticed, some directors will treat their cameras like slaves, like fascists. And I think that's so wrong! The camera becomes an *object of power*, like they're wielding a gun. I've noticed that attitude on a lot of sets. But I haven't thought about it until you raised this question today. It's interesting. Because obviously all our politics, our emotions, our sex lives are all there, aren't they, in our relationship to our cameras.

So you're looking for what might be described as an "unrepressive" camera style.

Yes! Totally free. I never saw this before. And I've tried a lot, if you look at the pictures, an enormous number of different moves. It's very complicated stuff, too, that we've tried. On *Born*, Bob [Robert Richardson, Stone's cinematographer] and I were really out there. On *The Doors*, too. It's gotten wilder! Bernardo Bertolucci came up to me after *Wall Street* and gave me a wonderful compliment I'll never forget. He just said, "I love what you do with your camera in *Wall Street*." And he's an expert of the technique, he has a love of camera, you feel it.

Some people react differently. Instead of being elated by so much movement, they find it—

[Strongly.] It's not about movement. He was saying, "I love the camera, what it did." It's not about a move, it's about what it did. Even when it's standing still, you pick that moment to stand still.

Some people feel that your camera is pushy, that they almost need to wear a seatbelt watching your films.

That's their problem. The world is spinning much faster than my camera and myself. Some people probably find it too slow. I think movies have to break through the three dimensions, as close as you can get. I think you go for every fucking thing you can to make it *live*. You can't shoot Buñuel-style anymore. You can, if you have very little money you can do that; I'd do it if I didn't have the money. But it's not enough. We're into new technology. Use everything you can. Make it breathe, make it coil, make it live.

On the other hand, I just want to say that if the movement is wrong, it's bad movement. If it's still and it's wrong, it's wrong. It's not about movement, it's about the camera doing the right thing. And there's a right thing for every scene, for every shot, for every moment. And if you're a good director you might hit it more than sixty percent of the time. But sometimes you can make a film and your camera is in the wrong place twenty-five percent of the time. And you know it. Maybe it's not that interesting unless you're a real buff, but I know where it's in the wrong spot. I can see a movie for three minutes and if the camera is always in the wrong spot, I know it, and I know I'm not going to like the movie. I think filmmakers have a thing—they can tell a bad movie from shot number three or shot number five. It's that precise.

Louis Kahn, the great American architect, talked about trying to make each building "what it wants to be."

Yes. And each film, each character dictates its own specificity to me. I have a kind of blank-slate approach to it. I walk out of the editing room, I say a bunch of things to the editors. I walk back the next day and I've forgotten what I said. I want to rediscover the same thing with the camera. I've forgotten the last way I shot a film. And that's what makes it so interesting and fresh to me, because the next time every camera movement is discovered for the first time. Not knowing how I'm going to do it is so much a part of the pleasure of making a film. In my earlier days, I would often rush to get all the shots the way I wanted and to get everything defined, and I think I lost a lot of the magic and feeling.

You're learning more about jazz, then.

Yeah. The nature of improvisation. Definitely.

Let's take another protagonist, Barry Champlain.

He's a . . . I would say—I feel very stupid talking like this because sometimes I'm repressing things that are there, that I don't see—but I would think that he's the furthest away from me. [Big laugh.] I could never get on the air and do that, that blatant confessionalism.

But it's a show for him—

Yeah, that's what's interesting.

In his big speech, he says, "I'm a hypocrite. I ask for sincerity as I lie. I denounce the system as I embrace it. I want money, power, and prestige. I want ratings and success."

Yeah, that's a very bald speech. That's an embarrassing speech. You'd think after that confession he'd get fired, but they love it. They love it. That's the new media age. You can go further and further until you hang yourself on the air. I should have had him shot in the studio, you see; that was stupid.

He also says his greatest fear is being boring. That's a fear of yours, no?

I think my greatest fear is being *bored*. [Laughs.] Marianne Moore had a great line, "The best solution for loneliness is solitude." So boredom is something you fight, and it's important you fight it by finding some other aspect, some other level that you're not paying attention to. One of the most recent boring things I've done—going to a cocktail party, I find it so boring. The conversation is never very interesting, it's always about surface things. And I always get asked the same questions, what am I doing, what have I done? People know more about me, through my films, than I know about them. I prefer to do most of the talking—I prefer to inquire about other people than to have to answer questions about myself. Gore Vidal said that to be interesting you have to be interested.

But Barry is too much on the nose. He's too out there. Anybody who has to do a talk show has got to be suspect. What do you think Johnny Carson's mind is like at this stage?

Let's not even hazard to guess. Why did you pick that project? It was so clearly someone else's vision—Eric Bogosian's—maybe there was a kind of freedom for you in doing it.

Maybe there was. It was an alien vision, and yet I loved the mood and the atmosphere, and I loved the concept of being able to say anything I wanted to say politically, about the state of the country. I loved the concept of not seeing the calls, of playing off audio. I loved the concept of making a movie in a claustrophobic space. Like *Das Boot* or an elevator movie, *Lifeboat*. I saw it at the time as a film noir, very much a film noir of the late forties. No hope. Claustrophobia. Despair. Protagonist being killed. Destructive affairs with women in his life.

And yet, he's offered a rope, speaking of Lifeboat, *by the Ellen Greene character.*

Yeah, she's sort of like a B-character from the forties, a Veronica Lake type. The woman in the dark who comes in, the ex-wife, who offers you a lifeline and you don't take it, because you're Edmund O'Brien in *D.O.A.*

And why not? Because as a woman caller suggests, Barry doesn't love himself. That the reason he creates so much misery for other people, and is so mean to them, is because he doesn't love himself. That's not in Bogosian's original play.

No, that's not in the play. I think I realized that through the years. I suppose I was like Barry—you're right, I'm hiding it. When I was younger, I was very dark, I was a B-film character, driven by a lot of self-loathing. And I think Elizabeth, my wife, has made me more aware of that, and made me a happier person, too. And my son Sean has. I'm getting sentimental, I don't want to get that. [Laughs. Stone calls Rosa, the housekeeper, and says, "Agua."]

I want to ask you about the videocassette of Platoon.

Jesus, here you go again. This is exhausting!

Now, in The Doors *you are rightly horrified at the notion of the band selling "Light My Fire" for a car commercial, and yet there's a Chrysler commercial at the beginning of the* Platoon *cassette. Lee Iaccoca comes on and says, "Platoon is a memorial, not to war, but to all the men and women in a time and in a place nobody really understood, who knew only one thing: they were called, and they went. It was the same from the first musket fired at Concord to the rice paddies of the Mekong delta. They were called, and they went. That, in the truest sense, is the spirit of America."*

[Stone laughs.] Is that so dishonest?

Fuck that!

Is that so dishonest? Isn't it true?

That's the spirit of America for you, Oliver? That citizens are just the mindless body attached to a head telling them to do something that may or may not be just, right? I was staggered at the notion of picking up a copy of Platoon *and seeing this guy doing a fucking commercial—first of all, just that fact, but then for him to politicize the commercial by saying the "true spirit of America" is to be called and to go. To me, that's not the spirit of America. The spirit of America is questioning, skeptical. If it weren't, we would never have broken away from the British, we wouldn't even be a country.*

We went around on that, you know. The first copy [for the ad] was unacceptable. The first copy dealt with Americans only. I think the opening line is about . . . what is the first line?

"This Jeep is a museum piece, a relic of war. Normandy, Anzio, Guadalcanal, Korea, Vietnam. I hope we will never have to build another Jeep for war. This film, Platoon, *is a memorial, not to war, but to all the men and women in a time and in a place nobody really understood," etcetera.*

I think you're right. I think I shouldn't have done that.

What was it doing there? The film made $180 million!

It was a small English company, and it had a lot to do with the video release of the film. It was a good guarantee for Hemdale. And I wasn't that involved. I didn't take a stand on it. I just changed the copy. I said, "This copy is unacceptable," and they came back three or four times with different copy, and I finally signed off on it. I was probably wrong. The copy should have been better. I learned a lesson.

What about the actual act itself of selling a product, or in this more sophisticated case, the image of a company, and attaching that to a work of art?

[Long pause.] Yeah. In America, we've been so packaged. You go to a theatre and you see the distributing company logo, and you see Universal's logo. You accept labeling, you accept being packaged. The videocassette comes in a wrapper and it's being advertised like Kellogg's cereal. They're patrons for artists; it's like working for the pope.

But you seem to be embracing it, not merely accepting it.

No, they came to us.

But the whole idea of attaching a corporate identity to a work that was so personal, and so political; and it seems like in The Doors *you really come down on Morrison's side about this song, to the point where you—*

Well, it happened that way. He was very sensitive about that issue.

I know, but Oliver, there are all sorts of ways you could have presented that material. And if you hadn't thought that Jim was correct, I don't think you would have made a special point of it, to the point of showing a commercial in the movie that never was actually made!

Well, it was trivialized, see: they took the music that he had written. [Robby Krieger actually wrote the music.] They didn't do that in this case, they didn't take *Platoon* and turn it into a commercial. They separated the two.

I understand the difference.

I'd rather have *Born on the Fourth of July* on television with schlock commercials in between than not have it on at all. We've grown up with such a corporate culture that one doesn't think twice about it.

What about posing for the Gap ad? Did you think twice about that?

The Gap ad I enjoyed doing, in terms of just a vanity/ego thing, I suppose. I got paid $700. I didn't do it for money. I was at a certain age, I thought those photographs were incredible and I'd like to have a decent photograph of myself at the age of forty-three in my life. Just as a marker. I like the clothes. They're cheap. It's not like working for Armani. They gave off an image of playfulness, an egalitarian image. What did I do wrong? [Laughs.]

I just wonder if you consider how you "commodify" yourself?

I agree. Yeah. But there's some interest in doing it. I have an Andy Warhol attitude—we're postmodernists. Look at Andy, he sold everything. He sold his toilet paper, probably.

But he didn't win all the "Man-with-Most-Integrity of the Year" awards that you do, Mr. International Integrity!

[Laughs.] Does that means that I have to have integrity?

Do you?

[Laughs.] Give me a break! Somebody gives me an award, so now I have to have integrity?

You get a lot of awards, man.

I don't solicit them.

Do they mean anything to you?

I can't remember which one it is. Some of them do.

Do you feel the same way about your work that Warhol felt? You're selling one idea today, another one tomorrow. No need for consistency, integrity? Are you interested in the Warhol ethic?

I don't want integrity to block my creative growth. Each time I've worked on a film I've put my whole being into it, and hopefully there will be some kind of consistency at the end of the day.

But I know how strongly you identify with Morrison, and I can't see him posing for a Gap ad.

That was the sixties and they were very anti. The war was on, too. There was a different feeling. Look at the way movies are made. Who makes them? Chryslers, Jeeps, whatever? It's the same thing. What does a filmmaker do? He goes to the highest bidder and he whores out his services. He gives his privatest fantasies public being—he prostitutes. So I don't have a very high self-esteem, maybe that's what you're saying. Maybe because I see myself as . . . an artist basically begging for a patron. I think there's a lot of that in me, that I feel very lucky each time I get the money to make a picture.

When you read me those lines now, they certainly sound like they're in bad taste—that Americans should just go and serve. I think the text is wrong. But is the act of having done it for Chrysler any different than the act of having done it for Matsushita?

Does the irony of your being at Carolco impress you—since they were the people who brought us Rambo?

That's the nature of the business. In the thirties and the forties they would make the potboilers, the formula fare, and then occasionally they'd take a shot at something else. I'd rather be allied with a successful company that can get it out in the marketplace. The irony of it? Yeah. I think that Mario Kassar [the head of Carolco] was certainly aware of it, because he made his fortune with Stallone. [Laughs.]

The very thing that you despise and oppose.

[Long pause.] Listen, I can't say I despise it. I said *Rambo* is a comic book,

I never took it beyond that. I did not do *Platoon* as an antidote to *Rambo;* I wrote *Platoon* way before *Rambo* ever fucking existed.

You said, I quote, "Platoon is an antidote to Top Gun *and* Rambo. *It will make them think twice before they go marching off to another war." And then you called* Top Gun *fascist, and I assume you thought* Rambo *was equally fascist.*

It was. It was a fascist comic book.

As you know, Oliver, people are always most interesting in their contradictions. As you are probing some of Morrison's, it only seems fair that we probe some of yours.

I like Carolco because they put up the money quickly, and they gambled. And there's not much interference. There's one man, that's Mario. He's like an old-time filmmaker. He's the boss. And it's great to deal with him instead of a bureaucracy; that's why I'm there. He likes directors. He likes movies. He really enjoys watching them. He watches his own movies, the ones he produces, six, seven, eight, nine times. He sits there, and he gets a lot of the details.

A question about verisimilitude: the demands and responsibilities of doing historical fiction. You've been criticized for taking too many liberties with certain things.

Such as?

The death squad burial site in Salvador, which I don't think works in the context of the film, because if you had that image, hundreds and hundreds of bodies spread out at a burial site, it would be on every front page of the world. That's not what those burial sites looked like, so I thought the inaccuracy compromised the integrity of the film. And people also complained about your putting the rebels on horseback, as a shameless romanticization of the rebels. I know you're going to get criticism for the Doors film over the commercial, which you show on TV, but which Morrison stopped before it ever became a commercial. So I'm curious as to the process of justification: how you justify—or don't justify—altering reality so that it will play differently in the film.

I justify it . . . I suppose [pause] with *Born*, for instance, I justified it at the time as being true to the spirit of the times. Ron was not actually wounded in Miami—gassed and beaten in the street—but he was gassed and beaten other places. But there were riots in Miami and many people were arrested, vets. There was fighting. I think I did the right thing. There was no riot at Syracuse, and the Syracuse police department got all upset, but there were riots that week at many colleges all over the country because of Kent State and the Cambodia invasion. He never went to Georgia to confess his crime, but he wrote about it in his book, didn't he? Which was a confession to him, a very strong confession. So I took the liberty of taking that confession—which was the most important thing in the book, the theme of the book—and externalizing it, having him go to Georgia and telling these people that he killed their son.

Why are we never aware that Ron Kovic/Tom Cruise is conscious of the selfishness of that action?

I think he is aware of it. I think he knows he's hurting those people. I think he's so desperate that he has to; he has to either save himself or hurt them. But it's more important that he save himself. And they're not going to die from it. I think those people would get over it. I think anybody knows that you go to war, you go to war; if you're killed by friendly fire, or enemy fire, does it really make a difference?

In their minds it probably did. They had a certain kind of illusion about what happened to him.

Maybe we should shatter their illusion. War shouldn't be illusion. They should see the corpses. Therefore, it was the greater good versus the greater horror. Ron had to save himself, he did it. He subordinated the harm done to them to the greater good it did him.

I'm more interested in how you grapple with subjects that are very rooted in history, and how you make decisions on when to stray in service of your fictionalized narrative.

I would probably do the two *Salvador* things differently now. I think at that time, being an unknown filmmaker, I wanted to have maximum impact right away for a subject that would not interest most Americans. I probably got carried away. I put the rebels on horseback because I loved the imagery of the tank versus the horse. I used the maximum number of people in the death field because it would have visual impact. I would probably do those scenes differently.

In The Doors, *Morrison's line "I'm not mad—I'm interested in freedom" is like an epitaph for this film. He's not mad as in "crazy," but he is mad in the sense of "angry," isn't he? My question is, if you need to rebel, to shock authority, to piss on people's carpets—and it seems like Morrison had that emotional or pyschological need—are you really free at all? Aren't you just a slave to something else— your own rebellion perhaps—just as much as people who are slaves to conformity?*

Contrary dependence? The role of the rebel as essentially a slave?

Maybe. I don't doubt that Morrison was interested in freedom, but he was most certainly quite mad—at least in the sense of angry. There's all sorts of hostility radiating out of this guy; that's one of the things that makes him so interesting.

He was interested in freedom from his own madness.

Maybe that's the resolution. He was very conscious of his own will to self-destruction. After Joplin and Hendrix died, he'd tell his friends, "You're drinking with number three."

Yeah. Yeah. I would like to believe that he went out smiling, he liked it, he enjoyed it as it happened, because he was in love with the death experience. He wanted to experience it, and he did. He had busted the limits on sex, for himself; on drugs, he'd taken every kind of drug; on the law, he busted the law, which I think hurt him the most, the trial really beat him down and tired him out, made him more aware of orthodoxy and the inevitable triumph of orthodoxy; and I think he busted through on the concept of success. He had success, he was God on earth for a while, he had everything he wanted, and he got bored with it. I think he became enamored of failure. He went on a failure trip, too, and I think he enjoyed busting through on the failure trip, by making a fool of himself in public, many times. He wanted to be an asshole, he wanted to be hated.

Because maybe then other people's opinion of him would confirm his opinion of himself?

Partly. And when he was a young lion he had a higher opinion of himself.

Where did all his meanness come from, his abusiveness?

Meanness? Abusiveness? The only abusiveness I know of—from all the witnesses—was when he was drinking. The Irish asshole side, the Dylan Thomas side, would come out, and he'd rant and rave and get into fake fights. And he got his ass busted a couple of times by guys who took him seriously. He would make an asshole of himself in public to go through all forms of experience. He wasn't about reserve and dignity, which his father had represented to him.

It seems, though, that when he was sober, or was on other drugs, that he would be one of the gentlest souls. Everyone would refer to how gentle he was, how sensitive, how well-spoken, how shy. He certainly had two sides: he'd go from being the most sensitive, loving, caring person, who talked to everybody—he was very democratic in his approach to life, which I love—and then when he performed, he would go into a shamanistic, devil thing, and then when he was drinking, he would be a monster at times. I also heard that when he was drunk sometimes he would behave very sweetly. So everybody attests to Jim's kindness. He gave away everything, you know. There was a Jesus quality about Jim. He gave of himself: his body, his life, his possessions. Nothing was his. He was a sharing person. It's the Irish dichotomy, I suppose.

Were you trying to dramatize that dichotomy in the film?

We tried, you know. That's the hardest stuff to do. To show the holy and the fool at the same time. I tried. Probably, people might say I didn't get enough holy.

Do you view your task as an artist as more demythologizing him or remythologizing him?

That's a good question. Aren't they the same thing?

Oh, no.

Give me some help here.

Demythologizing is stripping away the myths that have been built up around him, either by the person himself or by the forces of the day, media, friends, some of which he may have been trapped by himself; stripping those away to show the real human underneath them, in all his spectacular peculiarity—the person. Remythologizing is taking the corpus of Morrison, twenty years later, with the Doors selling more records than ever, and glorifying and glamorizing the artist as victim, as hero—the myths which Morrison himself was conscious of. He says, "We got to make the myths, we got to make the myths." Well, you're a myth-maker too, you're a filmmaker.

I suppose my answer to that is that we were remythologizing, keeping the myth. Keeping the myth. But to me it includes demythologizing at the same time. I don't know why, it just does. It's not like he's any less a person for being demythologized. We show, certainly, the asshole part of Jim, but to me it only makes him more mythological. So they perform the same function for me, I don't know why. If you try to strip away from a person, you end up making him greater. By the fact that you're trying to strip. Why? You think you're taking layers away, you may be adding layers. [Laughs.] You understand what I'm saying?

"The road to excess leads to the palace of wisdom." How can we be so sure?

Go. Go.

Maybe it leads to the palace of disintegration? Of psychic fracturing? Of death?

You need strong *cojones* to take that medicine. You risk becoming larger than life. I guess you could become grotesque. It's a road to travel warily, no question.

Are you at the palace? You've certainly lived through a lot of excess.

I don't know. I'm at mid-life in my journey, that's for sure. [Laughs.] I'm in a dark wood, babe. I feel often like a neophyte on the road, I really do. I don't say that immodestly. I still feel very innocent, in many ways.

Do you feel like a great artist?

[Long pause.] God, if I told you my true feelings about that, they'd never let go of me—I'd just be setting myself up.

You're thinking about what "they" are going to think. I want to know what you think. I want your true feelings.

My true feelings? [Pause.] I never doubted it, from day one. When I was eighteen, I just felt like I had a call. Like I had a call. And living up to that call has been the hardest part. I've got a lot of work to do on myself, on what I'm doing, on my craft, but I never had a doubt.

That confidence must be a gift.

Yeah, I'm sure it is. Oh, I've had periods of doubt and lack of confidence. I wasn't prepared for all the shit that's thrown on people by others. I always thought it would be just a celebration of joy to do good work. I didn't realize that doing good work is often not enough, that there's a fashion to the times. And there's such a thing as luck. We get buffeted by the storms of temperament—they send us astray for months, sometimes years, at a time. But we all must naturally return to our natural temperament. And when we do, we find ourselves again. Our life is the working out of our destiny, our character. I believe you have a certain character.

4

SPIKE LEE

SPIKE LEE FILMOGRAPHY

1977   Last Hustle in Brooklyn (short)
1980   The Answer (short)
1981   Sarah (short)
1982   Joe's Bed-Study Barbershop: We Cut Heads
1986   She's Gotta Have It
1988   School Daze
1989   Do the Right Thing
1990   Mo' Better Blues
1991   Jungle Fever
1992   Malcolm X
1994   Crooklyn
1995   Clockers
1996   Girl 6
1996   Get on the Bus

Spike Lee

Marketeer, provocateur, propagandist, genius, racist, humorist, writer, actor, director, producer, pitchman, chauvinist, homophobe, hoop fan, hype artist, egotist, entrepreneur, caricaturist, visionary, radical, reactionary: Spike Lee has been called all these things. What he wants you to know, though, is that he is a Strong Black Man. You can call him anything you like.

Born Shelton Jackson Lee in 1957, he was called Spike by his mother, a schoolteacher. His father, who's scored many of his films, is a bass player and composer. They raised the family of five, uncomfortably middle-class, in Brooklyn – for a time in an all-white neighborhood. Lee's sister Joie and his brother David have been fixtures on his pictures: Joie as an actress, David as set photographer. His brother Cinque is also an actor and aspiring filmmaker.

After being graduated from Morehouse College, Lee elbowed his way through NYU film school, along with Ernest Dickerson, his cinematographer. Lee's hour-long thesis film, *Joe's Bed-Stuy Barbershop: We Cut Heads,* was a sharp-witted and wholly convincing take on one man's involvement in the numbers racket; a sort of spare, thoughtful gangster picture about choice and responsibility. His next project, *The Messenger,* fell apart for lack of funding in the summer of 1984, after which he redoubled his efforts. Begging, borrowing, pleading, and sweet-talking, he raised $175,000 and made *She's Gotta Have It,* a black-and-white black-only sex farce that was bold but lighthearted. A blizzard of rave reviews and some $8 million in box office receipts later, Spike Lee was a star, as much because of his persona as because of his film. (He'd cagily cast himself as a wonderfully comic b-boy nebbish, which led to a lot of unfortunate "black Woody Allen" comparisons.) A hero to the black community, an intriguing character to white media (which embraced him), and a politically correct moneymaker to the hipper studios, Lee started making movies at a furious pace, and has not let up.

School Daze was a critical failure, but a commercial success. An ambitious if uneven musical airing the dirty laundry of color consciousness at a black college, its radical shifts in tone and style would become an integral part of Lee's work: fascinating to his supporters, irritating to his detractors. *Do the*

Right Thing, his best and best-known picture, focused on race relations during the hottest day of the year in one Brooklyn neighborhood, presenting a tragedy of Greek proportion and American character. *Mo' Better Blues* was a retreat from the contentious terrain of race into the fragrant world of jazz, where a famous trumpet player (Denzel Washington) pursues and is pursued by two women—a suprisingly conventional, ham-fisted piece of work. He sprang back into racial politics (and also, this time, sexual and class politics) in his next film, *Jungle Fever,* which took a cold look at the crack epidemic over the shoulder of its main theme—interracial lust, love, and marriage. And *Jungle Fever* would be but a prelude to the full movement of *Malcolm X,* a film Lee feels he was born to make, but which he had to fight to make.

Strong though somewhat superficial, dramatic but often corny, combative yet humorous, his films have all made good dollars if not always good sense. While Lee's refrain that he "wuz robbed" whenever one of his films fails to win a desired award grows tiresome, and his continual racial rationalizations cry wolf, his positive energy and impact on American film cannot be, and should not be, denied. At the very least, the visibility and profitability of his work helped open the floodgates for many other black filmmakers: Robert Townsend, the Hudlin Brothers, Mario Van Peebles, Julie Dash, John Singleton, Charles Burnett, Matty Rich, Bill Duke.

In addition to directing and acting in his feature films, Lee has been busy on many other fronts. His TV commercials for Levi's 501 jeans and for Nike's Air Jordan sneakers (which feature his Mars Blackmon character from *She's Gotta Have It*) have been nothing short of fabulous. His ad for Jesse Jackson's campaign in the 1988 New York presidential primary, however, was frighteningly shaky—indeed, almost disturbing in its political naiveté. Lee has published companion books to his first four commercial films (featuring journals, scripts, essays, interviews, storyboards, photos, and so on) as well as a restrospective look at his oeuvre, *Five for Five,* upon the release of his fifth. Lee has also shot more than a dozen music videos, often in connection with the promotion of a film. His relentless marketing savvy has found its ultimate expression not in his Brooklyn retail outlet, Spike's Joint, which sells T-shirts, sweatshirts, buttons, books, postcards, posters, and hats advertising his work, but in the nationwide toll-free number set up to allow fans to access the *"authentic* memorabilia" and to discourage imitations. While Lee's place at the forefront of American film may be debatable on strictly aesthetic terms, he's certainly the only auteur in the history of cinema with his own 800 number.

We talked twice in April of 1991, in New York City. Our first session took place in the Brill Building, where he was mixing sound for *Jungle Fever.* For the second session, Lee strolled us down Broadway to a Chinese restaurant, where he ate his dinner and my questions.

SESSION ONE

I want to talk a little bit about your family, because that hasn't been talked about very much. Yours was the first black family in an all-white neighborhood, Cobble Hill in Brooklyn. Was that a shaping experience in some kind of way?

No. I mean, we got called "nigger" on the first day, but after that we weren't deemed a threat, because we were the only black family in the neighborhood.

How long were you there?

We moved there in 1961 or '62, up until October of '69, when my parents bought a brownstone in Fort Greene.

What were your friends like at that time?

Mostly Italian.

You've been dealing with Scorsese's group in the last couple of films more than he's ever dealt with yours.

I gave him a book—when *The Last Temptation of Christ* came out—and I inscribed it, "Jesus Christ was a black man. Love, Spike Lee." [Laughs.] He laughed.

You were a late bloomer. You've described yourself as looking like a thirteen-year-old your freshman year of college. How do you feel you were affected by that?

Well, when you're like that—when you look that young—people tend to ignore you. So I've always been very observant, and quiet, also.

Was there any insecurity that came along with that?

No, because I knew that I would look my age eventually.

Let's talk about your mom. Her death was pretty sudden.

Yeah, it was pretty sudden. She got sick, and went into the hospital, and she passed two weeks after that. We suspected that she was sick for a while and didn't tell anybody.

What are your memories of going through that?

I was nineteen going on twenty, at college. And I remember they told me to come home, so I came home for a week. Then I went back to school, and came back the day she died. She was in a coma.

What was the connection between your mom's passing and your being a film-maker?

I don't know. My mother was the one that really pushed us—all my siblings. My father, anything we wanted to do was fine with him. He wasn't the disciplinarian, he wasn't the one that really motivated us—it was our mother. She encouraged us to do well, whatever you wanted to do. She was the one that started taking me to movies when I was little. She took me to see *Mean Streets*.

But the whole process of making films was magical to you, you thought they just appeared in the theatre.

Yeah, I didn't know that people—especially any black people—had a job making films.

Your maternal grandmother, whom you refer to in your journals, was quoted as saying that if your mom hadn't died, maybe you wouldn't have been a filmmaker. Where does that come from?

I don't know. My grandmother is very religious, so maybe she felt her daughter had to be sacrificed for me to be successful.

Your first movie, Last Hustle in Brooklyn, *came the year after her death, 1977. What was that like?*

It was Super-8 mishmash. I didn't have a job that summer. I walked around with a Super-8 camera and filmed New York City. That was the first summer of the big disco craze. Everybody was having block parties on the street, where they'd hook up their systems to street lamps. I filmed a lot of that. It was also the summer of the blackout, so I intercut a lot of looting with the dancing, and stuff like that. It was forty-five minutes.

Was there a story line, or was it kind of documentary?

It was kind of documentary, but I wrote some narration too. I haven't seen it in a long, long time. I don't even know where it is.

What moved you to pick up the camera?

I don't know. I just bought a Super-8 camera.

Had you been taking stills?

No, not really.

Just out of the blue, you decided to get a Super-8?

[No answer.]

Looking back on it, does it make any sense to you, when you made the move to film?

Well, it had to be something to do with the arts, because that's just the environment in which we were raised. My father was a musician, and my mother taught English and art sometimes. For me it's no accident that a lot of my siblings and myself are artists. It's in the genes. You know, it comes with exposure, if you're exposed to art at a very young age.

Now, your father remarried a woman named Susan Kaplan. Is she a black woman or a—

She's Jewish.

White woman, I assume. But of course, there are a lot of dudes in Ethiopia who think they are the original Jews—

She's not a black Jew.

What's that experience been like?

Well, I mean, that's his wife, so I really don't have nothing to say about it. [Pause.] We don't get along that good, but that's his wife, so . . . that's that.

Since you were an adult by then, it's not like she was your stepmother.

She hasn't been nobody's stepmother.

But you have a half brother by her.

Arnold, yeah, he's five.

Did this figure at all into your consciousness in making Jungle Fever, *the intermarriage within your family?*

No, not because of my father. I mean, it wasn't done solely because of my father. Intermarriage has been with us since slaves were brought over here from Africa. So that was not done as an answer to my father marrying a white woman at all.

What's your relationship with your father like?

[Slyly.] Oh, we get along every now and then.

In your journal for She's Gotta Have It, *you wrote, "Daddy and I can barely speak without getting into an argument."*

Well, sometimes that happens between fathers and sons. I was glad that we were able to do the four films we did together.

Your brother David takes stills for your films. Has he done others as well?

He did *The Long Walk Home.* And he is a free-lance photographer.

Joie we know about, and Cinque is a filmmaker and actor. What kind of films does he make?

He's the black David Lynch. [Laughs.]

Do you like Cinque's work?

He's very avant-garde. He has a good cinematic eye, but he needs to learn how to tell a story better.

It's interesting that because you work with your family as much as you do, there are some parallels between you and Francis Coppola.

Hey, [laughs] I love Francis to death, but I would not have cast Sofia in that role [in *Godfather III*]! I wouldn't have done it. And luckily, I don't think I've made a mistake like that using my family, my siblings.

Nonetheless, it adds another level of complication to dealing with aesthetic issues.

Well, not really, because I'm the director on my films, and what I say goes. They might be disappointed, they might bitch and moan, but what I say is gonna go. Not my father or anyone in my family has ever expected anything. They know that if they're right for the part or the job they'll do it.

As far as your being a filmmaker, you've said any number of times and in any number of ways that you were "put here to make films." That suggests a sort of divine intervention: that you were chosen for it.

Oh, I believe it, because too many things have happened that just weren't luck. I mean, a lot of things steered me in this direction. My father has great talent, but I don't think we're ever going to see the day where he's going to get the kind of recognition he deserves. In a way, maybe that's why I've been able to do what I've done—maybe that's why I've gotten what I've got— because of what was denied him.

Your dad has an awful lot in the drawers and closets—eight or nine operas, two unpublished novels—and you've been able to realize a lot of the things that he wasn't able to.

Well, that really just goes to show you that talent is not everything. My father is a terrible businessman. Terrible. If he would surround himself with people who know what they're doing, who have some administrative skills and could utilize my father's talent, it would work great, but he doesn't want to do that. Opera is not opera if it stays undone. But talent has never been a factor. He has all the talent in the world. It's the other shit.

He must feel a great deal of pride in you. He's called you "the Charlie Parker of the movies."

[Laughs.] He must have just cashed a check from me that day!

GIMDAD—"God is my defense and deliverance." You would write that when you were really up against the wall trying to raise money to make She's Gotta Have It.

Oh, that was given to me by a woman, one of my mother's close friends, Amy

Olatunji, the wife of Baba, the African drummer. She's a very spiritual person. You write it down—GIMDAD. It worked, and it's been working.

What's your spiritual hookup?

I've never been a very religious person, as far as going to church. The only time I really went to church was when I spent the summers down South, where we had to go to church with both my grandmothers. My parents in New York never made us go to church.

Nonetheless, you have some relation to—

Yeah, I do believe that. For me it's a very personal thing. I do believe that there is something greater than us.

Greater than Spike Lee? You're going to blow your image.

Greater than humanity. [Laughs.] You're just fucking with me.

What were the prayers you were saying every night? You referred to them a number of times.

"Where are we going to get this money? Please, Lord, please."

Now, you weren't asking the blond, blue-eyed Jesus Christ for that?

Hey, Buddha, Allah, Jesus—we weren't risking anything! [Laughs.] I think if *She's Gotta Have It* had been a failure I still would have been successful, but it would have taken another three, four, or even five years to rebound from that.

What's your feeling about organized religion? A lot of religious themes bubble up in Jungle Fever.

Well, that's really because of who I wrote it for. Ossie Davis is an ordained minister. So I really wanted to bring that flavor to this film. You see that more in older black people. That's all we did: get on our knees and pray, and sing to the high heavens. But I'm not too up on organized religion.

You think the Church was used to hold black folk down in this country?

All over the world. The Bible in one hand and the gun in the other.

But it kind of backfired, because—

Backfired? How?

Because in some ways the white Southerners, who forced Christianity down the slaves' throats, didn't realize that the personal empowerment Christianity gave the slaves led to a kind of self-esteem that the white people themselves didn't get from the religion, because they didn't take their religion as seriously as the slaves did.

Well, it gave us something. It gave us the strength to go on. I don't know that it backfired. But it also kept us praying to Jesus and worrying about the hereafter instead of what was happening now: getting our asses kicked! We were worrying about trying to get into heaven. Malcolm said the white man's heaven is the black man's hell. We want our heaven here on earth! So in a lot of ways religion has been used to oppress people.

Speaking of saviors, one of the things you wrote even before She's Gotta Have It *became a hit was that you were "determined not to let other people turn you into a savior."*

Well, that just happens when any black person is successful in any field— there's so few of us that when we do break through, the weight of the whole race is thrust upon our shoulders. And it can't be done by one person.

Do you feel the burden of that responsibility?

Not as much as I used to, because now I'm not the only one out there. I'm so happy that everyone else is coming up now. I never wanted to be the only black filmmaker, because no one of my films can satisfy thirty million African-Americans. Our taste is just as diverse as anybody else's. A lot of people do not like my films but nonetheless still want to go to see movies. Black parents talk to me all the time, and they wish I would make children's movies—movies they could take their children to—but that's not the type of movies I've made up to this point. I mean, the Hudlins' *House Party* was made specifically for black teenagers. That was a need that should be fulfilled and it was. That's why it made $29 million.

[A young white woman comes over to us and says, "I know you guys are doing an interview, but thanks for *Do the Right Thing*. It's one of the best movies I ever saw." Lee thanks her and I ask to move to another room to get away from the traffic. We move to a booth in the mixing room.]

What does it say on your passport?

Shelton Jackson Spike Lee.

Occupation?

Filmmaker.

Some filmmakers feel that they are first and foremost writers, and the way they realize their writing is with cinema.

I'm a filmmaker.

Do you ever think you'll write not specifically for the screen?

Like a novel or something? No. I've written essays, but I'm a filmmaker.

And a Harvard professor.

[Laughs.] Assistant professor.

What will you be teaching?

Contemporary American Cinema.

In the film department or the Afro-Am department?

In Afro-Am. Dr. Henry Louis Gates is taking over the department, so he asked me to teach a course there.

Let's talk about your relationship with women, outside the frame. You fairly self-consciously wrote in your journal on Mo' Better Blues *that you knew everybody would be asking how much of you was in this Bleek character [Denzel Washington], and you wrote, "All I can say is I love film more than Bleek loves jazz." Which would lead me to believe that you experience the same kind of difficulty maintaining—*

No, not true at all. Because I don't let relationships get to the point where it's a problem, where it starts to deter your work. That's something that Bleek had trouble balancing. But I don't think I do.

Do you still look forward to having a family?

Yeah.

Five kids?

All boys! [Laughs.]

What is this "all boys" stuff? Nola in She's Gotta Have It *wants "five rusty-butt boys."* Bleek wants a boy in Mo' Better Blues.

Well, I wouldn't throw a girl back in the ocean. But I want all sons. One girl would be all right.

Is it that you like boys more than girls?

I think there should be definitely more black men, that's for sure. Start to even it up.

Why, because there are more black women than black men?

Yeah, but also the assault on black men, where if they live to be twenty-five, that's a feat.

The life expectancy of young urban black males is frightening. It's like in a Third World country.

[Pause.] It's true.

Would a family slow down your pace of work? You talk about wanting to make another thirty-three, thirty-four films.

I know myself I can't keep up this pace. *Jungle Fever* will be the fifth film we've done in the last six years. I can't keep that up, nor do I want to.

Have things ever gotten rushed on account of this pace?

I don't think things have ever gotten rushed. There was an opportunity to get these films done, I was given the money; I felt these films should be made at that time, on the subjects that we did. Most black filmmakers, in the past, might get that first film out, but the follow-up took forever. I was determined not to let that happen to me.

When people have accused you of doing a "love story," as in the case of Mo' Better Blues, *you've responded by saying, "I don't do love stories."*

Well, I don't like that word.

Why not?

Just the whole image of love stories in my mind—I never liked it. It's a relationship film.

What about in your own life? Are you comfortable with the idea of love, or being in love?

Yeah, if that's what it is. But if it's not, I don't want to delude myself or anybody else.

Do you fall in love, hard?

Yeah, it's happened once in a while.

When was the last time?

When was the lunar eclipse? [Laughs.]

I mean, the end of Mo' Better *is like a—*

A Hallmark card? [Laughs.]

Well, it's certainly a celebration of love—the affirming, redemptive qualities of love.

Well, also family. I think that's it.

But if love's not there, then "family" can be a horror show—it can make everything worse.

That's true.

Do you still feel, as you once did, that you get too emotional for your own good?

One should hold in his feelings, sometimes. I happen to have more self-control. Instead of blowing up all the time, just listening. But I don't want to get ulcers either. You've got to pick your battles. You can't have a war every single time out.

Do you feel you're an angry person?

Not at all. [Pause.] The funny thing to me is when white people accuse blacks, when they see somebody black who's angry, they say, "Why are you so angry?" [Laughs.] If they don't know why black people are angry, then there's *no* hope. I mean, it's a miracle that black Americans are as complacent and happy-go-lucky as we are.

Malcolm said, "Yes, I'm an extremist. The black race in America is in extremely bad condition. You show me a black man who isn't an extremist and I'll show you one who needs psychiatric attention."

Or is dead. But I don't think I have that much anger. I don't think I'm angrier than I have a right to be.

You get angry on a personal level though—like at Cannes when you said Do the Right Thing *was "robbed" of an award.*

It was really anger at Wim Wenders, that's who.

"I have a Louisville slugger baseball bat deep in my closet with Wim Wenders' name written on it," is what you wrote.

[Laughs.] I just said that. I would never hit him in the head with a bat. What I was talking about was that it got back to me that the reason Wim Wenders didn't like the film was that he considered what Mookie does [throwing a garbage can through the window of a pizzeria and triggering a riot] as unheroic. But the James Spader character in *sex, lies, and videotape,* what's heroic about jerking off with an 8-millimeter camera? I didn't understand that thinking. [Soderbergh's *sex, lies, and videotape* won the award.]

Yeah, but that wasn't a movie about heroism. I mean, that wasn't even an issue in that movie.

But why have two separate rules?

Do the Right Thing, *even in its very title, sets up a moral universe and a code, so it's going to provoke a kind of scrutiny on the action that a movie in which things are more relative will not.*

See, I never buy that shit. Because I want my shit—I mean, if you're going to critique my work use the same motherfucking standards for everybody. Don't let shit slide and call me anti-Semitic every single way and then the shit goes by and nobody says nothing about the other stuff, work that's just racist in general.

I was trying to say that the film itself, within its own universe, sets up an expectation of moral action and heroism, and—

All I'm saying is that they gave out twelve or thirteen awards. Thirteen films got awards that year and we didn't get one.

I know you've complained about not receiving Oscars as well, but don't you ever feel that your work is more validated by not receiving the awards than if you were everybody's favorite?

I understand that. See, I'm not saying that awards are validating my work, saying it's great. But if you win an Academy Award, you know how much money a film makes after it wins one? That's it. Studios don't spend a million dollars on a campaign just to get the award, but because they know the award will bring in a lot more revenue. That's why I wanted it for *Do the Right Thing.*

But don't you think that if a conservative, regressive body like the Academy embraced your work—

Nah, I don't think that people would have liked it any less had we gotten an Academy nomination.

It's like, if an artist prides himself on doing work that is anticorporate, but the work is being supported by a grant from Exxon, maybe he's got to wonder if the work is threatening anybody. America always sucks up its most radical appendage.

I don't know about that.

As far as your image, people think of you as a hustler. Now, we know that everybody has to hustle to make it as an artist—

Do people accuse Madonna of hustling? I'm asking.

But it's got a different spin with you. In other cases it's, "So-and-so is hardworking," or "So-and-so has so much energy," but when you do it it's—

Self-promotion.

Are you conscious of that?

Look, I know there are two sets of rules. So, that's just the way it is. I just have to keep doing what I do best, and know what I have to do, and pursue that. I can't let other people dictate the agenda.

Would you say you're pedantic, Professor Lee?

Assistant Professor. [Laughs.] I don't know. I don't try to put labels on myself saying I'm this way or that way.

Cynda Williams, the young actress opposite Denzel Washington in Mo' Better, *said you gave it to her pretty heavy: "Do you know who Marcus Garvey is? Do you know this? Do you know that?" She felt like she was being tested all the time.*

I mean, if black people don't know . . . it's not like I was asking her who someone ten million years ago was. I felt, with Cynda, she had just moved from Indiana, and she didn't *know* anything. She had never been to any movies, hadn't really read any books. And I don't see how you can be an artist in any field without reading, or being exposed to as much stuff as you can. That's what that was about. I wasn't testing. It could make her acting better if she knows something. Not to say that she was a complete imbecile, but she just grew up in Muncie and she didn't know. John Coltrane was a big influence on that film and she didn't even know who the guy was. Trying to educate her, steer her. So I gave her a list of books to read, a lot of video-tapes from my library.

Maybe she was reacting more to your manner than to her need to learn?

Well, that could have happened. [Laughs.] "What are you, an idiot? Are you retarded? You haven't heard of Marcus Garvey? What are you, a retard?" That's probably what she was talking about. I will admit, I could've probably been more diplomatic.

Diplomacy may never be your strong suit.

Some of us don't have patience!

Do you feel that you are held for so much more accountability, both within and outside the frame, by white folk and by black folk, than a white director would be?

I agree. We got the most negative criticism out of the black community on *School Daze*, for airing the laundry. And white critics try to impose a higher moral standard on me than on others. They use the same tired line. "Well, you're a better filmmaker, so therefore we should have higher standards for you than for everybody else." That's bullshit! As I said before, there's two standards and two rules. It's not that I accept it, it's just that's the way it is.

Do you think you can change it in any way?

No. No.

What do you think could change that?

Just the way white people think. [Pause.]

So you try to operate within the double standards and create as much elbowroom for yourself as you can?

That's it. You ask any successful black person, and they're all doing the same thing. They all know when they embark on what they're doing they can't be as good as the white person—they have to be ten times better. It's not fair, but that's just the way it is. When I went to film school, at NYU, me and Ernest Dickerson knew that we'd have to bust our ass, that we'd have to be head and shoulders above the rest of these motherfuckers. That's just the way it is.

That's a pattern that a lot of minority groups have gone through in this country.

Yeah, it's not exclusively black.

Let's turn to your writing now. You're fast, very fast. You do a lot of prepara-tion, but you write quickly [ten to fifteen days for a screenplay]. Has that changed at all?

No, it hasn't. It's gotten faster. More disciplined. I block out four, five hours a day, and that's all I do.

How personal is the act of writing for you?

That's the most personal thing I do under all the heading of filmmaker. Everything else is really a collaborative effort.

I mean, do you search your soul a lot, when you sit down to write a film?

Search my soul?

Do you get confused?

Writing? I don't think so. Because when I sit down it's really thought out, by that time.

Is it your goal to make great art or to make massive entertainments?

I think what I've done is always a combination of the two. For me, it's not a conflict. I don't want to make mindless entertainment, but at the same time I don't want to make shit no one understands either.

Who's making shit nobody understands?

Uh, I'm not going say anything bad about anyone. There was a time when I did. But a lot of this has come with maturity. If you don't have anything good to say about people, for the most part don't say it.

Now, if you made what you felt was a beautifully realized film, but it did at the box office only what Charles Burnett's To Sleep with Anger *did, and you could remove from the mix any negative repercussions this would have on the budget of your next film, could you still be happy with the piece?*

With the piece, yeah. But there's plenty of artists who think they made a great record, a great movie, a great play, but it just didn't connect with the audience.

Do you still see your function as a filmmaker, as you once did, as one of "shedding light on problems" so they can get discussed and understood?

Not every film, not every film. It depends on the subject matter. I think we start to get in trouble if we expect the artist to have answers all the time. For instance, *School Daze* was the examination of petty, superficial differences that still keep black people apart. To me, we are the most un-unified people on the face of the earth. Skin differences, hair types.

Yet there are the same differentiations within a lot of cultures.

Yeah, but they ain't in the shape that we're in. We're not in the same boat. We don't have the same liberties as other people. And to me, we are the most un-unified people in the world.

There's a struggle, a tension, maybe a fundamental contradiction, between uni-fication and diversity. How do you deal with that?

I think Jewish people are very diverse but they are very unified, on a lot of things. You talk about Israel: Jewish people are unified on the State of Israel.

You've never heard people argue like Jews argue about what to do about it, or how to deal with Israel.

I know Jewish people are more unified than black people, I know that.

Why do you think that is the case, historically?

I don't want to get into the whole Jewish-black thing.

I'm not asking about Jewish-black relations, I'm asking why you think Jews are more unified than black people.

As far as America is concerned? Because I don't think Jews have ever been taught to hate themselves the way black people have. I mean that's the whole key: self-hatred. That's not to say that Jewish people haven't been persecuted. I'm not saying that. But they haven't been taught to hate themselves to the level black people have been. When you're persecuted, it's natural for people to come together; but when you're also taught at the same time that you're the lowest form of life on earth, that you're subhuman, then why would you want to get together with other people like that? Who do you hate? Yourself.

What do you think is the most interesting thing about your life?

That I'm making the art that I want to make, with a freedom that very few filmmakers have in general, let alone black filmmakers. Filmmakers period.

I'd like to walk through each of the films, starting with your student work.

The Answer was my first film, about a struggling black screenwriter who's hired to direct the $50 million remake of *Birth of a Nation*.

What about Sarah?

Worst film I made in my entire life. Too sentimental! I really did it for my grandma. She was saying, "Why don't you do a nice little film?" That's what I did. That's the only time I ever did something I didn't want to do.

Do you keep your defenses up against sentimentality?

Not if it's real. But when it's manufactured, I don't like that.

Let's talk about Joe's Bed-Stuy Barbershop: We Cut Heads, *your thesis film. There's a line in it: "Brother Homer, wake up, the black man has been sleeping for four hundred years." That "wake up" theme is going to keep coming back in your films, over and over. How did you engineer that theme into that piece? In other words, how does the action of that story—*

Well, that was really just put in the mouth of Nicholas Lovejoy, the numbers man, who's a pseudo black freedom fighter: one of these guys who give turkeys away at Thanksgiving and is received as a hero. Like Nikki Barnes; people in Harlem thought he was a hero. Big car, gave away turkeys, real successful. I guess people didn't think about all the damage he was doing with the drugs he was selling.

Though I must say Nicholas Lovejoy doesn't come across too badly in the film: his manner, his calmness, his level of articulation, his strength.

He's smooth.

Do you agree with him when he says, "We're ninety-nine percent consumers. We don't produce anything."

I agree.

"Color TV in every room."

That's a slight exaggeration, but black people do watch more TV than anybody.

A study was just published that showed the average black household watches over seventy-seven hours of TV a week. The average white household watches fifty. It's a race—

And we're winning it, hands down! And it's not a race you want to win either. TV is the cheapest form of entertainment, but it's definitely detrimental. I believe that figure; it's true.

And not only that, but sixty percent of white households have cable, but only forty percent of black households, which means that blacks watch for more hours while receiving less information.

And you know cable is going to come to black neighborhoods last.

Joe's Bed-Stuy brings up the problem of economic self-reliance. What kind of economic—

I don't really have a program. All I'm saying is that black people for too long haven't really thought of owning businesses. That's the key. Because when you own businesses, you have more control. That was one of the key things about *Do the Right Thing*: the whole thing about Sal's Famous Pizzeria, between Sal [Danny Aiello] and Buggin' Out [Giancarlo Esposito]. Buggin' Out rightfully felt that Sal should have the decency to at least have some black people up on the Wall of Fame, since all his income is derived from people in the community, who are black and Hispanic. Sal had, to me, a more valid point: this is my motherfucking pizzeria and I can do what I want to do. When you open your own restaurant, you can do what you want. Of course, now Buggin' Out countered by trying to organize a boycott of Sal's, which has always been one of our ways of fighting that type of thinking. But in the case of Buggin' Out, it didn't work.

A boycott takes patience, organization, determination—

And more than rhetoric, and that's something that Buggin' Out didn't have.

It's sad that the fight is over a symbol when the economic realities are so much more significant. You can spend all your time trying to boycott a Korean fruit stand in Brooklyn—

Black people should have their *own* fruit and vegetable stands in Flatbush. I'd be crazy to spend a year out there boycotting that one Korean place! That doesn't make any sense to me.

Let's go to She's Gotta Have It. *The film is set up to answer a question that you were continually asking yourself, during the writing of it: "Why does Nola do all this loving?" In your journal, a couple of times you write: "I better know the answer."*

Well, I don't know that I ever really found out the answer. She was really just trying to explore. All she was doing was living her life as men lead theirs. And in most circles, women cannot do it without being labeled a prostitute or a whore or a nymphomaniac.

But what she does is make love to men, and not much more.

She does other things, [laughs] but this is what we showed! I mean, sex is a large part of her life. That's what makes her happy. And doing it with different men, not just one same old guy.

But do you feel the film ever does answer the question why? Why that's true for her, true for her character?

I think people make up their own minds on a lot of my films. It's very rare where there's one answer that explains everything or satisfies everybody.

Well, there's ambiguity, but there's also vagueness, the downside of having under-written characters.

I don't think *she* was underwritten.

There were some black feminists—I know you're very popular with them—who felt—

[Sarcastically.] I got a lot of friends! [Laughs.]

Now, you were on the edge of pornography in She's Gotta Have It.

Yeah, you think so?

Well, you said you wanted to be on the edge of it, because that was the only way a film like this was going to get noticed: to sidle up to the edge of porn.

Well, I don't know if we were that close, but there was more sex in that film than in any other film I've done to date. And I'll probably never do another film that has as much as that film. But we had to get noticed. I wanted the sex to be tasteful, not pornographic.

How do you respond to the criticism that the three men, although they are not as central to the film as Nola, are actually more definite characters, whereas she is more of a body to be explored and fought over?

Well, I don't see it like that. For me, the film is about how *men* react to a woman like this. And I don't have any problem if there was a female filmmaker who could write better female characters, more developed than the male characters. Every filmmaker has a weakness, and this is something I've had to work on since *She's Gotta Have It*. I feel there has been growth on my part, as far as the female characters in my films.

Why did you feel that you would be "in the mud" with black women when that film came out?

Because there would be a section of black women who would think that I was saying that all black women were like this, therefore I'm just reinforcing the stereotype that black women are loose. Period.

The Rolling Stones' "black girls just wanna fuck all night" stereotype.

Exactly.

Eddie Murphy, in fact, said to you that if he had done that exact film, he'd be accused of perpetuating that myth, but that the context was different with you doing it.

[Laughs.] Every artist brings their own particular baggage. But he's done that anyway, in his films!

Michelle Wallace, the black feminist, wrote that "the film is about a black woman who couldn't get enough of the old phallus and who therefore had to be raped."

She couldn't get enough, so she had to be raped?

When she refused to marry Jamie, he punishes her with violent sex.

For me that scene is not a stamp of approval of rape. Hopefully, it was my intent to show how horrible it is. So if people have problems with it, you could say it was in the execution of it, but it was never my intent.

But if it was so horrible, why did you write in your journal that "it's there that she decides it's Jamie she truly loves."

So what does that mean?

So a woman who is being raped decides at that point that it's the rapist she actually loves?

I always wanted it to be ambiguous whether that was a rape or not anyway.

She calls it a "near-rape" in the following park scene.

But I don't think she decides she loves him because of the rape, though. This is something she's been thinking about. When you're dealing with that many people, you are always judging—each person up against the other. She felt that he was the one that cared about her the most.

Why did you decide not to actually have a lesbian sex scene?

That would have been too much. Nola Darling was wild enough. The reason we had the lesbian things was that we wanted to show that Nola had that much going for her—that women were after her too, not only men.

Now, at the end of the film, after the credits, come the words, "This film contains No Jheri Curls! No Drugs!" Why?

Because we made She's Gotta Have It like it was going to be our last film. So we put everything in there. That statement was mine and it still is mine. That's the way I feel about drugs and Jheri curls, and blue contact lenses and nose jobs.

Let's turn to School Daze. *A rape functions as the climax of that film as well.*

Uh-huh.

Were you conscious that you had done that on your first film and here, on your second, it was going to be the climax again?

Yeah, I was conscious of it, because that whole film, a lot of it has to do with sex. And the way this particular fraternity was using women. That was my experience in college. We could have shown guys running a train on her.

I know at one point you considered doing that.

That would have been too much. But that stuff happened all the time, so it wouldn't have been like we were making that up.

Let's talk about the "wake up" ending, where Dap [Larry Fishburne] calls out those words, and people walk towards him from all across the campus.

The whole ending is surreal.

Did you feel there was a risk to the film from changing tone so much at the very end?

I didn't feel that.

Did you get a difference of opinion on it in the script stage and during shooting?

Some people felt the ending didn't work, but it worked for me and that's why it's in.

You wrote: "People get out of bed not because he's calling them but because they realize something." What is it they realize?

For me, the whole film is about the petty, superficial differences that keep black people from being a more unified people. And we're using the black college campus as a microcosm of black society as a whole. And that whole ending was shot in a blinding light, using the metaphor of light being the truth and saying, "Look, we got to stop this shit, this dumb, ignorant shit we're doing."

You got criticized by some who felt the film wasn't so much a critique of sexism and color-consciousness as a display of it.

No, I think it was definitely a critique. It was showing how stupid it is. Numbers like "Straight and Nappy," where the two factions sing a song about which hair is better; it was definitely a critique of these petty, superficial differences.

But you got criticized by some women saying that the men in the film were concerned with ideas and politics, divestiture and what have you, while the women were concerned only with looks.

I wouldn't say that. I would say that the balance was more in the male parts, not the female parts, but I wouldn't say that they were complete bimbos, the females.

I know you think there's self-hatred in black women wearing colored contacts and hair weaves. Does a white woman who gets a fat-lip operation evidence self-hatred by doing that?

No, she just wants to be black. She wants those full lips. [Laughs.] See, but that's not my major concern, what white people are doing to themselves. I can't worry about that.

Silly-ass white people!

[Laughs.] If they want to sit in the sun and bake themselves and get skin cancer to get black, let 'em! That's not my priority. Black people, for me, that's a priority. Any race is going to say that their own race is a priority. Now, at the same time, it doesn't mean that you should do that by oppressing other people.

Did you feel the film was anti-gay, or were you just portraying what you felt was real?

Portraying what's real. How is it that Martin Scorsese can sit in the back of a cab in *Taxi Driver* and say, "See my wife up there. She's up there with a nigger. You ever seen what a .44 Magnum does to a pussy?"? I have never read one article saying Martin Scorsese is a racist because he played that character talking about his wife up there in the apartment with the nigger and he's going to blow her pussy up with a .44. I mean, I like his films a lot, but nobody ever says nothing about that.

But you would defend his right to play that character—

Yes! And I didn't say he was racist because of that, either. But nobody has ever written that. I presented the way it is with a lot of black males, but I don't think I'm a homophobe.

Why do people have that idea?

[Laughs.] Because I have a character saying "fag." *All* my thoughts don't come out of *every* single character I write.

Let's go to the main issue: color-consciousness among blacks. Why do you feel that black men are more interested in light-skinned black women?

Why? Because they're closer to white. It's common sense. I mean why, why, why do little black kids—if they have a choice between a white doll and a black doll—why do they pick a white doll? Same thing.

What would you say about a fair-skinned white man who's interested in dark white women or black women?

I can't answer that question.

Dap has that speech about going through the ghetto on a bus, and that if you say "Free chicken! Free drugs!" all the black people will get on the bus.

Larry Fishburne ad-libbed that, I didn't write it.

So we're left with the question, at the end of that film, given the "wake up" ending: How do you get off that bus?

[Long pause.] That's what we're all trying to find out. That's what everybody has been trying to find out. I don't have the answer. But the first step is to realize that there's a bus you're on! [Laughs.] The second step is you got to realize you've got to get off, and then you've got to figure out how to do that. But people don't even know they're on the bus.

Do you think your films are part of the way people might find out they're on the bus?

Hopefully. First you got to get them into the theatre, and then when they're in the theatre, hopefully they'll get it.

How many people have asked you, "Does Mookie do the right thing?"

[Laughs.] How many people are there in New York City?

And what's your answer to them?

Black people never ask me that. It's only white people.

Why's that?

Because black people understand perfectly why Mookie threw the garbage can through the window. No black person has ever asked me, "Did Mookie do the right thing?" Never. Only white people. White people are like, "Oh, I like Mookie so much up to that point. He's a nice character. Why'd he have to throw the garbage can through the window?" Black people, there's no question in their minds why he does that.

Yeah, but why one does something and whether what one does is right are very different things. I know why he does it, but—

But only white people want to know why he does it. I spoke at twenty-five universities last year and that's all I ever got asked. "Did Mookie do the right thing?"

What do you tell them?

I feel at the time he did. Mookie is doing it in response to the police murdering Radio Raheem, with the infamous Michael Stewart choke hold, in front of his face—also knowing this is not the first time that something like this has happened, nor will it be the last. What people have to understand is that almost every riot that's happened here in America involving black people has happened because of some small incident like that: cops killing somebody, cops beating up a pregnant black woman. It's incidents like that that have sparked riots across America. And that's all we were doing was using history. Mookie cannot lash out against the police, because the police were gone. As soon as Radio Raheem was dead, they threw his ass in the back of car and got the hell out of there so they could make up their story.

What about attacking Sal?

I think he likes Sal too much. For Mookie, in my mind, Sal's Pizzeria represents everything, and that's why he lashed out against it. It was Mayor Koch, it was the cops—everything.

That's "the power" to him?

It's the power at the moment. But when it's burnt down, he's back to square one, even worse. Look at all those riots: black people weren't burning down downtown, they were burning down their own neighborhoods.

You end up with no place to have pizza; that's the net effect of the whole action. You haven't stopped the police, you haven't—

That's the irony. Because that's the only way they can really fight. They felt very powerful that moment, but it was fleeting.

There's great empowerment when normally alienated people come together for a purpose.

They all saw Radio Raheem get murdered by the police, New York City's finest. Which is one of the reasons we get very little cooperation from the movie cops here in New York ever since that film. They don't do shit for us.

Malcolm X said that whether you're using ballots or bullets, your aim has to be true, and you don't aim for the puppet, you aim for the puppeteer. Isn't everybody on the corner there in Do the Right Thing *aiming for just a puppet, and not a very powerful puppet at that?*

That's true. But Mayor Koch is not in front of them. Rarely do you get a chance where you get to actively engage the enemy, and the closest there was was Sal's Pizzeria.

One of the disturbing things to me about the reaction to that film is that people focused on the burning of the pizzeria and not the death of Radio Raheem, and there might be a reason for that other than just hog-calling racism.

The thing I liked about *Do the Right Thing*, especially for critics, is that it was a litmus test. I think you could really tell how people thought and who they were. And if I read a review and all it talked about was the stupidity of burning the pizzeria, the stupidity of the violence, the looting, the burning, and not one mention of the murder of Radio Raheem, I knew *exactly* where they were coming from. Because people that write like that, who think like that, do not put any value on black life, especially the life of young black males. They put more importance on property, white-owned property.

I'm going to assume that that's true, that those people don't put the value on black life. Let me suggest, though, another reason why the burning of the pizzeria becomes the centerpiece of the picture and not the death of Raheem. I think there are aesthetic, as opposed to racial, reasons. For me, the most dramatic thing is the taking of a life, that's much more important than a pizza oven going up in flames, and yet when I left the film, the riot stood out in my mind more than the death. Two reasons: one, Radio Raheem is not a fully-drawn character—he's a caricature. He's a type, albeit a new type for many people. But the audience doesn't really develop an empathy for him.

I don't know if I agree with that. I think a life is a life.

It is, but Mookie's life would have meant more to the audience because they knew Mookie better. The second reason is that the burning reads as the climax of the film in terms of the way it's shot and structured.

You know, what you're saying are both two good points. What you just explained makes sense. But I'm talking about people who don't even think about the death of Radio Raheem. What's important to them is that the pizzeria was burnt. For them, Sal is the cavalry. Fort Apache, among savages. That's who their interest is with.

Let's look at something else. You gave Spielberg's The Color Purple *a great deal of criticism, but couldn't it be argued that the neighborhood you paint in Bed-Stuy is as unrealistic a portrayal of Bed-Stuy—in terms of material conditions, if not behavior—as Spielberg's portrayal of black Southern life was, where the house was too big, everything was too clean . . .*

We did not paint the grass, we did not paint the flowers.

But you did get asked, and I know you felt the questions were racist, "Why weren't there any drugs in this movie?"

Why do you have to have drugs in films about black people? Why am I the only filmmaker in the history of cinema that's been asked, "Why are there no drugs in your films"?

You yourself wrote, Spike, that it might be "a serious omission," to use your exact words, a serious omission, not to deal with drugs in that film; and then you backed off for aesthetic reasons — you felt it might be too much to handle for that film, and didn't want to pay lip service to the problem. But when people asked questions about it, rather than admit that it was an issue, you were very defensive and said that the question was racist.

I didn't say that all the time. I can tell how questions come. And how questions are asked, how people are thinking. So that's where that came from.

Does the ending of the film — I know it was much discussed in production, Sal and Mookie in front of the burned out pizzeria — does it ring true to you?

Yeah, I think it rings true. I mean, some people at Universal felt that Mookie shouldn't pick up the money.

I felt that Mookie would be too proud to go ask for his money, or that if he did do it because he needed the bread, there would be no way in the world that Sal would give him his money! He'd just provoked the destruction of Sal's entire business.

Well, I saw otherwise. I felt that to belittle him, he could hurt Mookie more by giving him the money and throwing it in his face.

"You're a rich man, Mookie! You're a real Rockefeller!"

"This money means nothing to me. I have the business, what do you have?"

Where's the sliver of realization?

The what?

The sliver of realization.

I used that phrase?

You know that. Yes, you said you wanted Sal to have a sliver of realization, you wanted his consciousness advanced to some degree and you wanted us to see that.

Oh, Sal. I think that everybody in the film, except for the cops, is not the same person they were the day before. I think that Sal's grown and Mookie's grown also. I think that Sal will think twice before he takes a Louisville Slugger to somebody's box, that's for sure.

What does Buggin' Out learn?

Maybe he might not have learned anything. He has good intentions, but he's not focused.

Did you feel you were making a comment on the dearth of responsible black leadership by making the only leader on the block a guy who is a misdirected hot-head?

Yeah. You know what that was alluding to? When the whole Howard Beach incident happened, there were some black leaders here in New York City who wanted to boycott pizza—which I thought was idiotic. That ain't doing nothing for nobody to boycott pizza because of Howard Beach.

With the quotes at the end of the movie, aren't you making almost a false opposition between Martin Luther King and Malcolm X?

I don't think it was a false opposition. The most important thing for me about Martin Luther King and Malcom X is that they both wanted the same thing for black people, it's just that they chose very different routes to arrive there. This has always been a choice that black people have had to make: which way to go to achieve our freedom? It doesn't have to be either/or; it can be a synthesis.

Right. But the way it reads in the film is that it's either/or.

All I can say is, that's your interpretation. But I always saw it as a synthesis of both.

But the way you close your journal on the film is with the words: "We have a choice, Malcolm or King. I know who I'm down with."

Right, I'm leaning more toward Malcolm X because my thing is more in line with what he was trying to do. But that does not negate what Martin did either. He did a lot too.

Who would not agree that self-defense is—

Martin Luther King would! He did. Kiss 'em.

You sure that's not strategy, instead of ideology?

No, there's no strategy in just standing there and getting whupped upside the head with a club. I'm sorry.

There were gains that came because of it.

Not merely because of that, though.

Not merely, no. But in certain cases nonviolence can work as a strategy, no?

[Surprised.] Oh, I agree with that.

It wasn't going to work against the Nazis, because they were going to throw your nonviolent ass into a cattle car.

Yeah, but when black people are trying to achieve their freedom, we're always saddled with, "Why don't you be nonviolent?" Well, how come we always got to get stuck with the nonviolent tactic? [Laughs.] While everybody else is doing what they have to do.

Yet the quote you use from Malcolm is something that Abraham Lincoln or Thomas Jefferson could have said themselves.

Yeah! If you would have Wited-Out "Malcolm X" and put "Abraham Lincoln" or "Thomas Jefferson," people would have had no problems with that. Like I said, it depends on who's saying what, or who's doing what.

Would you call the burning of the pizzeria "self-defense"?

I don't think that quote was alluding in particular to the burning and looting of Sal's pizzeria, just in general.

Some felt the turning of the firemen's hoses on the people involved in the rioting, which brings up a conscious association with Birmingham and Montgomery, Bull Connor and all that, really did a disservice to the people who had the hoses turned against them in the South.

How?

Because they were fighting for something that was positive, hard-won, and often going down on account of it, whereas the people on your block, all they were doing was rioting, stealing cash, and burning down a pizzeria.

But what sparked that, though?

Injustice.

Thank you. And this is the only way they could respond to it.

How can the response become more efficacious?

What? I don't know what you mean. [Laughing.] Look, I'm an *assistant* professor at Harvard, not a professor. You got to use that in the article: "I'm an assistant professor at Harvard, I don't got the full shit yet."

Okay, you would admit that the burning of a pizzeria is not the most effective means of combatting injustice. How could the response be more effective in authoring some kind of constructive change?

That's a very difficult question. I don't have the answer to that. I guess when people feel they're getting adequate housing and employment and health care and their vote means something—they're not getting fucked around—then I guess that's when we won't choose the other avenues of "artistic" expression. When people feel they're getting a piece of the American pie.

One of Malcolm X's favorite quotes was by Goethe: "Nothing is more terrible than ignorance in action." If Malcolm was watching that scene go down, would he have felt it was ignorance in action?

[Pause.] He might. But he would have perfectly understood why they were doing what they did. See, Malcolm never condemned the victim. And the people who were burning down the pizzeria were the victims, in that film.

I mean, the unfortunate thing about *Do the Right Thing* were the people, the critics, that said it was going to cause riots and stuff. It stopped a lot of people from seeing the film in the theatre where they could have enjoyed it the most. Instead, they saw it on videotape.

Specifically white people, you are talking about?

Yeah, because no black person was afraid of going to the theatre.

Have you talked to white people who were afraid?

A lot of white people told me they were scared for their safety because of what they read, so they waited until it came out on videotape. People did predict that it was going to cause riots across the country.

What did you learn from that whole experience?

That the media can fuck you up. [Laughs.]

Don't you feel in some way it made the film a bigger cause célèbre?

Nah. That hurt us. There is nothing positive that came out of that at all.

You had a PR firm doing "damage control" for the film when that whole thing went down.

I'm totally ignorant of this. Who are these people? Maybe Universal hired them, I don't know. I don't remember. Tom Pollack did not want a repeat of *Last Temptation of Christ*.

Was Universal supportive when this happened?

Very much so. They stood behind the film all the way.

Are you happy with the commercial success you've had?

I'm very happy. I would not have been able to make the films I've wanted to make if my films had not achieved some level of commercial success.

They don't pay you to lose money.

Not young black filmmakers. That's for sure.

SESSION TWO

How do you feel you take criticism?

That depends what kind of criticism it is and who it's coming from.

I know you wrote a letter to the New York Times *in response to Janet Maslin's review of* School Daze.

She used me as an example of filmmakers who, as long as they are given a limited budget and are able to make films with relatives and friends, are all right; but when they're given some real money, then they don't know anything about the craft. I used other examples. The motherfucker who directed *Leonard, Part VI*—that was his first film, too. That film cost $27 million.

At the end of your letter you suggested that she might not have rhythm and could not dance.

I said she couldn't even dance. Because she was trying to tell me that the musical numbers weren't staged well.

Did you stop reading the criticism that came with School Daze? *After the overwhelmingly positive response to the first film—*

Well, I knew there was no way we were going to duplicate the reviews for *She's Gotta Have It.* That's human nature. Whether it's music, or athletes' rookie season, second season they start looking for the chinks in the armor.

Have you ever learned anything from criticism about your own work?

Well, I think the best criticism I've read has been about my female characters.

You've taken that to heart.

You know, that was on the mark.

How would you assess your strengths and weaknesses as a person?

You talking about filmmaking?

No, first as a person.

Hmmm. Weakness. I probably don't have enough patience. I should have more. On the other hand, a lot of times I give people too much slack, so it goes either way. As far as a filmmaker, as far as a weakness, I try to concentrate on having stronger female characters. I think the strength I have is not just filmmaking ability but the ability to market my films, to promote.

How would you say you've grown as a filmmaker, from She's Gotta Have It *to* Jungle Fever, *in terms of the craft?*

It's evident if you look at the work. If you screened the films in a row, it's evident. The thing that's most visible is that there's better acting. I work better with actors now.

You're known for being pretty open with actors, not very controlling, giving them a lot of room to invent their own stuff.

It depends on the actor. Not all actors can do that. Not all actors can improvise. If they can't improvise, you're wasting time keeping the camera rolling; they're coming up with one dead line after another.

Do you feel you go as deep with the actors as some other directors?

I can't comment on that. Some directors—you've heard about Mamet and Sayles—don't let actors change one word. That's what I'm told. I'm not as possessive of the words. A lot of times once an actor puts in his own words, it's better.

And their creation of a back story for themselves can make the role a lot richer than you may have originally thought.

Exactly.

I'm thinking, in Do the Right Thing, *of what Roger Smith did with Smiley, and Danny Aiello did with Sal.*

[Testy.] What did Danny Aiello do with Sal?

Well, I don't know exactly, but—

But according to Danny Aiello he wrote the whole role himself.

I would not suggest that at all—

Danny Aiello . . . we were friends, we talked about this numerous times—he tells people that he wrote that role himself.

Well, he didn't write the script. You think he was trying to cop more credit for it, making the character more sympathetic, less of a racist?

See, if Danny had his way totally, Sal would have been the most sympathetic pizzeria owner in the world. And that was not the character I envisioned. I mean, in the climactic scene in the movie, he didn't even want to call Buggin' Out a nigger. He was having trouble saying the word nigger, and I knew, we all knew, that he had used that word before. [Laughs.] It's only when Buggin' Out called him a fat guinea bastard, that's when Danny opened up and all these words became familiar to his tongue again.

Annabella Sciorra [Angie in Jungle Fever] *was just quoted talking about the work that he had done on that character. I was broaching this as a positive, not a negative thing.*

Let me ask you, what great actor, what good actor worth their salt is gonna come to a film and not add anything? You think I want to hire directors [Freudian slip] who are going to do exactly what is written and bring nothing else? That's . . . I don't understand it. What did Annabella say?

That you kept things fairly simple in dealing with actors.

With actors, or with her?

Maybe she was just sharing her own experience. And she referred to the Danny Aiello character.

Well, God bless her, that's all I have to say.

Is there not a warm vibe between the two of you?

Oh, we love each other.

Come on, man, who are you kidding? I know you've got to do publicity for the movie, but—

No, I think she did a very good job. All that matters is performance up on the screen. And I'm very happy with her performance and that's it.

Sometimes if you don't get along with someone, it can bring something else to the work.

Yeah, but I don't suggest that way of working.

Do you have time still to study and to read?

I read all the time.

What are you most curious about?

History. Of all my shortcomings, I feel my biggest one is that I can't speak another language. And I'm never going to learn another language. I've been taking Spanish and French since third grade and I still don't know a word. Americans get so wrapped up in thinking everything revolves around America, everything revolves around English. I love to travel. It's my loss only being able to speak English. That's the one regret I have. But history, everything I learn, is going to end up helping me in some form or another, in some movie maybe fifteen years down the line. That's why I can't understand any artist not being on top of things: reading, just being alive in the world, not being shut off and holed up in some cavern.

Your inspiration comes very much from the real world, whereas some artists are primarily inspired by other art, the imaginative world.

See, I wasn't really raised on movies. I went to see them, but I wasn't like Spielberg and the rest of these guys. They wanted to be filmmakers when they were still in Pampers. That wasn't my case. And in a lot of ways this might be an advantage, because for a lot of these guys, their films are about films they've seen. Their films are *about* films. Not to say that's bad all the time.

It's limited.

It can be. Unless you're Spielberg.

What's your opinion of your own work? There is a retrospective book of photos and essays on your first five films, Five for Five. *Now, nobody bats 1.000.*

Well, I have my own Elias Sports Bureau, you have yours. [Laughter.] I have my own statistician.

That's why they call them "fantasy leagues," Spike! I'm just curious about how you look back at your work. Some artists find it painful to look at their early work.

For me, the only film I can't look at is *School Daze* — I mean, *She's Gotta Have It.* It's painful for me to watch that film. The filmmaking, the acting. Any time you see bad acting in a film it's the director's fault. And at that stage I was really not at ease working with actors. [To waiter.] Can I have some rice please, brown vegetable rice.

Uh oh, this Muslim thing is starting to happen.

[Playing along.] I haven't eaten swine in nine years!

Are you comfortable delineating influences? Scorsese is an obvious influence, but other than that?

That's about it, as far as filmmaking. A great film for me to see was Jim Jarmusch's *Stranger Than Paradise.* It opened up to me what the possibilities could be. 'Specially since I knew Jim; he was ahead of me in film school. I knew I could do this now.

Do you enjoy the whole process of filmmaking, or just the finished product? There's a quote about writing: "I don't like writing, I like having written."

I like, I love filmmaking. But making a film, even though I love it, is still murder. It's absolutely murder: when you're in production, doing a movie, the toll, the physical toll; and really it's more your mind that gets tired, because a director is asked five million questions every single day. And you've got to make all these decisions, very fast. And over the course of eight, nine, ten weeks, an accumulation of the wrong choices and your movie is fucked up! [Wild laughter.]

Do you feel there's evolving in your work a kind of Afro-American aesthetic?

In my work? I don't get into stuff like that.

We could make parallels with music. If you look at bebop, bebop was a language, a change in the language from swing. So I'm wondering if you think some of the structural or stylistic things you do are becoming a certain kind of grammar.

I have a style, I think. I don't know that you can call it an Afro-American aesthetic. For me there is no Afro-American style of filmmaking. First of all, there's not enough filmmakers doing it.

There's a compelling difference between the way blacks have dominated music and sport, and their contribution to our visual culture, and I wonder now, with the rise of these black American directors, if there will be a similar influence on the visual, in film art?

I think so. I think there are so many young black kids out there now that want to get into TV, that want to get into films, that want to get into the visual arts, because now they see young black people like themselves doing it—where before there were no role models. I think there's a whole lot of black kids playing golf now just because Michael Jordan plays golf!

It takes that.

It takes that. "Oh, Michael Jordan's playing golf. Hey, it must be cool then." In a way, it's kind of stupid, because you're waiting for somebody else to put the stamp of approval on it.

Why do you think historically there's been less black presence in visual arts in this country than in music or in sport?

We have a lot of great black painters. But for film, there's a very simple answer: film costs millions and millions of dollars. It would be very hard to have a Motown in film. Berry Gordy, who'd he borrow money from, his sister?

We know where he got the money from . . .

Well, I like my kneecaps! [Wild laughter.] See, he started Motown with like five hundred dollars. You can't start a movie company with five hundred dollars. The economics of movies are just astronomical.

Have you thought about a black studio?

It's killing me just to keep the little shit I got going myself.

But in the interview you did with Eddie Murphy, you talked about attempting to unify the very powerful, increasingly wealthy black entertainers and athletes for some purpose—which you left vague.

Well, you have to realize filmmaking is a very risky business. Now, if I was talking about all of us going in on a liquor store, it'd be different. [Laughs.]

What were you thinking about, all you sitting down and talking?

I think the battle, the great thing would be to get everybody sitting down to talk. It's going to come.

What do you hope would come out of it? Anything tangible?

Alliances. Unity, you know.

In your own work, there's frequently conflict within a single film between different styles, which is unusual for mainstream, narrative American cinema —

I wouldn't use the word "conflict."

Juxtaposition?

Yes, that's better.

— Between a presentational style and a dramatic style, between a documentary style and a realistic style, or even between a kind of romantic tone and a satirical, edgy tone.

It doesn't bother me to mix stuff like that up, because I don't think I make genre films. I don't think I make films that can be classified in one specific cubbyhole. I think the better question might be: do you think you've been successful with the juxtaposition? I really couldn't do a film that's one thing all the way through. That wouldn't be very interesting for me.

It does create certain kinds of collisions that people are not used to.

Most of the movies that people are used to suck anyway! They're the same old tried and true formula, and at the end of the movie everything is wrapped up in a nice little bow. And very rarely do those movies ever make you think, and once you leave the theatre, by the time you're back on the subway or driving home, you've forgotten what you watched. It's like disposable entertainment. You sit there for two hours, and it washes over you and that's it.

You like your endings to be really open-ended.

Not all the time. I just don't think everything has to be resolved.

Do you feel that's the work for audiences, to build a resolution in their heads?

Yes, I feel that. But not just to build a resolution, but to think. I think we don't demand enough of the audience. No subtlety, playing down to the lowest common dominator all the time, making films for an intelligence level of retarded twelve-year-olds.

Well, there's something about narrative itself that conditions people to want a period at the end of a sentence.

The condition comes from Hollywood and people who've been force-fed films like that. Not narrative.

Let's talk more about black film. You said, in the documentary on the making of Do the Right Thing, *"The number-one concern is to try to be the best filmmaker you can be and not be out there bullshitting, saying you're a black filmmaker."*

I think it holds true more now than when I said that.

Are there people out there bullshitting, saying, "I'm a black filmmaker, love me!"

Not "love me," but a lot of people are getting deals now to make films, and I'm not begrudging anybody, but we'll find out the contenders from the pretenders.

You were quoted as saying, "If you're black and have a camera in your hand, you can get a deal now." The subtext of that sounds almost a little bitter, like you had to struggle, and now—

No, no way. That was taken totally out of context. It was a funny statement, an exaggeration. I'm ecstatic if any black person gets a chance to direct a film.

Do you feel that this surge of black film could crest, like a wave?

If the films aren't good and people don't go, definitely. We'll be back to square one.

Hence your concern for how good these films are and for filmmakers taking their position very seriously.

Yeah. And also how well these companies market them. I don't think Fox did a good job on [Robert Townsend's] *Five Heartbeats*. That was a big blow, to all of us. The film never opened. You open on eight hundred screens and you average six hundred per screen, in Hollywood they say you never opened.

Do you still want to be seen as a "black" filmmaker, or a filmmaker first, who happens to be black? It's a subtle but important distinction.

To me, I don't think there's ever going to be a time in America where a white person looks at a black person and they don't see that they're black. That day ain't coming very soon. Don't hold your breath. So that's a given. So why am I going to get blue in the face, worrying about that? For me that's one of the most important things Malcolm X said: "What do you call a black man with a Ph.D.? 'Nigger.' " That's it. So why am I going to spend time and energy saying "Don't call me a *black* filmmaker, I'm a filmmaker"? I'm not getting into that argument. I'll leave that to the other *Negroes*. [Laughs.] The other so-called Negroes.

Do you still feel that when you write, you are writing for a black audience? Right up front you said, "Look, Woody Allen writes for intellectual New York City Jews and I write for blacks."

Yes, but that does not exclude everybody else. I like Woody Allen's films, but there's stuff in those films I don't get, and the person next to me is *dying!*

I don't get it. But that does not detract from my enjoyment of the film. I think the same is true of me. Black people be rolling in the aisle, and white folks don't understand it. They may not get everything, all the nuances, but they still enjoy the film. So I don't think there's any crime in writing for a specific audience.

I think people were surprised, maybe because of their own naiveté, that you would do that, that you would want to—

See, that's that whole crossover motherfucker that motherfuckers fall into. That's because any time they see the word black, they see a negative connotation. I wasn't raised like that. That wasn't my upbringing. So I'm never going to run from the word "black."

"Walk on stage and act-like-a-tree shit. That's what white people call art." What is that walk on stage and act-like-a-tree shit you're talking about?

[Laughs.] You have to realize a lot of these statements are not indictments of every single white person. But it's just . . . you know that avant-garde stuff people call art. Damn, what is that? You know what I'm saying.

Like Robert Wilson's "the CIVIL warS: a tree is best measured when it is down" and that kind of shit?

Andy Warhol movie of a man sleeping for eight hours.

"Conceptual art" I think is what white folks call it.

That's the name for it? [Laughs.]

And then there's "performance art," too!

Oh, I don't like that shit, either. Is Laurie Anderson a performer artist?

Come on, you haven't seen Karen Finley take off her clothes and smear herself with chocolate? You haven't lived, my man!

The Knicks were on that night! [Wild laughter.] I got season tickets, so I missed that. The Miami Heat were in town. I don't even know who that artist is, the one you just mentioned, because I don't want her sending no letter-bomb to my house.

You've written: "Black people are the most creative people on this earth."

I agree. I think so. I still agree.

How can you say that one race of being is more creative than another race?

Easy, I just said it. But I guess that makes me a racist now.

We'll get to that. Are you speaking of all black people or American blacks?

Black people. Africans. Everybody black. Not just American blacks.

You've stated, though, that you think "black people have let black artists get away with too much." Go to it.

Well, I think that a lot of times black artists are not held accountable as they should be. I don't feel that just because we are successful artists we should be let off the hook, to do whatever we want to do pertaining to some matters: performing in South Africa, or like Eazy-E, having lunch with President Bush and being a member of the Inner Circle and donating $2500 to the Republican party and at the same time being a member of a rap group [NWA] that says "Fuck the Police." What kind of reasoning is that?

Do you feel that all art is political?

I think so. I think even the absence of politics in a piece is a political move: we got to make as much money as we can so let's leave all the politics out. That's a political move. That's a political decision. Let's not rock the boat.

Let's hit sexuality for a second. Probably other than race, sexuality is the dominant concern of your work. I'd like you to speak about how you would define male sexuality. In the first film you have the "dogs"; in the second, you have Dap, who's "snakin'" because that's his "nature" as a man; in the third, Mookie presents a glorious objectification of Tina's gorgeous body parts, but at the same time pretty much ignores Tina and what she needs; in the fourth film, we get Bleek's famous statement, "It's a dick thing"; and in your fifth, the women sit around and one says that if a man sees a pussy he looks around and then has to get it. So male sexuality—

What about it?

Is it just "a dick thing"?

No, that line is definitely not the way I feel. I don't feel Bleek feels that at the end of the movie either. He ends up messed up because of thinking like that. I don't know how else to answer that question. [Pause.] I think that when you grow up black you never see people kissing on the screen. It's something I wanted to have, just have some type of sexuality in my films. And have the characters think the way people think; now, whether this is right or wrong the way they're thinking, now that's another matter.

One of the things I asked Coppola about is his work's reticence when it comes to sex—

Come on, Sonny was boning that girl standing up [in the classic James Caan scene in *The Godfather*]!

And that's about it. You ain't gonna find many other scenes in his work.

And what did he say?

He said because he takes sex so seriously and is so sensitive about it, it's very difficult for him to show.

Oh, and he's not sensitive about murder so he can do that all the time? Just have bodies riddled by bullets? See, the thing about it for me is I just want to have characters in my films that are real, and sexuality is part of your being.

In 1986, you wrote about racism: "We're all tired about white-man this, white-man that. Fuck dat! It's on us." No more excuses. But if you ask white people if you had said that, given your persona, they would be surprised.

Yeah, but where are they getting their perceptions from? [Laughs.] From TV, magazines, and newspapers.

And are you coming across in a way that's not truthful to who you are?

Yeah, because the way the media portrays me is as an angry black man. See, that statement is not a complete statement. You got to have a two-part program. On one hand, you have to say you cannot deny the injustices that have been against you as a people. On the other hand, you cannot use as an excuse, "Well, I really would have liked to have done that, but Mr. Charlie was blocking me every single time." I think that's the more complete statement.

You've said you don't think blacks can be racist.

Right.

Are you speaking of black Americans?

In this case, I am speaking of black Americans. And then, what I always say, and people never print, is that for me there's a difference between racism and prejudice. Black people can be prejudiced. But to me, racism is the *institution*. Black people have never enacted laws saying that white folks cannot own property, white folks can't intermarry, white folks can't vote. You got to have power to do that. That's what racism is, an institution.

Institutionally hindering an entire people.

Yeah. Me calling you "white motherfucker," I don't think that's racism, I think that's prejudice. That's just racial slurs. That ain't gonna hurt nobody.

Prejudice itself can come as a reaction to the racism that engenders it.

That can come as a reaction, but anybody can be prejudiced. That's the complete statement. But that never gets printed.

I see racism all over the world: one tribe to another tribe, the Japanese to the Chinese, and so on. It's incredibly complicated and incredibly sad, and so I can't buy your statement, "White people invented racism."

Where did it start, then?

I don't know where it started. What do you think caused it?

They wanted to exploit people. Colonization. Why do you think there's no Native Americans? Why do you think they're on reservations?

You think that was the beginning of racism? The 1600s?

No, way before that.

We're talking about history now, and I'm curious as to whether you've thought about what the origins of prejudice, the origins of racism are. I assume before there was the institution of racism, locked into place to keep certain people from realizing their potential as individuals and their goals as a group, that there was prejudice. It had to come out of thinking that the "other" was not as good as you; or out of being afraid of the "other"; or out of scarcity, where there was not enough to go around so you had to fight the "other" for it; or tribal shit. But to me, "White people invented racism" makes it seem like you believe there was a grand conspiracy to deny the fruits of the planet to everybody else by a group of unified people sitting in a room in Amsterdam in 1619.

You don't think there was a plan to wipe out the Indians?

I think that's certainly what happened, but I don't think it was drawn up like the Magna Carta.

Look, that shit had to be planned. There's no way. They saw the riches this land had, and they took over. And that's what the Afrikaners did in South Africa. And before that, that's what all of Europe did when they split up Africa into colonies. I mean, [pause] maybe white people didn't invent the patent on racism, but they sure perfected that motherfucker! They got that shit down to a science and it's being implemented now, full throttle.

You don't see any decline in it, do you?

What, racism? No. I don't smoke crack. [Laughs.] If anything, it's on the upswing—with eight years of Reagan, and now Bush. And now this Gulf War, America's in this patriotic fever. I went to the Super Bowl, man, I wish I hadn't gone. I was nauseous with all that flag-waving and airplanes flying overhead. God bless America.

It's fascistic!

It was like being in Nazi Germany at that Super Bowl game! Instead of Leni Riefenstahl—

—you had NFL Films!

You had NFL Films and "Up with People." [Laughs wildly, then to waiter:] More tea—and make it hot! And Whitney Houston lip-synching the national anthem. That marred the game for me.

When there's economic contraction, which there is now, people's prejudice comes to the fore, and racism stiffens, because if the pie is shrinking no one wants to give a bigger piece to anybody else. And I think it might get worse, because this is the first generation of middle-class white Americans that actually figures to live worse than their parents did.

[Long pause.] Welcome to the Terrordome!

Where do you think it comes from, Spike? Prejudice.

Where? I can't answer. I'm not a theologian.

You think it's a theological answer?

It might be. But who's to say that there's ever really been true peace on this earth? It's something we hope will happen some day, maybe in our grand-children's children's time.

God knows there are tribes in Africa that loathe other tribes, and always have, predating the white man's arrival.

That's true. But did you ever read a quote or a statement from me saying that black people don't fight among themselves? We kill, we kill each other—shit, white people don't even have to do anything. I mean, black males are killing each other at an alarming rate now. White people can just sit back and watch.

And keep score. You talked yesterday about the assault on black men. For every Los Angeles police idiocy, there are fifty black men assaulting other black men.

So that makes it all right what the cops do?

No, no, no. But the amount of black-on-black crime must be a bitter pill for you to swallow, as a black man.

You bet. I mean we're killing each other.

Do you care that some people feel you hide behind the shield of racism, that you're quick to call people racists to deflect criticism of yourself?

No. That doesn't bother me, not at all.

When you opened your retail shop, some dude from MTV asked you, "Spike, what are you going to do with the profits from this store?" And in what didn't get bleeped out, you said, "You don't ask motherfucking Robert De Niro what he does with the profits from his restaurant." So you were assuming that he was asking you because you're black and you were opening your own business. I won't come to his defense, because I don't know what was in his mind asking the question—but look, Robert De Niro is not at all a political guy, but there are white artists who—

That is bullshit! That is complete bullshit. No white person who's opened up a motherfucking business has *ever* been asked, "What are you gonna do with your profits?"

But people like Sting and Bono, who are political—

That is bullshit, that is bullshit. You're telling me people ask Sting, if his album goes triple platinum, "What are you going to do with your profits?" This is motherfucking America. When black people start to make some money then it becomes a fucking problem. [Very upset, yelling, standing up beside our table.] No . . . tell me a time when a white artist was asked, "What are you going to do with your profits?"

I've asked white—

That is bullshit! No one would ever come to someone's restaurant opening, book coming out, building, and say, "Mr. White Person, what are you going to do with your profits?" I don't care what you say, that shit don't happen.

I'm telling you, I've asked white artists, who have political points of view, okay, whether it be on the rain forest or the Irish problem, if they're doing something about it. I've asked them.

That is not the same thing, David. I'm talking about the first day the store is open, and he has a microphone in my face, "What are you going to do with your profits?" It was a racist question. The night the motherfucking Tribeca Grill opened, they do not ask Robert De Niro, "What are you gonna do with your profits?" It's plain and simple.

Are you comfortable saying you're a capitalist?

[Pause.] Am I a capitalist? [Pause.] We all are over here. And I'm just trying to get the power to do what I have to do. To get that power you have to accumulate some type of bank. And that's what I've done. I've always tried to be in an entrepreneurial mode of thinking. Ownership is what's needed amongst Afro-Americans. Ownership. Own stuff.

Politically, do you favor a more socialistic framework?

I think that would be better, for everyone concerned. But that's never going to happen in the United States.

The most overt political thing you've done is the commercial for Jesse Jackson in the 1988 New York presidential primary.

I think *Do the Right Thing* had a lot to do with Ed Koch losing [the New York City mayoral election]. I think it helped David Dinkins a lot. I'm not saying that the film put him in office, but I think we had a positive effect on that mayor's race.

You offered to do a commercial for Dinkins. What happened?

I just put it out there, I never asked him. I *did* the commercial: Do the Right Thing.

What did you learn from doing the Jesse Jackson ad?

What did I learn? [Pause.] Where the secret servicemen hide their machine guns.

Would you like to do more political, commercial work in the future?

It depends on the candidate.

Your least political film is Mo' Better Blues. *You had a kind of negative motivation for making that film, two-pronged. One was the jazz films that had come just before, which you had found grossly lacking: Bertrand Tavernier's* Round Midnight *and Clint Eastwood's* Bird. *Two, you heard Woody Allen might be making a jazz film and you had to beat him to it.*

That was a joke. I'm not going to do a jazz film so I could beat Woody Allen. The reaction to the other films was not the main impetus, though. The number-one thing was that my father was a great jazz musician and I grew up around the music. Also, after *Do the Right Thing,* I didn't want to do something that was overtly political, that was confrontational, or had to do with racism, with racial politics.

It seemed that part of your take on those two films was that they didn't get it right; they didn't get what the experience of being a jazz musician truly is.

No, that is not it. With *Round Midnight,* it was the romanticism it had, with Dexter Gordon's character, and him being alcoholic, and the sincere French man taking care of him like he's a little child. And with *Bird,* of the three main characters, how are two of them going to be white? How is Red Rodney going to have more screen time than Dizzy Gillespie? But at the same time I was glad that Tavernier and Clint Eastwood made those films because otherwise those films wouldn't have gotten made.

Your film didn't suffer from those shortcomings—the nice white character who clears the path for the black genius—but there were elements of your film that were not particularly realistic, as far as what the jazz scene is, in New York City.

Like what?

Like—

The club?

Like the club.

First of all, that's a stylistic choice. Most clubs—

It was a realistic film, Spike.

[Excited.] Who said anything about realism?

You did.

No, no, no. Any director should be able to make stylistic choices. If I want to shoot a film that's very stylistic, that has grand sweeping camera movements, I cannot have a fucking club the size of a cubbyhole. You just can't do it. "Oh, Bleek Gilliam, no jazz musician has a loft like that!" Have those people ever been to Wynton Marsalis's house or Branford Marsalis's house?

There are a couple. Very, very few jazz musicians—the skinny top of the pyramid —live like that, even among successful jazz musicians; dress like that, live like that, have that kind of rehearsal loft. The jazz musicians I know thought it was funny Bleek was trying to renegotiate his contract at the club: who did he think he was, Patrick Ewing? Jazz musicians are not usually in a position to renegotiate a deal, nor would they be playing a club for however long Bleek was playing there. Musicians don't play clubs for six weeks. Something else struck a wrong chord: a musician as proud as Bleek, who was very much a "Wynton type" and had that kind of carriage and demeanor, would not trade sets with a chitlin circuit comedian. I couldn't imagine Wynton trading sets with that guy.

You're wrong, because there's been a long history of jazz and comedy. Dick Gregory, Bill Cosby used to open up for jazz musicians all the time, in the Village.

Yeah, a long time ago!

Why am I not given the same artistic leverage other motherfuckers are given?

Because it's set in the present!

How many motherfucking white heavyweight boxing champions are there? *Rocky* is the most motherfucking Walt Disney movie, ever.

And that's fantasy. And maybe what you're saying is that you wanted to make sort of a jazz fantasy—

See, where was it printed that Spike said I was going to make the number-one realistic movie about jazz, ever? I never said that. If I said that, we wouldn't have that jazz club. [Exercised.] I'm not gonna shoot a scene where I don't have room—where I can't get a Louma crane in, and it's all gonna be static shots of people playing on the bandstand. That shit is boring! That's boring! Let's talk about facts. Martin Scorsese, ask him the fucking size of the ring in *Raging Bull*. They had a fucking ring that was huge because that's what they needed to get the shots the way he wanted. Okay! "Oh, there's no jazz clubs that big in New York." So what? So what? So what? But the same people won't say diddly-shit about *Bird*: "Why is Red Rodney in this movie more than Dizzy Gillespie? How come there's no mention of Charlie Parker's other black wives? Why does it seem like this woman Chan is his only wife?" Shit like that is like over everybody's head.

Certain parts of the movie are very realistic and other parts are less realistic, and—

All you can say is—

And other parts are—

Look, let me finish—

Go on! You're building up steam, man.

[Laughing.] Nobody said—

[Laughing.] Tie me to the tracks!

All I can say is, this is the way I saw the film and if somebody doesn't believe it, if it rings false to them, then in their eyes I was unsuccessful. *But,* what I'm saying is, people got two different standards, though. For other shit, for other motherfuckers, that shit goes by . . .

You hate corniness. You say you hate corniness, and fight to keep it away. To me, a lot of stuff in that movie felt corny.

Like what?

Like the "happy family" montage at the end, the musician names, the two-women-in-the-same-dress scene. A lot of stuff seemed like 1930s, 1940s. Bleek calling out the name of the wrong woman while making love. Those are such clichés I was surprised they showed up in a Spike Lee movie.

I didn't see them like clichés. What names were clichés?

A drummer named "Rhythm Jones." Modern jazz musicians don't have names like that. Left-hand, Rhythm. Very 1940s, very pre-bebop, sort of swing era stuff.

And how were they dressed?

There was definitely a retro thing happening there too, so it was blended. Now the montage at the end: you hammer on Disney, the love-can-conquer-everything shit, but that ending! Yesterday you talked about "earned" sentiment rather than "manufactured" sentimentality. I didn't feel that the movie, built up through the characters, had earned those moments. I wasn't moved by those moments.

Look, that's your opinion, I can't argue with that. I don't think the montage "A Love Supreme" was corny at all.

The music they were playing was pretty conservative—1960s hard bop music, essentially. What was your thinking, making the music very mainstream jazz as opposed to music pushing the boundaries, like Parker in his time?

I was thinking about people coming to the film who don't know anything about jazz. That was the main consideration. The people who are jazz enthusiasts make up a very small number of the movie-going audience.

The club owners, Moe and Josh, got a lot of attention. I'm not saying I expected them to be like Max Gordon, beloved owner of the Village Vanguard, but in your romantic ideal of a jazz world (which is I think the phrase you use), the owners of the club are certainly no romantic ideal for anybody. There's a clash here between one kind of tone, one kind of film going on, and these guys, who fly in from what seems like a different movie, an over-the-top satire—the tight-fisted, money-grubbing, Jewish businessmen. It was discordant. Not because I think you were making an anti-Semitic broadside (because we know jazz musicians often have been taken advantage of, I accept that), but the style in which you did it struck me as discordant, and curious. What was behind it?

What's behind what?

What's behind the way you presented them, where the manner and mode of characterization was so different from anything else in the film?

But David, there's not *one type* of thing in the film. The two guys who beat up Bleek were different from everybody else in the film. The band. The two guys who work for Moe and Josh. It's not like the whole movie is complete here and then out in left field you got Moe and Josh. I just don't see it like that.

You wrote an op-ed piece for The New York Times *in response to accusations that you were anti-Semitic. Will you share what you related in that?*

I'm trying to remember. I just gave various examples of double standards. I just listed several recent instances where no charges of being a racist were leveled against these films and these filmmakers, and why is it you can never have any negative Jewish characters in a piece of art? [Pause.] I forget what I wrote, most of it.

Were you aware as you wrote and shot those scenes that you were playing with a stereotype that was going to inflame people?

To me, I did not see that as a stereotype. First of all, that's like when the NAACP came out with that statement that most of Hollywood is run by Jewish people. Jewish people were upset. I don't see what the big deal was. It's the *truth*. Now the Japanese are buying it up, but the people that run things are Jewish. The entertainment industry, and particularly the film industry. And in this particular case, Moe and Josh, these guys owned the Beneath the Underdog club, were Jewish, and were tight, and they exploited artists. And this was not to say that every single Jewish person exploits artists, or that every single Jewish person in the world is like that. In this case, these guys were. And that's all there was to it.

Did they strike you as caricatures, more than characters?

Not me.

Not to make it overly simplistic, but did you feel there was a message in Mo' Better Blues *about the demands of art?*

That the great artists probably have a very hard time with their personal life. 'Cause a great artist is going to devote every single waking minute to their art, and that family is always going to suffer for it.

Present company excluded?

Well, hopefully, it won't be the same for me. Knock on wood. [Raps the table.] With the whole Moe and Josh thing: if people want to say that the characters were flat, you know, that's all right. But to say that Spike is anti-Semitic, and "Don't you know that Jews walked side by side with Martin Luther King during the civil rights movement?" and all that other shit, that has nothing to do with the movie. I really didn't want to be swept up in that whole black-Jewish relations thing.

You know, I think there's a thinking among a lot of Jewish people that there's some great black conspiracy against Jewish people. First of all, black people don't see it like that: it's not just Jewish people, for the most part it's just white people. Because how do you know who's Jewish? You just can't look at somebody.

A yarmulke is usually a tip-off.

That's not always the case.

That's a nice segue into Jungle Fever. *You shot film, to start the movie, of you on a crane, talking to the camera and saying: "People say I'm anti-Semitic. They can kiss my black ass, two times."*

But that was not the whole statement. That was the end of it.

The rest of it was more about not having answers.

Yeah. The statement was really like a prologue to the movie.

It's not there anymore. How come?

Well, you know, over time I saw it didn't need it.

What taught you that?

I mean, it's like any other scene in the film. The first cut was two hours, forty-five minutes. Now it's 2:03. We see what works, what moves the film forward, and stuff that doesn't, hopefully that's what you take out.

Did your research screenings give you a feeling about the Spike-talks-to-the-camera shot?

A lot of people laughed at it, thought it was funny.

The focus of Jungle Fever *is not so much on the interracial relationship itself as on the environment in which they have to operate. Why did you make that choice?*

Because in this case, these two people came together for probably the wrong reasons. It really wasn't love. Even though Angie I think grows to love Flipper [Wesley Snipes]. But that's not the same case for him. And it's the two neighborhoods they're from, Harlem and Bensonhurst, and the boundaries that are crossed, and what happens to you when you cross those boundaries—how you're looked upon by friends, family, and the two neighborhoods they come from.

It's pretty despairing in that regard.

It is. Again, this is not to say that is going to be the case, or is the case, with every interracial couple, but I think that with the dynamics today—especially here in New York City, and again, with those two neighborhoods—it's fairly accurate.

I loved the chain-link backgrounds in the parallel scenes where each tells their friends about the relationship. It's such a beautiful metaphor for the sense of being fenced in by your surroundings.

I think that's true, but I think Angie is much more fenced in than Flipper is. She's trapped. She's trapped in that neighborhood, that environment of Bensonhurst. And Flipper is her one way out.

Flipper can move more fluidly than she can. Is that a function of class? He's upper middle class, and she's lower middle class.

Class. Yes. The difference between this film and *Do the Right Thing* is that was mainly about race, and in this you add class and sex to that. For me, that's a much more combustible combination. Race, class, and sex.

In the Italian neighborhood scenes, with the counterpoint of Sinatra singing so sweetly while all the verbal violence and other violence is going on, there's a heavy tension between image and reality.

Three great songs by Frankie baby! Old Blue Eyes! "Once Upon a Time," "Hello, Young Lovers," and "It Was a Very Good Year."

Did you have any trouble getting permissions?

We had a little difficulty, because we used Frank Sinatra's picture on the "Wall of Fame" in Sal's Famous Pizzeria in *Do the Right Thing*. So they reminded me of that when I called to ask permission for these three songs. [Laughs.] I talked to his daughter, Tina Sinatra, and she was very gracious, and hopefully Frank will like it. [Wild laughter.]

There's a whole kind of "in-group" freedom Scorsese has in depicting Italians, or you have in depicting blacks.

I understand it. I understand exactly what you're talking about.

The myths you're basically dealing with are—

Sexual myths.

Right. The myths that the white woman is the ideal of beauty—

The epitome of beauty.

Okay, the epitome of beauty, and that the black man is the epitome of sexual performance. So that works for black men and white women. But what about interracial couples where it's a white man and a black woman? They're not operating with those myths.

Yeah, but we were only handling that in this film.

Do you think there are equivalent myths operating for those couples? You take pains to show, at Bloomingdales, two consecutive interracial couples: white men, black women.

[Happy.] You picked that up! After only one showing! Well, I think that for black women, today, it has become more of necessity. Because they just can't find—there are no black men out there for them. With all the black men in prison, or not on their economic or social level, black women can't find mates! And they're stepping outside, you know. On the other hand, why wouldn't a white male want to have a beautiful black woman! [Laughs.] I don't blame 'em for that. They know it's good!

Does the film not want to allow for the possibility that there could be love between Flipper and Angie, or is it just Flipper that doesn't want to allow for that?

I think it's Flipper. But you have to realize, Flipper is the one who's married. I really do think there comes a point in the film where Angie loves Flipper. She's younger than him, too.

In your own personal life, you've had a little experience with some of the dynamics here, with your infamous lunch with Kim Basinger. [Lee laughs.] The quote was, "I wouldn't want fifteen million black women to think I had gone astray."

I said that facetiously. Let's talk about the whole incident, so we don't take it out of context. The 1989 Academy Awards, Kim Basinger is naming the five films for best film. She felt the best film wasn't mentioned, and she called out *Do the Right Thing*. And I was shocked when she said that. Nobody knew she was going to do that. So I thought it was a very courageous act for her to do. She caught a lot of flak behind that. Then her agent called me and said, "She would like to meet you." I said, "Fine, next time she comes to New York I'll meet with her." So she comes to New York—and I know how this stuff is, so I make a point of bringing a black woman with me. [Laughs.] So it's me, my friend, Kim, and her assistant. So there's four of us sitting at a restaurant. Two days later, there's a column in the *Daily News:* "Spike Lee! Kim Basinger! Sitting across from each other, making goo-goo eyes! Romantically linked!" All kinds of shit. There were four of us at the table! So, I called the columnist and said that was not the case at all and I explained. Anyway, sort of like a tag line, I said, "I don't want the wrath of twenty million black women on my ass, thinking I had went astray." And that was the end of that; it was a joke.

I just wanted to focus on the words "going astray." Is it your personal feeling that to marry outside the race is "going astray"?

I wouldn't do it, I wouldn't do it. But if two people are in love with each other, that's it. But I don't think I would marry anybody other than a black woman.

For political reasons or because you're simply not attracted to white women?

Exactly.

Which?

Both.

This movie is the first time you've dealt with drugs. The film ends with more focus on that than on the racial relationship. Were you ever afraid that the drug sub-plot was going to come up and eat the rest of the movie because it's so strong?

No, because I saw it as one unified unit. Now, some other people might not see it that way. It did not bother me that the last note of the film was not about Flipper and Angie, the relationship. For me, the film is not really about this interracial relationship, and not drugs, but about this particular person: Flipper Purify. And we're looking at his life in this very specific time frame, where a whole lot of stuff is happening to his life.

What about the name "Purify"? Are we to make too much of that as a metaphor?

No. It was there for that reason.

Both wives of the black men in the film are mulatto. Is there anything positive about mixing, blending black and white?

I think that mulatto children are very interesting. I know a whole lot of them. Some think they're one hundred percent black, and you may find somebody as white as this tablecloth, and they're "blacker" than anybody. And others, you know, they go the other way: they're *passing*. Then you have the ones who say, [silly advertising voice] "I'm not black, I'm not white, I'm a combi-nation of the two!" I think it really depends on how people see themselves. Some people might think that they have the best of both worlds.

That's what Quincy Jones told me about his children.

Well, how many white wives did Quincy have? He *would* answer like that. The reason why I did this in this film is that this color issue is dynamic. In the dialogue in the movie, Flipper's wife says to Flipper, "White people hate black people because they aren't black." Then Flipper answers, "Does your black father hate your white mother?" And she says, "Are you talking about my family?" And he says, "See, color has you fucked up too." And that's a big dynamic right there: the issue of blood and color. That's something we wanted to have in *Jungle Fever*.

Do you think the idea of a "colorblind" society is something that's even positive to shoot for, or is just stupid?

I don't think Utopia is going to be a society where everybody's blood is mixed up. Hopefully, we can live a peaceful existence, and people can still have their distinct nationalities or backgrounds or races or whatever.

Would you call yourself an integrationist?

Not necessarily. I'm not going to break my neck to piss in the same urinal next to some white guy. That battle's been won. I don't think the battle anymore is living next to a white person, or going to the same school. The battle to me should be on the economic front.

What about the revived Black Nationalism today?

What, move back to Africa?

Not necessarily that, but it doesn't really advocate mixing; it advocates mixing as little as possible, even in a social way.

Do I advocate that? I think you should be around who you're comfortable with. I'm very comfortable around white people, so I have no qualms about it. I'm not calling for no separate state, or nothing like that.

If America gave black people a separate state it would be North Dakota.

It's never been feasible anyway.

I'm thinking of Sterling Brown's line in favor of integration: "An integer is a whole number."

I think that at a time that was something we had to fight for, to sit at the same lunch counter. But that stuff is over with now. You got to move on, progress.

One more thing about the film. One of the interesting things about your handling of the Italians is that Vinny is very dark, has kind of kinky hair—

And listens to Public Enemy!

Yeah, he's really confused.

I wouldn't say that. Because those kids in Bensonhurst love Public Enemy. They like the music, but I guess they're definitely not listening to the lyrics. The beat is there. When I went to Bensonhurst on the invitation of this writer from *Newsday*, three or four days after Yusuf Hawkins was murdered—you wouldn't believe all those Italian kids come up to me, "Yo, Spike, can you sign an autograph? Woo! Bring Michael Jordan! Where's Flavor Flav! Where's Chuck D?" They love rap. But at the same time [laughs] they will take a baseball bat to a black kid's head, if they feel he's not supposed to be in that neighborhood.

I mean, that's the crazy thing. That's the paradox about racism. America. They could hate black people, yet at the same time they will buy Michael Jackson, they will watch Bill Cosby, they will love Michael Jordan to death. They don't classify those particular people as black, they are classed as exceptions. The perfect example is that scene in *Do the Right Thing* between Pino and Mookie. Pino loves Prince, Magic Johnson, Eddie Murphy— they're not niggers, they're different. That shit is true.

There's a sense that Vinny may be secretly terrified of having some black blood in him. There's a real sense—

I'm not a psychiatrist, but I think that's one of the reasons that there's always been a lot of static between black people and Italian-Americans. Italy is very close to Africa. Hey, you know what's up! [Laughs.]

Now, as to Malcolm X, *you were quoted as saying that you would be "crazy to let white people determine the outcome of this film." Even if you had black producers, wouldn't you still think it would be crazy to let them determine the outcome?*

Yeah, but I produce it myself. It's white people at the studio. We're talking about Hollywood today. No black people run Hollywood. So what are you talking about?

I was trying to understand exactly what you meant by—

I'm talking 'bout the real world, not some make-believe shit. No black person runs a motherfucking studio. There's no black studio executive who can green-light a picture.

I'm aware of that.

So when I make a statement like that, that's what I'm talking about.

If there were though, I'm asking you a theoretical—

Oh, now let's talk about the theoretical world.

Yes, let's. If there were, wouldn't you still insist on complete control?

Yes.

Okay. That's all.

But that's not the point though.

That's not your point. I get it, I'm not that slow. [Pause.] When you said, "Only a black should be able to write and direct Malcolm X," *did you get flak about that?*

No. You know, August Wilson got a lot of flak when he wrote an article about it. There's always been that debate. James Earl Jones, [laughs] he's made several comments saying that it doesn't matter. But I still feel that way. I feel a film like this . . . even Norman Jewison told me that he always felt a black person should direct this. At the time he was going to direct it, he says he didn't see any black people out there qualified to do it.

Can you appreciate how that argument could be turned against you, against blacks, by racists?

That doesn't bother me, because you could turn anything any which way you want to.

What does Malcolm X represent to you? Why was the project so important to you?

[Pause.] Because I want this film to do justice to his legacy. I feel, Denzel feels, everybody that's working on it feels, this has to be a great film. It can't be all right, it can't be a good film. It has to be our obligation, our duty to make a great, great, great movie. Because he deserves it. And it would be a great testimony for what he stood for and what he died for, and what we still have to do as a people.

Are you fighting over what kind of film Warner Bros. will let you make?

There's never been any debate on the content, it's the length. I told them from the get-go, from jump street, this is a three-hour motherfucking movie.

Are they nervous about it?

Yeah, they're nervous about it. Yeah, they're nervous about a three-hour movie. This movie can't be done for under $30 million.

Do they accept that, yet?

[Pause.] Well, they can believe what they want to believe, but it can't be done for under thirty.

Because this is a big jump in the history of black cinema. It would be the first time that kind of major money—

You're right! That's why they're nervous about it! This is the same studio that did you-know-what, *Bonfire of the Vanities*. They lost a bundle on that. So they're kind of nervous.

The producer, Marvin Worth, used to road-manage Billie Holiday, didn't he?

That's what he says. I believe him.

He also did a documentary on Malcolm X.

In the early seventies. He bought the rights directly from Betty Shabazz, Malcolm's widow, and Alex Haley, back in 1969, and has been trying to get the film made ever since.

Would you feel more comfortable with a black producer?

It don't matter now. I try to keep grounded in the real world. The fact is, I produce my own films and I'm gonna have the same creative control I've had on all my films.

So will he be co-producer, or executive producer?

I haven't really decided what the terminology is, but I know the way it's going to run, though. [Laughs, sly smile.] I know what the program's gonna be.

There have been five scripts.

Five or six.

David Mamet—

He wrote his for Sidney Lumet.

You're working off the original, with Baldwin and Arnold Perl. Who was Perl?

He was a writer who got blacklisted in the 1950s. See, James Baldwin started out, but he was having trouble, so Marvin brought Arnold Perl in. They're both deceased. That's what I'm rewriting.

You felt that was the best script?

In my opinion, it was.

Do you plan to act in this film as well?

Yeah, I might.

That will be a trip, to see you in a historical film.

Yeah, with my conk. [Laughs.]

You've appeared in all of your films, and have such a persona now outside them, don't you worry that—

I think it's worked to my advantage. If I thought it would be a deterrent to the movie, I wouldn't do it. But I don't think it will be.

Good luck with it. Is there anything else on your mind?

Yeah, hire some black writers at *Rolling Stone.* Now I got to try to get a cab to go to Brooklyn.

5

DAVID CRONENBERG

DAVID CRONENBERG FILMOGRAPHY

1966	Transfer (short)
1967	From the Drain (short)
1969	Stereo
1970	Crimes of the Future
1975	Shivers (also known as: They Came from Within)
1976	Rabid
1979	Fast Company
1979	The Brood
1980	Scanners
1982	Videodrome
1983	The Dead Zone
1986	The Fly
1988	Dead Ringers
1991	Naked Lunch
1993	M. Butterfly
1996	Crash

for television

1972	Secret Weapons
1976	The Victim / The Lie Chair / The Italian Machine
1990	Regina Versus Horvath / Regina Versus Logan (episodes of Scales of Justice)

David Cronenberg

When you enter the world of David Cronenberg, there are no bad men with knives in the closet. No one pops up out of the bathtub after a certain drowning. The wind doesn't rattle the windows or make the curtains billow like death shrouds. No. The horror in the world of David Cronenberg is not the easy, external horror of the slasher, but the far creepier, insidious horror of the self, of self-consciousness. I think, therefore I might not be.

It's out of such a disturbing state of mind (and body) that Cronenberg has fashioned his work. First came two provocative but pretentious "underground" science fiction films in the late sixties, *Stereo* and *Crimes of the Future*, in which Cronenberg already displayed an interest in sexuality, control, and the social order. His long wait for a commercial feature—funding is difficult in Canada and often involves the government—ended with *They Came from Within*, where the repressed residents of a sterile high-rise become infected with parasites that sex them up in most unusual ways. A full-scale debate in Canada's Parliament about the suitability of government support for such a film followed (no doubt to Cronenberg's dismay and delight) and indicated what he was up against in the great white north. Enter former Ivory Snow girl and porn star Marilyn Chambers, sporting an underarm phallic spike in *Rabid*, an entertaining essay in which, as in so many of Cronenberg's works, cutting-edge science and somatic desire perform a romantically tragic pas de deux. Next, Cronenberg made a skidding detour onto the drag strip for the formulaic, forgettable *Fast Company*.

It wasn't until the 1980s that he really hit stride. *The Brood* was a minimasterpiece about the horror of the fraying family; *Scanners* brought Cronenberg his drive-in audience, with its famous exploding head and sci-fi subtext; *Videodrome* was a complicated, polyoptic exploration of the connection between image, power, and flesh, starring James Woods in an emotionally intricate role; *The Dead Zone* found Cronenberg boiling down the Stephen King bestseller and extracting the best performance of Christopher Walken's career. And then *The Fly* put him squarely over the top. Featuring Jeff Goldblum and Geena Davis, Cronenberg's reworking of the laughable little 1950s original was masterful: tight, vicious, disgusting, metaphorically rich and intellectually rigorous, it was slamming yet subtle, like the best of all his work. After *The Fly,* he turned down the temperature with *Dead Ringers,* a stainless-steel-on-skin story of self-destructive identical twin gynecologists (both played brilliantly by Jeremy Irons) which scraped to the core of the problem of identity—how we separate self from other. Indeed, considering these six films, an argument can be made for Cronenberg as the most consistently interesting filmmaker of the 1980s.

He'd been scheming, dreaming, and fretting over his next work for many years—the unfilmable film, *Naked Lunch.* William Burroughs was always one of Cronenberg's greatest influences (indeed, much of his thematic imagery strongly parallels that of Burroughs) and *Naked Lunch* provided him with his long-wished-for fusion of their visions. It's quite a strange film, hardly the free-for-all that is the Burroughs novel. Rather, it's dry as dust, slow as sun, bristly in its intelligence and unsettling in its aura: it's like a visit to the mental dentist. It is also one of the few pictures that generously rewards—and almost, like *Videodrome,* necessitates—a second screening.

Born in Toronto in 1943, Cronenberg was gearing up for a career in science when English stole his brain at the University of Toronto. He wrote a few stories that won him some attention, and shot his first experimental shorts. He made do without film school. Early in his career, Cronenberg was lumped together with a number of other young horror filmmakers, most notably George Romero and John Carpenter, but they've been inappropriate company for at least the last ten years. In addition to his feature films, he has done work for Canadian television and a couple of terrific commercials for Nike and Cadbury's Caramilk chocolate bars.

I met with Cronenberg in November of 1991 in Toronto, where he still makes his pictures and lives, quietly (when he's not racing cars), with his second wife and his three children. We talked in his small, spartan office as the snow swirled outside. The man himself is calm, thoughtful, and focused; he's deadly serious but not at all deadly.

SESSION ONE

Let's go back to the beginning. There's very little written about your childhood, and your family. I'd like you to describe it.

I was brought up in a kind of immigrant section of Toronto: Jews that had not yet moved out to the suburbs, Turks, Italians, Greeks. My father was a bibliophile and a writer, and my house was always full of books. Literally, walls made out of books. I never really saw the real walls of the house, because we had so many books; there were actually corridors made out of books. To me this was all perfectly normal, of course, since it was there from first consciousness. And he was also very much the music buff, and a bit of a gadget freak. I remember we had an Altec speaker that was much taller than I ever was. It must have been a studio-size speaker. He had a Quad amplifier. Down a street, around the corner was the record store, and my father was always down there, previewing records. And my mother was a pianist—for the ballet, for choirs, for violinists and their teachers, and opera singers and their teachers, who would come to the house.

I was exposed to culture, but I was never into studying it, so I know tons of music in my head note for note, but I don't know who composed it and have no idea who played it. They weren't just into that kind of culture though, they were both very eclectic. I remember an album of recordings from all over the world. The original African recording of "The Lion Sleeps Tonight," which is better than anything that ever came after. Fantastic, incredible. And old blues records. And folk. So it was a very eclectic culture, not just classical.

What were your folks like as parents?

Great. They were very sweet. Very supportive. I think that has always been there for me, underneath. Very approving, very easy, very sweet people.

Did they want you to be a scientist?

Well, the truth is, they wanted me to be whatever I wanted to be. I'm sure they had discussions at night, very worried about my latest girlfriend, or my latest philosophy of life, whatever—but I wasn't really exposed to much negativity, I have to say. Basically, if I decided I wanted to go into science, my father would immediately present me with twenty books on biochemistry, and be enthusiastic. And if a year later I decided to drop out of science—which I did—and went into English, then we would talk about literary criticism, and I'd get twenty books on literary criticism. And he'd be equally excited by that. I never felt I had to please them. It seemed like whatever I did pleased them.

Sounds ideal.

It was, it was. I mean, obviously, life being life and humans being humans, there was angst and anguish that they had to deal with that I didn't know much about. They basically did not lay that on me at all. I mean, my father's mother-in-law was in the house, my grandmother, and she had a leg amputated, so I grew up with this wonderful wheelchair in the house that I could do wheelies in, and go up and down the halls in. I *know* that must have caused huge stress and strain—because she was a mother-in-law and an invalid, and in this very tiny house and there's not much money and all of that—but I didn't know all that. Nobody screamed and yelled.

It's been said that children live out the unexpressed emotions of their parents.

I don't think that's true. I think children have a desire for things to be wonderful, and given half a chance, they will experience them that way. I don't think they're looking for bad times. That's my experience of it. I can be back there in a flash. I can be back living at home, instantly.

Well, I flash on you living there with this grandmother figure and her amputated leg, and think of your body consciousness—

Well, it's not impossible. I mean, this leg is something I would see. We'd talk about it. She'd tell me about the phantom leg, how she'd feel pain where her leg used to be. It was all pretty mysterious at the time. Although I'm not sure she was the most sweet, forgiving woman at the time, she was a real grandmother to me. She wasn't a huge part of my life, but I definitely do remember that stuff. There was not a sense of sickness about her, despite the amputated leg. The wheelchair was great. I couldn't see why anybody wouldn't want to wheel around in that. On a conscious level, I was pretty oblivious to the anguish that must have been hers.

Maybe the wheelchair was your first car.

For sure, it was. I had a red tricycle, which I preferred, because I could take that outside.

What about your sibs? You have a sister named Denise?

That's right. She's been the costume designer on the last few movies. She's four years older than I am. So we had that kind of relationship. When she became a teenager and I wasn't, I didn't see her that much, because she'd be out doing teenage-type things. We use to put on plays at the house, she'd organize those. I still remember we did "Little Red Riding Hood." I was the hunter that popped up at the end and shot the wolf at the last minute. I had to stay behind the piano hiding for the whole thing. We had seats set up in the living room, for people to come in and watch the play.

What were your childhood obsessions? I know you had the car bug fairly early, and then also the bug bug—

Well, the bug bug I think preceded the cars. In fact, I do remember a period when I was really down on cars, because I was into animals. I hated to see squirrels run over by '53 Buicks, because there's not much left of the squirrel after that. So there was definitely a period when I was not crazy about cars, and my father didn't have a car, we didn't have a car in the family. I'd walk everywhere. Everything I needed was accessible by walking or bicycle. I remember my father had a car for about ten minutes once. I remember he bought it, and we were driving around the corner, and we had to get out—the car was dead. I never saw it again. My mother never drove and my father almost never drove.

The first 8-millimeter film you ever shot as a teenager—your train arriving in the train station, as it were—was of auto racing, right?

That's correct. Not only that, but a guy, a CBC [Canadian Broadcasting Company] producer, was killed in the first race that I shot, and I have that on film. He rolled his Triumph TR3 in the chicane at Harewood Acres.

So in your very first film you unified your obsession with death, your love of technology, and your ambivalence about TV!

Probably. [Laughs.] Maybe just producers in general.

Every kid has fears. It's almost a cliché that your horror is the horror of the adult and not of the child, but I'm wondering, what was the dark stuff of your childhood?

I think it was pretty garden-variety stuff. The scariest movie I ever saw as a kid was *Blue Lagoon*, with Gene Simmons and Joan Hall. That was the movie that kept me up with the lights on for at least a week, maybe more. Normally, I liked the dark. I wasn't a kid that was afraid of the dark. But this was separation from your parents—that was the scary thing. And *Bambi* was terrifying. And *Babar the Elephant* was terrifying. *The Blue Lagoon* was terrifying because it was about two kids on a boat, and the boat catches fire, and the boat sinks, and the two kids are on this island with this drunken sailor, who eventually falls out of a skull-shaped cave and dies, and so the two kids are totally alone and have to invent their own culture. That was the part that was terrifying—separation from parents. And when people get hysterical now about children and terror and film, they really are looking at it from an adult point of view. I think kids can take a lot of things that adults find terrifying, but what is almost universally terrifying for a kid is the idea of being separated from his parents.

You've had to live out that fear in two different ways: first, in going through the death of both your parents, and second, in being separated from your child when your first marriage ended. Let's talk first about your parents, because I know that was a real shaper. When did your father die?

Well . . . I don't know. This is the most bizarre thing. I actually don't, I can't, I can't remember the dates of my parents' deaths. But my mother died . . . my father died first. My father had been sick, had this mysterious illness, but my mother had always been absolutely healthy. I never remember her even having a cold. Not ever. I was in London, when I got a phone call from my sister, totally hysterical and destroyed, saying that both of my parents were in the hospital. Now, my father wasn't a surprise, but my mother – that was a total shock. She'd had a stroke, and I think it was the stress of my father's illness.

He had a illness where he couldn't process calcium, his bones were so brittle he could break a rib turning over in bed.

Yeah, that was just one of the more horrifying aspects of it. It was a kind of general disintegration. At a certain point his body just started to let go. And suddenly I had two parents in the hospital, and I had to come back, and it was just sort of downhill from there. My father died. My mother was relatively okay for roughly another ten years, but she was never totally right. She had heart trouble.

Did you have to take care of her?

Yeah, basically. She could live on her own till the end, but she was constantly having to have blood transfusions because she had an anemic condition. I can tell you when Giles Villeneuve [a race car driver] died but I can't tell you about my father.

There's a television journalist here who for about twenty years has tried to make huge connections between my work and the death of my parents. Unfortunately, she happened to be sitting behind me and my parents when I had my first screening of *Stereo*. And then she later interviewed me, and said, "Weren't you really in this film trying to say, 'Look at me, mom and dad, I can make a film that you can't understand'?" And I said, "My parents understood that film perfectly well. You're the one that didn't understand." Then, after my father died, she said the death of my father was the theme of all my films, and then when my mother died, her death. It isn't that simple.

It's reductive for one thing.

It's reductive, and also, it ignores the stuff I did when my parents were perfectly healthy, which was also fairly death-obsessed. I mean, you don't have to have your parents die: you can anticipate your parents dying, you can anticipate your kids dying, and you can anticipate yourself dying—if you have half an imagination and decide to let it go in that direction. You don't have to have an actual death in your family to traumatize you. In truth, the deaths of both parents had a fairly long lead time. They didn't come out of the blue to shatter some kind of security I had. I *never* had that kind of security, in my understanding of the human condition. This was always a given that I couldn't accept. Let's put it this way: the death of my parents has sort of confirmed all the bad things that I thought about the world. It just confirmed it. It wasn't induced by that. They could still be alive and I'd be making exactly the same movies.

Let's touch on your Jewishness, briefly.

What it is, is simply this: my parents were basically non- to anti-religious. Now, they weren't non- to anti-*Jewish*. In fact, my mother, in a mysterious way, taught me a fair amount of Yiddish. And she was absolutely not anybody's stereotype of a Jewish mother. Yes, she made chicken soup—I have to give her that. She was a second-generation Canadian Jewish girl. One brother was a violinist with the Toronto Symphony Orchestra and had gone to Germany to be educated, and her other brother had a Ph.D. and taught German. So it was not the normal idea of a thirties and forties Jewish family stereotype.

But as far as religion went, she was in fact more virulently anti-religious than my father. All very quiet, I have to say. They were very sweet and non-vindictive people. But over the years I came to realize she had great disdain and contempt for the religious structures. At a certain point I remember her asking me if I wanted a bar mitzvah. And I asked her what was involved in that. And she said, "Well, you'd have to go to Jewish school." And I said, "You mean that school that you go to after you come back from regular school." And she said yeah. So I said forget it. So I didn't. And from my friends at school I learned what Jewish school was, and what went on there. They'd tell me all these escapades and crazy things. It was completely alien to me. I had no knowledge and no desire to know anything about it.

Were your parents both atheists?

Yeah, they were. The word "atheist" almost suggests you buy the religious system. Beyond atheism, they were simply non-believers. To me, to say you're an atheist almost suggests *theism*. You can't have atheism without theism, and I'd go beyond that. Non-belief. Period. And therefore all the structures that go with it. And this did not mean that my parents had a disdain for Jewish North American culture. They didn't. Quite the contrary. But it was really totally secular.

So what was celebrated was humanism and science, the rational mind?

That's right. Maybe with an emphasis on the humanism, because neither parent was anything like a technocrat.

Your father's newspaper column of thirty years was about stamps. So there was a certain obsessiveness there—

Oh yes. Oh yes. He was a collector, he was a rabid collector. He was a squirrel. He collected anything that was collectable. They didn't drink, my parents. I think I saw my father slightly drunk, twice, in my entire life, and my mother never. But he collected whiskey bottles! It was the bottles he was collecting, not the whiskey. He had a whole cabinet of bottles and he would show it to people.

It's a bit like you collecting images of disturbing things, but not the reality.

Well, there's probably some truth to that: I have my cabinet that I can open and show you, yeah, but I don't drink.

You may be no more paranoid than the next intellectual, but you've said you never thought you'd be put in jail for your Jewishness; you thought you'd be put in jail for your art. Why did you feel you'd be put in jail for your art?

I think I said it's more likely.

Well, you suggested the possibility.

Yes, yes. Well, because I can see what's happening in the world. I have been censored, and you just have to have that experience once and you understand what the implications are. If an artist has got anything to sell at all, it's his antennae, which pick up the most subtle vibes, and from that you make inferences, and you understand the implications of things perhaps better than other people—possibly just because that's become your field. You deliberately sensitize yourself to things that some people choose not to be sensitive to. Let's take this century. Salman Rushdie's situation is the ultimate paranoid situation. Absolute ultimate most perfect artist's paranoid situation, and it *exists*. The truth is, it could happen to anybody that performs any art. The idea that some fanatic would hire a sort of universal hit squad to come get you, wherever you are, because of your art, is absolutely perfect. To live in fear and terror, it's very Kafkaesque, but it's even beyond Kafka.

I suppose what I was saying in that particular parallel was in response to friends of mine who were ardent Zionists, and who would talk to me for hours about the party line, which was that a Jew cannot possibly feel secure anywhere but Israel. And that's when I said that the boots at the door, the knocking of the fists on the door, probably would come more because of my art than because I'm Jewish.

I don't walk around wracked by fear. And I know there are people who are, and more lately than before. Just about our world: you name it, pollution, the ozone layer. I know people who are actually getting ulcers because of this. And whatever paranoia I might have—and I must tell you I don't think of myself as being particularly paranoid—but whatever paranoia I might have is not giving me ulcers or keeping me up at night.

But it's my understanding of art as being subversive of civilization. I think it is. And yet, it's a paradox, because in the Freudian equation civilization *is* repression. Now I'm simplifying it, but basically, you don't get civilization without repression of the unconscious, of the id. And the basic appeal of art is to the unconscious. Therefore art is somewhat subversive of civilization. And yet at the same time it seems to be necessary for civilization. You don't get civilization without art.

It's a sign you have civilization to begin with. If you go back into a culture, archaeologically, and you see the writing on the wall, so to speak, it's a sign you've got a civilization, as opposed to a bunch of hominids just trying to survive.

That's right. That's right. The first moment there is time to do more than just survive, art is created. So it's a necessity we have, to do it. But it's a very strange, uneasy alliance between the two, which you constantly see being played out in the corridors of power. On the one hand, politicians want to align themselves with artists of various types; but the instant the art gets a little out of control, or unfocused, or cannot be used for political reasons, then suddenly it becomes an enemy. It becomes a source of hostility or political embarrassment. And whenever you see artists of any kind flirting with politics you get a very strange dissonance happening, and I think that's just natural, given the nature of the two things.

How do you feel your films are subversive?

Really by suggesting other realities than the ones that are normally accepted as realities. And by insisting on the equal reality of these other states of mind.

There's a dissenting tradition of criticism of your work which suggests that your films are hardly subversive, but are in fact bulwarks of the conservative order.

There's only one person who's ever said that, Robin Wood.

I've read a couple of critics who think you are essentially conservative: morally conservative, emotionally conservative.

I think that's a misreading of what I'm saying. I don't insist on an image of a brigand, of some sort of outsider, because I don't live a life like that. But some of the most subversive writers lived very bourgeois lives. One French writer said that to be subversive you *must* live a bourgeois life, because that's the perfect disguise. And I'm not in the sixties tradition, looking for chaos and a complete disassembly of society or anything like that—

Though some of these critics obviously wish you were.

Yeah. From that point of view, I guess I'm conservative and that's all right. I accept that. But to the extent that they're misreading me, that's just annoying.

I'll give you the most classic, straightforward example by Robin Wood, who accuses me of being reactionary, not just conservative: the ending of *Shivers*, my first feature. All the crazed people, who are infested by venereal parasites that cause them to become quite mad and erotically irresponsible, to say the least—at the end of the film these people go out into the city. And they look very cool and calm and they're well-disguised, and they're going out to infect the entire city and perhaps the world.

Wood takes this straight and seriously, as if I am presenting this as a hideous, scary thing, without any redeeming qualities whatsoever. And since he identifies with the crazies as gay, as Marxist, as whatever, he therefore thinks that I'm a reactionary. What he's totally missing is the humor and the irony, and it's obvious that everybody who watches the movie on one level identifies with the crazies, and wants to be a crazy. In fact, we were living in that highrise apartment, and it drove us mad. By the end of the shoot we all were running down the halls naked, and banging on people's doors and being stoned. So our identification was also with the crazies. I believe that's in the film. And the thrill of it comes with that, the sort of illicit identification and pleasure you get watching the crazies tearing this stuffy little middle-class place apart. He seems to give no weight to that, or chooses to ignore it for schematic reasons. For me, the ending is a happy ending. It's scary, and chaotic, but it's happy: it's liberating, it's cathartic. And for him, it's only reactionary and fearful.

The reading of your work as conservative is hardly limited to that movie.

No, I just wanted to give you the most obvious example. But, on the other hand, in *The Brood*, where I'm talking about the transmission of destructive neurosis from generation to generation, and I'm making it physical—as a metaphorical reading of it—to pick up that I find it negative, that's correct. That's a correct reading of *The Brood*. But I wonder if Robin really does identify with the little creatures? You'd have to, if those are the radicals and the rebels. They're an expression of rage. Now, if you're a Black Panther in the sixties you can say, "We creatures exist as an expression of rage, of our substratum of society, because of the frustrations of being black in our society." Yes. But I give them their due, as well, in the film. Nola [the woman who gives birth to the "children of her rage"] is a heroic figure. She's grotesque, but she's heroic—and her rage is real. I don't say that her rage is not real. I don't say it's reprehensible.

A feminist critique might suggest you're showing the woman's anger as dangerous, and ridiculous, and that the film is misogynistic.

If they're plugged into the movie do they not see what I'm showing: a kind of tragic trap that this girl at the end of the film is in, having to bear the sins of her mother, and not just her mother, but her parents? Is that not realistic? And is it not tragic? I don't think that this serves to bolster the status quo. I see this stuff transmitting from parent to child, from parent to child, it's a cycle that seems unbreakable, and should we not break it? That, to me, is not being conservative. I don't really have much respect for schematic criticism.

The Brood *is the closest you've come to autobiography. You were in the midst of a divorce and a custody fight for your daughter.*

Really, relative to what friends of mine have gone through and what I've read about, what I went through was very unspectacular and very straightforward, and relatively civilized. But that was the part that disturbed me: the fact that it was relatively civilized and straightforward. There was not shouting and screaming and yelling and stabbing and shooting, and it still was hideous. Even given that it was relatively Canadian and civilized, it was hideous, and really horrifying to me. Part of it had to do with an ideal of the family which was being ripped apart, and in that, one can detect a kind of heartbreak in something that was hoped for, and anticipated. Definitely, that was there, and I'm sure it had to do with my own family. I was not able to replicate what my family situation was. And I liked what my family situation had been. I thought it was good. I thought it was healthy. I thought it was productive. Whatever strength I have comes very much out of that. So I would have wanted to be able to give that to my own kids, and to the extent that in that case I was failing, it was quite a hideous failure. I'm actually not really very good with guilt. My first response to things is not ever guilt.

Boy, you're not Jewish.

[Laughs.] Well, that is one of the constructions of North American Jewishness. I'm not so sure they did the same thing in the old country. But you're right, you're absolutely right: I had to learn about guilt, people had to teach me. It's not native to me. I think it undoubtedly had to do with my parents, who did not lay guilt trips, period. They really didn't. And I don't think guilt is a natural thing, I think it's a neurotic thing. It has to be learned; how good you are at guilt depends on how good your teachers are and how early they start on you. Still, I was feeling guilt in this situation.

I mean, where I grew up, the destination signs on the Greyhound buses down at the station all said "GUILT."

[Laughs.] Did you take the express? This was something I learned from my friends. They had to tell me about it. I didn't realize until later that guilt was a crippling disease for some people, that some people can never get out from under it. So here I am in a situation feeling that I failed to give my kid the kind of security that I had as a kid. And I did feel guilty about that. And I didn't like that feeling. So here we come to theory-meets-practice. Now, I don't know what Robin Wood's experience of childhood was—

Let's not let him dominate this interview, please.

No, I'm using him as a metaphor also.

As a whipping boy.

[Deadpan.] I wouldn't want to give him that pleasure. Actually, he's a very nice man. Very sweet. The point is, my approach to things tends not to be political. I'm not trying to make a political statement. I'm thinking that politics is like art in that it's an attempt to make order out of chaos. And in order to do that, like art, it has to simplify and create symbols and metaphors. And I suppose when I'm creating my own art, the imposition of political symbols and structures is always going to be awkward. It's not going to be a nice, cozy fit. I think art is too complex for politics, but you still have to try politics. And perhaps life is too complex for art, but you have to try art.

Did you want to kill your ex-wife, when you were going through this divorce?

No. No.

You didn't have the urge to kill her, or strangle her?

No. But I'm just not violent. That's not my first impulse.

Let me quote you something you said ten years ago, at the time of The Brood, *about the scene where the husband finally strangles his wife to death: "I can't tell you how satisfying that scene is, I wanted to strangle my ex-wife."*

Yes, of course. Yes. Once again, it's metaphorical. When people are in favor of censorship, let's say for feminist reasons as opposed to strictly totalitarian reasons, there's a confusion of art with life that normally they don't make but for convenience they choose to make. That is to say, what's on the screen suddenly is *real,* and people who see what's on-screen will imitate that behavior; that images exist out of context, and there should be image police. You get this argument all the time. I never wanted to strangle my ex-wife literally, but at the moments that I chose to blame her for everything that was going on, I would have liked her to disappear. Everybody has that feeling. It's like saying, "I could've killed that guy."

Well, if you're in touch with that rage that everyone else is suppressing, why apologize for it?

No, but these days there are people who go to McDonald's and shoot forty human beings; you have to now be a little careful in insisting upon the metaphorical aspect of this.

Were you uncomfortable making something that was so closely autobiographical?

No, I wasn't the slightest bit uncomfortable.

Why then did you, after you had the experience, say that you didn't ever want to get that close again to autobiography?

Because it involved a kind of balancing act that I didn't think was all that productive. Art as therapy is not something that I think is terrifically worthwhile. The closer you come to its being therapeutic, the less valuable it's going to be.

Why is that?

Because you have to make choices in your art that eventually have only to do with the art itself. Let me give you an example, which simplifies. You're doing a scene which is not exactly a scene from a marriage but it's got some resonances, and suddenly you find you've got the impulse to put the exact words someone said, let's say your ex-wife, into the mouth of your character, despite the fact that those words are pushing your entire scene out of shape. And those words only have cathartic value. They only allow you to continue the argument, on screen. When in fact, another line of dialogue might be more potent for the audience, might be much more cathartic for the audience, given the structure you've created. And I found myself that it took a lot longer to make a decent movie out of this. There had to be a cooling off time for the film not to be like a guy wandering down the street muttering to himself and shouting and going over and over these arguments that he's gone over for years. I don't think that that's art. I think there's an artful mixture, an alchemy, of personal things and schematic things that ends up being something you could call art. If it's only a replication of life, it's not much.

If you don't believe in art as therapy, do you believe in therapy as therapy?

I think it's conceivable, yeah. But I don't think the deepest, most profound Freudian paradigms really work. It would be nice if they did. It's a wonderful fantasy. I think Freud was a wonderful philosophical writer, but I don't think he was a great medical writer. I just don't think the structures work. I don't think it's enough to bring certain things to consciousness. What *is* enough I don't know. But Freud invented the unconscious—that's a brilliant invention, which just about everybody in Western culture has bought. And the unfolding of the biblical paradigm, "The child is the father of the man";

it's true that before Freud, people didn't take childhood seriously. That was an incredible breakthrough in human consciousness. But in terms of the therapeutic structure, I think people are just too slippery, too perverse. The therapeutic situation immediately becomes perverse. It becomes an arena of personality, or power struggle, and so on. Because the analyst cannot be nothing, cannot be a cipher. And as soon as you get that, you must wonder, why bring another person into this, when you desperately need some objectivity? So that's why I don't think it works.

Have you gone through this experience?

No, no.

Because you're too balanced and too well adjusted!

That's right. I mean, I would end up trying to psychoanalyze the therapist.

Parenthetically, did you win your custody fight for your daughter?

Well, it wasn't even "win." At a certain point, my ex-wife just signed her over to me and left town. That was really the issue: whether to take her out of Toronto and go live somewhere else; and when she realized it was going to be a court battle and take a long time, she basically signed her over to me and left.

Did your wife change dramatically from the time you fell in love with her and married her to the time you were divorced?

Uh, no.

She didn't mutate or transform?

No.

Her ears didn't fall off?

No. They might be burning right now, but they didn't fall off.

Nola, in The Brood, *says, "I seem like a very special person in the middle of a strange adventure."*

You can hear that echoed in *The Fly*.

It occurs to me that that's, one, what a person in therapy feels, and two, what a director must feel making a movie.

Yes, absolutely. And I'm glad you've mentioned that, because that's one point where Nola is saying something real and more interesting than anybody else in the film is saying. Critics who think I'm making Nola the bad person should really listen to what I give her to say. She's very similar, in saying that, to Seth Brundle [Jeff Goldblum] in *The Fly*, who says, "I know what the disease wants." In other words, you find yourself in a situation that normally you would consider pathological, but now you're in it, it's your new reality; are you just going to succumb, to lie down and die, or are you going to try, as humans tend to, to encompass it with your mind and try to make sense of it, something positive out of it? It's like the people that survived the concentration camps—they somehow had the will to do that. And the ones who didn't, succumbed. I'm not talking about the physical impossibilities of surviving, but the psychological ones, which were even greater. Yet somehow people managed to do it, by force of will, in absolute defiance of the reality they found themselves in. And I'm really giving Nola the same will I give Seth Brundle. It's scary, but very human.

I made a joke about you being so well balanced before and—

And I took it completely seriously!

But you indeed have indicated that you are "afflicted" by the curse of balance.

Well, maybe this is what people mean when they say my films are conservative. Theatrically, it's wonderful to see someone who's unbalanced. Actors would always prefer to play a villain, because it allows them to express that obsessive craziness which, despite the danger of it, is still rather admired in our culture.

Evil is usually more interesting, cinematically, than good.

But I'm not even thinking in terms of evil. Evil is a whole other thing. The minute you say evil, I think: Christianity. I don't throw that word around, and it may not be something I even believe in. But let's say cinematic evil. Okay, I'm willing to go that far. Yeah, it's more interesting. Because it illuminates things, partly, and partly because it's cathartic. A villain in a bizarre, twisted way is always a Christlike figure: you know he's going to die, and he's dying for your sins, for your rage, for your craziness; he's doing it for you, so you don't have to do it.

But your movies never give us an easy evil. They always present both sides of every situation. And it almost leads to a kind of analysis paralysis.

And yet, I don't think of myself as being particularly indecisive. I mean, even on the set, there are directors who are very indecisive, even though making decisions is the *essence* of directing—a lot of them, and really fast, thousands every day. But I do think it's a Canadian thing, this balance. Up to a point it's a virtue, and beyond that, it's neurotic.

And beyond that point a "hard-won equilibrium can become a kind of morbid stasis," as Adrian Tripod of Crimes of the Future *says.*

Well put. I did wrestle with that in the early days of my career. It came out of an inability to act. I didn't have access yet to the machinery of my art. There was a huge limbo time where I really wanted to act and could not act. And like the Jewish philosophers in the shtetls—and there is a theory that

Jews of Europe became so philosophically adept and so clever and complex because they did not have access to real political machinery—I was in that situation in the beginning of my career. I had a script [*Shivers*]. I had a company that wanted to make it. And I had to wait three years before I could do it. And there's a kind of forced paralysis which you fill with philosophy. But I don't find it in my life now.

I do know people who are so self-obsessed and so self-analytical and so self-critical that they could sit in a room talking to themselves for years, and never allow themselves to act, because they would anticipate the exfoliation, the elaboration of the situation. Anticipating an affair, for example. A simple thing. At university. They would think, I could call her. But then this could happen. I could arrange an accidental meeting, I could bump into her at the cafeteria, but then this could happen. And on and on and on. To the point where no action would ever be taken.

And thus they personify—Canada!

And thus they would, to me. To a certain extent. At its worst, not at its best.

While the United States of America is already contemplating date rape!

[Laughs.] Yes, exactly. That's right. No, not contemplating—*doing* it.

Thus the attraction of Canadians to things American, but also the repulsion?

That's exactly right. It's definitely a love-hate relationship.

And where do you find yourself in that nexus, as a Canadian filmmaker whose largest audience is American?

Right in the middle. Right in the middle. It's a very interesting place to be. It's a Canadian place to be.

Are you a contradictory fellow?

No, I don't think so.

At one point you said the reason you're so secure is because you're so nuts. You've described yourself as sweet and warm and personable, but yet you make these diseased, grotesque, disgusting movies. There's a contradiction. And your character Tripod says of Antoine Rouge that he was "once a fierce sensualist, but is now a pure metaphysician." I wonder if you have these same sorts of oppositions?

Well, I think they're all reasonably well integrated in me. This is the reason I don't think I'm contradictory. From the inside out, my films feel completely like *me*. And yet I will resist the attempts of people to identify me with characters in the films or attitudes in the films, because I think that's misunderstanding the nature of art, of narrative art. I don't feel they're contradictory, I feel quite well integrated.

I'm aware there are apparent contradictions, like the well-known Marty Scorsese thing: after I met him, he said in an interview that he had been terrified to meet me, though he had wanted to meet me. This is the guy who made *Taxi Driver* and he's afraid to meet me! This is a guy who knows from the inside out that there's a complex relationship between someone who makes films and his films. But he still was taking the films at face value and equating me with them, and the craziness he saw in the films, and the disturbing things he saw in the films, he felt would be the essence of me as a person. And so he was amazed to meet a guy who, as he later said, "looked like a Beverly Hills gynecologist." And I was not anything like he thought I was going to be.

So I guess we can forgive critics who have never made a film for making the same mistake. And this is not a real contradiction, but just a humorous social contradiction. I feel very integrated with my films and my life.

Let's turn to the horror genre, which is where you and your films come from, if it's not in fact where you're going. At one point you described your project as a director as "making mental things physical." I would hazard that if we add a comma — "making mental, things physical" — then we would get a better idea of both sides of your equation. Is this as front and center in your consciousness as it was ten years ago?

Well, I've been thinking about the problem of the literary cinema, which is: how do you make a metaphor on screen? But it's the same discussion, really. You have to do it physically somehow. Eisenstein tried to do the literal thing. You know, the crowd roared like a lion. Here's a shot of the crowd, then cut to the lion roaring. And it was laughable and it didn't work and no one ever used it again. The attempt to literally do metaphor on screen did not work, and has not become part of the language of cinema, whereas it still works beautifully in literature. You're not talking about symbolism, you're talking about making a metaphor. The answer is that you have to make it physical, on screen, without being literal, and that's a trick. It's the same problem your quote addresses, a problem of communication.

You've said that all horror springs from the Latin phrase "Timor mortis conturbat mea," The fear of death disturbs me. Was there any way for you to resolve your fear of death other than making movies about it, or have you not resolved it, even with the movies?

I don't know if it's really resolvable for me, but we'll see. I think it would have to be through art, and I think in one sense that is what all art is. I don't mean to be reductive, but I don't think that's so reductive, because the question of death is not a simple question. It's not just fear of death, it's meaning of life — it's the same question. Is there a meaning to life? If you're religious, you talk about what God might be like, what the nature of God is. The question of human mortality is not a simple question.

Are you positing "art against death"?

I'm positing art as a means of coming to terms with death. Yes. I guess I'm putting art in opposition to religion, or as a replacement for religion, in the sense that if religion is used to allow you to come to terms with death, and also to guide you in how to live your life, then I think that art can do the same thing. But in a much less schematic way, in a much less rigid and absolute way, which is why it appeals to me and religion doesn't.

You once said, "I don't think it's the purpose of art to tell us how we should live." Maybe you were talking about how we should vote?

That's what I was talking about.

Because on a deeper level it seems that is exactly what art does address: how should we live?

Yes, it does. There I was reacting to an attack on me and other makers of horror films, really. It was my attempt to say, "My films are beyond politics," when other people were saying, "Nothing is beyond politics." I'm saying, "No, no, there are a lot of things that are beyond politics." Yes, teaching us how to live—it's not the *way* to live, but it's teaching us how we can go on living. That's what I'm talking about. You're right; there I was talking about how we should vote and how we should organize society—no, that's not the purpose of art.

You don't feel that art's just a reflexive mirror? I've not gotten that sense from your work.

No, no I don't. No, it's not nearly that passive.

Speaking of your horror, more specifically, it's never been a situational horror (the-man-in-the-basement-with-the-knife) as much as an existential, philosophical horror. Where does that come from?

I really think it comes from what I need art for. I don't need the story around the campfire; there's a couple of great campfire-type horror stories. But they are basically the-man-in-the-basement-with-the-knife. To the extent that that can be cathartic and entertaining, fine. But it's not enough for me. I want, I need more from what I do: I need more complexity, I need more philosophy, and I need more of a struggle in my art than that. More of a struggle with myself.

I think there are levels of filmmaking, just as there are levels of novel-writing. We know the difference between Elmore Leonard and Saul Bellow. There's a big difference.

Yeah, Elmore Leonard writes more convincing dialogue.

I'm not all that sure, actually. It depends. You put an Elmore Leonard character in a Saul Bellow novel, I'm not sure he'd be that convincing. But that's why my films are immediately more complex, even from the very beginning, when I didn't have the technical know-how to make them work wonderfully and I didn't have the money or the structure. I was still trying a lot of difficult things, often in dialogue, because even if you can't move the things around physically and cinematically the way you hope you one day will, you can still have the dialogue. The characters can still be complex.

Didn't you think at one point that dialogue was your weakness? That your scenarios and structures were strong, but that your dialogue wasn't convincing?

No. I tell you exactly what it was. I think I'm really good with dialogue. I think it's obvious in my last few films that I'm really quite okay directing actors; more than that, I'd say. But it was quite straightforward: when we started to make *Shivers* we had this discussion. We said, look, this movie has got a lot of effects, and they take a lot of time and we don't have a lot of time—we have fifteen days to make the entire movie—so the scenes where people just talk you have ten minutes to shoot. So that is exactly what happened.

Then, of course, there are the B-movie obsessives who love the dialogue to be bad. They love *Plan X from Outer Space*. And they would project that onto my films even when it was quite obvious that the films had gone to a different place. They *want* the acting to be bad. They have great affection for that. They don't want Gregory Peck to be in *The Omen*. So I suffered, not greatly, from that, because people were not looking at the movies. They were not seeing that Oliver Reed [Dr. Raglan] was quite interesting and that Samantha Eggar [Nola Carveth] was actually quite terrific in *The Brood*. They'd rather not know that. And they'd rather concentrate on the small character role that maybe wasn't so great because you didn't have the time.

Dialogue was always important to me. It was extremely important. Have I gotten better at writing and directing it? Yeah, I hope so. The words are important. And this comes from my writing. I have an ear for it. You either have it or you don't, it's like music: you're tone-deaf or you're not tone-deaf. And there are some directors who are tone-deaf; they have to depend on the actors or somebody else to tell them whether it's in tune or not. I think I've always had that ear. It's just that I haven't always been able to do anything about it because of the circumstances of making a movie.

Let's go back to "timor mortis." Are you terribly afraid of your own dying?

I don't think more so than most people. But I'm willing to discuss it with myself more than most people. And earlier than most people. I think it's something that everybody thinks about and anticipates. You can't help but do that. But I think most people basically repress the whole concept of it. Certainly in Western culture. There are other cultures where death is more integrated, but not in the West.

I think my consideration of death shows my philosophical bent, rather than something neurotic. I'm saying, "Well, okay, here we go again: death? Now, what about death? Well, we've all got to die." Now, physically that makes sense. You look at the cycles of nature and evolution, and you say, of course, individuals of a species have to die, and it happens in the insect world viciously and without the slightest bit of remorse on nature's part. But here we are with this consciousness, with this awareness of death, that no other creature has—probably in the universe.

We're not sure. Some scientists think elephants may have consciousness of death.

I don't think they do. We're projecting, quite frankly. I'm not saying animals don't have affection and fear and neurosis and all that, they do. But I really think it's something else. I'm not saying that an elephant seeing a dead body of another elephant is not perplexed and disturbed because they expect movement and motion and some kind of response and they're not getting it. That's still not understanding that you too, elephant, Babar, are going to die. I don't think they come to that inevitability, I don't think they have that in their heads.

We don't know what most animals really have in their heads. We're looking from the outside in.

Absolutely. Experientially, that's true. But one of the things we can do is project ourselves into other creatures, and I feel pretty confident that elephants don't know they're going to die. I really do. Part of the thing is language. You need to be able to manipulate abstract thoughts and communicate them.

You need language for thought?

You need language for thought. And you need language to anticipate death.

No thought without language?

No abstract thought without language. And no anticipation. I do think the anticipation of death without language would be impossible. Maybe that's another reason why language in my films is important. Even silent films had language. I don't think of film as being a specifically visual medium at all. I just think that's one of many elements that you've got. Language has always been important to me. So I think, "Well, death? What about death?" And it's not necessarily always out of *fear* of my own mortality at all. But it's very difficult to imagine one's own nonexistence. And it's been so recent that I didn't exist! Only forty-nine years.

Have you been close to nonexisting again?

No, not anywhere near it.

Even in your car racing?

Never. You really exist a lot when you race cars.

Never a time when you thought "I might die right here"?

Oh, yeah. But I didn't. When you say, "I might die right here," the instant you say *I* you are very far from nonexistence. Normally, I say, "This is going to hurt," or, "This is going to cost a lot of money," and not usually, "This is going to kill me." Really the closest to nonexistence is before you're born, and it's very hard to put yourself in that state. And it's kind of an unacceptable thing, even though you know it's perfectly acceptable to the universe and to the structure of the world. It's more than acceptable, it's inevitable. That's the conundrum. I think nonexistence is a difficult one.

If there's a horror in confronting the inevitability of death — and we all carry our little mini horror film around with us in the shape of our own deaths — wouldn't eternal life be an even greater horror?

Oh, yeah. There's no way out, that's one of the problems. No one *really* wants to live forever, not really. But on a theoretical level, by apposition, you don't want to die, so you really are saying you want to live forever — even though you know that's not going to work.

Now, the other thing is that I've had moments where the inevitability of death is an absolute strength, it's an escape, it's a freedom. And certainly for people who find themselves in a hideous situation, like the concentration camps, there's a point where death is truly a release. So the idea that death is merciful, that's not only a schematic concept to me, I can feel it as an emotional reality as well.

At the beginning of *Naked Lunch* is the quote: "Nothing is true, everything is permitted." Although I don't think it was originally conceived by Hassan I. Sabbah as an existentialist statement, in a way it is. It's saying, because death is inevitable, we are free to invent our own reality. We are part of a culture, we are part of an ethical and moral system, but all we have to do is take one step outside it, and we see that none of that is absolute. Nothing is true. It's not an absolute. It's only a human construct, very definitely able to change and susceptible to rethinking. And you can then be free. Free to be unethical, immoral, out of society, an agent of some other power, never belonging.

Ultimately, if you are an existentialist and you don't believe in God and the judgment after death, then you can do anything you want: you can kill if you want to kill, you can do whatever society considers the most taboo thing.

Including suicide.

Including suicide.

The Dead Zone *ends essentially with a suicide; Max Renn kills himself at the end of* Videodrome; *Brundlefly at the end of* The Fly *asks for a mercy killing, and the Mantle twins end* Dead Ringers *with what is basically a double suicide. Your last four pictures all end with suicide, so it's obviously something you've given a lot of thought to.*

Yeah. It's probably the only way we can give our death a meaning. Because otherwise it's completely arbitrary. It comes because of some small bodily malfunction or some accident—a safe falls on your head. You're Krazy Kat and a safe falls on your head. And it doesn't mean anything! It means fuck-all! And so you say, I don't like this. I don't like the fact that death, which is a pretty important moment in my life, I don't like this to have no meaning. The only way you can do anything about that is to control the moment and the means of your death. And that means suicide, basically.

In opposition to this you have a built-in, genetically programmed desire to survive and stay alive at all costs no matter how hideous the circumstances. To survive and to live no matter what. In the West, suicide is basically considered a cowardly thing that comes out of despair or hopelessness, and is something you should have therapy or take pills for, so you won't do it. I think I've had to find my own way through that. I knew some people who committed suicide in my youth, and I didn't think those were *right* suicides. Now I'm beginning to wonder. I thought, like everybody else, that these were some kind of tragedy that came out of neurosis, or imbalance, or craziness, or drugs; and now I think it's not necessarily a bad thing.

I was shocked when Hemingway committed suicide, because he obviously could have lived a lot longer. But his very Hemingwayesque statement that all that mattered to him was fucking and writing and hunting and fishing, and that he couldn't do any of them worth a damn anymore, so why be alive?—as you get older you say, he has a point, he really does. If your life has meaning, then it can also cease to have meaning. And if you're still alive after that point, what are you? And I also believe that the only meaning that there is in the universe comes from the human brain. I don't think that there is a God, or that there is an external system of meaning out there that exists apart from human beings. So, from that point of view, it's even more cogent, the possibility that suicide is an elegant and properly structured way out of life—that it could be, anyway. And whether I could ever do that, under certain circumstances, or could overcome the will to be alive, which is strong, I don't know.

But doing the kind of thing that I can't help doing, when I heard that Hemingway had died, I *became* Hemingway. I imagined him taking the shotgun, I imagined him the way he did it, and the feel. Did the barrel clink on his teeth? How did it feel? I tried to imagine the moment of death. Whenever I read about a suicide I do that. And, in a sense, whenever I'm having a character in my films die, I'm rehearsing my own death. I truly believe it. It's trying things out, saying, "Well, how would it feel under these circumstances, to do this? In what way?" If somebody dies, if somebody commits suicide, the first think I always think is: how? People say, well what does it matter? And I say, no, it really does matter, especially in a suicide. It says a lot of things about what was going on in the person at the time.

It's also socially coded: men choose more violent means, women choose more passive means.

But that's statistics. It's also a body thing. Die young and leave a beautiful corpse.

That kind of vanity is encoded for women, too.

Yes, they don't want to mess their hair, which putting a shotgun in your mouth and pulling the trigger definitely will do. It'll mess your hair. Now, if you've already gone bald, maybe you *want* to mess up your head a bit. I think it says a lot of things. See, my first impulse is not to do what you did, which is to think of it statistically. I don't think of it as why women do this, why men do that—I think of a specific moment. Everybody knows Sylvia Plath—she made breakfast for her kids first, that's stunning. She's more known for her death than her poetry. That's the first thing: I'm seeing that apartment, I'm seeing that room, I'm seeing the breakfast. I want to know what she made, was it her kids' favorite thing? I'm looking for the meaning there, not because it's morbid.

You and your work are pretty obsessed with the nature of control. It's interesting that you used the word "control" to talk about suicide. I think your work suggests that almost none of us is in control, even when we think we're in control; and what's present is the illusion, or perhaps more discouragingly, the delusion, of control.

I think it's true. In all of my films there is some type of discussion, whether it's subliminal or up front, of free will versus predestination. Whether it's religious predestination or genetic predestination doesn't really matter. It's that the feeling of free will is so palpable and so tangible, and yet the evidence against the real existence of free will is quite compelling. How do you juggle these two things?

As a director, I *know* that control is a delusion. I mean, it's an illusion and a delusion. Orson Welles said that a director is "someone who presides over a series of accidents." I live that. And yet, you can see, there's a director who's really got no control, and here's a director who really has a lot of control.

Isn't it disingenuous for you to suggest that you're presiding over these "accidents," when in fact what the director is doing is taking the chaos that exists in the world and creating, on the table that is his movie, an orderly miniature?

Yeah, but you see, you become very aware, when you focus on the table, that you can't control it. That the phenomenological world is not controllable. It's a focusing down, and an abstracting, out of the chaos, some things; but you're not really abstracting *order* out of it. And it's true on the set. It always pleases me when there are people who have been on the set, and read the script, and they still don't know what the movie is. They still have no idea what's on the screen—even when they look at the monitors. Because they are not really able to abstract that rectangle of film out of the chaos. And you as a director, that's all you're there for. That's your only function on the set.

Don't you need that rectangle of control in contradistinction to how messy this non-rectangle is, out this window of your office? Isn't that part of your desire?

But you see, I am the same as a writer, who is trying to control chaos with words, and knows that still it's only words. And to me that rectangle begins with real things. Here's a real actor, a human being, and he's drinking this real cup of coffee, which someone had to go and get, and decide that it would be this shape and color, and would the coffee be steaming or not, and is it going to be hot, and is the actor going to play out of it being hot, or is he going to ignore that? It's real.

But by the time it's on-screen it's no longer real, it's as abstract as words are. And I'm aware that the reality of it is mitigated totally by the cultural structures that are necessary for it to have meaning; just as words have no meaning unless you have language, and you have a culture behind that language, and a history behind the culture behind the language. And that can shift, and disappear, and the language that you are using can disappear. Well, I feel the same way about the film. The film can disappear, the frame can disappear, the meaning of the frame can disappear. It's very volatile, it's very fragile and ephemeral. Anybody who's writing has to know that, and ignore it nonetheless, because you'd drive yourself mad, and it would lead to paralysis if you obsessed about it. It's an illusion to think it's any different for the filmmaker just because he gets physical things to play with and the writer doesn't.

But the process is different. The process of a writer sitting at a typewriter or computer writing a sestina involves control only of his own mind and the words; the process of you making a $20 million film involves an inordinate amount of control, over even your artificially constructed reality.

However, however, if you think about it . . . it's true you're forced to interface with your society a lot more. You can't be as reclusive, being a filmmaker. You're forced to be a social animal. Because you have to deal with the economy of the times and the finance of the times and the banks, and you have to deal with the logistics, and the unions, and the politics of the unions, and so on and so on. And all of that is no more than a writer learning how to use his computer or his typewriter, and to learn the language, and having to hone his sensitivity to language, and having to learn the form of the novel or the sonnet, and understand its history, and understand where we are now in its history, for your novel to actually make sense and be relevant. It's easier to ignore the enormous amount of work and patterning and growth and awareness that goes into writing, because you see the guy and he's sitting alone in a room, and it's not much. Compared to a guy on the set with all this *stuff*. But I tell you, at bottom, it's the same act. The same act. An abstract act that only has meaning and force because of the circumstances of the times, and those circumstances can shift so quickly as to make everything you've written completely irrelevant, or inaccessible.

And yet, you've indicated that when you write you want to put aside the whole idea of the time in which you live, that you want the vacuum.

In a certain sense. You can't create art in a vacuum. There's no such thing. But once again, I think I was speaking in response to people who were trying to suggest that *relevant* filmmaking, filmmaking that meant something, that had power, had to be bound up in the politics of the time. And I'm saying that that is a peripheral thing, that there are things you can deal with that are more universal than that, more basic than that. But the peripheries of the art are very much bound up in the culture.

Where does your need come from? We're talking about the need to do this—the need for that rectangle. What's the genesis of your need? You once said that film is not something you're "doing to" the audience, but something that has been "done to" you, which you feel the need to share.

Well, it's a classic need. It's the need to communicate and to involve other people in your experiences and to share them. I think everybody does it. Children do it. Children *insist*; it's an innate thing for children to insist that you be involved in their experience. Children refuse to exist in a vacuum, and if they're forced to, then it becomes a totally pathological situation. And why should that be in human beings, and not be in the case of, let's not say elephants, but maybe mole crickets or beetles? Why do beetles not seem to need to involve other beetles in their experiences?

To find the common ground but also to convey the uniqueness of our experiences, as well. We do that all the time. And when you want to do that to an extent that goes beyond your immediate social circle, then it becomes art. And certainly everybody on TV on a talk show is doing it.

Why do you think we need that? Does it come out of the insecurity of consciousness?

[Pause.] That's a big question. That's central to the impulse to make art, and yet it's universal. I think it's partly to confirm your own existence as an individual, and at the same time, to confirm your existence as part of a whole. The two, at once. It's a bit of a paradox. And I don't think all species do that. I think we're quite unique, in that we insist on our individuality and at the same time insist on our community. It would be very easy if you only needed to confirm your individuality. But part of it is to transcend yourself as an individual. And I wouldn't necessarily say that that is immediately an attempt to become immortal, but I think there is a lot of that in art.

There is an awareness in your work of what I would call "the horror of sharing." Brundle in The Fly *is very wrapped up in trying to get Veronica [Geena Davis] to share his experience. If she doesn't "go through" it's less of an experience for him. He needs her to confirm what he's done, and of course, we've all been through that in relationships. For the Mantle twins in* Dead Ringers, *it's writ large, more obviously, that one doesn't even have an experience unless the other shares it. It's almost a fascism of sharing, where the absorptive ego goes out and needs to bring the other into its world. And we could even say for John Smith [Christopher Walken] in* The Dead Zone *that his sharing of others' experiences, in a way, in the future, present, or past, is a kind of terrifying thing, a very unpleasant thing. So while we tend to put "sharing" on a very high order of human experience — it's good, like a white Christmas or the family gathered together around the dinner table for Thanksgiving, sharing is good — there's a dark side to it, too.*

Yeah, there's a real paradox. It's a very ambivalent situation. Because the situations we're talking about are forced sharing. And as an artist, who does not want to be forced to share, myself, to me it's like totalitarianism, which is a forced sharing of ideals — whether you want to or not!

Like emotional proselytizing.

Yes. Yes. So, what do you do when everybody has the impulse to share? [Laughs.]

You have writers' colonies.

That's right, you have writers' colonies where they don't want to read anybody else's work [laughing] but they *have* to read their own, to everybody. And everybody has to listen to everybody.

But I suppose that's the gropings of the beginning of an understanding of the individual in society — that's a theme in a lot of the stuff that I'm doing. It's an uneasy relationship that one has, which mirrors the relationship of an artist to his civilization. Somehow, they're both necessary, but it's not necessarily an easy or obvious symbiotic relationship. Because, I think, people have the need to transcend themselves, and that's why they attach themselves to the Blue Jays ball team on one level. They feel they are a part of something greater. And it can be quite aggressive and scary when it's in some militant religion, where the desire to immerse your individuality, to annihilate it in favor of the huger part, becomes quite aggressive and destructive. And yet the desire to transcend oneself seems to be as innate as the desire to insist on your individuality. It's a conundrum. It's strange. Beetles don't have to deal with it.

Do you buy artists'—painters, filmmakers, whoever—saying that what they are doing they are basically doing for themselves, because they want to see it. Obviously, a filmmaker needs an audience more than a painter does in a garret, but do you buy this at all?

No, not at all. I think it's just a rationalization, because of whatever failure or your fear that you'll be rejected. But in fact, you desperately, you *desperately* want an audience. My films don't exist without an audience. They absolutely do not exist without an audience. They might as well never have been made. If I no longer had an audience, in film, for whatever reason, and I decided that I would write novels, for example, I would still be writing for an audience. And the fact that the audience never appeared, never materialized, never connected, would be a failure of that process. It would be an interruption, it would be a perversion of that process. You've got to have the audience.

You might have it in a hundred years—

You might, and like Kafka, you might not know your audience. But I mean, Kafka also desperately wanted an audience. He was also terrified of it. He was terrified that he was no good, that he was a failure, and that the audience would materialize and laugh at him, or not understand him. It didn't mean that what he desperately wanted wasn't an audience that loved him and understood him. That's what he wanted. And that's what he got, without knowing it. I often wonder what he would think—

Kafka, soon a major motion picture!

Soon a major philosophical excursion! I mean, the word "Kafkaesque" is a word that has a very specific meaning.

Well, some of the more academic critics have already coined "Cronenbergian."

I think it was a toss-up between Cronenbergesque and Cronenbergian. Cronenbourgeois.

Like Antoniennui.

That's very good.

Before we stop for the day, I want to go back to something you've touched on a number of times: the issue of catharsis. You routinely insist on catharsis in your films as a benefit and as a raison d'être for horror as a genre, and yet I've rarely consumed an artist's work that leaves me feeling less catharsis than yours.

Yeah. Yeah. Well, it's the catharsis of the ambivalent. Maybe that's what I'm selling to you here. If you're simplistic, or your work is simplistic, or you choose to make it simple, then there can be a simple catharsis; and you get that in soap operas, you get it in the traditional comedy, where things are tied up in the end, and everything feels all right after you've gone through some perilous moments. And maybe the catharsis in my films is more complex, in that it is my reconfirming that things are not simple, not easily—perhaps not ever—resolvable. When I need a book, when I need a particular kind of book, I don't want a book in which everything is sweet and neat and nice. What book do you take to the island with you? What really consoles you? Is it something that tells you everything is all right? Is that really consolation? I feel that it's not.

But it seems like one could provide the intellectual ramifications of doubt, which your work does, and still provide the audience more release and recovery than your work does.

This sounds like trout fishing. [Laughs.] Catch and release! It's that whole trout fishing thing, where you don't keep the fish anymore. You catch them, say "Hi!" and throw them back.

You've caught them in the theatre—your audience as trout!

And maybe I don't want to let them go. Maybe catharsis is, literally, letting them off the hook too easily!

I'm not insisting that catharsis is the be-all and end-all, I'm just pointing out that it's a mechanism that seems to be there. And obviously, it can vary hugely from work to work. But certainly, when you begin to mix your blood with the characters' in the film, or if it's a scary film and you're mixing your own anxieties with the anxieties that are being played out in the film, the catharsis does not purge, it makes clear. I suppose my version of it is not totally classical. It's like the frame isolating things out of the chaos on the set. It's sort of saying, "For the moment we're going to concentrate on *this*. I'm not saying this is the whole world, but for the next two hours it's going to be your world, it's going to be our world together, we're really going to dive in deep, and we're going to explore all the aspects of it." To me, that is cathartic, right there. It doesn't have anything to do with whether there is a happy ending, or a solution, or anything else.

Your work is certainly less classically cathartic than, let's say, a filmmaker like Oliver Stone's, to make maybe the boldest, capital letter example: Platoon, *where at the end of the film, if it works, there's a wash of emotion—you've really bathed in that bath of feelings.*

[Laughs.] Are you trying to say that his films are bathetic?

Or you may be very upset in Born on the Fourth of July *that Tom Cruise has a terrible experience in the VA hospital, but by the end, you've recovered, because in the grand—*

Well, that's because Oliver Stone is afraid to say the truth. That's really my feeling. For all the shouting and screaming, he's still not quite able to deliver the final blow, which is that he had these horrible experiences in the VA hospital and it didn't mean *anything*. And it didn't have to happen. And it really has fucked the guy's life, and nothing can be done about it. That's the truth. That's the truth that maybe is not speakable for Oliver Stone, I don't know. It's a hard truth. And the truth does not really lend itself to the dramatic structures that are immediately available to the Hollywood filmmaker. I'm not saying absolute truth, because I don't think there is absolute truth, but in the particular construct you are dealing with for these two hours, there can be relative truths that mean something.

To the extent that you are a Hollywood filmmaker, you have to buy the several suits that are on the rack. And you have to expand or contract to fit them. And it's very rare that it allows you to tell the truth. Because the Hollywood structures, the forms, were never created for the truth—that's never what they were there for. And so you *have* to work in a different form. I mean, Oliver Stone—why pick him?

Well, let's take even David Lynch, who falls back into an ironic stance when confronted with this structure. The other brilliant movie of 1986, in addition to The Fly, *of course, was* Blue Velvet. *At the end, you have the insect in the robin's beak and you have the happy ending. Now, Lynch may be putting quotes around it in a postmodern way, and he may be teasing you with the resolution, and yet, you get resolution. Whereas in a Cronenberg movie, the bird and the insect are still far apart at the end and we are hovering between them, and you want us hovering, it seems.*

Well, when Brundle is shot, is killed, in *The Fly*, to me that's a cathartic moment emotionally. It's a release, it's a release from *his* pain and his agony. It's not a classic cathartic moment because there is no regeneration. I suppose in classic Shakespearean tragedy, you can kill any number of people hideously, but there's always some sense that society goes on, life goes on, something good will come of Hamlet's death, ultimately. And I'm not giving you that. Although I must say, in *Blue Velvet*, the quotes are so huge, and the bird is such an obvious stuffed bird, that you do feel that the classic structure is definitely being mocked.

Mocked and loved in sort of a strange way.

That's right. There's a qualification on it.

Whereas Lynch leaves us with the happy couple, you leave us with Veronica weeping and her ex-lover with his foot and hand eaten away by acid, which may be the best catharsis you can manage. I think it's catharsis for you as a film-maker—

Oh, definitely.

—But I think there's a key distinction between what's cathartic for you, unveiling these fantasies, and what's cathartic for your audience.

Yeah, well, as I suppose I'm insisting on my version of optimism, I'm also insisting on my version of catharsis. It's saying, this is as bad as it is, and if we are to have optimism, we have to be very tough, we have to be very tough in our understanding of what reality is, and what life's possibilities are, and we have to create our optimism out of that. Because if we create it out of pie-in-the-sky, if we create it out of some willed delusion, then it also is a delusion.

I suppose I'm really trying to get through the fog to the reality. It's like tearing aside a veil to see what Moby Dick really is. And I'm kind of being ruthless with myself and with the audience, to get to that. See, I don't think my films are pessimistic, but they're insisting on redefining what optimism is, I suppose. I think too often optimism is an invention, it's a fantasy.

And the function of that fantasy is?

I think avoidance of pain more than anything else. But it's a complex pain. It's not physical, it's many kinds of pain. It's almost a cultural pain. It's a question of expectations that we think are innate, but I don't think are innate. Expectations of what life is and can be and should be are very delusory in the West. I don't know if they are any better in the East.

Has someone sold us this?

I think we developed it ourselves. See, one of the reasons I'm not a true paranoid is because I think there is an optimism built into paranoia. See, if you're a wonderful paranoid, you believe that someone is in control, and to me that's optimistic. You think that someone somewhere has figured it out, has managed to control it, and has a vision of how things should be. To me, that's *optimistic*. So I'm not even allowing myself the optimism of paranoia. When the crazy fascists talk about the Zionist conspiracy, and talk about how the Jews control the world and all the money and that they're all rich, I say, "Where is this conspiracy? I'm Jewish, why haven't they contacted me?"

Ah, but David, you own the means of production of images. There are ways to see these things, you know.

Well, I want control and I want the abdication of control at the same time. It's a difficult trick. And one of the ways I do it is by not working within the accepted forms. The instant you want to invent your own forms, you are immediately abdicating some control and at the same time gaining control, because within these new forms you can do other things that no one has done before. But at the same time they're not as easily absorbed and accepted. It's funny. If you say, "I want to be a mainstream, Hollywood director," you'll get a lot more people seeing your movies, and responding to what you do, but you're much more limited in what you can do. It's a dilemma.

And I'm already balancing on a strange tightrope. I went to Rotterdam, where they did a retrospective of my films. It was very interesting. To them, I'm a total sell-out Hollywood mainstream moviemaker, because they show Chilean underground films, beyond art films, films seen by five people at most.

Things that would make Stereo *look like* It's a Wonderful Life.

Yeah, exactly. Although that is a very strange movie, *It's a Wonderful Life*. You know, two hours of torture for one minute of catharsis. I'm not sure it's a trade-off. People who think it's a wonderful, warm comedy, I don't know what they're seeing.

It's a vicious movie.

It's fucking vicious! And it betrays a mind that really is, I think, misanthropic. That truly is misanthropic. That's been more critical of human beings and America than almost all of William Burroughs, in a way. It's just so nasty. And what a weird approach most people have: what a wonderful Christmas picture!

See, it's the payoff. We go back to catharsis, because if you didn't have that—

If you didn't have that, you'd see the movie as it really was. That's a fake! That's a fake! The movie's not a fake, but the ending is a fake.

Anyway, in Rotterdam it's very interesting. Here, I'm considered marginal, by Hollywood in particular. Marginal, but somehow I'm allowed to plug into it a little bit. There, I'm completely Hollywood! It was a big scandal—there was derision and laughter and disbelief when it was announced that the subject of that year's retrospective was Cronenberg's films. To them, my films are traditional narrative films; they are big-budget; they are distributed by major studios; they are reviewed by normal newspapers. Most of the films that they dealt with were only shown at obscure festivals.

And it makes me realize in no uncertain terms that I am walking a very strange tightrope, a very fine line, in my filmmaking. Because I want it all, really. I want a huge audience. I want to be able to use the machinery of Hollywood to distribute my films and even make the films, but I don't want to accept the Hollywood forms. I don't want to work within those forms, because they're just too restrictive.

You're still willing to accept beginning, middle, and end: traditional narrative structure.

Yeah, but I don't find that to be an acceptance of something from outside. I like that. I actually think that narrative . . . I remember when color first came out.

[Looking out the window, at the swirling snow.] I would imagine that color would have been a good thing to you, growing up in Toronto!

Well, you weren't here in the summer, it was great. But Bergman didn't want to use color at first. He didn't trust that he could control the color, and he wasn't sure of how he would use it. And Kubrick, he still has not made a stereo film, you realize that? He distrusts stereo, still. And in the early days, people mourned the death of the silent film because that was the "pure" film form. And part of the reason was that when you had to keep cameras quiet for sound, it made films rather static—they had to build big booths for them—but it wasn't innate in sound. And as the French critic André Bazin said, and it was considered very heretical at the time, film was always *waiting* for sound, it was never a complete form until sound. And you could say the same thing about color. It was never a complete form until color.

For me, narrative is the same. I love narrative. I think narrative is an additional arrow in your quiver. You can use it to turn back on itself, to illuminate things, to engage questions. So not doing narrative, to me, is not necessarily good. I don't feel trapped by narrative. The narrative of *Naked Lunch* is pretty strange by Hollywood standards, although it's narrative compared to the book.

And you tend to end your narratives with ellipses . . . instead of with periods.

Because it's turning back. I see it as cyclical and turning back on itself and re-reflecting. So I would give up narrative reluctantly. Now, you can approach film strictly as an artist in the sense of painting and sculpture, the way Michael Snow does, that it's rhythms and it's time and it's musical, and it's completely non-narrative. There's nothing wrong with that, but for me, that's not a necessity of freedom, whereas with the Hollywood forms, it is necessary to abandon those if you're really going to have freedom. But narrative is not one of those things I would abandon. There are many versions of narrative.

And some have argued that simply because one page follows another, and one frame of film follows another, you have the insistence of narrative—

Yes, in time, you definitely have a sequence in time. You can say the film has to be linear—all films—because it has a beginning, middle, and end, even if it starts at second one, and ends at second thirty, and second fifteen is in the middle. There is some truth to that, in that it plays through time.

Now, video is interesting because it allows film to be more like literature. Because the audience—I would say consumer but it has bad connotations— can control it. The audience for video has more control over the image and therefore can be more involved.

And less involved, as well, than in a theatre.

Well, I wonder.

The phone rings, the sun sets outside, the kids come in—

But I see that as more involved, not less.

How so?

Because in a cinema you are abstracting yourself from your daily life to have this special moment, this sacrament. And people can get very excited about that and mourn its passing, as it does seem to be passing. But the very fact that you have abstracted yourself from your everyday life means you have disinvolved yourself, the process, from your life. The fact that you listen to music while you're doing a bunch of other things means the music can work itself into the nooks and crannies and crevices of your life.

It may mean that you're not really listening to it either, though it may appeal to your unconscious in some ways.

But maybe that's the best way for it to appeal.

It could—if you want someone to watch your film and miss whole chunks of dialogue. Over the last month and a half, I've seen everything you've done, twice, on videocassette at home, and while it's nice to be able to start and stop, and go back, and watch the head explode in Scanners *in stop-frame, which is really quite beautiful—*

Yeah, it is.

—It's like Kubrick's atomic bombs exploding at the end of Strangelove, *but I would still rather go to a cinema and sit in the dark and have the image projected large and fill my vision, and not be interrupted by the phone or the Federal Express guy, because I want to be more involved, not less. I don't think it's removing yourself from your daily life to go to the theatre; I think it's like ritual. When you stop crushing millet because you're going to form a circle with your other tribesmen to engage in a dance, it's not that the dance is not a part of your daily life and your daily life is only crushing the millet—it's because this is the time for ritual.*

Yes. But nobody ever reads a book like that. Nobody ever reads a book like the way we go to cinema.

Right! And part of the power of cinema is that the audience does not have the control over time that it does in literature. In literature, we can stop, skip, back

*up a page, whereas cinema is something that is "done to us." Which leads to some
people's suspicions about the passive consumer of images . . .*

But video, once again, you can speed through the parts that don't interest
you and hook up with the parts that do. Which is like rereading your favorite
passages and scenes in a book, or skipping a chapter if you find it boring.
It's really a toss-up, I think, as to whether that's more or less involving. It
certainly is, as you say, taking control away from me, the filmmaker. I've got
less control, there's no question. But maybe I'm more willing to give up that
control than you are. Maybe I'm not seeing it as such a bad thing. I'm not
sure. It's happening though, it's a fact of life. I've never shot in wide-screen,
and I don't think I ever will, and the reason is because I want the film to
translate to television easily. And I've done that right from the very beginning.

It's almost unthinkable now, that you did not have access to films except
when they came out in the cinema and maybe disappeared forever. There
was a time when there were not rep cinemas, so when Hollywood movies
came out, you saw them that weekend, or you didn't see them. That was it.
And your references to them and your remembrances of them were all based
on that one Saturday when you went to the theatre and saw it.

Now you can "own" the film.

Now you can own it. And I think, ultimately, maybe not experience for experience, but maybe over ten years, twenty years, when you can have access
to a film for twenty years because it's in your drawer, and you can take it
out and look at it, ultimately, maybe there will be more involvement. And
the abdication of some responsibility and some control by the director of the
film will be balanced by the involvement over a long period of time by the
person seeing the film.

SESSION TWO

I'm wondering, as we were talking about order and chaos: you once talked about something "overwhelming and incredibly potent, and you don't ever really recover once it hits you" in connection with Sartre's nausea, and I was wondering if there was anything that hit you in your wonder years—

I'm in them now!

—that you never recovered from, in any kind of way?

Sure. C. S. Lewis's book, *Allegory of Love*. Technically, it's an analysis of medieval literature, particularly Chaucer, but he cleverly and slyly discusses romantic love as a literary invention and basically, in a very quiet, scholarly, and genteel manner, makes it very clear that much of what we take to be a given of human nature—as it relates to love—is in fact a literary invention of about the eleventh century. And that in fact, prior to that, it's easily demonstrable that romantic love did not exist. Period. Now that was shocking!

When you did you read that?

I read that in university. And he shows how in the whole idea of putting a woman on a pedestal—now this is kind of amusing, but certainly in the fifties, and sixties as well, it was very much in force, and still is really, maybe not on the leading edge of cultural invention but certainly underneath that—romantic love lives. And he points out how that was based on the feudal system: the idea of the feudal lord, and how the woman becomes like the feudal lord, and the swain, the lover, the man, becomes the courtier, the man who courts the woman and puts her on a pedestal and sort of worships her from afar. The Victorian era was heavily into that; the woman you married was a goddess, the one on the pedestal. Of course, it meant you couldn't fuck her, because how could she be a goddess and be this slut that you really wanted? So there was difficulty there and a lot of men had mistresses—you couldn't solve the duality with one woman.

That's still a huge part of our cultural heritage. And the idea is still that you will find *the one* that you will live with and worship and grow old with. And C. S. Lewis is kind of saying, this is just a literary invention, and human beings didn't expect that or even understand that before then. And it goes back to the poems of Catullus–I studied Latin for about eleven years and this was very accessible to me–which show that the real friendship and real love, in many societies, was between the same sex. Men for men, women for women. And that heterosexuality was really for making babies and doing that social thing, but not really where you go for real love. And that's kind of interesting, a whole other amazing take on human nature.

Did you buy into the ideal of romantic love in your first marriage?

I'm sure I wasn't any more immune to that than anyone else, though in the late sixties and early seventies things were hipper. I figured it was a marriage and you do that and you expect to stay together a really long time–to that extent, I suppose I did. But that's not why this was shocking. I was reading this before my first marriage. It was really a one-two to the head and then the gut, it was kind of an intellectual and visceral blow. And that had a huge impact on me, a huge impact. Certainly the fifties were structured around romantic love as an ideal. No question, absolutely no question.

The transformational aspects of love, relationship, and the body itself–the mutating possibilities–are something that you have verbally endorsed as exciting, inventive, interesting, attractive; and yet your films always show those sorts of mutations and transformations in a quite horrific light.

Hmm, once again it's a question of aesthetics and a few other things. Dramatically, of course, something that goes wrong is always more interesting than something that goes right. I have to confess to being part of that structure. It's Shavian: conflict is the essence of drama. I mean, if a guy transforms into a fly and it's really nice and everybody likes it, you know, what have you got? You've got a comedy on TV. But you don't have heavy-duty dramatic stuff. So that's part of it.

And the other part is that I'm perhaps admitting in the films that what might be potentially positive in theory is maybe quite difficult to manipulate to the point where it's positive in practice. Like communism, for example. And many other things political and emotional. The theory can be manipulated, but the reality can't always be. So when I'm verbalizing, I very well may be giving you the theory, and in the films I'm giving you the possible outcome of the practice. Now, do I contradict myself? Well, very well then, I do.

I'm trying to explore it; I'm trying to say, well, what happens when we put this theory into practice? That's the extent to which my films are my little lab experiments. Let's try it out, let's see what happens. Here's a guy who's transforming into *this*, and uh oh, I see a problem, it's not turning out so nice, what's he going to do? In a way, it's play. It's the way children play to try things out.

Children have consciousness of their play, but there's not a cautionary tone to it, while in your work—

No, no, there's not a cautionary tone, but there is an experimental tone. It's a glee in trying it out, knowing at the same time that you're not living it. Kids can get quite thrilled playing scary stuff, in safety, knowing that they can back out. And that's what's similar to some of the things that happen on the set. I mean, there you are with your actors and you've got this playpen and you've got a drawer full of costumes and you start putting on the costumes and you play around. We all feel that. However seriously we take it because it's our profession, there is a sense of play there, too.

Do you have the same attraction to the inventive and the extreme in your own life that you do in your films?

No! Definitely not.

What if you couldn't sublimate it into your work—or project it?

I think it's more like a projection. Sublimation is a whole other thing. What if I couldn't? I don't know if the pressure would get to the point where I'd have to "act out"—those terrible words. Or whether it would just remain repressed and I'd end up being a somewhat hazily dissatisfied, not very fulfilled person, but not necessarily doing anything particularly antisocial or spectacular. I really don't know.

Does your art keep you sane the way Ben Pierce's art keeps him sane in Scanners?

Yeah, but we know that he's wrong when he says that. Because he's completely mad, isn't he?

I know. And your cover story is that you're completely sane, and not only completely sane, but have no touch of neurosis.

Yeah, well, I won't say no touch. But, relatively speaking, I think that's all true. Because from the very beginning, the first little glimmer of artistic stirrings, I assumed that I would find my art form and that I would be relatively successful in practicing it. And I have had some shaky moments when I started to doubt, but not too many of those moments, I have to say. So I have never had to deal with what the consequences might be of not being able to practice my art. And I'm very curious about filmmakers in particular, but writers and any other artists as well, I'm fascinated by any artist that suddenly stops. For any reason. Because he is physically incapable of continuing; or because the circumstances of practicing his art have shifted and he can no longer do it anymore—when his art form disappears. If you're a great radio writer and there's no radio to write anymore, what do you do? I am fascinated by that, and am very interested to read about that, and obviously the reason I'm fascinated is because I'm wondering what I would do under those circumstances.

What have you fantasized?

I think it's very possible, for one, to not be physically able to take the demands of filmmaking. It is rough. I like to think that I will be something like John Huston. I look forward to the wheelchair and the oxygen mask, [breathes heavily] saying "Cut!" That would be good. I would like to drop dead on the set. I think that would be great. Now, if it doesn't happen, then I think for me it would be very natural to write. I know that Jean Renoir wrote some novels when he could no longer get films made. I've never read the novels. That disturbs me, that they're not that well known. But on the other hand, it is something that would come naturally to me. So I wouldn't feel like "no movies" means "no access to art."

I know you started as a fiction writer. Do you have a couple of novels in the drawer?

No, never got that far. Never got that far. A lot of attempted novels that no longer exist. I didn't keep them in the drawer.

Do you ever write in a way that's not connected with the filmic process?

No. I don't. I'm constantly tempted to, though. I just like literary things. It pleases me. I go through waves when I read a lot of novels and try to plug into what's going on in the art of the novel, and then there are periods when I just don't read at all, anything but magazines, let's say. At the moment, I'm going through a fairly intensely literary phase. But I love the act of writing and the idea of writing. I like it a lot. If I keep making movies I might have to be forced into trying my hand at a novel or I may never do it.

What do you do when you're not working?

I'm never not working.

You're working all day, every day, seven days a week?

Well, in a really irresponsible, non-specific way, yeah, I think I am.

The myth of the writer on holiday is that he's never on holiday because he's always working.

I guess that's what I'm saying, and I think it to be true. So much of what a filmmaker does is not making a film. Right now, I'm being a post-production supervisor, producer, worrying about where the prints are going, worrying about the theatres and how they're set up, worrying about the processing of the first twenty prints. I'm going to be spending time in the screening room looking at a couple of reels of each of several prints at random, trying to make sure that the corpse is in the right condition, and ready to be presented, so that it will give the simulation of life, let's say. And yet it's part of the filmmaking process; it's not really a creative part, but it's a necessary part. I get dirt under my fingernails. I'm a mechanic. And it's okay. It's necessary. And talking to you is work. And not only work because I have to do it to promote the film, but also because you ask me questions that force me to be analytical about what I'm doing, which I'm not normally. I'm not analytical when I'm doing it. And it makes me start to think about my next film, and so that's work, too.

Now, I don't know if anyone can really shut off from work. In a way it's my sophistry to say I'm never not working. On the more pragmatic front, I almost never take a holiday. I don't go away for two weeks.

Is the car racing your holiday?

The car racing is a very intense, compressed little holiday.

How long have you been doing it?

Since about '81. I used to do it in the sixties, but I came back to it in '81.

How many cars do you own?

I have four race cars that are all from the late fifties, early sixties.

Are you good at it?

I'm pretty good at it, yeah. In the world of club racing, I'm a competent club racer. I'm okay.

Is there anything else you're passionately interested in?

Not to the same extent. Not on the hobby front, no.

I know the body is more than a hobby for you. At one point you went so far as to say that you'd really like the project of redesigning the human body. Of course, I guess you do that in your films.

I do try, yeah. The screen is littered with failed experiments.

How would you redesign the body?

You should have given me the weekend to think about that one.

It's an extra credit question.

[Pause.] It's a good question. I really can't answer it spontaneously. Anything I say in the context of an interview has huge implications.

Do you ever feel trapped by your own reputation of going further than other people will go? Trapped by the idea that the audience carries with them a certain expectation when they go to see a Cronenberg film?

No, I love disappointing people's expectations. I really do. It's a perverse power trip for me. So, in fact, no, I don't feel the slightest bit trapped. I'm very stubborn. And I really just do what I fucking well want, is the truth. Which is why I say I take full responsibility for what I put up on the screen.

And in truth, I feel that's what any filmmaker ultimately wants to be able to say. I don't want to say I was forced to do it by the producer any more than I was forced to do it by the critics or by my public. I want to say I was forced to do it by myself. That's why I've done it.

So you don't still feel the kind of compulsion to show the unshowable and speak the unspeakable that you did earlier?

Not if I don't feel like it. Not if I don't feel like it that day. And I might feel like it tomorrow. But today I don't. The artist's duty to himself is a culmination of immense responsibility and immense irresponsibility. I think those two interlock.

Does the artist have any moral or social responsibility?

No. No. Still doesn't, after all these years. Still irresponsible, after all these years. As a citizen, of course; as a parent, of course. But as an artist, that's where the paradox is, your responsibility is to be irresponsible. As soon as you talk about social or political responsibility, you've amputated the best limbs you've got as an artist. You are plugging into a very restrictive system that is going to push and pull and mold you, and is going to make your art totally useless and ineffective.

You spoke the other day about Hollywood "limiting." How is it limiting you if you are making exactly the films you want to make?

But I haven't made my films within Hollywood. I flirt with it, I want to use the machine, I want the machinery of Fox to distribute *Naked Lunch* in the United States. The closest I came was with *The Fly*, which was the only studio film I've done; it was a Mel Brooks, Brooksfilm production, although it was already understood it was going to be a Fox picture. And in a way *Videodrome* was; oddly, it was a Universal picture, one of the most conservative studios that ever existed. But, if you can slip through the cracks, and you feel you can manipulate the machine without being manipulated back, it's a dangerous game, but you can try it. It's difficult to make a film these days, even as an independent, without some connection with the Hollywood machine, even if it's just in terms of US distribution. But how close can you come to the flame without being burned? That's really the question.

If there's pleasure in the image (and I think we're all agreed here in Western civilization that there's pleasure in the image) I would think there would be, for someone as wrapped up in it as you, pain as well, if the image is not exactly as you want it to be. You once spoke of becoming physically ill when you looked through the viewfinder and found an improperly composed image.

That's true. That's still true. And that's why I'm so obsessive about the interpos, the interneg, the check print. Making sure they're all right, and that the release prints are going to properly represent the film. The prints that are made from the negative are called answer prints. And they are the closest generation to the original negative. But then you can only make so many prints from that, so you get into duplicate negatives, and second and third generation prints. And the further you go from the image you captured, the more pain there is. That's why I get obsessive about it. You try not to over-obsess, because you could drive yourself mad, and could spend the rest of your life tracking the one movie you made and making sure that every screening was perfect, and only screening it in one theatre at a time and being there every time. You could do that. And most directors who are serious have the impulse to do that. You have to suppress that.

Didn't you spend $7,000 of your own money in Toronto once, making sure that The Dead Zone *had the right sound in the theatre?*

Yeah, because it wasn't going to be played in stereo and it was my first stereo picture. And Cineplex was distributing here and they did not put it in a stereo cinema. And that meant that there was nowhere in Toronto, my home town, where you could see the film and hear it the way it was supposed to be. Now that drove me *mad.* It was not something I wanted to do, but it was a very informative experience to run my own theatre. And as soon as I did that, Cineplex switched it into a stereo cinema, because it was in the press and was embarrassing to them. That's the power politics of movies. I couldn't force them to put it in a stereo theatre until I competed with them.

On set, what percentage of your time filming do you actually spend at the TV monitor?

During shooting, it's an incredibly valuable tool. I can't imagine shooting a film without it. It just gives me more power. I love the video tap, the monitor system. It's a very interesting subject. I did do some videotape shooting for TV, back in the old days, and you'd use three or four cameras, and you'd run your TV show like a play, from beginning to end, and switch, while you were playing it, from camera to camera. That's how you did your cutting. You did it right there, on the spot.

And so it wasn't such a shock to me when I first used the video tap on a feature. I think it was on *The Fly.* It seems incredible to me now, because I can't imagine working without it. It just means that you are riding the camera at all times. Imagine a moving shot: I'm on the dolly, and I'm operating the camera, but I don't know when the cameraman does it that he's doing the same moves at the same time as I was, if I can't see what he's doing. And so the composition during the course of a moving shot, for example, is something that I have no idea is right until the rushes the next day, when it might be too late to re-shoot it.

With video, you're watching as it's being shot. You can see the composition. And if you don't like it, you can say, "Let's do it again, but *this* way."

It's not minor stuff, it's the essence of your art: the composition, the framing, the movement. To not have that precise control over it is a real liability. And it's fantastic to have that power.

Now, a lot of cameramen are very paranoid about it, because suddenly, what used to be an intimate thing—between themselves and the camera—is up for grabs. *Everybody* can see it; there are monitors all over the set. I mean, once you've got one monitor, you can have any number.

They replicate.

They replicate. They're viral. And I, for example, having had the experience of shooting a couple of TV shows on Betacam, would walk around with a pocket TV set that I could flip up at any time and see what was being done on the set. I love that. I love the commonality of it. I'm not afraid of it, and I don't feel I need the secrecy of the old way—where only the people who got to peep through the lens really knew what was going on. And it is so efficient, it saves so much time, too. Now the props guy doesn't have to say, "Should I worry about what's under the table? Can you see that in the shot?" He looks at the monitor and he knows. He doesn't have to ask. It really increases the sense of community among the people making the film. And of course it also gives visiting journalists the illusion that they're getting an idea of what the film is going to be. And of course they have no idea.

See, in a way, you still have that secrecy. Because no one is really putting it together the way you, the director, are putting all the shots together, and noticing all the nuances or subtleties. Everybody is looking at the monitor for something else, and only the director is looking at it for everything. Which is as it should be.

Is there any way you would define the way you frame images as being uniquely yours?

No. I can't. It's nothing that I can come close to articulating. But it's interesting. I love it; when someone came up to me over *Dead Ringers* and said, "Your bizarre visual sense is so strong," and so on, he was talking about composition. And I said, "You know, I never put the camera on the floor and shoot up somebody's nose, I don't do those sort of Orson Wellesian things, I never have the camera tilted off axis, it's always actually pretty level." And most of the shots in *Dead Ringers* are close-ups shot with a very conventional 50-millimeter lens, I don't do like 9.8-millimeter close-ups. He said, "You know, you're right. Well then, how did you achieve that?" I said, "I don't know." [Laughs.] It's everything. It's the dialogue as much as the composition.

You're more willing to stick with a tight, controlled frame—more willing to show "talking heads" than a lot of other auteurs are.

Yeah. Yeah. To me, the "talking head" is the *essence* of cinema. If you look at a baby, the most fascinating thing to a baby, a newborn, is the human face. The baby will look at your face and watch your face move and want to touch it; it gives you a whole other insight into what a face is. We get very used to them, but in fact, if it's a fantastic head, and what it's talking about is fantastic, then you can't have anything better. It's the best! So I'm not afraid of it. I'm not afraid to sit on a close-up and let it happen. If you've got the right face saying the right things at the right moment, you've got everything cinema can offer.

Is there an insecurity among certain filmmakers, who may not have written their piece themselves, who are jealous of the power of the word?

Absolutely. It's such a cliché, but I think it absolutely is true. And it's demonstrably true in some movies, where the camera is wandering all over the place, and craning, and doing this or that, and what you really fucking want to see is that face saying that stuff to this other face. That's what you want to see. But the director is not letting you see it.

Let's take your friend Martin Scorsese, in The Color of Money, *for instance, where the amount of camera movement seemed almost gratuitous for what is a very conventional story, which he didn't author.*

Yeah, well, it's conceivable that his solution to getting all of the juice possible out of that story was to put a lot of energy into stuff that was sort of peripheral to the story itself. It might not even be a bad ploy, in that case. And whether it works or not depends on a zillion different things. But we've all seen films where the camera is just not where you want it to be, and often it's the director's own stubborn refusal to be there, because for some reason he's insecure.

Your screenplays are quite detailed, full of description, but are completely bereft of camera instructions.

That's true. Often, the detail is to convey something to people who are reading: a tone, or something subtle that can only be revealed by detail, which maybe I'll decide to change on the day of shooting, but which at least gives you an idea of what the tone is. And I want it to read well, I want it to read more like fiction than something else. But I've read other scripts, let's say those of Robert Towne, that go much further than what I would bother to do.

But the lack of camera instruction, and your unwillingness to storyboard anything but technical sequences, I assume provides you with a kind of freedom on set to make it up as you go.

Well, the reason I don't put the camera instructions in there is because I *know* I'm going to make it up on the set, so why waste my time pretending?

There are one or two moments per script where I give a bit of a camera indication, just because it needs to be clarified because of context. But I want to make it up on the set. It's very palpable and tangible to me. It's not an abstract thing at all. I wouldn't know how to make a storyboard of a scene of two people in a room, which is a dialogue scene, unless I have the room and have the people. I want to involve my actors in the choreography of the scene. Why manipulate them like puppets when I've hired them because they're wonderful actors? One of the things an actor does is use his body. They're like dancers. A moment of dialogue at the window with the head turned away from us, and then suddenly on a certain phrase turn back to us, has a totally different effect than the same dialogue delivered sitting in front of the window. I want to work with the actors. I want them to surprise me. I want them to show me some possibilities that I haven't thought of. I'm not so arrogant that I think I can anticipate every possibility, and choose the best one, and storyboard it, before I've ever been in the room with the real actors. A lot of storyboards are done before actors are cast.

Nonetheless, do you have a lot in your mind's eye on each day's shoot, or a blank slate?

Blank. Very blank. Often, though, something that I've done in earlier parts of the shoot starts to suggest something else. Parallels and interconnections. Really, the Orson Welles statement about "presiding over a series of accidents" is only coy and arch from a distance. When you're on the set, it's really a pretty accurate description of what goes on. The accidents are often very small, little things. Somebody will be standing at the window, and you say, "I like that! What happens if you do the dialogue there?" And everything snaps into place. Well, that's an accident. If the actor hadn't stood there, you might not have thought of it. Why resist that? Why cut those possibilities out?

Storyboarding, to me, is a control-freak thing or a security blanket. I don't condemn it, because for some people it obviously works, and it's fine. I don't promote my system as *the* system. Also, I know that a lot of people storyboard who know they are going to change the storyboards, but they like to have it as kind of a security, so if they suddenly come up blank one day, they at least have got this stuff to work with. I just like to go out without a net.

A great deal of scientific discovery comes through happy accident.

For sure; it's the same creative process.

In fact, there's a parallel between the scientist and the artist, because neither has complete control over what is created.

See, that's something that's very misunderstood about my scientists. People think I'm standing apart from them, and showing them as sort of evil and misguided. No. They're my artists. They're my heroes. Because I think the process is the same. A brilliant scientist is as creative as a brilliant artist. Books are full of the inventions and the inspirations that came out of dreams, out of drug use, out of everything—that then later became hard-core scientific dogma.

And neither scientist nor artist is fully responsible for what happens with their creation?

I've never said that.

Well, are they? Are you as an artist responsible fully for your creation?

Yes, you are.

But once it gets out there, it may be interpreted in all sorts of ways, including ways which you might be violently opposed to.

That's right.

Let's attach this question to your work. Videodrome, *for example. Are you responsible if some people read the film, for two reasons, as a very conservative, reactionary approach to mass media? One, it posits a direct link between image and action, and two, it shows a breakdown in the distinction between image and reality. Now, those are two of the greatest concerns of the people who are in favor of censorship. So, one could say that* Videodrome *is a good argument for censorship. Are you responsible for that?*

Well, I'm not sure I agree with that reading.

No, I know you don't, but—

We should really cut to the chase. Your example is subtle. Let's take the most obvious example: what if you made a movie that actually induced people to kill other people? That's really what we're talking about, the fact that an art object, an artifact, can be misinterpreted or interpreted and can be plugged into a political system in many ways that you perhaps could never imagine but that are absolutely contrary to what you would want or believe: *that* can't stop you. Because it's uncontrollable, and unanticipatable. And also, you just know that people—out of sheer orneriness—are going to do that, and maybe even gleefully. But that just stimulates debate. And to me, that's always healthy. The real question could be, getting simplistic about it, what if you could make a movie that would actually cause people to kill other people? A direct, causal link; these people would not have killed anybody if they had not seen the movie. The movie triggers off a psychosis, or something—

There are lawsuits, right now, having to do with that same principle, regarding heavy metal music and teen suicide.

That's right. And the question to the artist has to be, let's say you spent three years writing this book, and somehow it can be shown to you that reading this book will cause one person out of a hundred to commit suicide—it's a direct causal link—what do you do? Do you publish the book anyway? Do you destroy the book? Do you suppress the book? Do you hold it back until circumstances have changed and this won't happen anymore? Do you deny the reality of this thing that's been proved? It's an interesting question. Because only *there* is there a direct link between the artist's responsibility and the citizen's social responsibility. The problem is, of course, when are you ever going to have direct proof of anything, especially something as complex as that? That's the problem.

I don't know what I would do. I might end up saying, "You know what, even if a thousand people died because of my movie, it's worth it. Not just to me, but to society." So maybe that's a rationalization. Who knows? But it's not likely I'm ever going to find out. The world being what it is, there's almost never one use or one effect from one thing, whether it's the A-bomb or atomic energy or drugs or a gun or anything else. Multiple effects.

Let's get into one of your very favorite subjects: sexual politics.

Let's go down to the bar and have a few drinks and discuss sexual politics. [Laughs.]

You've been asked before about the "sexual humiliation" of women in your films, and I'll just read you one of your responses, which is maybe the best way into this discussion: "I think it certainly has to do with the fact that I am male, and my fantasies and my unconscious are male. I think I give a reasonable amount of expression to the female part of me, but I still think that I'm basically heterosexual male. . . . I have no reason to think that I have to give equal time to all sexual fantasies whether they're my own or not. Let those people make their own movies—leave me alone to make mine. . . . If I'm going to get into scenes of bondage and torture, I'll show a female instead of a male. . . . Fantasies are sexual, not sexist."

I say "basically heterosexual." I was recently talking to a journalist who was making a very cogent point of the gayness that goes through all my work. And I said, well, you know, I'm interested in sexuality, and in my normal fashion, I don't want to limit myself to what I might *live* out of. One of the reasons you do art is to live other people's lives and to plug into other modalities. One of the reasons actors act is to be other people. So I'm not afraid of homosexuality, and I'm not afraid of exploring those things. And I have explored those things in the films. There are a few men I sort of whip and torture in the movies, too.

Interestingly enough, one of the reasons you said, years ago, that you were "not one hundred percent with Burroughs," was that his fantasies of hanging boys being sodomized were not your fantasies.

I understand that buggering a hanging boy is not exactly a sexual fantasy of William Burroughs'. Because I know where that comes from. It's being flippant to say, "That's his fantasy, not mine." In fact, it's as much my fantasy as his, in the sense that when I read it, he managed to make it erotic for me. He managed to make it a fantasy of mine when I read it. What is normally repulsive to you is suddenly seductive and erotic: that's my reading of Burroughs. A lot of people respond to the surface, and turn away, saying, "Oh this is disgusting, I don't want anything to do with it!" But if you get into it and don't fight it, you allow the book access to your unconscious, you find it appeals to a lot of places that are disturbing.

When I'm making a film, I'm no longer a reader of the book, I'm now the creator of this world that I'm going to put up on the screen. I'm operating from a different place. I talked to William [Burroughs] about not being sure what I wanted the sexuality of *Naked Lunch* to be, because my sexuality is different from his. I could not guarantee him that the film would portray, or duplicate, his sensibility of sexuality. And he said it was okay because he's not very censorious.

Do you find the scene in the parrot cage in the film, with a similar image, erotic?

No.

That's the most explicitly gay image of sexuality in the film and it's horrifying and bloody and very disturbing.

Yes, and before I'm attacked for this, "Cronenberg is portraying gay sex as the image of the old queen sucking the life out of the fresh young boy"—

And there is vampiric imagery earlier in that same sequence. Get ready for The Advocate.

Yes. I'm ready. But, but, there will be, necessarily, a willful misunderstanding of the movie in order for them to carry out the political attack with full gusto. Because I think it's very clear that at this point in the movie I'm still having the lead character not fully come to terms with himself in terms of his sexuality. Basically, the guy is gay. He creates a world in which everybody recognizes him as gay, and in fact, people proposition him and set him up with other men. But he's not ready to accept it. He keeps saying, "I don't want to fuck him."

We're to think that that's his cover story. I'm not sure the audience gets the received meaning that the guy is gay.

But who is telling him it's his cover story? It's his own fucking typewriter. When he talks to his typewriter he's talking to himself, just as any writer who's writing is talking to himself. And so imagine allowing the typewriter to become your unconscious, and it's saying, "You're going to have to engage in homosexual acts. We know you're willing to go through with this, you're going to have to do it because it's your cover story." [My and Cronenberg's feet brush accidentally under the table.] I noticed you just touched me there. It's a very delicate moment for this to happen.

I'm sorry, David.

[Returning to the subject.] And you say, "Oh gee, do I really have to get fucked by a guy?" Who's saying it? He's saying it to himself. He's forcing himself to come to terms with what he is; that's the structure of the movie. Now, if you don't get the structure of the movie you don't understand it. You see everything as literal, even though it's obvious that much of the movie is not realistic, impossible. There is no giant centipede. And what is he seeing in that cage, in that bedroom?

I give you the clue. When he walks by, we hear Kiki and Cloquet in sexual ecstasy. We hear orgasmic moanings and groanings. We hear Kiki's voice going, "Oh, oh." And we hear Cloquet actually say, "Kiki, oh Kiki." But Lee [Peter Weller] has gone off and taken this drug and is totally stoned, and he thinks he's coming back like twenty seconds later, but it's probably an hour later, and he's walking by the master bedroom, and he hears Kiki and Cloquet fucking each other. And so he's feeling guilty and jealous, because Kiki is his lover, and now he opens the door and what is he really seeing? I think, it should be obvious, maybe not the first time through, I'll admit that, but when you understand the film, he's seeing Kiki and Cloquet fucking. They are naked in bed and they're fucking. But he has to construct a horrific, unbearable, repulsive image around it for him to respond to—because his response is revulsion, guilt, fear. So he hallucinates this thing that he can run away from, and sort of disconnect from. Kiki is already decaying, the giant centipede has eaten him.

That to me is the mechanism that's going on. It's not at all saying that gay sex involves a kind of centipede-like sexuality. What it is, is I'm insisting that you stay in there with my characters, and not immediately jump to political imagery from the outside. Within the movie, it's perfectly conceivable that Kiki and Cloquet are having perfectly wonderful sex. The more wonderful the sex, the more horrific and disgusting it is for Lee.

Let's retreat from Naked Lunch, *briefly—*

That's a good title, *Retreat from Naked Lunch.* I can see the sequel.

You have a kind of—I don't know if we want to say—"repressed" homosexuality in a lot of your work. In the first two films you did, Stereo *and* Crimes of the Future, *your lead actor certainly had a gay presence; and then you gave Marilyn Chambers an underarm phallus in* Rabid—

But I gave her a vagina; I gave her a cunt, too! First there's the cunt, and then the phallus—it's both, you got everything! I gave her everything!

And you give Max Renn [James Woods] a vagina in his stomach in Video-drome, *and vagina dentata as well. So obviously there's a sort of bisexual play through the work. Has this always been a part of your consciousness? You were just talking about Catullus and same-sex love.*

Yeah. I think it has been. I think we start off with what Freud called a poly-morphous perverseness, which is not a negative thing. It's a child's sexuality before it becomes specific and genitalized and acculturated. We have what I called an "omnisexuality," which does not recognize the sorts of normal barriers and liaisons and taboos. And to the extent that I'm interested in ex-ploring stuff that's beyond taboo, I would explore not just bisexuality, but any kind of sexuality. Dog sexuality. Animal sexuality. Insect sexuality. Whatever. The sexuality of food or touch or words. So I don't think I'm limiting myself to bisexuality. It's just that that's the most obvious to people. They might not see some of the other things I do as sexual, and I do.

The sex blob in *Naked Lunch,* that the typewriter becomes, is a kind of all-purpose sexual *thing.* It has every genital part that you could imagine plus a few that you couldn't imagine. It's got vaginal sex, it's got anal sex, it's got about twenty different things going on. I hope the censors don't quite perceive it. I hope they don't stop-frame it. It's always moving, so it's a little hard to see.

It's humping the floor—

It's humping anything! It will hump anything! It's worse than your dog in heat. So I really think I'm looking beyond the normal structures that we ac-cept and that are easily recognizable. And I would say it's not just bisexual-ity. It's not gayness. It's more than that, that I'm looking for.

Have you experienced any of these things in your life, or only the world of the image?

Unfortunately not. Unfortunately, I haven't. Well, I won't say I haven't, but not in the sensationalist way that any journalist would of course want to dis-cover. I remember being at university with a woman, and talking to some professor, and he suggesting that we join him in this orgy that he was going to. And I said I had never done that before, but I had a feeling it wouldn't work. I had a feeling that the same old jealousies would come out—oh, she's fucking him, getting more attention, and all I got is this old guy over here and really I want that cute girl over there—and don't you find that that's a problem? And he said, "You're right," the orgies had not been working out very well. Despite the fact that everybody in the room had read Norman O. Brown's *Life Against Death* and was really ready to go the distance in trying to form a Dionysian consciousness and would take drugs together—it *still* wasn't fucking working out. People were being paranoid. People would feel neglected. People would feel jealous.

And you think that says something about human nature or just about our particular culture?

I think it says something about human nature. I think both, maybe. So I never really got into that stuff, because I could sort of anticipate, before I did, all the reasons why it wouldn't work out. I guess I was never a hippie in the true sense, because there was never a moment when the skepticism dropped away, or the cynicism dropped away, or just the honest doubt. I never bought into any of that stuff, but it was exhilarating to think that society was changing and it was possible.

Now, however, within the act of "normal," quote, heterosexual sex, you do have these Dionysian moments. And that I have experienced, definitely. Without the aid of drugs, I will add, because I really don't do that. Moments when you are not male or female, you are just sexual. And you don't know whether you are being fucked or you are fucking and it doesn't make any difference. I really feel that I have felt that. And at the best moments, that's the way it always is. You lose, to a huge extent, your individuality. And yet, it's the individuality that heightens the sexuality—you know who you're having sex with.

Now, I'm fascinated by scenes in *Prick Up Your Ears* where twenty guys would be fucking each other in a public toilet, with the lights out, not knowing who anybody was, or what anybody looked like. Part of me says, I'd love to try that. And if you're doing that, it doesn't matter if it's men or women or a combination of them or animals or fucking anything. But I also know what human beings are like. And I know what venereal diseases are like, too—they like to take advantage of those moments. And so I think the closest I've come to experiencing any of that stuff is just in what to an onlooker would be the straightest kind of normal, socially approved, possibly even missionary-position sex. But internally, there's a moment when you feel you are pure sexuality—neither male nor female. I think maybe that's the way. Maybe gays can experience heterosexuality through gay sex; maybe if you get to the purest form of whatever your specific sexuality is, that's where all the sexuality merges. And that's what it feels like I'm exploring in my movies. It doesn't then have anything to do with, "He should come out of the closet, it's obvious he should fuck guys." To me, I just shrug, and say, "Not really."

Can you identify with any same-sex feelings, let's say when you were prepubescent or pubescent?

I think so. I can remember a moment or two being sexually attracted to a guy who was very female. It was almost like he was a woman. So what does that mean? I remember acting in an underground film, in Toronto, where there was supposed to be an orgy, and I ended up hugging some guy and kind of kissing his cheek and stuff. And I was really quite turned off, by the hair on his legs, by his beard. It didn't do it for me. And yet, you have a man you love—your father, your brother—you hug them, and it's not exactly sexual, but it's physical and there's love involved, and at that moment, the beard and the hairy legs are fine. So it's not simple, that stuff.

Well, you're not nibbling on the beard or stroking the hairy legs in that kind of clinch.

No, no you're not. But you're feeling maleness, and you're taking comfort from that. I think it's like taking comfort from when you were a boy, hugging your father. It's not sexual in the obvious way. And then it becomes, where do you draw the line between sexuality and something else?

If everything is sexual, then nothing is sexual.

Then nothing is sexual. I agree. That's right.

What about the expression of what you called the "female part" of you? How would you define that?

Well, I can really define it against the most gross archetypes or clichés, that whole jock relationship of men. I must say, I have felt the pleasure in that: guys being guys together, playing a game together, racing cars together—

Life as Budweiser commercial.

Yeah. That really puts it in perspective, doesn't it? But basically, I find that repulsive and reductive and diminishing. Because my most interesting, satisfying relationships with men, even in sports, even in racing, have always been much more complex and sensitive and confessional and open than that. That jock thing is really a very defensive kind of relationship—a group of men agreeing not to go any further than *this* deep. I don't enjoy that, and even as a kid, it seemed to me very superficial and unreal and unsatisfying, that kind of maleness.

So the female for you is the open and the sensitive—

This a traditional kind of Jungian version of yin and yang, male and female. I must say I'm talking about it in those terms. I don't see that as being quintessentially female, but it's a traditional way of talking about it, so I'll talk about it that way. If you set up that dichotomy, most people think of the female part as the artistic, intuitive part. When I was a kid, I was playing the piano when other kids were out playing football. I played football, too. But I had a girlfriend when I was five. A very close, wonderful relationship with a girl, at a time when all the other boys would go, "Yuck! Girls!" They had not yet come to terms with the fact that girls could be kind of good companions, or even human. I guess all I'm really saying is that I felt fairly integrated.

Why do you think you're so attracted to images of sexual violence?

I don't think I am. Am I?

I think you are.

How many minutes of my films are devoted to that as opposed to, say, discussion?

I'm not saying just in your films, but maybe in what you want to watch, too.

I'm not. I'm definitely not.

In 1983 you said, "That isn't to say that I haven't noticed that I can be attracted to images of sexual violence and wonder what that means about myself." I'm just asking you the same question you ask yourself: what do you think it means about yourself?

Sure, I guess that was at the point of *Videodrome*, where I was actually creating some images of sexual violence, so I could be attracted to my own movie maybe. Well, sexuality is, as we've been discussing, a complex thing. As it becomes connected with various cultural dynamics it can start to express itself in various ways that we might call perverse, unnatural, or unacceptable, or politically incorrect maybe is what we'd say today. And yet they seem very forceful, these images or concepts. There are a lot of people who do play bondage in sex—*play* bondage. Of course, you're not supposed to talk about this. Not only is it unacceptable, but it's almost considered impossible. And yet I remember my cat—cat sex. In cat sex, the male cat seizes the female cat by the neck, he bites her neck to hold her down, and she's sort of struggling like she doesn't want to have any part of it. And then when she finally manages to get away, she sort of rolls around on the ground in a very flirtatious fashion and waits for him to come to her again.

That's the way lions are doing it in Africa, right now.

They are doing it this very moment, thank God, whatever few lions there are left. And you say, that comes from survival of the fittest: the most aggressive male is the one who is going to survive, so the female's got to make it difficult for him to get to her, and so on. And maybe there is still a holdover of that in human sexuality. And maybe there is something in female sexuality still that comes from that very primitive beginning, which wants a man to dominate, which wants a man to defeat other men in order to have this woman, and then she herself makes it a little difficult just to make sure that he's really serious, and really the most aggressive, dominant one—and has to pin her down or to tie a sash cord around her arm or wrist or just hold her down with force when they're having sex, and that's more satisfying. And you will probably not find any feminists who will admit that this is a possibility.

However, we have now taken our evolution into our own hands, we have done it long ago, we have mucked about with our environment, so that all of those factors that might have made survival of the fittest work don't necessarily work in our society, because we have "de-physicalized" our society. It's now no longer necessarily the guy who's physically strongest—it might be the guy who's the best at manipulating stocks on Wall Street who is the dominant one. But how does he express this dominance that is no longer physical?

By having the biggest house or having the fastest car—

That's exactly right. Or having the most mistresses. And we haven't sorted it out yet, because half the time we're denying that it's all true. But underneath it all, there might still be the desire in men to physically dominate women and the desire in women to be physically submissive to men through a bit of a struggle. A bit of a shadow struggle even then. With my cat—she was going to get fucked, and she knew it and he knew it, but they still had to go through the whole thing. Why is it so horrible if that is still a vestige that we have to deal with? It's only horrible because of political implications and cultural problems, and it becomes a political, cultural football. And it makes these people, who still must do these things, these poor men and women, all of us maybe, sublimate it or change it or shift it or jigger it around somehow in our mind so we don't have to feel ashamed of our sexual politics in bed and all that kind of stuff. It's interesting. And I am interested in exploring it. I think that well may be the reason why—hmm, a naked woman tied up? Do men respond to that sexually? Well, I think they do. I really do. Now it might vary from culture to culture. Certainly in Japan it's more accepted as a sort of ritual of sexuality embedded in the culture than it is here. But, I say yeah, I do respond to that. And I think I've begun to figure out why, and it's not deadly—it's not as deadly as one might think, and it doesn't mean that I hate women and want to kill them. I think it comes from someplace else.

There's a possibility that we're hardwired for a lot of stuff.

There's no doubt that we're hardwired. That's not just a pun, it's a pretty good metaphor. (When pun becomes metaphor, it's an exciting moment.) It's only sane to look at it as it is, and not futz the issue, and not cover it up with so much politicking. It is not the same thing that a man and a woman should want to do a little play bondage as that someone shoots seventeen women in Montreal. This is not the same thing.

But the image police would have us believe that—

The image police must make it the same thing, and the image police must make policy based on this. I think it's very destructive. And if my films shake things up and make people shake their fists at each other over that, then I say fine, because I think things need shaking up. I find that stuff very distressing. I myself have been accused by a writer in Toronto, in a *Toronto Star* article, of being a direct contributor to that massacre in Montreal, where a man shot seventeen young women and said, "The feminists made me do it." She said, in her article, that we have a misogynistic culture and it is constantly being fueled and created by video games, and a whole list of things with no names attached, and then she said, "and the films of David Cronenberg." And the only other name mentioned in the article, other than the name of this killer, was Adolf Hitler. She was comparing women to Jews and men to Nazis. I find *that* irresponsible.

You think of yourself as a feminist, don't you?

I am a feminist. I am a feminist in the sense that I agree that because of the structure that we are talking about—whether it's Christian medieval morality, and that's where it came from, or more basic things, like the man-woman split of responsibility for childbearing and all that—however it came about, I do believe that Western culture is relatively misogynistic and certainly gives women a very second-rate role in society. And that given the way things are now, there's no need for that, if there ever was; and I think there probably was at the time, just survival. And that we should say, "We don't like this anymore, it's not necessary anymore, so let's change it." To that extent, I'm a feminist. And I think that's the greatest extent you can be a feminist. But to then start to talk about men as evil and maleness as evil, and femaleness as all the good in the world—if you take a lot of what is being said in the extreme right wing of the feminist movement, that seems to be what the suggestion is. And I laugh at that. It means they don't understand human nature at all. Because any evil that is possible in human beings is very equally possible in men and women. If we are a different species, we do at least share that characteristic.

There's another element of your work I'd like to examine: the Cronenberg hero. Dr. St. Luc in Shivers, *Hart in* Rabid, *Frank in* The Brood, *John in* The Dead Zone, *Max in* Videodrome, *Brundle in* The Fly, *and the Mantles in* Dead Ringers, *and now Bill Lee in* Naked Lunch. *There's a certain—*

[Surprised.] They're all fucking repressed! Just as you give me this litany, I think, these are all really repressed guys. Which is maybe where some of the misunderstanding of the movies comes in. Because if you say this is the Cronenberg hero in the sense that Cronenberg posits this as the correct kind of human being to be, then you've immediately warped all of the films.

That would be a terrible misreading of the function of narrative art—to think that you are positing your hero as an example of humanity refined and perfected.

But it happens all the time. I have an ironic distance on these characters. I'm saying, there's always a part of me that's repressed, or undiscovered, and that's why I keep forcing myself to look and discover. Maybe these characters are a projection of that part of me, but they are not necessarily my model of ideal behavior. But a lot of people assume that. So many people identify you with your main character, it's scary.

Not only are your heroes repressed, but there's a kind of passivity in them: one could say, the passive, reactive Cronenberg hero, as opposed to active. They are often very ineffective and always on the defensive, all the way through Bill Lee.

I'd say you're absolutely right. Those are my guys, my boys . . . my *team!* My team. They're my team. My soccer team.

Your team—they all got picked last on the playground!

[Laughs.] They came in first in the *last* division. "We won, we won, we got a trophy!" Yeah, but it's the last division and there's only one team in that division.

And a fragile bunch, too. You know, everybody talks about the way you present women—if they're too aggressive, that's bad; if they're too vulnerable, that's bad; so you can't win on that—but they may not actually spend much time thinking about how you present men. You present masculinity as an extraordinarily fragile proposition.

I think that's true. I'm not actually presenting these guys as the embodiment of masculinity—they're male people, it's not quite the same thing. But if you want to reduce everything to sexual politics for the moment, I'd say yes, my vision of masculinity as revealed in the movies is not at all the sort of macho-insensitive rapist that all those feminist critiques present.

Or the in-control manipulator, or the powerful technocrat, or any of those models. None of them works in your pictures.

That's true. I like this, I like this line of reasoning. It's so obvious, I've never quite talked about it this way before. But I think it's good weaponry. I mean, I think it's true. But beyond that, I think I find that kind of character a very good basis for a film in which one explores human nature, rather than a guy who's very opinionated, very secure, very strong, very aggressive, very focused, very active. Certainly, there are any number of writers who start from that vantage point, with a character like that—Shakespeare did okay. But obviously, it works best for me to have a character much more like the ones we've been talking about. It's not conscious.

They're almost recessive. Just as Brundle recedes—

Like a hairline—

—Or a budget. Just as Brundle recedes from life as a man into an insect, and the Mantles recede, quite literally, into the chromework of their practice, and Bill

Lee—who's recessive to begin with—recedes into a kind of complicated wallpaper, there's a sense of the watching man, the man who sits and watches and is too late. I wonder, do you identify with that?

[Pause.] I think there's some truth in that. For example, I've never felt, until just recently, that I had any access to the political machinery of Canada. And yet I did run into some people—now this may seem like a strange place to start—some people who were born thinking that political involvement was sort of their birthright. Is this a particularly Jewish thing? Are we coming back to the shtetl? The Talmudic scholar who ties his brain in a knot because he is not allowed to act.

It's true that I have a real *horror* of passivity, in one sense. I don't like fantasy, in my life. Let's take the most Hollywood example: when I start to become obsessed with Ferraris, my friends know I'm going to get one. And maybe even race one. I'm not going to just think about it. A lot of people would drool over it and love it, but not find a way to get their hands on one. They know I'm going to do it. It was the same with writing and filmmaking. In some of those limbo moments of my life, for instance, when I had written the script to *Shivers* but was not able to get it made, I thought, will I just have this fantasy, a fantasy that I was a filmmaker, and never be able to realize it? I have an incredible abhorrence of that, and a real drive into reality. And I suppose I'm putting my characters in that difficult, passive position deliberately. To see what it takes to provoke them to action. I'm interested in that mechanism. So it is an issue with me, obviously.

And also your interest in the outsider in everyday life, the guy something is wrong with, or not quite right with—

Well, often his passivity is enforced. It's his circumstances which force a certain passivity on him, and let's see what he does, then. Which would also be the sort of shtetl situation. It's a given. It's an accident of circumstance. Even the John Smith character in *The Dead Zone* fits the pattern well: he starts off feeling like he's a full-fledged, legitimate member of society; he knows what his place is, he knows what his purpose is, he's going to marry this girl, he knows who his in-laws will be; and then suddenly—bango!—he's an outsider. He's forced to play the role of outsider, and what does he do then?

And of course, by the time we get to Bill Lee in *Naked Lunch*, we feel he has been an outsider, and he's making some small effort to not be that anymore. He's trying to go straight, as he says to the cops: "I was a troubled person then, now I'm straight, got a job, got a wife." But it doesn't work. He's going to force himself to be an outsider, if no one else will—he will do it himself. And needs that role for some reason. He feels that perhaps if he's not an outsider, he'll sink without a trace.

Which is a romantic kind of disposition.

Yeah, yeah. I've never denied that there's a romanticism in any of my films. I haven't talked about it much, in fact.

A certain astringent romanticism, perhaps.

Yes. The best kind. [Laughs.] We don't want to get too messy.

Acerbic romanticism.

Acerbic, yes. "Astringent" I like because it's more medical.

Your works from Stereo *in 1969 to* Videodrome *in 1983, with the small exception of* Fast Company, *were all from your original screenplays. But since* Videodrome, *all four films have been collaborations and adaptations, no original screenplays, and your next will based on the play "M. Butterfly." Do you make any sense of this?*

Not really. I can't find anything in me that has any recognition response to this. In the Middle Ages, you know, you got no points for originality. In fact, it was just about proscribed. You always built from the past, and you elaborated that into your own unique version. When you're young, I suppose there's a great ego necessity to say, "Hey, it's all original, I did it all myself!" It might simply be that. Even then, I knew that where the material comes from is almost irrelevant. Does it matter that it's a newspaper article?

There's a kind of friction that comes with adaptation and collaboration, which you don't get from your original work.

I don't have that in my collaboration. I've not really sat in a room with somebody and argued about lines of dialogue.

I don't mean friction in a negative sense, I mean friction in terms of heat—your consciousness up against the consciousness of someone else.

Yeah. There's a Hollywood version of collaboration, which can also be positive. I was very interested to see "Naked Hollywood" [the BBC series] about scriptwriting, seeing Sydney Pollack, and how he deals with a screenwriter, and vice versa. They live together for six months, they see each other for twelve hours a day, they go out and have meals and talk about everything and know everything about each other's lives. This is a very perverse thing to me. I watch this and I say, this is a guy who really wishes he could write the script himself, but he can't write it, so he's trying to fuse with the other guy, so it's almost like the other guy is *him* writing. And the other guy knows that it's perverse, because he knows that this is all for Sydney, it's not for him. That's how I read it. That kind of collaboration, that kind of perverseness, I haven't had to deal with.

But you run up against other things anyway, which is why I don't think it's that different from an original script. As soon as you start to introduce characters that fight back—you want to get rid of them and they won't go!—you're always collaborating with yourself, with projections of yourself. That's why I feel the metaphor of Bill Lee's typewriter—giving him orders, pushing him around, telling him what to write—is like normal writing to me. Whether there is another human being in the room or not, it feels the same.

I don't think I'm trying to rationalize anything here. As time goes on, it doesn't matter whether it's a dream I start with, or a newspaper article, or a story someone told me, or a story someone said actually happened, or a biographical incident, or somebody else's fictional work. It all seems like intake; it's narrative and conceptual intake and then you do something with it. Now, when you're starting out and you really have a lot to prove, and you have not yet necessarily found your cinema voice, and you are desperate not to dilute that, because it's so fragile, there might be a real pressure *not* to collaborate. "I'm the only guy who wrote this, I made it up, I didn't get it anywhere else." But what I'm doing now might be more pure and honest and straightforward than what I did then.

You read The Dead Zone *only once before making the movie. I assume you read* Naked Lunch *many times.*

Oh, many times, over many years. Quite a different situation.

You talk about a "fusion" of your work and Burroughs's work. I'm assuming it's at the molecular, genetic level?

Getting into the telepod together. Burroughs and I get into the telepod together and we come out of the other telepod, fused. That's how it feels. Half the time I don't know whether I invented this, or it's part Burroughs and part me, or it's all Burroughs. There are some moments in each case where it's clear to me, but I'm actually not sure about some of the stuff. And it felt like that while I was writing. It was pouring out of my fingertips, I'm sitting here reading it, laughing. I'm passive, I'm not doing this, I'm *willing* this to happen, but that's about it.

Do you normally write quickly?

Yeah, I normally write quickly, but this had a different feel.

You had thought about this for many years.

Yes, and so it makes sense therefore that it should come out easily.

The reservoir was about a thousand feet deep.

It was very deep. The pressure, at the bottom, where the tap was, was pretty intense. No question. But it also felt like Burroughs could have written this. Maybe Burroughs did write this. Maybe I just memorized it, and I couldn't even tell anymore. It was a very exciting feeling, and I think the film ended up exactly that way: it's nothing I would have done on my own. And it's nothing that Burroughs could have done on his own. It took the two of us.

The book Naked Lunch *is very much about control and the body, the algebra of need, need and addictions of all kinds. The film is really not about that.*

There's a bit of it. The proportions are very different. I think that's a consequence of stepping back from the page and including the act of writing as the center of the discussion.

But why a movie about writing? Writing about writing is one of the most boring things—

Totally boring.

Incredibly boring. And to extrapolate from that, film about writing—

Is worse, much worse.

So much so—

But that's the challenge.

—So much so that when we see the tale of the writer trying to write in Barton Fink, *the Coens are satirizing the writer as an "interesting" character—*

Because he's not.

And the process of creation is dreadfully interior, and from the exterior, boring.

You don't even need *Barton Fink*. You've got *Hammett*.

So don't you risk making a movie that is almost exclusively about itself in the way that Barton Fink *is about itself, or* Baron von Munchausen *is about itself? That's something I never think Cronenberg is about.*

But do you think that's what happened?

To some extent. I think it's very self-referential, and about the creative process. In that sense, it's about itself. I'm not saying that's exclusive of other meanings.

[Deadpan.] You're saying my movie is as boring as *Barton Fink?* Is that what you're saying? Even more boring? Thank God you're not writing a review.

See, I'm not wanting to do that. You do need internal reflections in a film. You are making a universe that has to hold true to itself. Even when you're pretending that's it's just like outside the theatre, everybody knows it isn't really.

Here are the rules we're going to play by, whatever they are.

That's exactly right. What I'm saying is that a film will be self-referential, if it works, no matter what. Has to be, to a certain extent. And the illusion is that it's not *only* self-referential, but that you are alluding to a wider meaning, and a wider universe, because you are only presenting this little universe. If it is only self-referential, it is an intricate game, within itself, as some novels are.

And the Coen brothers are good at that.

And the Coen brothers certainly did that in *Barton Fink*. But I myself would think the film was a failure if that's all it did.

But why a film about writing? Why focus on that? When all the other concerns of the book, which are fundamentally Cronenbergian concerns—

No, wrong. Wrong. Wrong. This *is* a very Cronenbergian concern, and here's what it is. In a way, coming to grips with writing, with being creative, I think I'm coming *closer* to the basics. And coming closer to the flame, by dealing directly with it. Because, what is writing but trying to order reality? Trying to make order out of chaos. To come to understand phenomena that are not really susceptible to understanding. To create your own reality. To come to terms with your own reality. I deal with this in all my films. All of my characters do this sort of thing. And here I'm coming to a distilled version of it, i.e., a writer. And the fact that it's a dangerous thing to do cinematically—because it's difficult to do well—is part of the thrill. Just like the difficulty in doing Burroughs because it's an impossible book to film is part of the thrill. I think you have to be slightly psychopathic to make movies anyway.

So, I'm trying to turn the writing process inside out, and show it from the inside out. So quite contrary to the notion that I'm distancing myself from anything dangerous by making a very self-referential, introspective film, I think I'm actually coming closer to the essence of some things. Despite the cliché possibilities of having chosen that subject matter, it's the destiny of the film at that point. I guess I feel there's a criticism you're aiming at me, and I'm trying to be defensive—in an entertaining way—but I guess I haven't really understood the attack. What's the criticism then?

Let me lampoon it: it's art about art, and not art about life, or only art about that part of life that has to do with art.

But to me, a perfectly legitimate conce..n. To me, if you are an artist, you are deliberately amputating a huge part of the stuff you can discuss firsthand if you never talk about your art. It is incestuous, it is sort of intra-cyclical, it can be a cliché. But nonetheless, it comes with the territory. If you're a filmmaker, a huge part of your energy and life is filmmaking. If you choose never to refer to it, what have you done to yourself?

But you can make film after film after film about the intersection of science and society—which in a way you have—whereas I can't see you making film after film after film about writing.

[Deadpan.] I intend to. That's what I plan to do. This is the beginning of a huge series. [Laughs.] How 'bout, instead of Cronenberg coming out of the closet as a bisexual, he comes out . . . as a writer! Or a filmmaker. Or an artist. Maybe unconsciously that was one of the things that drew me to *Naked Lunch*. I can't say which came first. I was very excited by the fact that this movie was going to be, in some part, about the artistic process.

I'm not saying it's not worthwhile. I'm saying it's difficult and perilous and —

And I fucked up! But other than that.

Because it's a very hermetic world.

No, see, that's the part of the attack I disagree with. Or the proposal, the proposition. I don't think it has to be a hermetically conceived system at all, it just depends on what your approach is.

It's hermetic because it's encapsulated within the brain of the character. So to begin with, you're going to need metaphor in a way you don't elsewhere. Let's look at the problem of metaphor, because this film slams you over the head — I'm not saying you're not subtle — with the difficulties of filmic metaphor.

I bet if you ask a hundred people coming out of the cinema if that's what they thought, I bet they wouldn't know what the fuck you were talking about. Never mind. It slams *me* over the head with that problem, and I have to figure out how to solve it.

And the first time through the film, I choked on some of the things that were metaphorical.

Like what?

To some extent, the talking typewriters. It seems to me that metaphor, to function successfully, requires an act of imagination. At its best, you need both to care about the object itself, in an intimate way, as well as to be able to entertain the idea of a larger or different significance for that object. For instance, in The Fly, *we care about the fly, as Brundle, and that's a baseline, and so then the fly works as a metaphor for other things — for AIDS, or disease, or contagion, or just the love for someone who's changing on you. Those things are rich and work metaphorically because the fundamental connection between ourselves and the object is there.*

What you're really saying is, because there's someone human under the rubber — why don't you get direct about it? — whereas *these* little guys are puppets. See, you weren't raised on "Sesame Street," that's your problem.

That's probably true.

I'm telling you it's true. And if you had been raised on "Sesame Street," loving Cookie Monster as I have, only because I had a kid that watched it all the time, it wouldn't be a problem. I mean, what you're saying, now that we've gotten to the bottom of it, is straightforward and not wrong. It really is a very specific response. Some people are definitely going to be turned off by the typewriters. A lot of actors are going to be turned off. Some actors who were involved in the film said, you know, I'm really happy with the acting, but I have difficulty with the scenes when there is an actor acting with a puppet.

Don't you feel there's a risk in making metaphors too literal?

Huge risk. What's literal here?

Let's say where Joan Frost [Judy Davis] is at the typewriter writing this uncivilized prose that leads to their fully clothed sex grope, and the typewriter literally sprouts an erection. Don't you feel we "get it" without a penis coming out of the typewriter? Don't you feel that you defuse, or vitiate, the metaphorical richness of it by making it too literal?

No, I think I'm making it funny. And playful. Maybe you're taking it more seriously than I intended. It's like the embodiment of their lust, it's this polymorphously perverse thing. It's beyond them fucking, it's just total sexuality.

It's not them fucking, they're fully clothed. Which is an interesting choice you make throughout the picture.

You're right, it is a choice.

People would expect a lot of flesh in this movie and there's basically none.

Like I told you, I love to disappoint people.

Why make the typewriters embody the characters' strange sexuality instead of the characters embodying their strange sexuality themselves?

Because I'm probably giving you the same sort of avoidance, the same sort of avoidance-denial level cinematically that I'm saying Lee is doing psycho-emotionally. That's what's happening. I'm saying Lee is denying and avoiding certain realities about himself. And to the extent that he is controlling his fantasies, they are also avoiding, denying fantasies. So that if he is squeezing mugwump jism into a glass, he is not allowing himself to see that he is really sucking Kiki's cock. I think it works. I think it's a structure that has never been used before. I've never seen it. I think I made some inroads in that direction in *Videodrome*, where I'm saying it's the character's point-of-view fantasy that is now controlling the reality.

It's a relentlessly first-person movie in the same way.

That's it. But in this case it's not as removed. Because you do get hints. I mean, when the sex blob jumps out of the window, it lands as the typewriter. And when Lee has the death scene with the typewriter/bug, we see that it is a typewriter, and that he's been sitting in the corner, typing. And when Kiki and Cloquet are centipeding, I give you some soundtrack that is letting you know what is really happening. It's not quite as relentless.

Now why did I choose that structure? Partly, I wanted to deny people their most ordinary expectations. Because I want to surprise them and confound them and intrigue them and jar them out of their expectations. That's one reason. I guess it's the anti-entertainment part of me. An entertainer wants to give you exactly what you want. A good entertainer gives you those good old songs that you want to hear. And an artist wants to give you what you *don't know* you want. Something you might know you want the next time, but you never knew you wanted before.

Do you watch your films with an audience?

Yes.

Do you take pleasure in it?

Yeah, because it's like rehearsing for three years and then doing the performance. I only want to do it a few times, and it's kind of confusing sometimes, because I end up watching it in Italian with an Italian audience, in French with a French audience. Basically, I need to do it. That's my catharsis. I don't get catharsis from a film until I've watched it with an audience.

What did the process of making this film teach you about the process of writing?

The real subject of the film is what I've dealt with before, that is, the necessity of human beings to create their own reality. That's beyond writing. Writing is just one way of doing it. And it's a well-known, socially accepted way, but it's not the only way. Drugs are another way.

You are fascinated with drugs.

Definitely, because to the same extent that our understanding of reality comes from our senses, and to the extent that the senses can be deranged by drugs, or that the function of the senses can be completely altered or skewed by drugs, then we alter our reality. I mean, I did do one acid trip. One. In the sixties, and it was a great trip. It had some sad moments, but it was great. And I would have assumed that I would take it a lot more times, but obviously, I must have felt that it was going to be too dangerous. Maybe it's like when you go to the race track and bet for the first time and win, then you should stop right there. But it really confirmed something I had known intellectually, it confirmed it viscerally: that the world was different. It was not the same world. I was someplace else. The colors were different, the shapes were different, time was different. It was fantastic. It didn't make me want to keep going there, what it made me do is realize how fragile and how invented our understanding of reality is. Even physically, the most basic kind of reality that we know. This shows you that that's not even nearly an absolute.

I started to think, yeah, what about a creature like any other human being, but born with LSD as part of his nervous system. Like an organ that produces acid. You could survive. But your understanding of the world would be totally, totally different from any other human being's. I'm sure the animals that we share our houses with—our dogs, our cats, our salamanders and turtles—they're all on acid! On their own particular kind of acid. They don't see the colors the way we do, if at all. We think it's a shared reality. It's not a shared reality. I think that's the real subject of the film.

And that's where the writing connects very directly with the drug-taking, with the fantasizing, with the will to control. All of those things are part of the same human urge. So I do make a case that *Naked Lunch* is not a film about writing. And I do feel that when I'm making a film, I'm doing the same thing: I'm creating a new reality.

6

ROBERT ALTMAN

ROBERT ALTMAN FILMOGRAPHY

1957	The Delinquents
1957	The James Dean Story
1964	Nightmare in Chicago
1968	Countdown
1969	That Cold Day in the Park
1970	M*A*S*H
1970	Brewster McCloud
1971	McCabe and Mrs. Miller
1972	Images
1973	The Long Goodbye
1974	Thieves Like Us
1974	California Split
1975	Nashville
1976	Buffalo Bill and the Indians, or Sitting Bull's History Lesson
1977	Three Women
1978	A Wedding
1979	Quintet
1979	A Perfect Couple
1980	Health
1980	Popeye
1982	Come Back to the Five and Dime, Jimmy Dean, Jimmy Dean
1983	Streamers
1984	Secret Honor
1986	Fool for Love
1987	Beyond Therapy
1987	O.C. and Stiggs (shot in 1983)
1988	Les Boreades (episode of Aria)
1990	Vincent and Theo
1992	The Player
1993	Short Cuts
1994	Ready To Wear [Pret-a-Porter]
1996	Kansas City

for television

1983	Precious Blood / Rattlesnake in a Cooler
1985	The Laundromat
1987	The Dumb Waiter / The Room
1988	The Caine Mutiny Court-Martial
1988	Tanner '88

as producer only

1977	Welcome to L.A.
1977	The Late Show
1978	Remember My Name
1979	Rich Kids

Robert Altman

Robert Altman makes memorable films. Some because they are sublime, some because they are ridiculous. A few are both. His best work, the work that established him as an anti-establishment figure and a loopily cockeyed auteur, came between 1970 and 1977. *M*A*S*H, McCabe and Mrs. Miller, Nashville, The Long Goodbye, Thieves Like Us, California Split, Buffalo Bill and the Indians,* and *Three Women* presented a swirling, hazy yet acute portrait of an America, past and present, that was Altman's very own. Digging for and then dynamiting all the myths and clichés that make Americans *Americans,* and make movies *movies,* the golden age of Altman's cinema presented a wry, sad-eyed but somehow energizing view of a culture bursting with tragic, and often laughable, desires. The films were also full of signature stylistic devices such as gauzy color, a wandering camera, overlapping voices, offhand acting, and parenthetical, episodic story structures. By the mid-seventies, Altman was revered by many as America's Fellini.

However, over the course (and the curse) of the next ten years, from 1977 to 1987, Altman lost his sense and sensibility. His work ranged from the pleasantly competent to the screamingly bad. The "good" films of that period were his taut but tame versions of a number of plays, most notably Sam Shepard's "Fool for Love" and David Rabe's "Streamers." But the bad work dominated: from the boring bluster of *Quintet* and *Health* and *A Wedding,* to the big-budget madness of *Popeye* (which banished him from Hollywood), to the pathetic unfunniness of *O.C. and Stiggs* and *Beyond Therapy,* it looked like Altman had in some way "had it."

But just when we thought we wouldn't have Robert Altman to kick around anymore, he came roaring back with three impressive pieces. First, HBO's "Tanner '88," in which he and Garry Trudeau ran a fictional character for president of the United States, proved a clever, compelling mix of fact and fiction. Then in 1990, *Vincent and Theo,* a slashing look at the bonds between a punkish Van Gogh and his bourgeois brother, resurrected Altman's high-art credentials. And finally, improbably, back to Hollywood waltzed this aging, acid dumpling of a man, where in 1992 he turned out a killer—*The Player*—masquerading as a fluffy comedy.

Altman was born into a prosperous Kansas City Catholic family in the winter of 1925. He was not scarred by the Depression; he may hardly have noticed it. He was lovingly surrounded by two sisters and four aunts and his mother, while his father was a larger-than-life insurance salesman, raconteur, and hustling ladies' man. (In his adult life, Altman surrounded himself with three wives, many mistresses, and five children.) His rascally performance in parochial and public school led to two years at a military academy, after which he found himself flying B-24s in the Pacific theatre of World War II. His first postwar screen credit (as a story contributor to an obscure RKO picture, *The Bodyguard*) came in 1948, but that was followed by a long apprenticeship making industrial films for the Calvin Company of Kansas City.

Producer, director, designer, cinematographer, editor, and writer, Altman learned his craft banging out close to sixty films in the 1950s on subjects ranging from highway safety to the rules of basketball. Throughout the late fifties and sixties, more lucrative dues-paying followed in Hollywood, as Altman directed countless episodes of over twenty different television shows. From "Combat" to "Bonanza," "Alfred Hitchcock Presents" to "The Millionaire," Altman learned all the formulas, backwards and forwards, while attempting to resist them. After three films failed to spark a bankable belief in his vision, Altman finally got a gig directing a small antiwar comedy that fifteen other directors had turned down: *M*A*S*H*. The rest, as he might say, is or is not history.

I talked to Altman on the last two days of 1991, in Santa Monica, in an empty conference room at Skywalker Sound, where he was sort of busy mixing *The Player* across the hallway. Over the course of two days, our interview was interrupted at least twenty times by assistants' queries, reports on card games, meals, phone calls, glances at the day's newspapers and mail, and his intermittent participation in his film's final sound mix. The breaks proved frustrating, and even Altman said at the end of the first session, "This is a terrible way to do it." But I later came to realize that the discontinuity, the roundabouts and cul-de-sacs, the vague narrative glitches and evasions (which I've largely edited out), were quite perfectly *Altman*. The only difference between this interview and an Altman film is that he would have kept all that good stuff in.

SESSION ONE

To start, I'm curious as to what moments in your films most thrill your soul? What moments do you cherish most?

The accidents. The things that happen that are totally uncalculated, unprepared for, unanticipated, and take on the guise of a discovery. That can happen at any time in the process. In fact, I count on it happening. It's the only time I'm truly put in the position of the audience, for whom I'm supposed to be monitoring all this activity. I'm supposed to be their ear, I'm supposed to represent the audience, until I pass it on to them. Right? I don't have any examples . . . yes, I do. The easiest one is when Shelly Duvall's yellow skirt got caught in the door of her car in *Three Women*, and everybody yelled "Cut" and "Stop the cameras." No, no, no – leave it there. And see that it happens every time. But those are the kinds of things that, when I finish the day's work, and change my temperature, I look back on and it puts a grin on my face.

It seems that surprise itself is fairly integral to what you think art is all about.

I think it is. If you anticipate it, you've already experienced it. It's only art if it's on a different range or level than what you've anticipated. If what you see is what you expect, then you've already done a better job than the event.

Given that bias, you prefer things that may not even make sense in a kind of linear or rational way, because that kind of making sense always confirms people's suspicions.

Well, it can happen in a linear, rational way, but it is unexpected, usually, because it is more *truthful* than we all want to be. And that's why I say they're mistakes, because most of our activity in bumping into each other, and just having intercourse with each other, is *disguising* a lot of truths. The Irish, their whole culture speaks that way: that everybody lies, all the time, but you're supposed to know that this guy is lying, and he knows that you know, and you know that he knows that you know, etcetera, and it's very difficult for someone who's not used to that culture to go deal with the Irish – like me. I get angry with these lies. I mean, I like my lies to be much more subtle.

So it isn't that it can't be written or planned or plotted, the surprise, but when it's a true surprise it's usually more truthful.

Are you aligning art with truth? Because it certainly can be aligned with lying.

Well, lies can be a truth. I'm aligning art with discovery. Maybe I mean discovery more than surprise, though each discovery is a surprise. You can go dig in the ruins and say, "I hope to discover an old broken pot." And you can discover it, and it can still be a surprise: not that you found it, or that it was there, but by what it is. And those are the moments that are the most gratifying, and we kind of set up all the machinery in order to allow them to happen.

I was surprised myself a number of months ago when you gave that talk in San Francisco, when you said that "the process of making the film is the only *value" in it. I mean, some artists are very attached to process, but that seemed extreme.*

Well, it probably is an exaggeration. But I think it probably is the only value. Selfishly—it's the only value to me. The afterglow, the afterburn of it is nice and it's memorable, but it doesn't . . . the process itself is being in the activity itself, while it's happening, and really being out of control. It starts with the preparation. The script, the casting, then the shooting process, then editing. Then the last stage is the sitting back and grinning, or denying that you had anything to do with it.

You also said that eighty-five to ninety-five percent of your creative work is done by the time the film has been cast.

I think by the time the cast is complete, most of the work that I'm going to do, most of the creative work, has been turned over to those people that I have cast.

But from that time to the end, there's a long road to hike, and if you really feel that way, doesn't it get boring, tedious?

No, because it's always full of these surprises. These surprises, these discoveries that take place are not boring. It's more orderly, it's more mechanical, it's more the workaday business kind of thing—the order of what has to be done, which way it has to be done. You know, this sound mixing we're doing right now: I sit there all day and play solitaire with the editor, and do crossword puzzles, and I make phone calls and jokes and I eat, and wish we were through with it. But it's something that has to be done, and in the *process* of doing it, invariably, five, six, seven times, during the whole thing, I will feel, "Wow! I didn't know that was going to be like that. That's good! Leave that!"

The real movie for you is the dailies.

Well, the best movie is all the dailies.

Was that Fellini's claim, originally?

Yeah. Bergman told me that Fellini told him that. 'Cause I had just told that to Bergman, for me. So let's give that to Fellini.

Why is that true for you?

Because you're seeing much more of the characters, the life of the film. You can liken it to your own computer, your own brain. All of the anticipation, all of the work you do is to bring you to an event, whatever the event is, whether it's lunch or a statement, until it becomes history—and the dailies are like that. Because these people in this film don't exist. Everything in this film is a lie. Everything. Then we show it to an audience as if it is a true thing—an event that happened, a piece of history.

So, in dailies, when you see the same scene being played seven times, eight times, and you see the little changes, the nuances, it's going into your brain as if those people were real, and as if there were more options available. Do you understand that? It's very hard to explain. So by saturating yourself with the dailies, it's saturating yourself with that event. And even though I decide to leave this out, it's still in my computer, my brain. I mean, I know things about a picture that you don't know. And that can be a trap. Because if I've seen too much of these dailies I may make assumptions that are wrong. But I just love all that saturation, because it helps me with the progression of the film.

Does it also give you the feeling that it's almost as if you are doing a documentary about real people?

Yes, that's what I am trying to do. I'm trying to do a documentary about these fictitious people. Documentaries are not real at all. In many ways, this is more real. Documentaries are not truthful.

They are a slant on the truth.

They are a slant on the truth, but they are a different kind—they are still picking and choosing.

They are just as constructed, even Fred Wiseman's.

Oh, absolutely! More so! And what we do is no different from what Fred Wiseman does. Fred Wiseman goes in and sees a bunch of old people chewing their food, and he's doing one of those documentaries, or they're singing in a church pew or something, and he uses that. That's no different from what I do when I see an actor acting those things. In fact, what I'm really trying to do with the actors is to get them to be less creative and just use their own natural selves more, as if they were the character in that circumstance.

Not so much "actorial" as behavorial.

Behaviorial. Behavior is what it is.

Your films are fascinated with catching that kind of behavior, in a way that sets them apart from the films of your peers.

Well, I don't know about that, but I know that seems to be the main thrust of all of this stuff.

Is it fair to say that some of your films are edited more than they are directed? I don't mean this as a slight—

Yeah. Absolutely! Absolutely, absolutely. I think what I try to do is simply create an event—and that event can be somebody pouring a cup of coffee, and spilling it, or not spilling it—creating that event, and then *documenting* it. And whether it's a riot, or a church fire, or a cup of coffee, I try to create the event, and then *not* manipulate everything to work for what you would like to have. And many times getting less than you would like to have. There has to be a whole different reason that would send me around and make a shot from the inside of a refrigerator as the door opened and somebody took something out. I mean, when I make that kind of a shot—I'm doing something else! That has very little to do with the event.

That's not Altman cinema.

No. That doesn't mean there's anything wrong with those shots, but for me to make that shot I may have to stay there in the dark and listen to the rest of the scene when he closes the door.

Is the kind of behavior you talk about seeking from actors—allowing them not to "act" in a way—one reason why you're distrustful of rehearsal?

Well, probably. Or maybe I just don't think there's anything to rehearse. Usually, I'm laying brick on top of brick, behavior on top of behavior, and whatever happens in the first thing that I do affects every other bit of it. Say a film is composed of two hundred elements, two hundred different scenes. The production manager will tell me the cheapest way to do this, the most efficient way, is to start with Scene 23 and then go to Scene 54 and then go to Scene 33, and blah blah blah. And I'll say, "I can't shoot that scene till later," and "I can't shoot that scene till later," but most of the others it doesn't make a lot of difference.

You prefer to shoot in sequence, I assume.

Oh, in continuity is much better, but the best things have happened when I've been forced to go out of continuity. Then, you're just shooting continuity, backwards. You're just building in different directions. But whatever the first day's shooting is, whatever the first thing we shoot, *that* affects every other shot that's made for that picture. So if we start on Scene 24, and then go on in any order you want to tumble, that film is going to end up a certain way. If we start with Scene 4, it's going to be different. The whole thing. So each film, if I went back and made the same thing, it would be a different film. And as many times as I would remake that film it would be a different film. And I think probably *surprisingly* different. The weather is never the same, the actors are never the same—they never feel the same, they never have the same amount of confidence, they never have the same amount of fear. So it's back to Einstein and relativity: everything is in movement in relationship to everything else, so nothing is ever the same.

The process on the back end—the rough-cut screening process you go through— may not be unique, but it's distinct. [Altman continually screens rough versions of a film to those both inside and outside his circle.] What do you learn by "reading the backs of people's heads," as you've said?

Well, I learn nothing, but I learn from my own embarrassment. I sit in that room the first time I show an assembly of film and I have twenty-five people in there, and I know who they are in most cases, or I know about them, and the film starts, and suddenly a scene goes up, and suddenly I go "Oh, Jesus!" and I cringe with embarrassment. Because I'm looking at this film for the first time through somebody else's eyes. So, through my own embarrassment or my own glee, I leave something in and enhance it or I take something out.

How do you know what their eyes are seeing, if you're not talking to them about it?

Because I'm the one that's seeing, but I'm seeing it from another standpoint. In other words, it's a way for me to try to get rid of all this knowledge that I have—so much more knowledge than you, the audience, have—because I've been exposed to so much more information. And also I have to come to that realization that none of you really gives a shit! You will, as long as I keep you entertained and interested and involved; but the minute it becomes boring to you and you say, "Listen I saw this about sixteen times last year in various forms," you're out of there.

And you can see, from the back of the room, by their body language, that they are "out of there"?

I feel it. It's not *them*—it's the fact that I know that they're there, that's a truth; so I suddenly have to become aware of those people, and I'm responding. I'm a different *me*. I've moved my position: from myself to myself-in-a-room-with-twenty-five-people-that-I-don't-want-to-be-embarrassed-in-front-of.

Isn't this process really Bob Altman's version of a focus group? Doesn't this serve the same function for you that the studios seek when they go out and test films?

Oh, absolutely. Absolutely. Only mine is more truthful. Because at least all the judgments that are being made about this thing are being made from the same point of view, not from several different points of view. I don't trust what anybody *tells* me at these screenings, any more than I would trust the people in the focus groups. 'Cause I know how much I lie about my very, very closest friends' work. I mean, the people that I truly love, I do not tell them my true feelings.

Why not?

I don't want to hurt their feelings . . .

If they've asked you for your opinion?

I don't believe they really want it. And I just don't have the courage to do it.

You think you're doing them any good by lying to them?

I think it's much more selfish than that. No, I think it would do them much more good if I were totally honest with them. But I'm not that way.

You just want to avoid the conflict?

I don't want the confrontation. Yes. [Pause.] I also don't trust what the audience tells me because they are not right. They're just looking at it from their standpoint: each element of the audience, individually, has all this information that they've gathered in their lifetime, everything that has ever happened in the vicinity of their senses is recorded, and filed, and cross-filed, and stuffed with other things. There is a lore there. And now I'm coming in with something new and it's reacting with their lore. They're shuffling the information that I'm giving them in with all this other information. There's no two people of the audience that are alike.

And no two people will have the same reading of a film.

None whatsoever. Absolutely. And I don't really much care about them. If suddenly you are zapped with a truth ray and you say, "I hate this fucking film," it doesn't make any difference to me. Now, if I've made this film that *nobody* gets, or nobody likes, or nobody understands, then it's a bad film. It's stupid for me to make a film and find one other person that thinks it's the greatest thing since hash. That's great for me, but it's kind of stupid to put out that much energy just to please one person, or to get to one person, or involve one person. So I'm trying to get to as many as possible. But if you got 'em all, then you know it would be pretty banal.

But you don't feel you've ever made a bad film.

I don't think I've ever made a bad film. I think I've made films that have not performed in an equation that justifies their manufacture. But I haven't made a film that isn't what we – the group – set out to do.

You once said you'd shoot yourself before you'd let a bad film out of the editing room.

I won't do it. I'd burn it. I'd hide it. I may do that one day, but I don't think so. Now, this is very subjective. I'm talking about how I feel.

Do you care about how "they" feel out there?

I would like them to like what I do.

Only because that will allow you to do more of it?

Yeah, and it makes me feel better. And then there is more attention turned to me. It's like—you know, Abner Dean the artist, the cartoonist, used to draw all those naked people. There are always masses of people in his drawings. There's one that shows a knoll, with a dead tree on it, and this lithe young man standing next to the tree. And coming around this knoll and going off into infinity is this absolutely endless line of people, trudging down this road. And they all have headbands on and they are all trudging, pulling these enormous boulders behind them. And on this tree is a board with a nail and a feather and a spring—some silly, eclectic kind of stuff—and he's trying to enlist their attention, and he's saying, "Look, I made this!" And I think *that's* the real artistic drive, that I want to say, "Look what I did!" [Chuckles.]

The projection of the ego out into the world?

Yeah, I suppose.

It's a useless thing you do. There's nothing more useless than a poem or a film.

Absolutely. Absolutely. But I made this. The author wants his signature on it. But that's what art is. Art is useless. It has no utilitarian purpose. It is only an enrichment, and then it becomes only a discovery or a surprise.

Have you ever felt like you've gotten enough ego gratification from your first thirty-odd films that you don't need to make a thirty-seventh or thirty-eighth?

No. No. I don't think so. When that happens, you don't do it anymore. Then it's drudgery.

You've never wanted not to do it, is what I'm asking.

Never came close to it. I do find that I'm more conservative now. I'm reading a lot of scripts now, because I'm looking for a film to make, or a theatre piece—and many of these things I turn down or I don't pursue, whereas twenty years ago I would have said, "Oh, this is almost impossible, let's do it! Let's just try to make it work."

Just for the perverseness—

No, but—a lot of it is that. But a lot of it is: anything can be done. Anything can work.

You've said that the content is there no matter what you do, and that your films are more exercises in style.

[Pause.] Yeah. Yeah.

In which case, you could almost take the phone directory and make an Altman film out of it.

Well, I think that's extreme, but it could be done. That's the idea. We could sit here and say, let's make a film called *The Yellow Pages*. You could figure it out. But now, some of these scripts tend to be too complicated, too already-worked-out, they're too high-concept.

There's not enough for you to discover in them.

Yeah, maybe that's it. It's education. By practice you learn what is a fruitless trip. I'm starting to think that each project is a pond of frozen ice, of thin ice. And I've got to walk—taking everything I have with me, all the people, the actors, all the musicians—we've got to walk from one side to the other, and there are all these steps that have to be taken. And one step that's too heavy, *one*, breaks the whole fucking ice, and everybody sinks. And you lose, if you make one bad step. So maybe I calculate more of the pitfalls and the traps and the places to take that heavy step, and I tend not to do these things. But if I got down to where I was trapped, if I said, "I've got to go to work tomorrow or they take away my washing machine," I would take any one of these twenty-five scripts and do them.

You're in a sort of unusual position, in that you're not as much of a writer as some others we think of as auteurs, and you've always struggled with your writing. So, in your dissatisfaction with these twenty-five scripts, don't you wonder why you don't do it yourself?

I think I'm probably much more of a writer than . . . or as much as, when you're making comparisons. I tend to do more writing than not.

Let me qualify: it's not the sitting-down-with-the-blank-piece-of-paper writing that you do, it's the interactive writing—the collision with your source material.

Yeah, I don't do very well at . . . I do better rewriting. I have to have the idea. Something has to make me believe that something is true. And *then* I can go in and adapt, and deal with it.

Why do you think that is?

I don't know. I just don't come up with imaginative ideas. Everything I've ever done has been off of something that somebody has done—that has already been there. Something exists.

Can you not make yourself believe that an original story of yours is true?

Well, to degrees. But once I find something that's true, you can't convince me that it isn't. And then I have the confidence to go ahead with it.

Last year you said, "I can't write alone. I have on occasion, but I've never been comfortable with it. I've had these little sessions with myself when I've said, 'Oh, screw 'em, I'll just take six months and I'll go and sit there and I'll write every word.' And I like the way I write, but it's too painful . . . and I always feel there's something missing. I'm dry. I don't have enough ideas."

Yeah, it's true.

What's the painful aspect of it?

The painful part is very simple. It becomes physically painful for me to sit at whatever device, a typewriter, a computer, by myself. I mean, I get pains in my body, and I wish I could go somewhere else and do something else, and I bite the inside of my mouth, because I want to get this done, and I get sort of lost in it, and time passes a lot. It's very much like painting. I find it's exactly the same thing.

You used to paint quite a bit.

I did at one time. I have spurts. Maybe it's just attention: maybe I just don't have the concentration.

You're never more alone than when you're writing. Is it uncomfortable for you to be alone?

Uh-huh. Yeah. I don't like that very much.

Has that been a lifelong thing, as far back as you can remember?

Oh, yeah. I'm very gregarious, and I always liked being with other people. There are times when I love to rest, to read, but the idea of going off and spending two, three days by a lake, by myself, would be torturous to me.

I know enough about you to know that you don't have a self-analytical bent, but do you ever wonder why that is?

No. No. What difference does it make? I hear people say, "I love to go spend time alone," and I think, God, don't you get bored? Maybe they're more interesting to themselves than I am. It's just a matter of accepting it. I don't think I can go back and change myself, and I don't see any reason to do that. I can envision a much better brain, but I think you have to start over.

So there was never a wish or a regret that you couldn't do that better?

I've never had a wish or a regret about anything that exists. It's like, I've had friends who have had strokes, and become paraplegics, and suffer situations, blindness, what a terrible thing. But really, when something like that happens to you, that's what's happened to you. I don't think there's anything you can do about it. I don't think what you like or don't like, or are happy with or unhappy with, makes a whole hell of a lot of difference. I don't think you have much control over it. It's what that is.

You've praised actors to the hilt throughout your career, and I've not seen the same kind of praise, or respect, for writers.

Well, I don't think the respect is the same. I praise actors because actors are thrown into a situation where they only have control over their own place on the table. They have nothing to do with the table. Writers I think of as more like myself: they're part of the main planning board, and they have more control, and they are doing pretty much the same thing I'm doing.

The Player, *which I loved—and I'm telling you the truth here, because I would certainly tell you which films of yours I didn't like if that would make things any more interesting—*

No, it would just hurt. I would think it would be a shame that you just didn't understand them. [Laughs.]

You'd feel sorry for me.

Absolutely.

The Player *has a sort of dim view of screenwriters and writing. Kahane, the screenwriter who's killed, is quite a bad writer—*

I never say he's a bad writer.

But June [Greta Scacchi] does, and of course what's read at his funeral, his screenplay about the underclass, which is not in the novel, makes him out to be kind of a ludicrous, comical guy; and the writer who writes the film-within-the-film is quick to sell out his ideas. Now, I know you have had your back-and-forths with writers; you certainly bring a lot of baggage to the movie when it comes to writers.

There are hundreds and hundreds of different kinds of writers and kinds of writing, but in none of them—when it comes to writing for film—are you dealing one-on-one with your work and an individual audience. When you write a short story or an article or a poem or a tome, there's a line between you and the audience and there is no interference. But the minute you write a play or an opera, where there are other people involved in interpreting and presenting that, you are a collaborator. You may be the main collaborator, but . . . you can take this thesis down to, "Okay, let's do a film about a circus." And so I hire Harold Pinter and he writes a thing about a circus. I can say, "I'm the original author of that, because that was my idea to do a thing about a circus." But there can be a billion different ideas come out of that circus. Now you can go even further with this, and I say, let's do something with a blind clown who doesn't want anyone to know that he's blind. And the guy takes that and writes it. So now, this is *more* my idea than it is the writer's. So now I say Paul Newman is going to play this blind clown in the circus, but I need dialogue for one scene when he comes in and they say, "You're blind, aren't you?" and for the first time he has to admit that he's blind, and he says . . . *something*. And I need someone to write that—I can't think of anything. And someone writes that one line. They are a writer, but they're just collaborating in this thing. So who's the writer? And why does there have to be the writer?

Someone has to get the credit.

The credit, yes, but why—back to this ego thing. Where's the artist? You go out and say, I was an actor on that picture. Or, I was a writer on that picture. Who made that picture? Sometimes, it's the star that makes the picture. There's an imbalance. But it's never one person. I get the credit for most of my pictures, but that credit is for selecting the people that I collaborated with. So I'm just really a manager. And you can strip me down to having no artistic input whatsoever, other than of selection.

Isn't that just a bit disingenuous, Bob, that you're just the guy who comes in and turns on the lights and says go?

It's very true, though. I think it's very, very true. It's just like this mixing thing. [Points across the hallway.] If I were in New York, then these people would all be doing what they thought I would like. This thing would be fine. It would be different than if I was here, but it would be as good or better.

This thing about who does what and who's who is very confusing. How come actors work with some directors and are good, and work with other directors and are bad? Is that the director's fault? Is that the actor's fault? There are a million reasons. So our egos get involved with it, our livelihoods get involved with it . . .

The kind of compendium of complaints by certain writers who have been your collaborators—

I have no sympathy for them!

—that one finds, for instance, in the biography of you [Patrick McGilligan's Robert Altman: Jumping Off the Cliff*]. Where does that come from? They don't understand the process?*

Well, it comes from, it comes from . . . well, the biggest, let's start with *M*A*S*H*. If Ring Lardner, Jr., hadn't written that script, there would have been no way I would have done that picture, because it was one of the worst books I ever read in my life. Talk about sexist, racist—

Hawkish!

Hawkish, oh, it was just dreadful. So when I read Lardner's script, I thought, there is a real side. What I saw in his script were those operations, these guys dying on those operating tables. When I read this, I said, I know how to make this film, because I'd been working five years on another project that used a similar technique. When Ring Lardner saw the first screening of that film in New York, he came out afterwards and he looked at me in the lobby of the theatre, and said, "You've *ruined* my script. Absolutely ruined it. This is not my script. I did not write this!" He was quite put out. When he won the Academy Award for Best Screenplay, he talked about a lot of people and a lot of things – he didn't say one word about me.

The next film I did, a guy named Billy Cannon wrote an original screenplay called *Brewster McCloud*, and Lou Adler had bought it, and brought this thing to me. And it was a dreadful piece of work. But there was some wonderful stuff in it, it sparked me, and I said, "I can do this, but I can't do this screenplay." So, everybody said fine, go do what you want to do. And I rewrote it while I did it. But in the process of making the deal with Billy Cannon, Lou Adler, as a part of his contract, had to pay a lot more money if someone else got screen credit. So I rewrote that script with lots of other people. There was lots of improvisation. And there was a book published of his screenplay and the transcript of the actual screenplay – some twenty-two-year-old guy wrote about what went on during the making of the picture – and it'll tell you what it's all about.

I don't want you to feel you need to defend yourself on a case-by-case basis –

I'm not, but I'm trying to tell you how this comes about. So Cannon was furious that I was writing on his work. After he saw the picture, and the picture was deemed successful by a certain group, Cannon wrote me a letter and said, "I really like what I saw, I think we can work together again."

Other than that, *McCabe and Mrs. Miller* was a book. I wrote the screenplay for *McCabe*. *Nashville* was written by Joan Tewkesbury, certainly, and myself. She was there all the time. I have writers on the set whenever I can. *A Wedding*, *Quintet*, *A Perfect Couple* – all kinds of films – I always have writers. I have two writers that worked on *The Player* that nobody knows about. The only reason that Michael Tolkin [the novel's author] and I didn't have a big blowout on this thing was 'cause of Tolkin's sensibility. He had written a screenplay. I said, "I want this to go in a different direction." And finally, I said, "The only way I can do this picture is to collaborate with your material, but I can't collaborate directly with you." He said, "Okay, I'm your producer." And he stepped back. I don't think I could have done that. And I made changes in his book, his material, the stuff he had written, which was the only way I could see how to drive it for myself. And that is going to happen forever.

And Harold Pinter. I did two Harold Pinter plays. Harold Pinter hates my guts because I changed the number on the door from 7 to 73 because I found a set that was already existing.

I did *The Caine Mutiny Court-Martial* – Herman Wouk – and I got the nicest letter I've ever had from anybody, and he said, "It's the first time any-body, including myself, ever really got what my play was about."

I know—you're a writer, and I know how you think and I know how I think. And if I write, and I give it to somebody and they change the goddamn thing, I am furious, I am furious about it.

It depends what the understandings are.

Yeah, but the understandings are mostly economic. Or they are career moves. I doubt that in most cases the writers who have disagreed with me—Ring Lardner, etcetera—would turn around and say, "If you're going to do that to my thing, you can't do it." The problem is, we're using this word "writer," which is what throws everybody off. A writer and a screenwriter are two different things. And I think if anything I'm probably more of a writer than I am a director. Because I do very little directing, and I do a lot of writing.

Go on with that. Tell me more.

Most of my directing—I don't *direct* people. It's a misnomer. I'm just calling the shots. I'm the one who says, "We have to start here today, and we end here, and we're going to do this now," or I can say, "We're not going to shoot that." In *Vincent and Theo,* in the sunflower scene, where he destroys the painting in the field of sunflowers: I drove by that field every day, and one day I said, "We got to go out and shoot that." Now, is that writing or is that directing? Julian Mitchell, who wrote the screenplay for *Vincent and Theo,* went along with everything I did and said, "Oh Bob, it's wonderful," hating every minute of it—but economically, he wouldn't have gotten his picture made [if he didn't]. And in the end, he got drunk and he said, "I want my name off of this picture, you've destroyed it, this isn't what I wrote" (which is true), and he's having a terrible time with himself. Because he's made these contradictory statements, he doesn't know what he wants.

The point is, he didn't *invent* Vincent Van Gogh. He wrote a script. And I wish people would *read* these scripts sometimes! I wish the audience would go ahead and read the scripts—and that's not to punish the writer or to say, "See what a great job I did with this script!" It's that no script is taken and translated directly to the film, and when it is, these films are terrible. You can tell it immediately.

And in theatre, when you go buy your Samuel French version of a play, that's not what the author wrote; that's what the actors, through rehearsal, and the director, and the writer, have sat there and rewritten. Most of the dialogue in "Fool for Love," for Eddie, was written by Ed Harris [not Sam Shepard]. Dialogue isn't necessarily writing, it's part of a process. This thing will never get ended.

I want to talk about your body of work. One of the things that strikes me is something that's not there. And that's the presence of the erotic. It's almost remarkable by its absence. What do you think accounts for this?

Well, I'm not aware of that. I never really thought of that before. I don't know. Maybe I'm not capable. Maybe I just don't do that. Maybe it's something . . . obviously all that I show you reflects my personality and all I see. I don't know. I thought the scene I did, the lovemaking scene in *The Player,* was erotic.

For you, given the landscape of your work, that's pretty demonstrably erotic. Maybe not for other films Greta Scacchi has been in. I don't know if it's because of your Catholic upbringing in the Midwest, or—

I don't know. But I tell you, primarily, most of what anybody does, is imitating. I imitate the things that I like and admire. I'm showing you what I like to see. And maybe I don't like that. Maybe I'm embarrassed by this.

I think it's true for Coppola as well, and he said something interesting: that maybe in inverse proportion to how important eros is in your private life, you can depict it in cinema. The more important it is, the less comfortable you are in presenting it.

Well, you can say it's in inverse proportion or in direct proportion. Each theory is just as valid. I don't know. Maybe he's lying to you, or to himself.

Well, you certainly, personally, don't have a reputation of being someone uncomfortable about sex. While there are certainly sexual situations in the films—I'm not saying they're prudish—they've never been comfortable with nudity, even in the seventies, when nudity was accepted. You really went against the grain.

Are you sure?

Yeah, I think so. I'm sure. Even in those situations when you do show nudity—like the shower scene in M*A*S*H *or the painful striptease in* Nashville—*it seems you're much more interested in depicting how you felt women were being depicted by our society, rather than delectating over them yourself.*

[Pause.] That's all I can think of to show. I don't know a circumstance. I can't think of a circumstance. I'm trying to think of something erotic? Whatever Francis does or whatever I do is a reflection of what we think is right. Eroticism for me ties more into voyeurism than participation. When you get into participation, suddenly the element of showing and watching doesn't enter into it. Very few people have their friends pull up a chair in their bedrooms to watch them fuck, and have a cup of coffee. Very few people. So it's not a natural condition.

The simplest answer is that it makes me uncomfortable. And in most cases, when I use nudity, I have a different attitude about it. A lot depends on what the person performing that will give you. I think of those scenes in Alan Parker's *Angel Heart*, some of those scenes with Lisa Bonet and Mickey Rourke—I don't think I could have ever done those scenes.

Where's the discomfort?

I don't know. It doesn't occur to me. I ask the actors and what they will show me, I'll photograph. That's back to the documentary kind of approach.

It's ironic, because in The Player *you're dealing with an actress who's become known for being comfortable with her nudity, and sexual situations.*

Well, she's comfortable with her nudity but during this picture she sure wasn't.

She's probably trying to get away from that.

Oh, she is. She hates it. You know, there's some show in England where they use those puppets—political things—and they made her one of the characters along with Reagan and Thatcher, and she's sitting around saying, "Oh, Dickie"—Richard Attenborough—"Oh, Dickie, when do I get to take my clothes off?" So she doesn't want to do that stuff. But I have to do a certain amount of sex in this film, because it's obligatory, because it's a film. But my whole point is to never show *her* nude. Which is why the girl who played Bonnie Sherow [Cynthia Stevenson], when I cast her, I said, "It's very important that you be nude in the hot tub for this scene." And she said, "No one ever asked me to be nude before." And I said, "I want it for just that reason." Because I want to give them the nudity—but I don't want to give them the nudity that they think they're going to see. Paul Newman's comment, after seeing the picture, was, "You don't get to see the tits you *want* to see, and you get to see the ones you *don't* want to see." And that was really the idea!

[Pause.] I think the erotic in film is a very tough situation. If you literally do arouse a sexual feeling, really arouse erectile tissue in an audience, and then, if it isn't relieved, we move on to the chase, and you're sitting there in your seat, and there's this other thing going on: the blood is still pounding in your temple, and you're not going to concentrate on what you're supposed to. So I've got a lot of questions about that.

You're known for having a healthy sexual appetite, throughout your career.

Well, yeah, but I've been married three times, and to Kathryn for thirty-two years, and that's most of my career. If you're implicating . . . if you're talking of me being a promiscuous carouser, it probably isn't as true as you think it is.

I'm going on what you've said in the past.

Or what's been said that I've said.

There's the famous quote, "I just giggle and give in."

Well, I like to say that.

Speaking of promiscuous—there's a nice transition—I'd like to talk about the more formal aspects of your craft. Let's look at a couple of Altman conventions: the overlapping sound, the zoom and reverse zoom, a disjointed or open narrative, the stuffed frame, and this kind of camera that "plays around," if we want to think of it in a promiscuous way, as opposed to focusing on—or valorizing, which is the code word now—the star, in iconic closeup. Do these things feel integral to you in your experience of your own films?

Well, they're the way that I like to make films. If somebody says, "You're going to make a film about a private eye," I say, okay, I'm going to show you what a private eye really is. It's not going to be the private eye you think it's going to be. If I make a film about a cowboy, it's not going to be about the cowboy you think it is. Or the banker, or the doctor, or whatever.

This camera thing—I love that, promiscuous camera, I love that. It's just a way, if people have a tradition, if people have a given—like if I say "whore," certain images flash in everybody's mind, so a lot of my work is done. A lot of my work is finished. Just by me saying "whore." So now, I go in there and I can say, "You're wrong about whores. Because this is also what a whore is, and this, and this." So I'm breaking down your preset ideas. And that's consciously done, because it interests me, and not for any other reason. I don't set out to make a genre-breaking film, but that certainly interests me.

Genre inversion.

Yeah, take *McCabe*. If I had not used Warren Beatty, if I had used an unknown actor as McCabe, that picture could not have been done the way it was done. I would have needed more information up front. But the minute you know it's Warren Beatty on that horse, you got preset ideas about him. I use that. That's part of my storytelling.

I don't think this promiscuous camera is any different. You know the camera is supposed to do a certain thing. If nobody had ever seen a movie and I took and I showed you any of my films, they would be horrendous. You couldn't follow them. But you've learned how to look at films by looking at films, and television. And now we're learning how to fracture more. The audience has that information. But if you start showing this to a strange audience, to a bunch of desert people out there in Iraq who have never seen a film before, they don't know what the fuck is going on. I mean, how can the rat be the size of an elephant? And the other thing is, we learned during World War II in teaching pilots how to fly an airplane that if you put sixty-four images on the screen at the same time, each with a different thing going on, the retention rate is greater than if you show them literally one image at a time.

Part of all of this that we're talking about has to do with what we call instinct. What it really is, is using all of your senses and all of your information. That's what we call hunches. And that's why I think the studios are going down the tubes. Nobody can follow their hunch. The little man inside of them can't tell them something. That is valid judgment: to say, "Jesus Christ, it just *feels* this way to me." You're getting information from everything. And you're probably closer to being correct, because you have all that judgment, than somebody who sits down and figures it out line by line.

Do you feel there's a politics to your style, to the style itself?

You mean, am I using it politically?

Whether you feel that there's a political bias in the structural way in which you order a film, or disorder it, as the case may be. The tradition in the criticism of your work is that by decentralizing the hero, the icon, and by concentrating on the periphery, and by flattening the playing field, the work is intrinsically democratic, left-leaning, less hierarchical.

Oh yeah, I think it's more . . . subversive. It's not revolutionary, but it's subversive.

What do you think you're subverting when you say your films are subversive?

Uh, set ideas. Fixed theses. Platitudes. Things that say: this is *this*. Commandments. Attitudes. Those kinds of things. I'm saying: it's not true. It's true, but it's not.

What gave you such a passion for debunkment?

I have no idea. I have absolutely no idea at all. It's just what interested me, and I'm talking after the fact. It's not like I sat around thirty years ago and said, "Ah, this is what I'm going to do." I'm trying to debunk *myself* as much as I'm debunking somebody else. Once again, everything builds on experience. Experience is just practice. Burning yourself on the hot stove. You don't do it again. Maybe you're making a terrible mistake. Maybe that stove was only hot once.

So you're like the general fighting the last war.

Yes. Always.

Fifteen years ago you claimed your films were essentially all about one thing: striving, cultural and social striving. I'd like you to reflect on that, with fifteen years' hindsight.

I don't know. If I said that today, I'd believe it. It sounds logical, reasonable. Striving has a lot to do with it, that's a good word. I probably wouldn't say it the same way today, but what I would say today probably means the same thing.

SESSION TWO

[Altman reads a personal letter while the tape rolls, glances at *The New York Times*, then tears up the letter.] Okay.

Okay. Before M*A*S*H you said you were "comfortable with failure." What did you mean by that?

Yes, I was. What I meant was that I was comfortable in my life, not having attained my own goals. I was happy. And I was doing lots of television and I had work and I could feed my family and buy party favors and life was okay.

With your having been in that place, I'm wondering what the big success of M*A*S*H did?

The success, or the surprise, of *M*A*S*H* gave me the power to do other things, and to stretch a lot more. *Brewster McCloud* is a picture that would never have been made had it not been made by someone like myself who nobody would interfere with. And the only reason they won't interfere with you is if you've had a previous success. This is true for all of us, Cronenberg and Soderbergh and Lynch. Everybody gets to do their own thing once they've kind of proved themselves. That gave me the power to make pictures that would have otherwise gone unmade. The mistake that you make in terms of corporal success is to stretch too far, and then many of these things—most of these things—are not acceptable to the audience, to a mass audience. So then you fall out of favor. It swings back and forth.

If not for the limitation on your freedom to keep making the pictures you want to make, would you care whether it was acceptable to a mass audience or not?

No. First of all, I wouldn't know what to do if I was going to set out to make a film that I even *think is* going to work for a mass audience. Usually I say, "I hope it works for a mass audience," but I am invariably kidding myself. My choices on who should be the president never agree with the mass audience. That's always going to happen with any artist. We fool ourselves in thinking that if you are an established artist—Picasso, let's say—you are popular. Picasso is the leading artist of the century, but he is certainly not popular. He is very popular amongst a very small number of people; the other people don't even know about him, or they know the name—he's a celebrity, not an artist.

One of your associates once said you were "ennobled by failure, and oppressed by success."

Well, that's another one of those nice statements that sounds good.

Is there any internal truth to that?

I think that's almost a truism for everybody. Failure—the word failure—implies an effort. You don't fail without trying. So that's noble. The effort is noble. And success is very dangerous because it leads to complacence. And the reason you can't have continued success in this kind of endeavor is because you strive to push beyond what you just did. I want to be more clever, more obtuse, more . . . I'm trying to show everybody who likes what I do something they've never seen before. So it's very difficult. If the second thing is a bigger success than the first, then on the third thing I'll push way out and then I'll fail, and I'll be forced back down to a plane that is understandable.

Well, if that's oppression, that's a very creative form of oppression.

Well, yeah. Absolutely.

Most people of my generation, I'm thirty-three, would be shocked to know that you were forty-five when you made M*A*S*H.

Forty-four. That's because everybody is youth-oriented.

Right. And the fifteen years you spent in Hollywood before that, doing mostly the TV work, what did that leave you with?

A lot of practice, a lot of rehearsal, a lot of study. I mean, I did hundreds of hours of television, and every bit of that is stored in my computer, as experience, to be used each time. It gave me a great edge on people who direct pictures, who are directing their first film, let's say an actor or writer. I had practice under adverse circumstances, I had practice working short of time and money, I had practice working for people who don't care about quality and I learned how to "sneak" it in. You learn how to work underground.

Was it at all an embittering experience, running into that wall, again and again?

No, never. Never. Never. When I first looked at the wall and said, "I'm going to go up and batter against it," I never had any idea of how long it was supposed to take. Time is relative. And being relative, who's to say it was a long time? You say it was a long time because you're thirty-three and I was forty-four when I made that picture. To me, what am I, sixty-six today?—it doesn't make any difference to me. I don't feel any different. I mean, I'm starting to realize that my body is wearing out, and things like that are happening, but I'm not any different than I was when I was thirty-three. I'm more experienced.

Did you have the expectation that you would succeed in doing what you wanted to do?

I never pictured myself at the end of any road. I mean, I've always been *on the road*, and I still am on the road. How could I envision myself? As some kind of king or something? Or sitting someplace where I could do any caprice, anything I wanted? I wouldn't know how to envision myself.

You once said that there's never been a time in your life when you weren't in debt. Is that still true?

That's true.

Do you set things up to be that way?

No, but I don't try to . . . I don't store money away. I never feel or think that I can't handle whatever it is I have to handle, one way or another, on a day-to-day basis. And I've lived all my life that way. So I have no . . . what can happen to me? [Quietly.] I'm not going to starve. I'm not in danger of being a homeless person. Although that could happen, I'm sure. Being in debt means you just borrow from the bank. If I don't go to work in a few months, it will be very uncomfortable for me. I'll have to do something. So I'll take a job. I'll take some kind of assignment. And every time I've done that (which is constantly) something very, very good has come out of it. The assignment has turned into some kind of a very, very good experience for me. Whether it's a successful experience in terms of somebody else's yardstick is a different thing.

But, if I had played safe and done things, protected myself, and say, had $10 million in the bank working for me, and was totally secure, well, so what? What does that do to my life? It doesn't mean anything.

Theoretically, maybe it gives you the freedom to turn down a job you don't want to do?

Well, I turn down the job I don't want to do until I can't turn it down. On the other hand, if I could turn down forever, maybe I'd be like Warren Beatty or these people who go every five years and make a picture, when they find one that's exactly right. And I think maybe that's a little too safe. And I think it's too dangerous. And when I see that everything is very safe, I think the picture's going to turn out just that way, as well. So I think it isn't any fun for me unless it's a real stretch, a real uphill climb, unless I'm doing something that I don't think can be done.

You've said, "If I could just say, 'Call the bank and tell them I wanted $12 million . . . make it $16 million to do this picture,' well, that would be ugly and horrendous because there's no opposition. There's no struggle. I mean, I have to have these obstacles to fight against or else it's not worth doing."

That's right.

Isn't trying to make something that's artful, that's great art, isn't that obstacle enough? You say "it's not worth doing" unless you have the opposition, from the financing sources, the banks, the studios—

L.A. Shortcuts is my current pet project, which I cannot get the money for. If suddenly I won the lottery and had $12 million and could do it myself, I would do that, because there would be a certain amount of adventure and derring-do to take my own money and do it. But if somebody came along and said, "Here's $30 million, make it for $30 million," that picture would be terrible. Because I could wait, and I wouldn't have that anxiety and that edge that I think is needed—that I at least think I need—in order to be creative. That's why I feel I can't work, or create anything, under drugs or alcohol or anything that changes my condition. I can't make it easy for myself. I have to really face the reality of it, and do my fantasy, but within a very hard reality.

So you wouldn't want the kind of situation that Woody Allen had for years at Orion, where he could do whatever project he wanted, within reason. That would not have been a healthy situation for you.

No, I would have liked it, if I was always pushing, and they gave me $10 million when I needed $12 million. But I think it hurt Woody Allen. I think there's a certain complacency in that. I think he begins to fall into similar situations, although I admire Woody Allen immensely, because I think he's one of the few people that operates as an artist. But I think the same thing happens to Rauschenberg and Jasper Johns—they can do anything that they choose to put the energy into.

Let's say I have a picture, and I can either put unknowns in it and scramble it through, or put in Dustin Hoffman and Robin Williams and Julia Roberts and Bob Hoskins and all those people. If you can have everything you want, there's something, there's some *energy*, some drive that disappears. That war, that struggle, where you have to gamble and you have to fight, to push through; out of that, it seems to me, the best art comes.

You mentioned drugs and booze. Would those things make it easier for you to work, and that's why you say you—

No, I say I couldn't do that. I mean, in that book that that kid wrote [McGilligan's *Robert Altman*] there were several places where he indicated I would come into work drunk. And it just is not true. I've never had a drink in my body in my life when I've worked. The last shot of every day, the crew would know it was the last shot, 'cause they would see someone bringing me a glass of wine. And I know people who do work on grass—millions of musicians do that. But I can't do it, because . . . I'm gone. There's something about

being there with your feet wet in a very hard reality. The minute your obliga-
tions and decisions are finished, then you can get as wasted as you want.

*Have you ever used alcohol or pot—not when you were shooting—but when you
were writing, or in collaboration, working on something?*

No. I mean, I've certainly been drunk and stoned and sat around and talked
about things, but that's a different thing.

Around Nashville, *you said, "I work a lot when I'm drunk and I trust that all
of it will eventually appear in my films."*

What I mean is, when I'm drunk or when I'm stoned, I'm talking and I'm
thinking about things, and I was that way most of my life. At the end of the
day, I don't sit around sober in the evenings, unless I'm working. What I
mean by that is that I'm working all that time—coming up with wild ideas
and having arguments and discussions and blah blah blah. But I've never sat
down at the typewriter and written anything, or never edited or done any
altering when I was in an altered state. Whenever I say "never" there's always
an exception. I'm sure I could find many times when it was the opposite of
that, but not when something can't be reversed.

That again has to do with my own personal situation. All the time, the
forty-five or fifty years I was drinking heavily—I say heavily and I did, I was
a very heavy drinker—I never drank at lunchtime. I couldn't do it. It's not
any moral judgment or anything, it's just simply like putting on a blindfold.
I've never done it. But these kind of statements come out and it indicates that
I'm floundering around on the set, saying do this and do that when I'm
chemicaled out, and I've never done that.

I think smoking grass, for the many years that I've done that, probably
the first fifteen or twenty minutes of getting stoned, some very, very creative
ideas have come out. And we've held onto them, and executed them.

So in that sense, you think it had a positive effect on your work?

Oh, absolutely. It's my life. It's the way I live my life. The way I live my
life is the only thing that has any effect on my work.

When did you stop drinking heavily?

About three years ago, heavily. And it's been about a year and a half that I
haven't had any alcohol at all.

Doctor's orders?

Yeah, it's my heart. My heart is enlarged. So I just stopped. I still smoke
grass when I can. That's medically advisable. And I sometimes turn around,
spin around the room to make myself dizzy. Try to change my temperature.

Was it painful to stop?

No, just boring. Not painful at all.

How's your health now?

Uh, it's okay. My eyesight is getting bad. I have a problem with my right eye. That's aggravating as hell, but it doesn't look like I'm going to be really handicapped by that. There's certain things I have to watch. My heart.

The years 1975 to 1985 were really the cocaine years in Hollywood—

Absolutely.

I'm wondering what was going on for you in those years?

Well, fortunately for me, I never liked coke. I don't like it. It didn't work for me. It made me very paranoid and made me feel very bad, and so I never got addicted. I can get addicted to anything, but I never did that. And it was just something I was lucky to have sidestepped. And also, during those ten years, I wasn't here very much. I was in Europe most of the time. But I have a lot of friends—the ones that didn't die—who were really destroyed by cocaine. Certainly a lot of artists were.

I used to go to those parties, like when we were shooting *Brewster McCloud* and through all that period, and there would be sugar bowls full of cocaine. My only reason for not participating in all that was that I just didn't like it. That was just fortunate. Because my personality is such that I would have become *the* cocaine addict of all time. My only experience with drugs, really, is marijuana and alcohol, and I suppose coffee, and years ago I smoked cigarettes.

You did opium a few times, didn't you?

No, never. Never. Never.

So that was misreported?

Absolutely. When we were shooting *McCabe,* my daughter was begging me to do opium. But I never had the opportunity.

It's become a cliché here, but do you feel you have an addictive personality?

Well, I think I have an excessive personality. I don't know if I'm addictive. I'm excessive.

Was the gambling on the same level as the drinking?

Well, it was on the level of the drinking, but I was never a gamble-oholic. In other words, I never lost a day's work from gambling or drinking, or any of those things. I've never stolen any money, I've never misappropriated, I've never lost any money, I've never put my family in any jeopardy or friends or anything like that. So whatever I did, in terms of that kind of recreation, all of my life, it's never gotten to the point where it's been damaging to anybody else. That is not to say that my *behavior* hasn't been damaging to other people, and probably a lot that I don't even know about, but I don't consider that an issue of any kind.

Was gambling something that brought you, or brings you, a lot of joy?

No. It just was something to do. It's something to do. I gamble at backgammon. I played football and baseball with the bookies for two or three or five years. Lost a measly amount of money. I don't do that any more. I quit that a couple of years ago just because I started feeling silly. I started feeling like a fool: why am I putting so much energy into this? I'm as involved with the football playoffs this year and the World Series as I ever have been, but not gambling.

All this stuff—the gambling, sex, drinking, drugs—all this has been put in some kind of category that these are all the bad things.

Well, let's correct that.

It's bullshit. Because they are not bad things. They can hurt people, but so can obesity. It's just, how you conduct your life and how you conduct your art is really your own choice. And these things I say about what I do, I'm telling you what I find from experience works for me and what doesn't work for me. That doesn't mean that's applicable for other artists. Or that's what Alan Rudolph does or David Lynch does. I don't much care what they do.

No, David collects body parts in fluid.

Well, okay. [Laughs.] Whatever it is, is fine, as long as he's not collecting my fluid!

Do you feel like Hollywood has changed in twenty years?

I think it's basically the same thing, it's just slid more. The power has been taken away from more people and the bottom line has become more strongly the power. I don't know anybody who runs any of these studios who could make a decision about what to put their money into and what not to who will follow their instincts.

Their avaricious instincts or their artistic instincts?

Their artistic instincts. Just to have a feeling, a hunch. Nobody follows hunches anymore. It's marketing, it's market research. And it works. They've figured out how to make a bad picture like *Robin Hood* go out there and generate big grosses by the way they market it, the kind of cartoon that it is. But so what? And now everybody is trying to do the same thing on all the pictures. You're considered not a success if you don't win the whole thing. So we've got films out there like *Ramblin' Rose* in direct competition with *Terminator 2*. That's all there is to it. The critics say the same things about them. It's like taking a Harold Robbins book or a Danielle Steele book and comparing it to an E. L. Doctorow book. I mean, they're both books, so consequently both have to achieve the same thing. It's just terrible what we do. It's all based on money. It's all based on how we measure, and not by the money you spend or how you increase your standard of living, but it's the money which says you're the most important because you've made the most. It's chips. It's markers at the table.

Hasn't it always been that way? Isn't that the American way?

It's become that way, it's become so refined at this point that there's not any room for any mistakes. The only good things that ever came out are in the mistakes. Every film that was a breakthrough film – that changed the way films are made, and changed the way audiences see films, that has affected audiences and changed them – has been an accident. *Easy Rider, M*A*S*H, Five Easy Pieces* – those are pictures that should not have succeeded. They were never *backed*. And you can probably name twenty-five other ones that were real benchmarks that changed things. The point is that different kinds of things do get made, and will continue to get made, but now, totally by mistake. It will be a total accident.

Were the old moguls better than the new moguls?

Absolutely. Because the old moguls had control and they had passion and they had hate. They could say, "I'm gonna burn this goddamn picture! This actor is never going to work again! That actor can go to another studio!" And then the other studio would make a big hit. It wasn't computerized. And now it is. You don't know, now, who is the boss at Columbia? Really? You don't know, and nobody can find out. It's a Japanese corporation. And maybe there isn't any person anymore that is the boss.

Maybe it's an accountant, sitting somewhere in some office.

Undoubtedly it is. Undoubtedly it is. So Hollywood has changed. I think the people working in Hollywood have changed. Everybody is playing by the rules – all the young people that come in all talk in this vein. I hear them, in my own office, talking about "concepts" and "marketing research" and putting this star with that star in this kind of a story, and happy endings – it's all what *The Player* is about. And it's dreadful! It's really dreadful! And that doesn't mean that it will succeed and the artist won't, because the artist *will* succeed. Because they keep growing and appearing and are not corruptible.

Twenty years ago did the executives like movies more than the executives do today?

Yes. I think so. Not a hell of a lot. But a little bit. Forty years ago, certainly. Thirty years ago, more so.

So maybe the old boy network, by comparison, doesn't look as bad now as it did at the time?

No, there was some humanism in it. They may not have made the pictures that you and I would have liked, but they made the pictures that they liked — and that's something.

And now they are making the films, not that they like, but that they think the sixteen-year-old at the mall will?

That's right. That's exactly what they have to do. A guy like Brandon Tartikoff has come out and said that. And that's his business, if that's the business he wants to do. But he's wrong, because what they don't know is that people tire of this stuff and they catch on very quickly. I'm sure if you make a *Hook* every year, it's going to disappear.

Does the audience really want to see something that they haven't seen before, or have they been so manipulated by now that what they want to see is what they've already seen, again and again?

No, that's all they can tell you that they want to see, because that's all they have in their experience. The audience will never sit there and say, "We want to see something we haven't seen before." But that *is* what they want to see. They want to be surprised. They also want some familiarity — it's comfortable to be familiar, it's comfortable to see Gene Hackman in a picture.

The part Hollywood gets wrong is that they are trying to service an existing market with the same material, rather than trying to create new markets. They're not doing that, which is why you have all these numbers after all of the titles. You take a clipboard and go out to one of these lines where they're lined up on Westwood Boulevard and say, "What movie would you like to see most?" And they will tell you a movie they have already seen. Because they can't tell you a movie they haven't seen. What actors do you want to see? Oh, I want to see Julia Roberts. They want to see someone that pleased them before. They don't know that there are six thousand actresses in the world that could please them more.

Cronenberg's take on this is that art gives you what you don't know you want, while entertainment gives you what you already know you want.

Well, that's true. But I don't know how much art there is in this and I don't know how much entertainment there is in this — it's become more. I think the big problem is that the audience knows too much about the manufacturing of it now. They know too much of people like me talking, there's too much bookkeeping — this picture cost $43 million, and this picture grossed such and such — I can't pick up the fucking paper or turn on the television without finding out what the "number-one picture of the week" is. And that's just free advertising for the wrong movie. It's them that has the most gets the most, and gets the most gets more.

Nothing succeeds like success.

Yeah. But it will fail. It is destined to fail. It cannot succeed.

Vincent Van Gogh says to brother Theo, "Don't tell me there's no market for my work, it's your job to make a market."

That's exactly right.

And I know you resist identifying with Van Gogh—

Because it's such a cheap shot. And also, it puts me in a position of equating myself with that sort of quality.

But if you're really honest, you've got to identify with him, on a number of important levels.

I identify with him more than I do . . . with Gaugin. Sure, I do. Because I know what his struggle is, and it's basically the same struggle that all artists go through. They want somebody to appreciate what they've done.

But if they're making a market for your work—that's marketing. And there's going to be some discomfort in that, isn't there?

There's all kinds of marketing. I guess basically it comes down to not underestimating the audience. Which most of these guys do. They say, "Oh, I like this, but everybody else won't." As soon as somebody tells you that, you're dealing with a fool, the minute they say they get it but nobody else will. They *don't* get it, is what they mean. Everybody is not equal. Certain people are not going to enjoy a Kurosawa film, certain people are. Certain people aren't going to "get" one of my films, certain people are. And the intention is *not* to get all of these people. It's there for all these people; it's up to them to make the effort, not for me to make the effort. They have to make the effort. They have to be educated. I mean, my own editor for this picture, she just said, "Gee, I rented *The Long Goodbye* last night, and I didn't like that picture when it first came out, but it's really good." Well, the picture hasn't changed one bit. She's changed.

You've spoken about trying to "train an audience," trying to bring an audience along with you—

Absolutely. This work doesn't exist unless an audience is half of it. If they come there and sit in front of their sets or in the theatre, and they don't go halfway with you, and take the material in front of them and process it through their own history, it's meaningless. Ideally, I want someone to walk out after one of my pictures and say, "I don't have any idea what that was about, but it was right."

Well, if they think it's right, doesn't that mean it just confirms what they already walked into the theatre with?

They can't literally explain why it's right. It's like looking at a painting that you're just in awe of. There are a lot of people that have never been in awe of any painting. 'Cause they don't allow themselves to be. Who's to say that the greatest poet in the world isn't the person who goes up and whispers one word into somebody's ear? And it startles them. It changes them. It scrambles their information. It augments or changes all the information they have. That's a poet.

So for you, the lack of articulation by the audience is a sign not of their passivity, but that they had an experience that they cannot place well?

That they cannot delineate to someone else. They only know that it fits. It's like a color.

And in time?

In time, yes, they learn that, but they have to do the learning. We can't teach. You can only allow someone to learn. That's what most teaching is: allowing someone to learn.

Did those hundreds of TV episodes and industrials before them make you intolerant of linearity, of cause and effect? Did all that nuts-and-bolts work propel you into a milieu where what you valued more would be oblique, or opaque, or not so definable?

I don't know. Maybe it did. But I know the films that I was impressed by during the time I was making those industrial films, and they are the same films I am impressed by now. I was trying to do something to emulate those things. I was trying to do something like that. Everything is a lesson. Every single thing you perceive stays in your computer, and becomes mixed and tainted by every other thing you've learned. Like a pond. You put in some red ink, and it affects every other thing there. We're all very, very similar, but none of us are the same. If somebody's mother dies—everybody feels exactly the same way, more or less. There's a certain amount of universal reaction. Now there are some people who might have killed their mothers.

We have communication, which the Bengal tiger doesn't have as completely. A Bengal tiger walks through a rain forest at sunset, and this fantastic light comes through the mist, and a parrot calls out, and the colored light is just so. He doesn't run home and say to the rest of the tigers, "Hey, you've got to see this sunset." I don't think they do that. But people do. And they go so far as to paint them. And they paint them for two reasons. One, they're amazed at their own skill of being able to do it. They're proud of their own skill, and they want approval from other people, to tell them how good they are at what they do. But also, they just love that sunset and think it's beautiful and want to show it to someone else. And all of those elements enter into art.

What fascinates you most about people?

The absolute differences between each individual and yet the sameness of them. I think of ants. I stand and see a little ant hill, and see a line of ants. And that's people. And every once in a while, you see one little ant that gets out of line—you see one of them out there, about an inch from the main line. In the main line, these guys are crawling on top of one another and some of them are hooking rides maybe. And the one that goes out by himself, usually he gets stepped on. They don't get out very far. But that's Picasso, and Einstein, and Hitler . . .

And the Altman ant?

The Altman ant is in the middle. Well, hopefully, I'm over to one of the edges of the main stream.

But not so far out that you'll feel someone's heel?

Well, I've never been out that far. If I get out that far I'll get stepped on.

How do you think of yourself?

I think pretty highly of myself, I think. I know that each individual is the center of the entire universe. And everything else spins around them. So everything that has ever happened in my life, in my experience, spins around me. But I'm spinning around somebody else. And I think that all my children think about is me, and all my wife thinks about is me, and everything is based on me, and I'm absolutely incorrect about that. I'm the only one who only thinks about me.

You're supposed to get past that stage at four or five—you're supposed to learn that the moon is not actually following you when you drive at night in a car.

Yeah, but you're stuck with where you are—you are stuck inside of yourself. And consequently, you are dealing with your own experiences. And with pain, you can deal with your own pain, and you can empathize with someone else's pain, and you can make pain for yourself because you feel so bad about that person's pain, but it's not the same pain. It's a different pain.

Do you think everyone is lonely, essentially?

Yeah, in a way. I think everyone is basically alone. I think everyone experiences that. When you're not alone, you say, "Oh I'm so lonesome, I want to be with someone else." What does that mean? Does that mean you want to share what you know with someone else? Do you want them to share what they know with you? Or do you just want them to cater to you? I think being alone is really dreadful. I don't like to be alone. I much prefer to be with people.

It strikes me that in your work, the most personal of your films are the ones that most strongly convey the sense not that we are connected, but how we are cut off from each other. I think of McCabe and Mrs. Miller. So much of that film is about what doesn't happen between them.

That's right. That's right. *McCabe* is about a loser. The only reason McCabe is the person you associate with in that film is because he's the one I pointed you at: "Oh, look at this one." It's like putting the tag on a dolphin. You catch a bunch of dolphins. Okay, let's tag one. Now we follow that dolphin, all the way to Japan and back. God, look what he did! He killed a shark over here, and he did this and did that. But we don't know what those other dolphins did—they probably did something very similar, and we probably could have been just as interested in them. It's pretty much the same as what I was saying about ourselves: the world centered around McCabe. In *The Player*, it's around Griffin [Tim Robbins].

Going back to Kansas City, what did growing up surrounded by women do to you?

I don't have any idea. Except it was a fact. I suppose I became manipulative, and comfortable with women, and not threatened by them.

Why manipulative?

Well. [Pause.] I think that's probably what people do like that. I'm sure I'm a much different person than if I had grown up with two brothers. It may not be discernible in my personality, but it certainly is discernible in my art. Not that as a specific thing, but anything that happened to me. Those are my basic chips. Nobody else can be me. And every experience that happens, every crossroads, the weather, whether it rained a certain night and didn't rain another night, somewhere is buried in this sphere that grows, that is you.

You've certainly been willing to give women more focus in your films than most directors of your generation.

I have, but I've never done that consciously, and I don't know why. I don't have any idea.

Why did you get married the first two times you did?

I got married because that's what you did. I mean, that was a progression, a goal. And I wanted to have children, and a wife, and a family, and I was in love with the person that I married. It's what everybody else did.

So you pretty much bought into the program?

Oh, I buy right into it. I'm very mainstream.

But you weren't fit for what comes with that, were you?

No, I think I romanticized. I had no realistic attitude about it. I can hardly even remember what my feelings or attitudes were. These were just things that happened.

If we were in for a session of Chinese Communist self-criticism, what would you say were your greatest weaknesses?

Probably egocentrism. I'm probably self-oriented. I probably misrepresent myself. I'm probably one of those people that think I know more than I actually do. All the normal things.

And as a director, your greatest strengths and weaknesses?

I don't know. I think that has to do with the other parties involved. I have worked with many many actors. I know that actors basically like me. Generally. I know there are some actors that don't like me at all, and I know there are actors that I can't communicate with. I am saying things and I am looking in their eyes and I can see that they don't "get it." That doesn't mean they're wrong, because I've seen their work, and they're terrific. But there are some people that you just cannot connect with. That's a lack, I think. Again, all the things I think are weaknesses about people are their own insecurities and trying to cover up for them.

Is it fair to say you have a problem with endings, or that endings are a problem for you?

But that's not a problem, that's a blessing.

Let's put the word "problem" in quotes.

I don't do satisfactory endings because I don't think anything stops. The only ending I know about is death.

The ultimate "cut."

Death is, to me, the only ending. People say I don't know how to do an ending. I probably don't know how to do that well. I don't think that well. I probably wouldn't like a good ending if it were presented to me—I'd probably reject it.

One of the frequent themes in your work is the space between image and reality, or the way we lie about ourselves. So I'm curious as to how you would assess the separation between your image—how you present yourself or have been presented to the public—and your reality.

It's probably the same as everybody else's. I present myself according to the existing circumstance. I try to be comfortable, and hold my position of power with whoever I'm dealing with.

How are you like Nixon?

How am *I* like Nixon?

How are you like Nixon?

I don't think I'm really anything like Nixon. No, I think I'm a little different species than Nixon.

You can't find any similarities?

Well, I'm sure I could find sympathetic areas. When I was doing *Secret Honor*, the Nixon piece, and thinking about Nixon a lot, I could find things that I could understand. Why do you ask?

I'm asking because one of the things I get from your sense of Nixon is that even when he was at the pinnacle of power, the ultimate insider, successful, he still felt completely like an outsider and a loser—

And will he always.

—And I wonder if you shared that.

I feel a little like an outsider. And not much like a loser, but I feel like I'm not *the* winner. I feel like there are always other winners, who are more winners than I am. I don't think of myself as a loser, though. I don't have the same opinion of myself that Nixon has of himself.

What about the anger?

[Pause.] My anger is . . . couched . . . my anger is in things that don't work out the way I want them to. And then I translate that into . . . I try to get other people . . . to support me.

It seems like your anger is generative—that it generates heat or something that's helpful to you.

Well, I might manipulate my anger a little bit. Rarely do I have a loss-of-control thing.

But at the end of Secret Honor, *Nixon's "Fuck 'em! Fuck 'em! Fuck 'em!"—directed at all his enemies—seems like it could almost be Bob Altman on a conference call, just having heard that some major studio has decided not to finance his picture.*

Oh, I could do that, yes. That was also Nixon's "Fuck 'em!" That was his personality. But I understand that. I admire that. I like that, the way that ends. See, there's a good ending.

And The Player *has quite a neat ending.*

The Player has a manipulated ending. It's the same ending as *M*A*S*H*. Those aren't endings, they are stopping places.

Which is why "Tanner '88," in looking at all six hours of it, feels kind of perfect to me—in that it goes on and it goes on and it goes on, and that's Altman, that's what you dig, really.

Yeah. That's right. That's what I'm showing. There aren't any endings.

The endless serial is a perfect form for you.

Yeah, it is.

Have you thought of doing more of it?

Oh, I've been trying to do this for forty years.

A serial movie?

Always. I remember, when I read *Tales of the South Pacific,* it was before the musical was ever done, I went crazy. I wanted to make a ten-hour picture of that. Five two-hour films. You could look at them in any order. There would be no Part I. It would just meld together. The form of *Nashville,* the form of *L.A. Shortcuts,* everything that I ever put together myself usually has that form where the edges of different stories touch. And I would love to do a never-ending story, a continual serial. And I'll do it. If someone gave me the television wherewithal to do it, I would probably rather do something for television than I would for film.

What did you learn doing "Tanner?" You said it was the "newest" work you had done?

Well, I think it was the most creative work that I've done. I think I broke more ground on "Tanner" than on anything else I've ever done.

In what sense?

In that style of crossing reality with the fiction characters. In other words, I made seven or eight characters—or Garry Trudeau and me, we made up these characters—then we take 'em out and put them into real situations, and very quickly those people become very real. *The Player* could not have existed if I had not done "Tanner."

How so?

Well, I think the whole idea of using real people—the way I use real celebrities and people—in connection with my fiction. And we did this in two ways: Julia Roberts plays herself, but she's playing Julia Roberts acting another character. And I never told anybody what to do. I didn't tell *anybody* what to do. I would never tell anybody what to do. I said, I have not got the right to tell you what to do because you are not being paid as an actor, you have been asked to perform as yourself—to be yourself. How can I tell you how to be yourself? Only you can tell you how to be yourself, and it's probably the hardest part you've ever had to play. It was never my intention to try to write anything for them.

You're willing to give up a lot of control that other directors hold on to very tightly.

Oh, yeah, I insist on it. But then, I don't know if that's giving up control. I mean, I'm still filling the space. I'm letting them color the space. And I'm making my adjustments according to what happens.

Filling the space is a painting phrase, really. A painter friend of mine used to talk about wanting to "fuck up the space." That was what painting was about.

It probably is!

And in a sense, what you are doing is "fucking up the space," not just filling it.

Yeah. It's letting that space . . . it's like doing a living mural. I'm going to do a mural. So I take a pigment—an actor—and I put her up there by the horses, and suddenly the horses are moving, though, and the actor decides to go this way, and she gets over there in the purple, and so I say shit, this composition isn't any good. Well, I can't stop these pigments from doing what they are doing, but I can throw more things up there that will change it. It's like a basketball game, I can throw a guard up there that will make this person turn and go the other way. I'm quickly sidestepping, I'm constantly moving. The minute the actor performs the first "act" I have to start moving my point of view, because it's not what I had in mind.

Why did you not concentrate more on your painting?

Oh, I'm not really very good at it. I think I probably could have been. But I was only fairly gifted in drawing and that sort of thing.

What's the work like?

It's very pedestrian.

Representational?

Yeah. I don't have the courage to do abstract. And also, there's so much knowledge I don't have. I want it to look like *this* and I can't get that, so I do something else. I'm very smug about things that I do.

Smug?

Yeah. Happy. You know, I like my work.

You say you've loved every film you've ever done.

Absolutely.

And the least successful all the more because it's like the parent loving the kid that's flunking out of school; he needs it more.

A lot of that is defensive. But basically, there will be pretty much of a quorum on the ones that are most successful. That doesn't mean that the others aren't what I set out to do, or aren't an improvement on what I set out to do.

Does it feel like there was ever a bad period, though?

Oh, there's bad periods. But I don't think you could know when those periods are, till after they've passed. It's pretty much like sitting at a poker table or the race track, and you get off, or you think you're off, and you just know that you're salty, that it's just a bad period and you make bad judgments, bad calls, and you lose.

Was O.C. and Stiggs *a bad call?*

It was probably a bad call going in. I probably did it for a lot of the wrong reasons.

It seemed sad to me that in it you were quoting things from earlier films: the bird droppings from Brewster, Hal Phillip Walker *from* Nashville, *it felt—*

See, I see no reason not to use those characters. The bird droppings was a steal, but . . . I thought *O.C. and Stiggs* was an adult satire. It was really my own outrage at teenage pictures.

But to make an uninvolving teen picture simply as a commentary on teen pictures is a very abstract and subtle business, isn't it?

Yeah, most people didn't like it. Although there are lots of people that really think that's a funny picture. I can sit and watch that picture any time with an audience. Any time!

What's funny about it to you?

Oh, the . . . I don't know if it's funny, but I like it. I love the dance sequence, when O.C. and what's-her-name go into that dance. I love that. I love her house, at the end. I don't want to get into defending that picture too much.

I am just trying to play Joe Audience here. I have a profound feeling for a lot of your work, and then I come across other films that I really have to struggle to get through.

Well, you don't like them. Because you've seen it already, and it's not new to you, and you can see my machinations. You can see their workings, and you don't like it. That's understandable. And kind of common.

Like when Beyond Therapy *came out, you said, "I think it's romantic and funny and bizarre. It's too sophisticated for most audiences. People are too lazy to get into it."*

Yeah, that's a defense. But I think *Beyond Therapy* failed and was thought badly of primarily because it came out about the time AIDS became public [1987], really public, and here was all this casual, bisexual sex, without any comments made on it. I didn't aggrandize the homosexuality and I didn't criticize it.

Let's put that off to the side, because—

Well, that's the main issue here. That's the main issue in that picture. Otherwise that picture doesn't . . . that picture, yeah, it's ill-conceived. The play [that it was based on] was not very good. I shot it in Paris to make it look like New York. I said, "I'll do that if I can shoot that in Paris."

What does the Paris period feel like to you?

Well, I was working there on projects that never got done.

Did you feel like an ex-pat?

No. Never. There were new things there. I learned new things. Different attitudes from different people, actors. And I edited over there. I did three films: *Beyond Therapy* and I did a little thing called *The Laundromat,* which I shot on a soundstage. The things like the two Harold Pinter plays I did—those are not successful really, but, to me, it became an exercise in building those sets that they were on. And taking this absurd play and presenting it in as unabsurd a way as I could find. Those aren't arresting pieces: nobody's going to sit there and say, "My God, you've got to go see this!" I don't think they are offensive pieces. They are exercises. They're like sketches. I could do those a hundred more times and they would never really succeed. I'd never find the key that makes everything work.

I think you did eight straight films that were written originally for the stage, which you shot for either TV or the cinema.

Well, that's because that's what I could get done.

Just on a purely economic level—

Well, just the work. Whether I needed the money—I didn't make much money on those things, but in order to work, I could not get anything else done. And those were quite challenging to do. To take a theatre piece and do it. I guess it started with "Jimmy Dean," and then once people saw that, everybody was bringing me their plays. "The Caine Mutiny Court-Martial" was much after that. That came up during the Iran-Contra trials. I was sitting and watching Oliver North and those people, for hours, for hundreds of hours. No rushing the action or anything. So somebody called me and asked, would I like to do "The Caine Mutiny Court-Martial." I said yeah.

*The Player *is essentially about a guy who doesn't get his phone call returned. You've been in that position, of having people not answering the phone when you've called them—*

Yeah. But again, I don't think there's anything in *The Player* that is any more personal to me than was in *M*A*S*H*. In fact, I think *The Player* is more like *M*A*S*H* than any other film that I've made.

Don't you think it's more like The Long Goodbye?

I think it looks more like *The Long Goodbye.* Yes, that film comes to mind the most. And in terms of the ending. But, to me, it feels more like *M*A*S*H*, and I don't know how to explain that, but it does. I never would have written that story. I never would have conceived that story. But when I read it, I said, "Oh, *this* is something to work on." I could empathize.

*When people stopped returning your calls, in the post-*Popeye *period, when you* *decided to get out and move to Paris, did you feel like whistling "Hurray for Hollywood" and leaving in a kind of a—*

No, I sold the studio [Lion's Gate]. I sold that, because I wanted to get out of it. I was also financially in trouble. I wasn't doing what I wanted to do. I did a couple of small plays after *Popeye*. I didn't have any big picture offers. I don't remember any. None that I took, certainly. I was always working on other projects. But I saw no reason to stay here.

"I know a cure," you said. "I know a cure. I'll go off to Paris and be rich and arrogant and look down on people."

Did I say that?

Yeah. Were you being wry?

I don't know what I was being, but that's not true.

But didn't you feel that there would be respect for you as an artist, which here had gotten discredited simply on the basis of the dollar?

I *never* had it here as you get it there. I'm sure that my going to Europe was because I was more welcome there. And so that's where I went. Yeah, I was more accepted. But I also had projects I wanted to do there. I had had the experience of working in Europe in 1972 when I did *Images*. And I like the fact that things are done differently, and it was a very attractive idea for me. I never really succeeded in Europe. In anything. My success, of all the work I did at that time, was all for US consumption.

It's funny because in America we think the audience is so sophisticated over there, compared to here—but fifteen years ago you said the audience in Europe still looked at movies as entertainment and not art, that they were twenty years behind us.

Absolutely. Absolutely.

Do you think that's still true?

Yes. I think they are the same twenty years behind.

Is that why Jerry Lewis and Mickey Rourke are the French cultural icons?

Oh, I don't think that's true. They create, from a very small group of people, they create their own heroes. And of course that spreads. You know, the French and Italian films we see here we think are such great films—they *fail* in their own countries. Fellini can hardly get a job in Italy!

So why, if films are seen as entertainment and not art, did you feel the reception would be so much better for you there, as an artist?

Well, the people who invest and buy the film and make the films worthwhile are more in tune with wanting to let the artist make the film. But their big audience is a very illiterate audience, just like it is here.

You think even worse? Even behind us?

I think everything over there is maybe twenty or fifteen years behind us.
Maybe in ten years it will only be ten years behind. It's like Canada! You
go there and you see cultural things—not that being in front means quality—
but you see that where the general American culture was fifteen years ago
is about where the culture in Canada, in Vancouver, in Toronto, is today.

*In Kamloops, in Moosejaw. What did directing for theatre in the post-*Popeye
period teach you? And what did it teach you about film?

I think that analytically, I figured out that the rehearsal time in theatre is
the equivalent to the editing time in film. You go in, and you edit and edit
and edit and edit: that's your rehearsal. And then you present it, and it's
finished. In film, you go in and shoot, and you're gathering all the raw material, and then you edit and edit and edit and edit—that's the rehearsal time.
You rehearse after you've shot. And you make the piece, and present it.

It's all the same thing, but in theatre you don't have the image manipulation that you have in film. You don't have the range. But you can be much
more imaginative. The words become more important. If I had to pick between theatre and film, I would stay with film. I think I would like to do one
more theatre piece.

*It's interesting that in your pre-theatre period you were known as being very open
about scripts—a screenplay was just a blueprint, and not more than that—but
then you went into a period where the scripts were as written in stone as they ever
could be, because not only were they finished, but they had been performed hundreds of times. So it was a complete 180 degrees from your relationship to scripts
previous to that.*

Yeah. That was a new experience for me. And I never saw any of these plays
performed. Except "Jimmy Dean" [which Altman directed]. I mean, I never
saw "Streamers" performed. At least I went into those things clean.

You didn't see "Fool for Love" before you shot it?

"Fool for Love" I saw performed. But "Fool for Love" is not a play . . . *Fool
for Love* is a film, and I think it's one of my best films. The words don't make
that much difference to me in films generally, so why should it make that
much difference to me whether they are words that somebody else wrote, or
words that somebody *else* wrote? I mean, it doesn't make any difference. If
the actor is comfortable saying the words, then why not?

What do you mean when you say the words don't make that much difference?

The dialogue. Usually, it depends what the intent is. It depends on what it
is we have to show. If it's radio, then the words are the only thing you have

to go on—the words and the sound effects. Nobody talks about radio drama, but there's a great art that was knocked out in its infancy by television.

In theatre the words are very important, too.

In theatre the words are more important, because . . .

The words are almost the "actions"—

Yes. In theatre, they are. It doesn't have to be one or the other. There are endless combinations of these things. And to me, it's almost kind of like doing the opera. I know exactly how long the opera is going to be. I cannot possibly let it go longer than the music, or shorter than the music. So when I go to do the opera, I can't say, "Oh, that's enough of that scene." I have to fill that time. And that's very unlike what I have to do with film.

Was it interesting for you to butt up against the restrictions of a script-in-stone?

Yeah. For instance, in *The Caine Mutiny Court-Martial*, I got Herman Wouk's message across, but I don't think any more of the dilemma of Barney Greenwald than I do of the dilemma of Queeg. Or the mutineer. I think they all have their own dilemmas. And I had *nothing to say* in that play.

But you never feel you have anything to say, do you?

It's true, it's true: I don't have anything to say!

So why say anything?

Oh, 'cause I'm saying what other people say, and I'm showing it to you in the context of the way it appears to me. It's like a painting. I'm not going to make up a sunset. I'm going to paint a sunset.

And that, in itself, gives you pleasure?

Yeah. Because I'm doing something different. It's inescapable that everything you see of mine is going to have my vague shape, like a cookie cutter, a gingerbread man, because all the material has been pushed through me. So it's going to have a vague resemblance.

Slightly rotund and fuzzy on the edges.

More than likely. It will be recognizable as my shape. But, I am not there telling you what my thoughts or my political ideas are. You will feel what they are, but mainly I'm letting everybody present themselves the way they want to present themselves.

Which is why Nashville *could be Julie Nixon Eisenhower's favorite film—*

Absolutely.

And which is why Nixon-lovers as well as Nixon-haters can really like Secret Honor.

Absolutely. Absolutely.

And which is why people who love Hollywood can love The Player *and people who despise Hollywood can love* The Player.

Absolutely. Because I didn't take "ankle shots" at people, cheap shots. My only real diabolical move—in my closet I can say I *got them*—is the agents. I took care of the agents in *The Player* because there aren't any.

Although I'm not sure that a Republican would enjoy "Tanner," since neither you nor Garry Trudeau—

Oh, I couldn't have done it as well with a Republican candidate. But I don't think the Democratic candidates came off too well. You know why they didn't come off well? Because they represented *themselves*. And to me, I'm not making propaganda. I'm making a film. And the film is art, and I think art is truthful. But propaganda—whether it's positive or negative propaganda—is something that isn't true, but you're trying to make people think it's true. So I believe every dog should have his day. And every time I see a character in any script I read or think I'm gonna do, and I see this great guy, I think: let's find all the bad things about him, and show them. Or vice versa. A guy who is so rotten—does that mean that he can't kiss his wife goodbye when he goes to catch the streetcar?

You're naturally a contrarian.

Yes, absolutely. Why don't you show the hero having fear? It's not serving a cause that I think I should believe in.

One of the things in that book [the biography] is that I call some guy "the Jew with the money." I say, "He didn't want to be the Jew with the money." Jesus Christ! That's a phrase I use with anybody. I don't think it's an anti-Semitic phrase unless the word "Jew" is.

I got a son, my youngest son is black. His father was black, and his mother was . . . he was adopted at birth. And I still find myself—I always—I talk about "niggers." And I have no racial problems.

Do you understand that that word is offensive to a lot of black people?

Yes, I understand. I understand also that everybody knows that word. The other day, I was in here and I thought of an old song. [Sings] "Here comes a nigger with a sack on his back, baby!" And someone said, "Shhh! You shouldn't say that!" And I said, "Why shouldn't I say that? That's what's in that song."

Well, there you are quoting something, you're not calling someone a nigger.

No, but most of the time when you use those phrases, you are using other people's phrases. You're not making those up.

Well, you're not making up the word—we don't make up much of our own vocabulary—but it's the way we use it that counts.

I'm talking about the way it's used. If you say, "That cotton-picking nigger this and that" . . . I don't . . . I remember the last time I was in Kansas City, I mean years ago, going to a cleaning store, I don't know how old I was, probably in my late twenties, and some guy said, "Just a minute, I'm sorry, it's not ready yet. Get the nigger to go get the such and such." And I was just shocked by that, that someone was referred to as a nigger, as if that was a profession. And I thought, Jesus, I grew up in this. I grew up in this! I grew up with a black woman being my nanny, and all of those things of course have to rub off, they're in your basic chips. But that doesn't mean that I'm a racist.

No, but if you're talking about Hollywood, would you call Denzel Washington a nigger? Would you say, "that nigger actor"?

Oh, absolutely not. Because it doesn't apply. It would apply only as if I called somebody "the Jew with the money."

Because he was Jewish and had money?

No, because there's a history of the Jews with the money, being the money people. It's just a phrase. It's the same phrase as "redneck." Calling someone a redneck. I wouldn't like to be thought of as a redneck, but people—I remember somebody once said I looked like a "redneck cop" to him. I was offended by that. I didn't want to look like a redneck cop.

Well, how does the Jew with the money feel about being called the Jew with the money?

I don't know. I said it to him, and I said it with humor. Bigotry is when you don't think somebody is really of the same species that you are. It's like disliking tall guys. When you're around tall guys, you say, "Hey, how's the weather up there?" And they don't like that. But that doesn't have anything to do with your own feelings of bigotry. If you want to see bigotry, go to Europe. Go to France, go to England, go to Canada—there's much more than there is in this country. Go to Montana, it's terrible. But this is tribal. This has nothing to do with—it's an overdone thing.

Let me cut back to Fool for Love, *then I'd like to focus on the last three things you've done. When you did* Fool for Love, *you said you didn't care if it was the worst film ever made, you were going to do it for the opportunity to work with Sam Shepard on a play he wrote, and have him in it.*

[Resigned.] Yeah, I said that. The idea of me making a film with the author of a play, and the author playing a part, to me was irresistible. And because I was in such a catbird's seat. And I thought it would be fun.

Cheerfully perverse.

Yeah, perverse and fun. It turned out to be not much fun at all.

You and Shepard had a tough time.

No, I didn't have too tough a time, and he didn't have a tough time. Any tough times we had, we gave ourselves. But I didn't like him very much and he, I'm sure, didn't like me. He just wasn't a very nice person during that time.

And that's why it was no fun?

Yeah. He wasn't nice. He was very self-oriented. Kim Basinger was just terrific, I'm crazy about her. And Sam, I think, is very, very good in that picture. As good as I wanted him to be.

How did he end up feeling about the picture?

Oh, he would never say. I'm sure he hated it. We'd show the dailies, and he could come in whenever he got up—we'd work all night—and we'd look at the dailies in the morning. He'd come in late in the afternoon and we'd run the dailies for him and he'd only look at the dailies that *he* was in. And of course, all the flashback stuff, all the storytelling illustrations that I did, he, to this day—he says he never saw the picture, and he probably hasn't—he didn't know what I was doing, nor did he care, that I was showing something different than what the characters were telling. And that, to me, that time warp in that picture, is what made that film so good. I think that was a terrific film, I really liked that film. I liked the structure of it, I liked the performances in it, I just liked the picture very much. The bizarreness of it. But Sam just wasn't very likable. I don't know why.

"Tanner '88." It occurs to me that although it's satirical about nearly everything in it, it's really most satirical not about politics per se as much as about how we "mediate" politics.

Yes, it was more about the media, about the press, than anything else, I would think.

And it worked best for me when I had no consciousness of anyone "acting" at all.

That's right.

In the beginning, there are some off notes, when it does seem "theatrical."

Yeah, a lot of them. But after we got going and kind of knew what we were doing, we got very good at it. In the beginning, we were very nervous, and we didn't quite know what we were doing—there was a lot of forcing in there. But I liked that a lot. That was a lot of fun. That was tough. There again is a case where we didn't have the resources to do anything more than we did. We have ten days to do each one of those shows.

It's funny: we like Tanner [Michael Murphy], and if you have a liberal drift, you want to like Tanner—but after six hours of it, we don't know what the hell Tanner stands for, except that John is his favorite Beatle.

Oh, he's a shell: he's a very empty character. And I don't know that having John Lennon as your favorite Beatle makes you anything.

It's obvious that it's written that way, that you didn't want to develop any political agenda.

No, because the minute Garry Trudeau and I start developing a political agenda, then we're doing propaganda. And I think I was more so than Garry. His writing was much more . . .

You didn't get writing credit on that, did you?

No. I never did write anything down. But in the doing of it, in the construction—we created the character, we created the backstory, we created the people. But he would have a half-hour script for each one of those, for each city we would go to. And if nothing happened, I would just do that script, that was our safety. But the minute I would find something there that I could push out into, that's what I would do. And something always happened.

There's a fascinating episode called "The Girlfriend Factor," which focused on inner-city Detroit—

That was the best one.

—And what was provocative about it is that the viewer feels he's getting reality almost "unmediated" by the camera and the people working on it, and yet there is completely an artificial construct around it, like a reality sandwich, to quote the beat phrase. So you're not sure what you're looking at. [In this episode, candidate Tanner travels to a ghetto neighborhood and listens to the residents talk about their problems.]

Well, the people who were doing that, who were in that forum, they thought they were on a talk show. It was like a talk show without a moderator. And we just let that stuff go. It just happened. We couldn't get the police to go into that neighborhood. They said it was too dangerous. So we just went in there, and went through SOSAD [Save Our Sons And Daughters], and these people just showed up. And we just photographed them.

Were you moved by what happened?

Absolutely. I was moved by the ridiculousness of it—that one guy showed up with a straw hat and a red bow tie and was a Reverend So-and-So, and he was one of those Bible-thumping niggers that did all that kind of neighborhood stuff, and was just a jerk of all time; there were confused, old drunks; there were really angry people there, who were women who had lost their children; and everybody there was doing their thing. And we did everything we could do not to interfere with that. And we gave it much, much more time than was ever allotted for it.

Did you intentionally bring the cassette to HBO late, so that they wouldn't screen it before they showed it?

Well, they got everything late. They never got to screen anything. We intentionally did that. It was also how close we were getting to airtime on those things.

At the end of that episode, when Tanner finds a dead kid in the bushes, that's not necessary. It felt like a false note.

It isn't necessary. See, that was written. And we did it. I'm not sure I like it. Yeah, it was weak.

Why aren't you running Tanner in 1992?

Nobody would give us the money to do it. We need about $1.2 million a show, an hour. And nobody can see it. There's nobody you can go to and say, "Listen, this has great shelf life. This is really a historical document." And they say, "Well, how can we sell it? We can't sell it for reruns, nobody is interested for this. It's not commercial."

Our plan was to come back, and in the very first episode, he was going to get ready to go to New Hampshire and run, he was going to find out that his daughter tested HIV-positive. His daughter has AIDS. And he decides not to run, but they take him anyway, and he runs. And so we have our soap-opera story: the daughter has AIDS, how did she get it? And all that stuff. And that would have allowed us to make AIDS an issue of the 1992 election, which it will not be, even with Magic Johnson. He jumped too soon. But AIDS may be the only issue in 1996. I think we would have had a terrific year.

See, it doesn't make any difference who Tanner is! Tanner is merely the calling card to get into the process. Again, the point is not to try to make the character make events go the way you want them to go, but make him whatever he wants. The *reaction* to him is what's interesting, and where it takes us. Some people said, "Oh, I wish we could vote for somebody like Tanner!" And I said, "This guy is *terrible*." And Michael Murphy got very embarrassed by it, because everybody got faked out, everybody thought Murphy could go in there with all those heavyweight politicians and talk. And he'd say, "Goddammit, I don't sound like I know what I'm talking about." So I said, "Well, get your ass out there and find out what you're talking about. You can talk about any goddamn thing you want." He got very hot one night. I said, "You're a shell, that's what you are, you don't have that knowledge." So Murphy was perfect: he's well-meaning, he's got the humor to laugh at himself, he looks good, he's the perfect candidate.

Now as to Vincent and Theo, *it seems the last thing that Bob Altman would want to do, the sacrosanct, PBS-style, great-artist-of-the-past thing. Was that more cheerful perverseness?*

No. It was a four-hour miniseries, the way it was written. Just like PBS, just like "Masterpiece Theater." It was a dreadful script. And these guys came and they wanted me to do it, and it just fit my time slot so well, and it intrigued me. I had tried to do a film on Jackson Pollock, and had another film I wanted to do about the art world today, a *Nashville* type of thing, sampling all kinds of people that are connected to it. And so I was in tune for that, so I said okay.

You're not too excited about Van Gogh as an artist: you've said he didn't have any ideas, he didn't have any imagination, that it was all his passion and energy, but that he was no visionary, that he was not that creative, really.

No, he wasn't. That's right. But again, I don't care. I'm not trying to make him up, I'm just trying to present what I see is there, and do it in a way that shows a little more of backstage.

Do you identify with him on that level—of not being the most imaginative guy? When we were talking about writing you admitted to not being imaginative in that way, yourself.

Yeah, a little bit. I don't think identifying, personally, with anybody is . . . I don't think I do that much anyway.

What was the juice for you in the project? The intersection of art and commerce?

The period, the culture, just the idea of being able to work in that arena. Commerce and art had something to do with it.

The film in a lot of ways can be seen as not about art, and the great artist, so much as about brotherhood, and the nature of that connection.

That Corsican brother kind of thing. The thing that makes *Vincent and Theo* about art and artists is that there isn't anything about art and artists in it, other than the passion involved in what they do.

Right. Theo never says, "I think you should use more yellow in your sky."

No. Artists I know don't sit around and talk about painting. From a gratification standpoint—artists, painters, comtemporary painters, amateur painters, big-name celebrity painters, and just painters *like* this picture. And that was important to me, that it not be bullshit. As little pretentiousness as possible. I totally stayed away from Van Gogh's letters. I think the letters are bullshit. I think the letters are part of his art, but I don't believe them, necessarily.

Have you ever had a family relationship with that sense of connectedness: Person A gets sick, so Person B throws up?

No. I had a connection like that with my father, but I don't know whether it was him hustling me or it was just an accident of time.

How did you have that with your dad?

Oh, I just remember a time when I was in real trouble and I was real sick. I had a boil on my foot and I was away at school. And my father called me, and said, "Are you all right?" I said I wasn't, how did he know? He said he had a dream, had a feeling that there was something wrong with my foot. And I never knew if he was hustling me—he would do that kind of thing.

Are you very much your father's son?

I don't know. I hope not.

Why not? B.C. was supposed to be a very grand character.

Well, you know, he was a nice guy, but he was kind of an asshole.

How so? In what way was he an asshole?

He was kind of . . . I don't know . . . he lived in a very narrow, very small world.

He was sort of a supersalesman and a hustler. You've described yourself as having kind of turned into a con man and a hustler.

Well, I can occasionally detect those traits in me. [Pause.] I find I'm shaving his face, occasionally.

Vincent and Theo *almost seems like your version of* Dead Ringers.

I didn't see it. I know the story.

Compared to Van Gogh, you're a lucky guy. You've succeeded, you've had people that have loved your work—

Oh, absolutely.

—All that, but on some level do you feel the unappreciated artist?

Not really. I mean, I never get enough, but I never had what he had. I mean, nobody liked this guy. Nobody appreciated anything he did. He came from this very wealthy family, and took that rebelling kind of thing, and he got off on this whole religion thing, which had to do with—you know, he had a brother, a first child born to that family, who was named Vincent. And he died within weeks, days after he was born. Buried right in that churchyard where his father was a pastor. And then, a year later to the day—same birthday—the next child was born and they named him Vincent, too. So this little kid grew up looking at this gravestone, watching his mother go out and put flowers on it, with his name on it. And I just envision that he took his younger brother by the hand and stood in front of that grave and said, "We have to make up for him!" And he told Theo, and Theo just believed him. And he had to have this connection.

It's so rich in irony, you coming back to Hollywood and making The Player.

Yeah, it is pretty loaded, isn't it? A lot is going to be made out of it, I'm afraid—I hope.

How does it feel?

Okay. I've enjoyed it. I think it's very dangerous. I find myself falling into the system in a way which at times I don't like, but I think that can be cured by being away from the proximity. I think it's like going to the beach: if you spend all your day on the beach, your skin is going to get brown.

What parts of the system do you feel uncomfortable sliding into?

Oh, I find myself talking about projects and whether they will be commercial or not. I find myself wondering whether anyone is going to buy this kind of a picture or story, and having a little taste of fear of failing. But, if I had the money for *L.A. Shortcuts,* I'd be here for another year.

Parenthetically, what's happened with that? I know what it's about, the Raymond Carver short stories linked together in a Nashville*-type way, and it was at Paramount for a while.*

I just have to find somebody who will give me the money to make the film. I've got a lot of foreign money. But I get the same platitude/answer: "Oh, it's too depressing!" They don't want to see downers.

Well, B. B. King records sell and that's the blues.

That's what I tell them.

What's The Player *about to you?*

It's a movie about itself. It's a movie of a movie that's about movies. It turns on itself; it's an essay. I'm sure if we took the ad and said "An Essay About Hollywood," nobody would go see it. But to me, it's an essay, a comment; it's a comment on itself, of itself, by itself—which makes it as bad as it is and as good as it is. It's probably a "bad" film.

Why do you say that?

Because it's about bad films. So it's a bad film the way the street people will say, "That's *bad!*" Meaning, "That's good." Because it's about all the worst parts of our culture, all the worst parts of this art. And if it succeeds, unfortunately, if it succeeds, it will succeed for all of the wrong reasons.

And those are?

All the things that you would assume I abhor, because I made this film, are the reasons why it will succeed if it succeeds as a film. In other words, it is a dilemma. I have created a dilemma. If people really like this film, they'll like it for the wrong reason.

I want to know what you think that reason is.

They'll like it for the ride, rather than the content. I can sit there and show this to everybody that I know, and they will love this film, most of them. Some of them will not like it at all, because they will feel too personally involved—they'll recognize something in it. But most people will see it because of the surprises in it, the discovery of the actors, the stars, the celebrities. It's just a film about itself.

One of the really rich things about it is the way it shows how desire is manipulated by film, in that the audience for The Player *cheers itself, and feels above and laughs at the "happy ending" that is provided by the film-within-the-film (we sneer at it because it's so ridiculous), while in the film itself, you deliver us—*

Exactly the same thing! Not disguised even thinly.

Which we take great pleasure in.

Which you enjoy. That's right. The target for this film is the people watching it. The bad guy in the film is the audience. The heavy is the audience. Not the studio executive, not the people that play the game, but the audience.

Do you think you're being critical or condescending to the audience?

I don't think I'm being condescending. I think I'm pretty much presenting it the way it is, I'm sorry to say.

And yet that's the same audience you align yourself with, saying this audience just wants to see something they haven't seen before, we're not the peons the marketers make us out to be?

Well, I'm showing them something they haven't seen before. But they won't recognize it as that. They will recognize the wrong thing. Because what they are seeing is a very, very well-constructed piece of work.

So, is it just the guile of artifice that's the thrill for you in making this?

It's just taking truthfulness about situations and molding it, so that while criticizing its content, or its morality, you're at the same time embracing it, and it seems to be okay. The best thing about this film is that it seems to have a very long aftertaste. And different people start getting the essay.

The Long Goodbye *was a goodbye to Hollywood and a kind of Hollywood picture—"Hurray for Hollywood" being whistled at the end—and I wonder where that puts you vis-à-vis this film, almost twenty years later?*

I don't know. [Chuckles.] I used all the Hollywood references in *The Long Goodbye* because it was there—but mainly I was doing the same sort of satire, if that's the word, that the people who created the mythical characters, as private eyes, did. The people who were disappointed with *The Long Goodbye* were disappointed not with my handling of Raymond Chandler, but because Humphrey Bogart wasn't in it. In other words, I was closer to Raymond Chandler than the people who criticized me for being so far away from Raymond Chandler. They were using as their model Humphrey Bogart in *The Big Sleep*. So part of my target, and satire, was on movies. And I took this character out of a deep sleep and put him in 1973.

And *The Player* is similar because there's bad stuff in there, intentionally heavy-handed, very blatant symbolism—but that's a *movie*. Suddenly this has turned into a movie within a movie within a movie. So there's no such thing as anything bad in it, because it's all on purpose. Whether it's performance or setup or lines or anything. In other words, I'm completely free. But this is a movie where I use movie scenes to illustrate what the movie is about, the thriller part of it. Those are "movie" scenes.

It's postmodern in that way, in that it's self-referential and ironic . . .

And it turns into itself and it turns on itself.

But isn't that a cul-de-sac, eventually?

It's spherical. It's enveloped. It's neatly wrapped up, like a little bag of shit.

And it chases its tail.

And its tail becomes its head. The pointed, thin end of it fans out and comes back and says, "This is the movie you have just seen."

Why is the audience the enemy?

Because the audience is the one that demands those kinds of movies.

Well, as you sit now at the Olympian heights of your sixty-six years—

[Laughs.] At the bottom of the crevice!

—How does your future look from here?

Oh, I'll get some more films made. Hopefully, I'll keep working. I have no agenda other than "one after the other."

Do you care how people think of your contribution?

Oh, sure.

Let's do a morbid thing—let's have you write your own obituary. That's perverse enough for Bob Altman. What's your contribution?

I don't know that. I just know that whatever it is, I won't be satisfied. It'll be wrong. Whatever they say will be the wrong thing. No matter how bad or how good, it will be wrong. But that's okay. I don't really much care. I don't think any of it makes that much difference. It's all gone, there's nothing to keep anyway.

Your sense that art is like a sand castle to be washed away with the evening's tide runs so contrary to the Western view of art—that that's what does last. Life is short, art is long.

The ideas are still there, the thoughts are still there. The actual symbol of what brings it to mind and kind of focuses it for a moment is what the piece of art itself is. It's all so selective. I'm speaking to a very minor, minority audience anyway. We're jacking off with this game. Sure, I like to be admired and I like people to like me and say "I love your stuff," and all that, but that's just a game.

You think truth is whatever gets the loudest applause?

No, I don't. I think that's the truth—but it's the other side of the truth. You're quoting Alan Rudolph now. [Laughs.]

I know, but your name is on the picture [Buffalo Bill and the Indians]. *Burt Lancaster, as Ned Buntline, says, in that film, "Even the least seasoned trappers will tell you, if you don't know what you're after, you're better off staying home." The funny thing is, that's contrary to the way you make films: you never know what you're after, yet you don't stay home.*

Because I'm very much like Buffalo Bill. And Buntline *invented* Buffalo Bill. He was criticizing Buffalo Bill, who went out and didn't know what he was going after.

And Buffalo Bill is a little bit like Willie Loman, isn't he?

He's like most of those sad characters. Buffalo Bill is very special, very special. My Buffalo Bill.

Why is Buffalo Bill sad and why are you sad? That's my last question.

He's a sorry, he's a sad person, because he tried to . . . he kind of . . . he was *made up* and grew to believe his legend, knowing it wasn't true, and consequently, in escaping that truth, he just became worse and worse and worse. He's kind of a sad character. But that's because he assisted in his legend—he gave interviews. And yet he knew the truth all the time.

7

TIM BURTON

TIM BURTON FILMOGRAPHY

1982	Vincent (short)
1984	Frankenweenie (short)
1985	Pee-wee's Big Adventure
1988	Beetlejuice
1989	Batman
1990	Edward Scissorhands
1992	Batman Returns
1994	Ed Wood
1996	Mars Attacks!

for television

1984	Hansel and Gretel
1985	Aladdin's Lamp (Faerie Tale Theater)
1985	The Jar

Tim Burton

Tim Burton, like his work, is a wonderful mess. He's falling-apart funny and completely alienated; he's morbid and ironic; he's the serious artist as goofball flake. A self-described "happy-go-lucky manic depressive," he's like a bright flashlight in a very dark place: the grim factory of Hollywood. Burton is a true visionary. Our culture usually doesn't use that word for people whose visions look like cartoons and go down like dessert, but Burton is spitting in the eye of our culture anyway, while simultaneously celebrating it. That's the fabulous, odd thing about his work: he's angrily spitting something sweet.

Tim Burton was born in Burbank, California, in 1958, and has lived near Hollywood all his life. He has a brother and two parents, from whom he's always felt distant. Growing up, he did feel close to Edgar Allan Poe and Vincent Price and many monsters from many bad movies. He also took sanctuary in the confines of his own imagination; for him, drawing was a refuge. Burton's first vehicle of public acceptance was a garbage truck: in ninth grade, he won first prize in a contest to design an anti-littering poster, and his work graced the refuse trucks of Burbank for a year. Wanting a career for which he wouldn't need too much schooling, he studied animation at the California Institute of Arts. Upon graduation, he went to work for Disney.

Unhappy on the animation assembly line, Burton eventually won some measure of freedom within the Disney kingdom, directing his first animated short, *Vincent,* in 1982. With narration by Vincent Price, this five-minute, black-and-white piece of stop-frame animation, heavy on German Expressionist sensibility, chronicled the miserable life and liberating fantasies of a seemingly normal but deeply disturbed suburban boy, quite like young Tim. A kung fu *Hansel and Gretel* with an all-Asian cast followed, to everyone's dissatisfaction. Then came *Frankenweenie,* a half-hour exploration of the Frankenstein myth come to the suburbs, starring Shelly Duvall, Daniel Stern, and a monster/dog named Sparky. This lovable little mutt of a movie, which announced the outsider-in-town theme Burton would later develop in *Edward Scissorhands,* was buried by Disney until 1992, when they released a home video version.

Burton's first full-length feature, *Pee-wee's Big Adventure*, was an inventive, well-modulated romp built around the singular, screechy talents of Paul Reubens, aka the prepubescent, grey-suited, rouge-cheeked Pee-wee Herman. The critics paid little attention, but the picture did great business. Next, Burton enlarged his visual signature on the campy, surreal *Beetlejuice*, a black laugh of a ghost story. Starring Geena Davis, Alec Baldwin, and Michael Keaton in a comic tour de force, the film was an over-the-top lob into the irrational, a cherry bomb tossed into the grey classroom of mortality. It didn't all coalesce (how could it?) but when it worked, Burton's pie-in-your-face existentialism worked like magic. The critics paid little attention, but the picture did fabulous business.

Never particularly a fan of comic books or cartoons, Burton was nonetheless chosen to direct *Batman*, one of those blockbuster properties that had been in development forever, with the studio executives clustered around it in dumb wonder, like cave men around their first fire. Burton went deep into the myth, and deep into the dark, and produced a flawed but fascinating pop epic. The movie had a grand, rotten urban texture and a brooding tone. It was weighty but not ponderous, and it was great fun—here Jack Nicholson had the comic turn—but the fun was somewhat submarined by awkward action, narrative glitches, and inappropriate music by Prince. The critics paid all sorts of attention, and the picture did historic business. This gave Burton the freedom to direct *Edward Scissorhands*, a profoundly personal project he'd first conceived as a teenager. A simple fairy tale gift-boxed in a sophisticated design package, the story concerned a castle-bound boy with shears for hands, who's plucked from the fortress of his solitude by an angelic Avon lady and thrust into the banal wonders of suburbia. Yearning and sentimental, the movie felt like Burton's ache, and was affectingly played by a cast that included Dianne Wiest, Winona Ryder, and Johnny Depp.

After waffling for some time, Burton decided to do the inevitable *Batman* sequel. (A sequel to *Beetlejuice* had also been proposed, and turned down.) He tried *Batman Returns* largely for the chances to take a whack at some new characters and to take the myth more in his own direction, exercising a control which the overwhelming success of the first movie brought him and which his added experience would naturally provide.

The first Batman film also brought him his wife, Lena Gieseke, a German painter, whom he met while filming in London and married in February of 1989. In addition to directing major motion pictures, Burton draws constantly and paints occasionally. A coffee-table book of his art is in the planning stage, as are some children's picture books he plans to author. He's also shot a documentary about Vincent Price, and is developing a full-length animated feature, *Nightmare Before Christmas*.

I spoke with Burton twice in March of 1991, in his production company office at Warner's Hollywood lot. Before our first session, he was in the midst of preparing *Batman Returns* to show to studio executives—he said he'd "rather show it to aliens"—and he was even more nervous than usual. Burton talks with his hands cutting the air, covering his face, pulling his hair. He struggles to make sense of himself, starting four or five sentences for every one he finishes, and dicing his words into bits. Indeed, he's been called "famously inarticulate" by the *Washington Post*. (I've chosen clarity in favor of interview verité in the editing and punctuation of our conversation, in hopes that what you lose in the *way* he thinks—his vegematic style of verbalization—you gain in actually understanding *what* he thinks.) The fact is, English seems like a foreign language for Burton: he thinks visually. Everything he says carries with it the burden of translation.

SESSION ONE

Why do think you are a director?

I never wanted to be. I never felt, I am going to be a director. It probably has more to do with having an idea and just wanting to control it a little bit. I've always kind of quietly had ideas and controlled them, maybe not in a demonstrative way. It really has to be that impulse. And it just lucked into movies. I started in animation, but I couldn't sustain that—because of my attention span. I have enough of an attention span for live-action movies, and enough of a temperament to work it out. And it's funny, there's this wonderful thing of having an idea and not being completely in control—in dealing with outside elements, which you have to do in movies, which I find quite exciting. The things that happen that are out of your control are quite energizing.

Is that tension, between what you can control and what you can't, the juice for you?

Yeah. Yeah! I think it becomes absurd and it becomes surreal. You are thrust, just in the nature of making a film, into a surreal situation, where there's a lot of passion. And I find that attractive. I think that's why I've always enjoyed Fellini films—he shows the beauty and surrealism behind the scenes, things you go through that people don't see. That's quite energizing.

Isn't the impulse to art, to draw, for you, an attempt to control your world?

Sure. I am very interiorized, and very private. I've never verbalized that aspect of working. I've chosen, and I choose, to protect it, in an intuitive way and not an intellectual way. So I'm kind of cagey about what I intellectualize.

Does the intellectualizing alienate you from your inspiration?

Yeah, because you are bombarded by outside elements: media, reviews, people. That's why I find myself interiorizing *more*. I don't want to hear what it is I do or I don't do, or start to analyze that too much. I feel my strength in my enjoyment is very private and interior. That's really the only thing I enjoy about it. And I try to protect that to some degree.

Everybody has a different way of thinking. And my way is with a certain amount of intellectualization of the themes, but there's a cut-off point—where I have a strong enough idea of what's going on, and then I cut it off and just try to deal with it intuitively. It's just your own barometer. I look at certain things—actors on the set—and I have my barometer of belief in what they are doing. 'Cause oftentimes when you are dealing with stupid-*looking* things, and all the sets look kind of ridiculous, you have to find that line of belief. I hate it where things just look ridiculous and people act funny, so it's just your own barometer. So I'm very cagey about it.

Let me stop you right there, because "cageyness" implies a kind of consciousness of what to reveal and what not to reveal, as opposed to a built-in censor.

Yeah. [Pause.] I guess the cageyness has to do with kind of fighting outside things. It's very hard to be in all of this—you really do have to fight to keep a certain kind of clarity. You see people turning into the most frightening creatures. I remember when I first got into this, and I'd see somebody yelling and screaming and bursting their blood vessels and I'd go, "Whoa! What's that guy's problem? Why he is reacting so strangely?" But being in it for a while, you tend to understand why. The whole situation perverts you. And it's a mistake to think that it doesn't. And I think it's a constant struggle to try to maintain what it is that you're doing, or what you're trying to do, and to keep that as simple as possible.

So the warding off is a self-protective measure?

It is, I think. It certainly feels that way to me.

David Lynch indicated that one of the reasons he never pursued psychoanalysis or therapy was that he was afraid it would block his creative process.

That can be interesting. I went through that process a little bit, and I completely *unraveled.* [Laughs.] There's so much about yourself and other people that's interesting, but I just unraveled too quickly! I had a therapist who was very good, and they'll tell you that one of their main concerns is not to let you unravel as you're recovering.

They want to let you hold onto your defenses until you have some new things to hold on to.

Exactly! And I just dived right in and immediately went to the bottom level of antidepressants and everything. I couldn't handle it. So I understand it. It's a true balancing act. Your mind plays funny tricks on you all the time.

How did the "shrinkage" relate to your work?

[With a Brooklyn accent, as an old-time director.] "Well, luckily I was in between pic-chahs!" [Laughs.] I was just a ball of yarn there. There are times in your life when you feel stuck. And I was wanting to burst through something, what it was I didn't know. Depression. Throughout my life, some form and level of depression has always hung over me. And I don't think it's bad necessarily, but sometimes when it gets bad—and there have been a few points—it keeps you kind of stuck.

How long did you stick with it, before it became intolerable?

A couple of years. I had a couple of shrinks. I had one guy, he didn't talk to me the whole time. [Manic laugh.] It was hilarious. *That* was my problem: I never spoke to anybody. So I found the perfect therapist, who just sat there for an hour and didn't speak. It was like being in any other relationship—I didn't say a word. So it was redundant in a way. He checked his watch every now and then. It was weird. We didn't say anything to each other. Maybe we were speaking Vulcan-style.

In the past, you've brought up making-films-as-therapy a number of times, both as a metaphor, and almost literally in the case of Vincent—*that it was therapy for you to make that film.*

People don't realize, because of the surface way the films look and the cartoonish nature of them, that the only thing that keeps me going through a movie is that these characters mean something to me. My process is that I look at all these characters and get a *feeling* out of them that I find to be very meaningful. And thematic, to me. That's the only way for me to approach it. I could never approach it like it's just a funny movie or it's a weird-looking movie.

It's not candy.

No, it's not, even if it may be perceived that way, and often is. Everything has quite a deep foundation, otherwise how could you really do something? The process is too difficult and it's too painful to not have some deeply rooted feelings in it. I wouldn't actually do it, I'm not proficient enough at it; I don't have that thing that some people have, that allows them to move from one picture to another, and be a very good director, and keep moving. Each thing to me is like the *last* thing: it's all very big and tragic and cathartic. "This is the next and last picture"—I really go through that quite grandly, in my own way.

Do you ever fear that because the superficial characteristics of your films are so strong—the surfaces are so brilliant, the edges are so sharp—the audience will be blinded to the elements underneath?

I believe that one hundred percent. I have found that to be true on everything I've done. For the first ten minutes, nobody knows what they're looking at. I think it's definitely true, but I also know that I have a reputation —and this comes from critics on down to studio people—that I am not America's Premier Storyteller. But who cares, really? Why does everything have to be the same?

Let's go back to the world of your childhood. I'm curious as to whether you think your character was almost fully shaped by the time you were five years old.

Number one, I really hate, more than almost anything—because it seems to be bubbling up—that fucking "child within" bullshit. Do you know what I mean? I don't know whether you've heard that shit. I've heard it related to me, where they say, "I've never lost that touch of the child." It's the remnant of some kind of yuppie bullshit, that whole "tapping into the child within you," and that it's important to make films that do that. And actually I find that a form of retardation. [Pause.] I am very interested in where you come from and what you are. What are you? That truly is a very interesting question. But not to the point where people perceive you as maintaining that "childish" quality. 'Cause I don't actually know any children, and I don't know what that's all about.

Well, in the past you've said that you were, in the films, working out or working from a lot of "childlike feelings" and that you felt you would move on from them.

Yeah, I find it very interesting, because I think it holds the key to everybody, that question of what you are. Children are not perverted, in a way. It has more to do with the culture. When children are drawing, everybody draws the same. Nobody draws better than everybody else. There's a certain amount of strength, there's a certain amount of passion, there's a certain amount of clarity. And then what happens is it gets beaten out of you. You're put into a cultural framework, which gets beaten into you. To punch through that framework you have to maintain a certain kind of strength and simplicity.

Do you think that when you were a kid there was an attempt to beat things out of you that you wanted to hold on to?

I think that in the atmosphere I grew up in, yes, there was a subtext of normalcy. I don't even know what the word means, but it's stuck in my brain. It's weird. I don't know if it's specifically American, or American in the time I grew up, but there's a very strong sense of categorization and conformity. I remember being forced to go to Sunday school, for a number of years, even though my parents were not religious. No one was really religious; it was just the framework. There was no *passion* for it. No passion for anything. Just a quiet, kind of floaty, kind of semi-oppressive, blank palette that you're living in.

How young were you when you felt that for the first time?

From very early on. As long as I can remember. My grandmother told me that before I could walk I always wanted to *leave*. I would just crawl away, I would crawl out the door. And then, when I was older, if anybody was going anywhere, I always wanted to go. I had that impulse. And I had the impulse for horror movies—that was a very strong thematic thing.

Young Vincent Malloy, in Vincent, *is "possessed by the house and can never leave it again." That must have been your greatest fear.*

Well, I think so. I think so. It's a funny thing, that. It has to do with this atmosphere. I don't think it even has to do so much with your parents. Just the kind of collective feeling. In some ways it's quite good. It's almost like dealing with a blank piece of paper. In some ways you had to create your own world.

You became quite private, and wanted to spend time alone.

Absolutely. Absolutely. To this day I'm happiest when I'm . . . I look forward to sleeping. And I did, even then, I liked sleep. And I love talking to people who like to sleep. There are a few things that just calm me down: when I hear about somebody making mashed potatoes, and when I hear about somebody sleeping, and liking to sleep. I get this sense of calm, and it's a wonderful feeling. And in Hollywood, nobody likes to sleep—they're losing out, they're not on top of it. There are a few people that enjoy sleep, and I love talking to them about it. People that like to sleep are able to talk about it in ways that are nice. There is something that's wonderful about it. I love to sleep.

But you don't remember your dreams.

No, I don't. I have like five dreams that I remember.

Do they repeat, consistently?

No, I only have one dream that's been recurring. It's a great dream. There was a little girl on my block, who I was in love with, and she moved away. Every ten years I'll have a dream about her, at the age we are now. We lost contact, but I have this very clear image of what she looks like and all that.

What are the other four dreams you remember?

I had a dream that—this is so weird, because it's like it actually happened. My parents went bowling, and there was this weird place that they stuck the kids. I guess it was like a day-care center, but it was all Gothic, it was all rotted wood. And there were a few of us morose kids sitting there, and we saw this light—a skeleton was coming in with this candle. And the skeleton looks at, and it opens a door, and I fall through a trapped door and I fall into my parents' bed. And I remember waking up in my parents' bed. Weird, huh? Whoa! [Manic laugh.]

I remember the ones that are so strong that I just couldn't forget them, and I remember each feeling, each detail. I remember one when I got into a Western axe fight with somebody. I remember every chop. I remember chopping off this person's face. None of us died, but we just went through this thing, in sort of a Western setting. There was another, where there was this horrible, [shudders] this horrible seaweed, like this tough purple rubberish sea plant, that was growing out of my mouth. And I kept tearing it away and it kept growing and growing and growing. That's all it was, a long dream about the feeling of that, and the wacky hijinks surrounding that.

But when you get deep into the middle of a film, nothing spills out of your unconscious about it?

No, my dreams then are the worst dreams in the world, which are dreams that I am actually awake and working. Nothing could be more nightmarish than that. The nightmare is that you're still working and you're still dealing with certain people. You wake up like you've just been through a day. Nothing is worse than that.

What was the kind of taste and smell of childhood for you?

This is funny, but I think I've always felt the same. I've never felt young, like I was a kid. I've never felt like I was a teenager. I never felt like I was an adult. I just have always felt the same. I guess if there was a flavor, I guess it was a kind of surreal, bright depression. I was never interested in what everybody else was interested in. I was very interiorized. I always felt kind of sad.

Were you lonely?

I never felt . . . yeah. Yeah. I've always likened it to that feeling, when you're a teenager, that grand feeling—which is why I liked punk or some people like heavy metal or Gothic. You've got to go through some kind of drama. I've always seen people who are well adjusted, and actually, they are not that well adjusted. Everybody is going to blow at some moment or other. In fact, the ones that come across as the most well adjusted are like human time bombs, waiting to go off. I just think that kind of dark catharsis, that kind of dark, dramatic, depressed, sad, moody thing, was kind of healthy.

When Edward Scissorhands *came out, you said of your youth that you were "perfectly happy" alone, in your own little world. When I read that, I didn't really buy it.*

I think my statement's a bit cavalier. I think that was a broad-stroke statement. Lookit, nothing is ever one way or the other. But I relate to that more than anything. Part of the problem when I'm doing a movie is that I never see things simplistically. People ask me if I'm happy. I never can answer that kind of question, because it's always too mixed, in a way. Well, I'm never going to be happy, but I feel absurdly lucky to be here.

Given this world, the fact that we're not starving makes us extremely lucky, but nonetheless, within your world, you have certain feelings.

Within an emotional world, nobody knows and nobody cares what sort of torments somebody might go through to do something. Maybe it's good not to talk about it so much. Fact is, who cares? Who cares? You can read about artists of the past, and you read about their dark, horrific struggles . . .

The painter in the garret.

Nobody in Hollywood is cutting off their ears.

Well, they are cutting up their breasts and faces.

[Laughs.] Yes, but it's more for beautification reasons than it is for dark, tormented reasons, although the result is pretty much the same.

I think there's plenty of dark torment beneath the need to do it.

Oh boy, you bet! It all ends up the same.

I'm curious about your attraction to the horrific: monsters, ghouls, demons, and so on. One take might be that in the kind of nothingness of suburbia—the almost slyly attractive no-feeling nothingness of suburbia—which you can project anything onto, the kind of deep feeling of the ghouls and demons and monsters is compelling.

Exactly. I love it. Lookit, all monster movies are basically one story. It's *Beauty and the Beast*. Monster movies are my form of myth, of fairy tale. The purpose of folk tales for me is a kind of extreme, symbolic version of life, of what you're going through. In America, in suburbia, there is no sense of culture, there is no sense of passion. So I think those served that very specific purpose for me. And I linked those monsters, and those Edgar Allan Poe things, to direct feelings. I didn't read fairy tales, I watched them. I wasn't watching them because I liked to be scared. From day one, I never was afraid of them, ever.

Did you identify with the monster?

Completely! Every kid does. They were always taking the monster and kind of prodding him and poking him, especially the ones of the fifties. The way those movies were structured, the heroes were always these bland actors, who had no emotion. They were the suburbanites to me.

And you were the creature from the black split-level.

Sure! Of course. Grand drama. You've got to feel, you've got to go for the drama. Because if I didn't, I just felt I would *explode*. I always felt it was healthy—I enjoyed the drama of that. I just felt it was saving me. You deal with it, and you create, or, you become it.

Is the alienation that was present between you and your folks, and you and your brother, a lifelong thing, or is there any possibility for repair?

It's one of those issues . . . my parents are good people. They are not bad people. But, I feel it's much more of a cultural phenomenon. I'm not the warmest of people, when it comes to that.

Do you see any of yourself in them, or any of them in you?

Yeah, I think so. I don't think I was adopted, or hatched from an egg or something. There is some connection there.

You've said you grew up at the end of the nuclear family experiment, and that it didn't work. Did you mean yours, or the whole idea?

I think the whole thing. There was no sense of connection to emotions. In our culture, what you were taught about America in school is the way things should be — success and family, what they call traditional family values — and you know, things are not that simple. So when it's not working, rather than going, "This isn't working, this is fucked," people just feel like they are failures.

And the last twelve years in Washington, they've been shoving that "family values" idea down our throats.

And it's completely frightening, because they don't understand. The same thing about "America." It's just bizarre to try to maintain this feeling about America. And you see it most strongly in Los Angeles. America to me always seems like a country that's based on a movie. Here you've got presidents spouting lines from Clint Eastwood movies, and it's getting more and more that way. It's hard to find people to work with because nobody wants to be what they *are*. "Oh, I'm sorry, I'm not this, because I'm really *this*." This level of success that's thrust upon you — you've got to be successful and you've got to be a certain way — nobody is what they are, because of this dream. And it's great to have a dream, and none of that should be taken away from people, because that's all people have, but not this materialistic dream. That's the problem, and everybody is fucked up from it.

Jim's dad in Edward Scissorhands *being case number one.*

[Manic laugh.] Absolutely, absolutely.

Do you remember when you first had the impulse to draw?

I think it started when it started for everyone. I'm just lucky that it wasn't beaten out of me. I was very lucky that I maintained a passion for it and didn't give a fuck what my third grade teacher thought of it.

And were your drawings stuck up on the fridge by your parents?

I got the normal parent routine. It's actually quite funny. You know, mom's reading a book, and you show her a drawing and she has X-ray vision through the book, where she can actually see your drawing without looking from her book. [Manic laugh.] That's the classic routine. I don't know what the whole deal was. My father was also a baseball player, in the minors, and he worked for the park and recreation district in Burbank, so there was a slight pushing in that direction. And my mother pushed me into the whole musical instrument routine. I think I played the clarinet, but I was never any good at it. So my drawing was always more *private*. I feel kind of lucky, because I think if they had supported it, I probably wouldn't have done it. Lookit, every kid is reacting against their parents. If the parents are radicals, the kid turns out to be a little accountant. It's not always the case, but that dynamic is pretty strong.

A couple of years ago you said you "freaked" because you didn't even know the most basic things about your parents, like where they were born. What caused you to freak about that?

I think it was that period of therapy, where I was trying to figure out what the fuck was going on. I felt a bit more depressed than usual. The fog got a little greyer. It's hard to see through it as it gets down a little bit closer to you. I was just not connecting to anybody. I was starting to feel a little too lonely and too isolated and too abstract and depressed. And it was around that time that it was pointed out to me that I didn't know anything about my parents. [Manic laugh.] It was kind of shocking.

Do you ever see them?

I see them occasionally. Not too much.

I know how important Vincent Price and his films were to you as a kid. You talk in terms of him getting things out of your system. What did he get out of your system that proved so helpful to you?

His movies probably spoke most directly to me. In fairy tales and myths, the symbolism is not so much intellectual as emotional. I could understand everything he was going through. Then, as I got older, I met the guy—and I still don't know him that well, and that's probably good in a way—and I realized that this connection made me feel good about my own intuition. Here you are, looking at a guy, and he's killing people and all this other stuff, but then you sense something else. It gave me a feeling, a human feeling, of intuition; and kind of a barometer of looking at people. There are very few moments like that that make you feel good. A little bit of a validating experience. A little bit of a reality check. A check on something that gets lost in the world.

Do you imagine depressed teenagers needing your work the way you needed his work?

I don't know. I've never really thought about that. You can't think about those things because it would be wrong. That's not the way things should happen. But if someone would say to me that that was the case, I would feel happy about it. I would feel an affinity for that, because of the way I felt, and feel.

How do you feel your background in animation shaped you as a director?

What I feel really good about, really happy about, is that I did *not* go to film school. I went to Cal Arts, and went through animation, where I got a very solid education. You learn design, you draw your own characters, you draw your own backgrounds, you draw your own scenes. You cut it, you shoot it. You learn the storyboarding process. It's everything, without the bullshit of film school. I can't even meet people from film school, because I feel like they've been in the industry for ten years. It's really frightening! Not to say that they are all that way, but I knew somebody who was at a studio and was going to look at a student's film, and then the student came in and said, "I'm not running this film, I need a *stereo* room!" The level of competition, of feeling like you're already in the industry, you don't get a chance to create.

But the torpor of being attached to the animator's desk was traumatic.

I couldn't handle it. At Disney, I almost went insane. I really did. I don't ever want to get that close to that certain kind of feeling that I had. Who knows what a nervous breakdown is? Or who knows what going off the edge is? I don't want to get that close again.

Was the monotony your biggest enemy?

Number one is, I was just not Disney material. I could just not draw cute foxes for the life of me. I couldn't do it. I *tried*. I tried, tried. The unholy alliance of animation is: you are called upon to be an artist—especially at Disney, where you are perceived as the artist, pure and simple, where your work flows from the artistic pencil to the paper, the total artist—but on the other hand, you are called upon to be a zombie factory worker. And for me, I could not integrate the two. I could not find that balance.

Also, at the time they were making kind of shitty movies. And it took them five or six years to make a movie. There's that cold, hard fact: do you want to spend six years of your life working on *The Fox and the Hound?* There's a soul-searching moment when the answer is pretty clear.

How do you react to the critical shorthand which suggests that your films are live-action cartoons?

You know what's weird? I never really liked animation. My attraction to it was: if I had the choice of being a court reporter or an animator, I would choose animation. [Laughs.]

That's right, your parents wanted you to be a court reporter.

There was a guy who lived near us, who was really creepy, who was a court reporter, and I remember I went to his office once to find out about it. It was creepy. So, beyond court reporting, I liked to draw—animation seemed good. But I'm not gung-ho about it.

So your connection to animation was really only that it was linked to drawing, which was something you did, and still do, obsessively and incessantly.

Well, sure. That's why the one thing I had to learn about live-action, which is still a struggle for me, is to *speak*. In animation, you would communicate through drawings, and I was perfectly happy to communicate that way, and not in any other way. So what you're saying is true: there was a direct link. You're able to maintain that privacy much more in that relationship, because there's nothing else happening, really.

Let's talk about the Disney work you did do. If you resist the connection between yourself and Edward Scissorhands, you can't really in good faith resist the connection between yourself and Vincent Malloy in Vincent?

No, I can't. It's probably the thing that is the most purely related to me, for sure.

And young Vince has some fairly aggressive fantasies: one of boiling his aunt in wax, and one of sending enough juice into his dog Abercrombie to turn him into a zombie.

Sure. All forms of experiments, yes.

So, did you have these kind of fantasies? And did you exorcise them by making the film?

I did both. But again, again, if you grow up in an environment that is not passionate, you have no choice but to have these dark fantasies. That's why I get so freaked out when I read about parents trying to stop their kids from listening to this or that music. It's like "Sesame Street"—I would never watch that. You got to understand, things are not perfect for children. There's a lot of darkness, there's a lot of abstraction. The only way to get through it is to explore it.

When you did all your drawing, did you do it to communicate with others, or just to pleasure yourself by doing it?

I pleased myself by doing it. I really did get enjoyment out of it, myself. I did these very big things. You know how kids would go out and play "army" or something like that—well, I would do it on paper. I would have these elaborate things where spaceships would attack, and so on, and by the end of it, it would turn into a gigantic mess. It wasn't even a drawing by the end. It looked like a collection of obliterated figures. I enjoyed it. It wasn't for anybody else.

If Vincent Price had not cooperated with you on the film and done the voice-over narration, in hindsight, do you think your life would have been different?

That's an interesting question. I remember going through those feelings at the time, thinking, "God, will he like this?" It's hard to say what would have happened, but I know how I felt about the thing: it was one hundred percent pure. It could have been like one of those things that you see: [imitating jaded star] "Hey, kid, get away from me! Get out of here!" Everything is based on your first impulse, and I didn't do the thing for his approval. *Vincent* is probably the only thing that I can watch and not have to turn away.

Of all your work? Or just that early work?

Of anything. I can watch parts of things. Sometimes I'll turn on something, if it's on TV, and I'll just watch a little bit of something, just to see what my own reaction will be. I feel like everything I do is part of me, but it's very hard for me to watch things. I can't sit back and enjoy it. I feel an affinity for it, but I can't enjoy it. It takes me about five years before I can really see it at all. I don't know what that's about.

Do you watch your films with audiences? Do you go to test screenings?

I have to. Those things are really hard for me. There's such importance placed on test screenings, by studios, and unrightly so, because they're complete bullshit. The reality of the situation is—and I don't care what anybody says—that if you show the movie to a group of people, you'll get an idea of what's working and what's not working. That's really all you need to do. You don't need to have this lab animal experiment, where you dissect the audience and dissect the film. That's complete, one hundred percent bullshit! And they are completely locked into it. If you put the audience in a lab experiment scenario, they're gonna turn into critics and they are going to turn into lab animals. So I believe, in the broad-stroke, in looking at a movie with an audience—and you don't have to ask them, who is your most favorite character, and who is your least favorite character? You can tell what's working and what's not. That's all you should do. And that's why I constantly try to fight this *fucked* system. It's so horrible. It doesn't help the movie.

But after the movie opens, I don't go. I get too freaked out. I can't enjoy it. It makes me wonder why I do it. I don't enjoy this, I don't enjoy that. I wish that I could, because I feel like I'm cutting myself out of part of it that's maybe nice. I get too nervous.

With hindsight, Frankenweenie *looks very much like a dress rehearsal for* Edward Scissorhands.

Yeah. I was very lucky at Disney to do things that meant something to me: A, to be able to do a short film in any studio situation, and B, to be able to do some things that were personally meaningful to me—that's unheard of. And everything is thematically meaningful to me. Even *Pee-wee.* Whether it shows up to anybody else, I don't know.

When Frankenweenie *got a PG rating instead of a G, Disney buried it in their vault, and from what I understand, they wouldn't even give you a personal copy of it.*

That's absolutely true. They were very weird about it.

And yet, now that you are a famous director, they are releasing it on video, before Batman Returns *comes out. It seems like Exhibit A of Hollywood cynicism.*

Exactly! And you know what, though, I don't even get upset with this shit, because it's the way it is. I understand it. I'm cynical enough about things just to be happy that they are releasing it. I have plenty of other things to get upset about and paranoid about.

Victor Frankenstein, in reading about how to bring his dog Sparky back to life, has Elizabeth Kubler-Ross's On Death and Dying *in his room. That's surely the only time that book has shown up in a Disney fairy tale.*

[Manic laugh.] Yes. It's all heavy.

And a lovable little monster is Sparky, and a monster who survives, and prospers. The monster is supposed to die in a monster movie, right, Tim?

Yeah, but they never do! Even when they die, they don't die. Even in *Creature from the Black Lagoon*, the creature dies, but he comes back in *Revenge of the Creature* and *The Creature Walks Among Us*. They never die. It's part of the mythology that they do. But they are always coming back. They're always fighting. They fight through the system, the system of bland B-actors.

After Disney, you had a couple of TV directing assignments: "Aladdin's Lamp," and "The Jar," for "Alfred Hitchcock Presents."

"Aladdin's Lamp" I guess was my first "directing" assignment. I did that right after *Frankenweenie*, for Shelly Duvall's Faerie Tale Theater. It was a three-camera video thing and I didn't know what the fuck I was doing. It came out looking like a Las Vegas show. "The Jar" was my only other assignment, a case where it didn't work out again. That's when I realized that nobody should treat me like a director, because I'm not. What we long for in the world is people doing their own thing. I don't consider myself a director. I don't have the capabilities. I can't use technique and proficiency, I can't hide behind those things, because I don't have them. My shortcomings will quickly come into play.

Do you still feel unaccomplished?

Well, I don't really care about that. I'm learning more and more, but I'm relatively new to the whole thing. It's a mistake for me, maybe, to try certain things.

You've admitted that your movies are "flawed" and that they could be shot full of holes.

I think it stems from *story*. It makes me a little sad sometimes. People peg you. And they don't know what you go through with studio people and executives, and they take their cue a lot from critics, and the feeling is that "Tim can't tell a story out of a paper bag." And when they peg you, then that's what they feed upon and that's their fight with you. And every time, when you're developing a script and you're talking to the studio and you have these stupid script meetings with them, I can say that if there is a problem with the movie it is *nothing* that you discussed. Nothing at all. So when you're fighting that, it does make you a little sad. And now, it's turning out to be a little boring. And *Beetlejuice* was kind of the one movie for me that gave me, again, that feeling of humanity, that *Fuck Everybody!* That made me feel very good, that the audience didn't need a certain kind of thing. Movies can be different things! Wouldn't it be great if the world allowed David Cronenberg to do his thing and people could tell the difference! And criticism would be on a whole other level! And the world would be on a whole other level!

But studios have the expectation that each film will be like one of those cookies coming off the cookie assembly line in Scissorhands, *and that there are only three or four different shapes of cookies allowed.*

Well, they're wrong! It's like with Warner Bros., because that's where my history has mainly been. I'm always amazed—movies that they fight tooth and nail, and are always the weirdest, those are the ones that end up making them all the money. All they have to do is look at their fucking slate of movies! The proof is there. Fuck! Fuck your system! Whoever's making the movie, give him a chance to make the movie, and you'll have a fifty percent chance of failing or succeeding, or working or not, and that's as good of a chance as you'll get on anything, and you're not going to do anything that's going to make it any better! So why not, if something is going to be flawed, why not have it be interestingly flawed, as opposed to boringly flawed? Why lower things? Why not let there be different things? Some people are better storytellers, some people are better at other things.

You don't feel that your "problem with narrative" is really a problem?

Well, I feel that less and less. Because now it's become redundant. And the fact is, I'm more interested in growing in ways I don't even know about. Maybe I'll become better at it, maybe things will become more abstract.

Would you junk narrative if you could? Because you indicated once that if you were left to your own devices, "the result will always be very commercial because that's the way I think."

Well, I don't even know what that is. It's best for me not to say, "Everybody says I can't tell a story, maybe I should really *try* here." I don't think I will ever consciously try to do that. But what's important is to keep moving and to hone in and to keep exploring. I don't know whether the storytelling will get better, or *worse*, more abstract or clearer, or whether it will become its own form—because the thing that's always been very important to me is the visuals as story. The images, for me, *are* the story. It's not that it looks great or funny or cartoony. If I were to hone myself, it would be: how could I make images feel a certain way, so that what you're looking at is the *thing?* That's a desire, that's a goal.

You got closer to that in Scissorhands, *where the feeling of the film is actually in the images themselves, rather than in the story.*

I feel that way. And I feel like that's the thing for me to try to do. That's the thing I'm interested in. That energizes me.

It's a very abstract and pure enterprise, that attempt.

Yeah, it is. See, the problem with Hollywood is that you're always fighting the *same* thing. It doesn't change. They don't change their tune. And it gets really boring.

So why not just use the machinery of Hollywood, but do your work more independently, as Cronenberg does?

Well, that's interesting, and I think I'm certainly in that area now to find out. See, I've never talked to somebody like him, and perhaps I should. I think I'm getting there, I do. The odd thing for me is that I grew up in the studio system. And it's been odd to feel like I could do what I want, and have had the ability to do what I want, in a system that doesn't seem to allow that very much. I always felt like, if you're not getting it from these guys, you're getting it from some French guy or something. There's always going to be some problem. But now I'm getting to the point where maybe it's time to deal with somebody *else*, because it's getting too retarded and inbred among these people. I can't hear these same things from these same people anymore. I'd rather hear it from some French guy!

What they don't understand, no matter how anybody perceives me in Hollywood, is you're still trying to make something—film is still an art form. And you go through the same anguish as any artist does creating something. But this doesn't enter into their thinking. You can go along with it for a while, and laugh your way through it, but then you have to move along, because it gets redundant and you get angrier and angrier. Where I wouldn't get angry before, now I get angry and start to see red in a split second. I just fly off the handle now. It's anti-creative. It's not helping anything. It doesn't even help them get the movie made! I understand their goal, their goal is simple: take this movie, make it commercial, make it good, we want to make a lot of money on it! I understand that, that's fine. But I can't go through it anymore.

Forgetting the "they" for a while, I'm interested in what you feel the flaws or weaknesses of your films are.

It's funny, there's two levels to that. On an emotional level, I never feel bad about it. I don't have children, but to me it's like giving your child plastic surgery. I accept them, and on a very weird level I *love* them for their flaws. Now, there's a technical side of me that sees I could have cut this, or that could have been shorter; that's the boring, technical side. But on the emotional side, you accept them. What if you had a five-year-old with a whatever —would you give him plastic surgery? I wouldn't do that, because part of the joy in life is in the flaws. I feel a very strong emotional connection to everything, and treat them as a part of myself. The only movie I feel colder about is the first *Batman*. I feel close to parts of it, but it's not as emotional a connection as to everything else.

In that movie, Vicki Vale [Kim Basinger] asks Bruce Wayne [Michael Keaton] about his mansion, because she thinks it doesn't seem like him, and he says, "Some of it is very much me and some of it isn't." And I felt that was Tim Burton talking there, about his movie.

[Laughs.] Sure! Sure. That's why I decided to do another one. Because I love the themes of it. I have to have those little links with it, because that's the only thing that really keeps me going, otherwise I couldn't do it. I don't have the technical talent to not have that.

Do you think you're disrespected by some people in the industry because you don't have that technical talent?

I don't know. Nobody is perceived any one way. I'm in an odd position. I'm looked at by independents as somebody in the studio system. And I'm looked at in the system as somebody who's very lucky. But I'm not in the system. I don't hang out with members of the Academy, so to speak. I'm not entrenched in it. So I don't have many friends in either world.

Do you feel any kind of simpatico vibration with silent film? It's not that dialogue doesn't matter in your work; it's that I can imagine your films without it, and with their great scores.

I think I know what you're saying. I actually don't like silent films. I never got into them, and to this day I don't get into them. I find them dated. I'm not into Charlie Chaplin. I guess though, the fact is, it *is* true, that I find dialogue and speaking kind of meaningless unless they're saying something. I think this has more to do with myself, my own feelings of verbalization and communication and what words mean to me. I am uncomfortable with dialogue. I do enjoy, when I'm working, scenes where people are *not* talking. I do feel more comfortable with that.

But the type of melodramatic emotions of the silents, the kind of overweening dramatic elements, has a kind of resonance with your work—

Yeah, but that maybe has more to do with the horror films, in a way. Because they always had that feeling, the Edgar Allan Poe thing. It doesn't come from silents, for me. They leave me cold. I actually find them kind of cold and calculated. Whereas the grand melodramatic emotion of horror movies was more of an attraction. I like dialogue to some degree. It's just that, like in life, what you say is not necessarily what you are *saying*. I just feel that too strongly to be able to do something where people are talking and it's being completely meaningful, because that's not the way I think and that's not my experience with people talking. God, all you've got to do is go to a studio executive meeting to understand that! [Manic laugh.]

Music is obviously hugely important to your work. The bond between your images and Danny Elfman's music is so tight that when I watch one of your movies I feel like I'm listening to them.

Well, exactly. Believe me, I feel I'm very lucky. I used to go see Oingo Boingo at clubs, when I was a student. It's like a dream come true to me to meet him, work with him. I'd sit there in the clubs and have this connection. There's nobody better for me. That's where a part of the idea of the silent film works—his music is part of the story. Every director will tell you, [as pretentious snob director:] "The sets and the music are part of the character of the film." It's bullshit! Nobody knows how important music is to my things better than me, I guarantee. It is as important as some of the actors or anything, if not more important. Danny is an actor in the films.

His music really does seem like the fuel that powers your films.

Let me tell you: I will now only test my films once the score is in. It's too painful the other way. I remember testing *Beetlejuice* with no music and then with music. The difference was shocking! And it really has to do with the fact that when you're doing a movie where people don't know what the fuck is going on, the music is the guidepost, it's the tone and the context. Danny and I don't even have to talk about it. We don't even have to intellectualize— which is good for both of us, we're both similar that way. We're very lucky to connect. It's one of the most fun aspects of filmmaking. That's one of the things I look forward to: walking onto the stage with an orchestra and seeing live music being played to certain images. It's something that no one will see and is actually so exciting!

Let's talk about screenwriting. Do you think you'll ever write your own screenplay?

That's an uncharted thing for me. I don't know how writers really feel about me. I'm respectful, and I do enjoy working with people, but then I get on a set, and things change, and I really don't go by what anybody says or writes. I have great effect on what I do. And I don't know how people really feel about that. Most of my friends are writers, because I identify with what they go through. In terms of the artistic pain, they're in a bad place in Hollywood. I can relate to them. I feel closer to them. But I don't know how they really feel about me, really.

Why don't you do the writing yourself? Even on Frankenweenie, *which was clearly your story, you had someone else write the screenplay, and also on* Scissorhands—*if ever there was a project where you would have been a natural choice to do it, that was it, and yet you didn't write it.*

I may need somebody else as a balancing point for myself, no matter how much I change or push or whatever. That is one thing I've certainly thought about and I am thinking about it, and I think I need to try to write one, just to see where it is I am. It's like on *Beetlejuice:* everything I've done I feel has equal parts writer, director, and actors. I think if you read original scripts of everything I've done, and looked at the film, you'd see lots and lots and lots of changes.

And yet you, for some bizarre reason, have insisted that you're not an auteur. You said, "I know I'm not an auteur because I try to listen to people," as if that would disqualify you? The fact is, if you can put your stamp on all these films without actually writing them, that's more of a sign that you are an auteur.

I think what that comment says is that I don't really know what the fuck I'm talking about. I think that sums the whole thing up. [Manic laugh.] Lookit, I'm relatively new to all of this, and I have a very tough time with words. A lot of words don't have meaning to me, because I have no context with them. The words "normal" or "auteur"—there are probably several words that actually I don't really know what they mean. Part of that is just my inexperience and naiveté. I *do* believe that the director has to be the person whose movie it is. Whose else is it? If it's the actor's movie, then you don't need a director—let the actor direct it. It's got to be the director.

Since you do have such a strong take on things, perhaps paradoxically it's helpful for you to rub up against someone else's material.

Perhaps it is. There's always that whole argument about artistic suffering. I've wavered on that. At one point, where I was near suicidal, I didn't want to be completely suffering to create. That's completely negative. So then you work more positive aspects into your life, but it comes back to butting up against something. Maybe it's just always there. There's no such thing as anything being perfect, so maybe if you got that, you'd be a zombie by that point. [Laughs.] If things were perfect, you wouldn't want to do anything.

Whether or not it's your thing [the story and screenplay], you have to walk into a picture feeling like it's your thing. I walked into *Pee-wee's Big Adventure* and I felt one hundred percent connected to it. I understood it and it was mine, even though here was a character that was already created. I couldn't have done it – even with the chance of doing a first film – unless that feeling was one hundred percent there.

So the question is, should I or can I write, because I've got a bunch of ideas which I'd like to do. I think my biggest problem is focusing, because I get a little scatterbrained. What I'm curious about is finding out whether you go through more in working with other people than what I would have to go through in doing something myself. I'd like to go through as little torment as possible, because it's all tormenting.

You're known as someone who will cast an actor without first seeing their work. Is that true?

Casting is the one area that's really down to taste and choice. You can sit in a room with studio executives and casting people and blah blah blah, and argue who's right for a part and who's wrong for a part. There are probably cases where people are right or people are wrong, but there's a whole big area where it finally comes down to a guess. Once you make a decision, I prefer not to think about their other work.

One thing I realize now is that I don't want to work with actors who care about anything other than what they are doing. People who care about how they look – it's not interesting. You've got to work with people whose passion makes it exciting. They are trying to take something that is absurd, and not real, and in whatever way, invest it with some sort of life. I find that very exciting. So their attitude is very important. I also like to *like* people; it's really kind of psychotic. Part of the energy, with me, is working through things with people, and liking them. I don't want to work with people who have a different agenda.

There were a number of hours of discussion with Tom Cruise about him playing Edward Scissorhands. And part of the issue was his concern about the virility, or lack thereof, of the character.

[Manic laugh.] I thought that was a little odd. It kind of struck me from left field, because I certainly wasn't thinking about that. I didn't think it was worth writing a scene where Edward goes to a bar with a bunch of guys and ogles the babes! Or scores with the chicks! Or we see him watching a Raiders game! There comes a point where actors have too many fears – there's too much intellectualizing about the process. I understand him wanting to understand the character, wanting to understand me – you have to go through quite a lot to get that – but there comes a point where their fears are too great, and it makes you realize they shouldn't do it. You need to work with people who will go, "Well, fuck it! Let's do it!" That's exciting.

But are there situations when you will cast someone without having seen his or her work?

I *prefer* not to have seen it. I didn't know Michael Keaton's work at all before *Beetlejuice.* I actually liked that. Because I felt like I was getting to know somebody, for myself, freshly, and that excited me. And with Kim Basinger on *Batman,* if I had seen her work, I probably would have said, "Ugh! No!" We needed someone in a time frame in that case and I ended up really liking her, I *liked* her, when I met her. People talk—"this person is an asshole" or "that person is a monster"—there is so much categorization and I prefer not to go through that, and just have my own feeling about somebody, and not listen to what everybody says.

As you don't have any theatre or acting background yourself, I'd guess the level of discussion between you and your actors can get fairly abstract.

Yes. Part of the luck I've had is to be around actors who have been willing to go through that with me. That's what the process is all about. Part of the enjoyment is to watch these people dressed up in their funny costumes trying to bring something to life.

SESSION TWO

I'd like to go through each of your five features, beginning with Pee-wee's Big Adventure. *Although that was perceived as a children's picture, there was a lot of very adult stuff in it.*

Well, I don't think of kids or adults. What's child? What's adult? Everybody is everything. It has more to do more with a feeling. You don't get rid of who you are or where you come from, but the point is: everybody is trying to get back to a certain kind of purity anyway. Why are people looking for escape in movies or drugs or drinking or going to amusement parks? Or anything? Why does anybody read? Because it's a form of escape, or a form of recapturing not a "childish" impulse, but a way of looking at the world as if it were fresh and interesting. It has less to do with being a child than with keeping an open, wonderful, twisted view of the world.

Did it occur to you during the process of making that movie how phallic the story is?

[Laughing.] I mean the whole thing . . . you strip down any story or any fairy tale and you pretty much come down to the same thing, don't you?

Yeah, but that was fairly relentlessly phallic.

I find that if those things come out, then it's pretty much what it was about anyway. It's the unconscious. The time to worry is when you're consciously thinking about that stuff.

Well, you would have to have been in a stupor not to have been thinking about it during the filming. There are many, many lines of dialogue that are explicitly sexual, not to mention the basic story of a boy obsessed with his bike. You couldn't have been shooting that and not been conscious of the implications.

I grew up with a fascination for people that were dangerous. Why a fascination with clowns? Why do I like clowns so much? Why are they so powerful to children? Probably because they are dangerous. That kind of danger is really what it's all about. It's playing with that to a degree. It's that kind of stuff that I think gets you through life. Those are the only things worth expressing, in some ways: danger, and presenting subversive subject matter in

346

a fun way. I link this stuff to the power of fairy tales. All roads lead to them, for me, because of what I think the purpose is of them.

What is the purpose and the function of fairy tales?

I think it does have to do with whatever that young impulse is – whatever you want to call that. Who are we? How are we created? What else is out there? What happens when you die? All that stuff is unknown. Life is unknown. Everything is under the umbrella of life and death and the unknown, and a mixture of good and bad, and funny and sad, and everything at once. It's weirdly complicated. And I find that fairy tales acknowledge that. They acknowledge the absurdity, they acknowledge the reality, but in a way that is beyond real. Therefore, I find *that* more real.

Does there need to be a moral, or something edifying, to make a fairy tale work?

Well, we're talking about the movie industry. There are things to be dealt with. I don't think it's necessary, personally. As a culture, and as an industry, people are looking for that, for sure. Especially the whole "happy ending" routine. They always like a happy ending.

Why do people seem to need that? You don't need it.

I don't need a happy ending. I feel much happier coming out of a movie like *Sid and Nancy* than I do . . . *Ghost* or something. I feel like: yes, I understand, and I love it and I get it, and because it acknowledges a certain way that I feel about life, I actually feel better. I see something like that and it makes me happy.

Because tragedy is what makes sense to you.

It does make sense. I think life ultimately is tragic, but in ultimately a very positive way. We all die. It is tragic. You go through many tragic things in your life, but that's not necessarily bad. That's what I love about playing with tragedy in a fun way. [Laughs.] That's what I loved about *Pee-wee*. He was into something, in a passionate way, and it didn't matter what it was about. He was into it.

Pee-wee says to the girl who desires him, brushing her off: "There's lots of things about me you wouldn't understand, you couldn't understand, you shouldn't understand."

[Manic laugh.] So I didn't ask! Because I understood.

It's interesting, because we could say the same thing about all your protagonists: Beetlejuice, Bruce Wayne, Edward Scissorhands, they're all misunderstood.

It's very true, I think. Definitely. Who can pretend to know about themselves? It's too complicated, there are too many crossed signals, there are too many split sides and dynamics. Does anybody know who they are, really? Does anybody feel integrated? I mean, I don't know anybody who does. I don't certainly pretend to know myself. So for me, I find this dynamic to be realistic. And I enjoy it. It's often fun not to know things about people.

What about, in Pee-wee, *the kind of sexual threat from women that hangs over the character during the whole odyssey he's on?*

I guess the Pee-wee character is immature. It does go back to childish impulses, in a way. My take on what he's doing is that it's a perversion, there's no question about it. That's what's great about it. This weird, alternative character that's protecting, that's fighting off things in the world—and has mutated into something that's *separate*. I just see him as an outside character dealing with the world, in a heightened way. It had less to do with his bike than it did with just the idea of passion about something that nobody else cares about. I kind of feel that way about . . . *the movies!* [Laughs.] I make these things that are very hard to make—that are not pictures with a message, by most people's standards—so I identify with a character who is passionate about something that nobody else really cares about.

Edward Scissorhands is also an "outside character dealing with the world." But you brought a lot more baggage to him, since you'd had the idea first in high school, and had lived with it, and there were clear correspondences between Tim Burton and Edward Scissorhands.

Yeah, well, it was a different thing for me, and I tried, very hard, not to be too self-involved. See, I saw that character more thematically than personally. Again, I saw it as much more fucked up. I tried to make it—you know what I'm saying.

Yes, you said you tried not to make it too personal because you wanted it to be universal. But the more personal you make something, whether it be a poem or a song or whatever, if it's true, if it's pure, the more universal it is. So why the fear that the tighter the bond between you and Edward, the less universal the picture?

I guess because I don't know enough about myself. I'm not integrated enough yet. I don't know if that will ever happen. It just shows you how unintegrated I am, because the kind of characters that I enjoy are the kind of characters that aren't integrated. [Laughs.] So that's about as personal as it could get. Let's put it this way: I'm interested in the personal, because I take everything personally. I take Pee-wee, and Beetlejuice and Edward and Batman—I feel very close to those characters. I really do. I feel like they are mutated children. They mean a lot to me.

It's clearly where you find meaning in the movies.

Exactly. But there again, these characters are all fucked up. They are impurely pure. If Batman got therapy, he probably wouldn't be doing this, he wouldn't be putting on this bat suit and we wouldn't have this weird guy running around in a cape. So there is a form of things not being integrated that is quite appealing. So I don't know if I'm *stuck* or if I *enjoy* being stuck at that moment. Know what I mean? There is a charm about characters that know not what they do, but do it purely. Even Beetlejuice is that way. There's a charm in that which I enjoy.

Let me play Satan's helper here. Edward Scissorhands is a pathetic, beautiful, ridiculous but funny character, whose heart is always breaking—it's Tim Burton saying how sensitive he is, that he's the oversensitive artist, who as a child could not touch, could not communicate, without hurting. That's obvious. That's an obvious reading of the film.

[Laughs.] Sure. Right.

How does it make you feel when you get that reading?

Well, I guess it makes me feel that I wasn't one hundred percent successful. When you do a fairy tale, you are a little bit at odds with yourself. Because a fairy tale is a romantic version of certain things. Taking something real and heightening it. So what you have is an inherent balancing problem between the real and the unreal. I think that's where I run into trouble a lot of the time, because of the unwieldy nature of it. And then you've got Johnny Depp [playing Edward] who brings a certain thing to it himself. Actually, it turned into more my perception of him, in a way—what I saw in him, what he goes through, how he's perceived—than even of myself. It's unwieldy, it's unbalanced, and there's a constant desire on my part to find the right balance. And you know what? I'll take the hit, and miss with it, because it's the only thing that really makes it fun. So that thing probably does make me uncomfortable, but I did it.

Well, it was a harder shoot for you, emotionally, because of that.

I was very moody. I was very interiorized. And I don't think it had completely to do with being in Florida, though that helped. That's a weird place. It really had a lot to do with how I felt about having the background that I did. It *was* personal. But whatever worked or didn't work is part of the nature of it.

Kim [Winona Ryder] at the beginning, as the old woman, says of Edward, "The man was left by himself, incomplete and all alone."

Well, there again, it's that tragic thing. There is that tragic element of fairy tales. Everybody can look at it and go, "Aww!" If that is the case, then I have not been successful in what I was trying to do. See, I'm interested in the grandeur of tragedy. And I didn't want people to look at that and go, "Aww! Poor character!" I see it as just like life: you're up against a lot. I see the ending not as, "Oh gee, the poor character doesn't get what he wants," I saw it more as, "This is the way things are. You get some good things and you get some bad things." It's not a happy ending, it's not a sad ending to me—it's more a symbolic ending. Some things work out and some things don't.

Why was it necessary to kill Kim's evil boyfriend, Jim? That shocked a lot of people—because the tone of the movie changed.

See, that's again how people misperceive fairy tales. I'm not interested in softening what that's all about. Yeah, I think it was completely necessary. And I think it's belittling the idea of a fairy tale—I think it's a mutation of our culture. People's idea of a fairy tale is that it's all white. Why don't they read one of them!

It's some of the nastiest stuff in the world.

Exactly. It's about as disturbing as it gets, for anything. And the point is, it has more to with the homogenization of our culture, and that needs to be fought, on all counts and by everybody.

The first words of a movie are usually important. Here, they are Kim saying, "Snuggle in, sweetie, it's cold out there." To me, that could almost be the epitaph to the entire film—and not because it's snowing.

Yeah. Everybody goes through it every day. It's not the most sensitive place. [Pause.] Lookit, if you analyze what you go through in a day, in your job, when is anything completely one way? And you know what, you can drive yourself crazy thinking about it. Good and bad. Positive and negative. Funny and sad. Every second is a flip-flop of some feeling. And ultimately, that's what it's all about. It's unbelievably complicated. *I don't get it, but I get it:* that, to me, is about as real as it gets. That's why I hate most movies. They kind of simplistically tell you what they are all about. They don't capture what life is about in any way. What am I talking about? I have no idea.

People are weird. And I think we forget, because we're so intelligent, that we are all basically animals. Animal instincts take over all the time, under the surface of things. People say to me, "Oh, you must be really happy!" Well, there's no sense of happiness, there's no connection to anybody, people aren't being nice to you because they really want to be, a lot of the time. You know who your friends are—people you like and respond to—and you know when it is complete bullshit. And most of the time it is bullshit. It's not like anybody acting real to you. Because there's no real context anymore. Especially, here, where it's all *business,* even the social. And America is founded on that principle—that's why everybody is over here to begin with. That's the whole point. It's frightening.

If these characters are the repositories of meaning for you, I'd like to talk about each of them. We've talked about Pee-wee already. What does Edward Scissorhands mean to you?

I loved the idea—and this did go with an impulse that I felt, and still feel, and I think a lot of people feel—of feeling misperceived, the feeling of being sensitive, and overly sensitive, and wanting things you can't get. I remember going through a very strong feeling, a very teenage feeling, of not being able to touch or communicate. I had that, very strongly. I've never been a very physical person. I didn't grow up in a way that was very physical. And I always resisted that. So there are simplistic things like that—which I would call the melodramatic teenage impulses. And then the subtext of presenting yourself in such a way that is not the way you are meaning. For me, I saw that character as all of that. He is a way that you feel: what you say is not coming across, what you want is misperceived. Just a way of seeing the world. I often feel, I look at things and see them in a way, and wonder if anybody else is seeing them that way. It's really just about each person feeling very individual. And just on a humorous level, I love a character that is open and sensitive to everything. There is something very funny and tragic about that. I've known people like that, that are overly sensitive, and you know what? It's *sad*. I've known five people in my life who are overly sensitive, and the pain and the torture they go through—it's almost funny.

You wouldn't include yourself in that group?

Again, I don't analyze myself. [Pause.] I have that tendency, yes.

Do you feel there's been some movement in you, away from that adolescent angst?

Do I feel like I've changed in that way? I think that you exorcise that, but I don't think you ever completely know if it's exorcised. I think it moves along a little bit.

Let's talk about some of the small, quirky things you put in Edward Scissorhands. *The striped, canvas house that's in a couple of early frames. Are they supposed to be fumigating it?*

That's just a little pest control.

It looks like a circus tent.

Yes. I have a lot of little things that nobody ever gets, but are there just for myself, like that. That was just the interlinking of the idea of a circus-like atmosphere, and the theme of getting rid of pests.

As they are going to want to get rid of Edward. There's also a soundtrack foreshadow, about a third of the way through. When the boys are up in the treehouse, listening to the baseball game on the radio, and Edward is below them, starting to cut his first hedges. The announcer describes a home run, and he says, "It's gone . . . it's out of here . . . it's history!" Now, I'm sure the first time through, nobody really gets that, but the second time through, it just leaps out: what's "out of there" and what's going to be "history" is him, Edward.

That's another theme that I love. I love the links between things. You take something that is a baseball game, that is in this world, and you make a direct link. Again, since we have no culture, it's just so interesting to explore things that way. It's too big to understand, but it is fun to see these links. Sometimes these things are planned, sometimes they are not. For me, they are the things that make me think it's great, that it's fun and it's worth doing. It makes you think that you're on some course.

What about Edward's "V" cap that he wears during and after the robbery that will be his downfall?

[Laughs silently.] We just had a couple of hats, and there was something about the image of that, something about that clicked. It was kind of like a weird, scissory peace sign. Something about that image, which has been used so many times before.

For "Victory," which this is not going to be!

Exactly. And it kind of points down to him. It was more of a feeling, in a way.

Many, many years ago you did a drawing of a gardener, without shears but with two long, sharp fingers on each hand, and he seems like a nascent Edward if there ever was one.

Yeah, yeah, yeah. It's an impulse from a long time ago, for sure.

What about the repeated offers to help Edward, in the film? Three different people tell him they know doctors who could help him, but nothing ever comes of it.

That's one of my favorite things. I've always loved that. That's Hollywood, isn't it? "Yeah, yeah, we'll do your script." Or, "Yeah, yeah, we'll do this or that." Again, is it the culture? They might as well be saying "Have a nice day!"

How do you say "Fuck you" to someone in Hollywood? "Trust me."

Yeah, exactly. The meaning of things, to me, has gone out of things. It's all like guilt—no one has any real intention of doing anything, but it's actually just a cultural thing. It's unfortunate, because it makes you not believe anything. And that's not a good place ever to get to.

In the script, or in the shooting, was there more between Edward and his inventor [Vincent Price] than there was in the finished film?

No, not really. I just wanted to keep it what it was. I didn't want to get into too literal a thing. It would have opened up a whole can of worms, basically. I just tried to treat it as an idea of what was going on. In some ways, the vagueness of all of that, or the blankness . . . I didn't want to go into that. It's tough with these kind of characters. Vagueness is a tough thing to get at, 'cause people don't quite know what to make of it.

Well, that's the second great criticism of your work. One is that you can't storytell your way out of a paper bag, and two is that your characters, while they are fascinating, tend to stay emblematic—

They're symbolic.

They tend not to grow, or push through, or develop in such a way that we come to understand them differently at the end of the movie than we did upon introduction.

Yeah. That may have a lot to do with my own problems. I may not be integrated enough to get at that yet. Take the *Beetlejuice* characters, for example, the ghosts [Alec Baldwin and Geena Davis]. I loved those characters, but they were perceived as the *bland* characters. I never saw them like that. The point is, they're stuck. They can only go so far, and that's part of their problem—in life and in death. It's all in this limited framework. And I thought that was part of the theme. But again, it gets lost.

They can't have children and their name is "Mait-land."

Things get misperceived in the broad-stroke of the visuals. [Resigned.] Sometime, maybe things will all work out. I'll just keep trying.

Where's the meaning for you in the Beetlejuice character?

He's a classic character, a true fantasy character, the good side of that. The good side of being labeled, and misperceived, and put in a box, is that even though that is being done to you, you also have, in some ways, a complete freedom.

You're not responsible to anybody's idea of you.

Yes. You can dress how you want. You can act however you want. You can be however you want. "Well, that's just Tim." The freedom that comes with that is a sad kind of freedom—there's a freakish quality to all of that—but, it's got its benefits. And I think Beetlejuice shows the complete positive side of being misperceived, and being categorized as something different. He can do whatever he wants! He's horrible and everybody knows it, so he's a complete fantasy of all of that. That's part of the lure of movies, in a simplistic way—just the freedom. People respond to it. And then you put him up against the other characters, which are really about repression.

About the tyranny of their desires.

Yeah, they've got their house, they've got their world. I just love the dynamic between them. It's just very much like life.

During the filming of Beetlejuice, *you apparently took a lot of flak from the studio about the "realism" of it. What were they talking about?*

I don't know. I have problems, to this day, understanding. I go through these meetings, and you know what? It's just so tiring, because on anything that I've ever done, there's nothing that they can ever say or have ever said that is meaningful to the outcome of the picture. They say their normal things— "The third act needs work," or "It's too dark"—they have a list of ten things in the Studio Executive List of Comments. None of it has any bearing on how the fucking thing turns out! So, on *Beetlejuice*, I was sitting there, thinking, realism? What do you mean, realism? The whole thing is fucking ridiculous. What are we talking about here? They often treat films as if they are radio shows. Unless every line says something, there are problems—almost as if they are doing a radio program. "You don't have to film it, we just can hear it!" So I had to fight that a lot.

I can't imagine anyone criticizing that movie for too much realism.

You'd be surprised. I went through a twenty-four-hour script meeting with them, over a two-day period, line by line, asking about this and that. Luckily, I bullshit my way through the whole thing. It's a big waste of time.

You said once that the things in your films which you really have to fight for turn out to be their shining moments. Like what?

Well, in *Beetlejuice*, little things that they would think were disturbing, like eating a cockroach. Anytime there was any kind of thing that was strong, in any way, shape, or form. Really, the movie industry, in my experience, rarely gets excited—they mainly approach things from a fearful point of view. That's why so many boring, bland things get made; they read ten scripts on a weekend, it's a good read, it's an easy read, you put the right elements in it, it's a great thing. The things that disturb them are things that jump out. It's almost why you get audited by the IRS! Things that jump out—whoa!—get you in trouble. The guy eats a cockroach? His head spins around? What's that coming out of Danny De Vito's mouth in *Batman Returns*? It's stuff that's based on fear. It's stuff that jumps out at 'em, really. And you know, it has a better chance of working if it's potentially risky than if it's not. Especially nowadays. It's proven itself.

Did you spend a lot of time when you were doing Beetlejuice *thinking about what death might be like?*

Sure! It's a classic. It occupies a little time, sure.

How much did your visual representation of the afterlife parallel what you actually think might go on?

What I'm reacting against is that people expect to be taken care of when they die. Which I find like giving up on life. I react very much against that impulse—these people that use religious belief as a way of disassociating themselves from their lives, and their responsibility for their lives. My feeling, in *Beetlejuice*, is a reaction against people doing that. I saw the Maitlands as those sort of people. I liked them, but they almost expected not to have to really deal with things because they'd be taken care of in the hereafter. And what I think is that basically you should never expect your problems to be taken care of, because they won't be. It's not necessarily bad, but it's an alternative universe where it's pretty much the same.

Hell is the continuation of life by other means.

[Laughs.] It's not necessarily hell. But they are experiencing hell, because they are expecting something nice and perhaps wonderful. That's the philosophy that I was most interested in, and that's what I enjoyed about it: they didn't get what they expected. If anything, why should the afterlife be any real different from *this?*

Let's turn to Batman, *the first one. Now there were, Tim, some rough narrative spots. There were periods on that shoot where the script was being changed every day and you didn't have time to reflect upon the changes —*

Yeah, it was bad.

—And you were, in your own words, "near death."

I was probably as sick as I've ever been, on a movie, all the time. I was out of it. I was sick. See, the problem is, it was my first big movie. There's all these people around. There's a different energy. There's no way to prepare. No way to prepare. More money. More tension. More fear. Everything: more, more, more. More. And I just let something happen which I'll try to never let happen again, which is to let the script unravel.

See, lookit, people in Hollywood, it's like territorialism, it's like animals peeing on little patches of ground. Unless somebody can do that, they don't think they're being creative. Hollywood is not *real,* it's not founded on reality, so there's a lot of subconscious paranoia. There's a lot of deep-down fear, people thinking: what's my worth? Am I necessary to this process? It's filled with that. And what happened on *Batman,* and I let it happen, is that the script unraveled. Here we started out with a script that everybody said — again, it's classic Hollywood — everybody goes, "Oh, it's a great script, it's a great script." But at the end of the day, they basically *shred* it. So it went from being the greatest script in the world to completely unraveling. And once it unravels, it unravels. You're there, you do it. I remember Jack Nicholson going, "Why am I going up the stairs?" I was like, "I don't know Jack, I'll tell you when you get up there." [Laughs.] And a lot of it had to do with dealing with the energies of the studio and the producers and everybody just being there and doing it. There was no one thing — it was a big animal.

What was the original ending, before you had to substitute the big deal in the tower?

God, I have no fucking idea. I have not a clue.

Well, a lot of those problems don't show up in the movie, or they show up, but we don't care about them, because we're swept forward by other things. But the one thing that everybody did care about is that the tension leading up to Vicki Vale finding out that Bruce Wayne is Batman is completely unresolved. She just walks into the Batcave and—

And obviously, that was one thing I got killed for. It was rough. I'll tell you exactly what the impulse was. The initial impulse, for me, and again, this is where I can go . . . 'cause I . . . I . . . my problem is, I can be a little belligerent. I can respond to things, like maybe when you read about those little kings in England or Egypt who go, when they're really young, [as petulant, spoiled child] "I don't care!" My impulse was, I said to myself, "Fuck this bullshit!" This is comic-book material. I thought, you know, who cares? Who really cares? But it was a mistake. It went too far.

We expect, at least, Bruce Wayne to play off of the fact that he is discovered there, by her, for the first time. But he doesn't. So the audience is left wondering, did he already know that she knew who he was? Did we miss something? And we don't know. So we're sort of thrust out of the narrative.

This is the trouble I have. This is where sometimes there will be big gaps in something that I do. I try very hard to create your own environment. And so far it's worked out. But sometimes there will be a leap that people don't buy, they don't buy, they don't buy. They go, "Whoa!" and it takes them out of it. I don't want to take people out of something. I spend a large time trying not to have that happen.

Because the rule you are playing by, until then, is that you do want the audience involved in her quest to figure out who Bruce Wayne is and who Batman is.

Yes. Yes. Part of the problem with that movie is that there are two things I made mistakes on. I think it has to do with the nature of a big, big movie. Number one, I said, on the effects, "Let's do the effects like on *Beetlejuice,* where they're just kind of fun and all." Well, that did not work at all! Because it's perceived as a big movie with cheesy effects, as opposed to a movie like *Beetlejuice,* which is a small movie, and cheesy, and so it fits. Mistake! Same thing with the structure. The original script was laid out like a grand kind of thing. And also, because the push was in that direction, I was playing into strengths I don't have. I think that's why I wanted to do another one: so I could look at *Batman Returns,* and whether or not it worked out, I could feel about it as I did about other things. I do feel differently about the first Batman movie.

One of the interesting things about that movie is that the action sequences are not nearly as interesting as the rest of the movie.

There's a zillion great action directors and I'm not one of them. Yet this is the genre. On this new thing, I feel better about the action. It's not James Cameron. There are a few people that can jack things up to that kind of level, and why try? I feel like, in the second one, I tried something a bit more representative of myself. I do feel better about it than I did about the first. The action feels more like a part of the movie, as opposed to: here's the movie, and here comes some action, and I've seen better action in my day.

The other thing in the first one that felt horribly intrusive was the Prince music. We're in this Tim Burton world, and all of a sudden, like him or not, in rides Prince.

Yeah, it's true. It's the unholy alliance of me and . . .

Warner Bros. marketing, pure and simple?

This is what happened. You learn something new every day. Now, here is a guy, Prince, who was one of my favorites. I had just gone to see two of his concerts in London and I felt they were like the best concerts I'd ever seen. Okay. So. They're saying to me, these record guys, it needs this and that, and they give you this whole thing about it's an expensive movie so you need it. And what happens is, you get engaged in this world, and then there's no way out. There's too much money. There's this guy you respect and is good and has got this thing going. It got to a point where there was no turning back. And I don't want to get into that situation again.

It had to be painful for you to put that music into that movie.

It was . . . it was . . . it completely lost me. And it tainted a lot. It tainted something that I don't want to taint, which is how you feel about an artist. So it tainted a lot for me. And actually, I liked his album. I wish I could listen to it without the feel of what had happened. And you know what? To tell you the truth, I understand the marketing side of it. I think it would be cleaner if you created cross-marketing, where you don't have that taint, but you can still do things. The idea of somebody looking at a movie and getting ideas about it and doing a musical interpretation of it is a potentially wonderful idea. But it needs big thinking, and it needs truly interesting, creative business people to do that, and it's not at that level. It would be great to crossover movies and opera and records and dance.

What's Batman about to you? Bruce Wayne's depression?

It's about depression and it's about lack of integration. It's about a character. Unfortunately, I always see it being about those things, not about some kind of hero who is saving the city from blah blah blah. If you asked me the plot of *Batman*, I couldn't tell you. It's about duality, it's about flip-sides, it's about a person who's completely fucked and doesn't know what he's doing. He's got good impulses, but he's not integrated. And it's about depression.

It's about going through life, thinking you're doing something, trying very hard. And the Joker represents somebody who gets to act however he wants.

He's playing the Beetlejuice character.

Yeah. There are two kinds of people, even with double personalities. The ones that are fucked and they're still trying to muddle through life, and then the ones that are fucked and get to be completely free, and scary. And they're basically two fantasies. There are two sides.

Which one are you closer to?

Well, I'm probably closer to the Bruce Wayne character, but I much prefer the fantasy of the other. That's much more the liberating side of it.

It's curious that Bruce Wayne/Batman is actually the only character in the movie who's not a cartoon character, but a human being.

I get the most gravity out of him. That's why I like Michael Keaton in it. He's got that—all you got to do is look at him, and he looks fucked up. So, for me, the context is immediately there. He's an unintegrated, kind of goofy, sad, passionate, strong, misguided, in some ways quite clear and in some ways completely out-to-lunch-type character.

Why didn't you explore that more in the movie?

Because, again, I always found that the deeper you went, the more of an intrusion it was. Maybe there's a way to do it which I haven't figured out yet. I always felt trying to figure him out more would be too intrusive.

You don't want to demystify?

Yeah, there's something about not knowing which I like. That was always the impulse.

I assume there was a challenge for you in directing the sequel. Because you said a number of times that sequels don't interest you, unless there is a challenge— something for you to discover which you know nothing about.

New characters. New characters. New characters. New characters. I like them very much. Catwoman, Penguin, and the Christopher Walken character, I like him too. It's a smaller cast. It's much more . . . uh . . .

Interpersonal?

Yeah! I don't know what it is, but there's a different energy about it. I didn't analyze it except to say, I don't feel about *Batman* the way I do about my other movies. It has to do with an energy and finding another field. And I feel good about that. I don't know what it means. It could be bad for the movie, I don't know. But I was much more interested in it. And I find these other characters very compelling.

Is it more open to interpretation? When you did Scissorhands, *you said it was nice to finally make a movie that was a little bit more open to interpretation than your first three pictures.*

I guess if people get it, no. And if they don't, yeah. I don't know. It's hard for me to predict. It could be a big, giant mistake. I have not a clue. Part of the good thing is not knowing what worked on the first one. I certainly know what didn't work.

This one feels more personal to you?

Well, I feel like there's more effect. I feel like I learned something. I feel better about this one. It sounds abstract, but it's really the only feeling I have about it. Lookit, it's an expensive movie, and they don't want you to say this kind of stuff, because it's like, "We're letting somebody do this, and he feels like *that?* Jesus!" Then they get more afraid, and it'll be harder the next movie.

I want to go back to talking about your filmmaking process. Do you draw everything first?

No, I don't get to the point where I draw every frame. I think the process is ongoing. I start by doing fairly naive sketches of characters, just for feeling, and then as it gets going, they get updated. It's more doodling. Sitting, talking on the phone, I do it. It's not that they are that elaborate, or that I say, [in deep, pretentious voice:] "I'm going to create this character." It's really a way for me to get my thought process out. It's really a way of thinking. I never used to even speak. That was the way I would speak. And I don't push it on people. It's really just a process I have.

You have such a strong visual sense that your production design and art direction people, whoever they are, have to be locked into that, otherwise—

It's meaningful, it's the one area that I feel, I guess, quite confident in. And I like working with people who are good, because they give you something. Most of the people who I've worked with have been very talented, and give you a lot. I prefer that, but I could do without.

Do you storyboard?

I used to, but I don't as much anymore. In fact, I'm getting anti-storyboard. I pretty much stopped on *Beetlejuice*. You storyboard things that need effects. I still do it to some degree. But certainly after the first *Batman*, I really stopped. And now, I can't even come up with—I'm getting very twisted about the whole thing. There's something about being spontaneous and working shots out. And when you work with these kind of actors—if they're good, you're just not going to give them a storyboard, and say, "Here." There's an energy and there's a working through things with people.

You're more comfortable with improvisation now?

Yeah. I've started to learn it. The most fun day I think I've ever had was on *Pee-wee's Big Adventure*, in the scene at the Alamo, with Jan Hooks, who played the guide. That was *all* improv, and it was so much fun. So I learned it on that, and that was Paul Reubens's background. And I realized that I loved it. And working with Michael Keaton and Catherine O'Hara on *Beetlejuice*—it was exciting, and it was a lot of fun! You get good stuff, sometimes. I think that kind of turned me into anti-storyboarding.

Are you a "first take" director?

No. It depends on the actors. I think my average is about seven to nine takes. There's always something technical fucked up and it depends on actors.

What's your favorite part of the process?

It's very private and it's very quiet. It's really the hardest part. It's the creation of being on the set and shooting. Right then and there. You're dealing with people that you like, and you're taking some weird idea and trying to make it work. You get that, with the layer of seeing stuff that people don't see, and the light, the way it hits the water, and a guy is sitting up there reading a cheesy magazine with this beautiful light behind him. And the people working on the movie are the greatest. Because they're the ones *working* on it. You're cutting through the bullshit of other things. That's the best thing about it. Those are the only people I can stand to be around.

I get the feeling that editing is fingernails-on-blackboards for you.

When I look at rushes I sometimes get chills because it reminds me of shooting, but editing? What can I tell you? I don't slap 'em together, but I'm not going to win any editing awards. It's okay. It's fine.

What about your camera? Do you feel it's as clunky as you used to?

Well, it's kind of moving around a little bit more. Things are happening. I'm getting a little more confident. I'm knowing about more things. But again, I never think about it too much. I'm getting much more now into looking at it, and trying to respond to it in the moment. Which gets me into trouble, with no storyboards . . .

Because it makes things technically more difficult.

It takes a little longer. I make up my mind very quickly, but I've got to do it when the time is right. Maybe I'm less professional. This is all stuff that worries people. Less professional, maybe more moody.

Do you go out to the movies?

I think because of living here—this sounds like a stupid cop-out but I don't have any other explanation, to tell you the truth—it just feels redundant. It's such a one-industry town. I grew up here, I live here, you go out and it's all movies. It just feels redundant.

So how do you see work you want to see? Go to screenings? Rent cassettes?

I guess, right now, I'm feeling kind of bad about it. For the past few years, I just don't go out and see movies very much. I rent things on videos, but not new stuff. I haven't seen much new stuff. Somehow, when I'm in a video store, I go to the *lowest* common denominator. When I walk into a video store, I'm not going for the latest Martin Scorsese, I'm looking for the latest *Chainsaw Massacre Babe-o-rama Fest*. I can't help it! There's something about video where you seek the level of the medium.

Is there anybody's work out there that you feel connected to, or are interested in?

Well, I don't have a good answer. My answer is bullshit in a way. I mean, I know who I'm *for*. I mean, I do like David Cronenberg. He's great. Basically, you got to like anybody who's doing their thing, don't you?

You and David Lynch sometimes get put together in the same sentence.

But, don't you think that's because of categorization?

Maybe comparison and not categorization. You both have strong visual arts backgrounds, you both really struggle with the language, you both have an interesting take on—

But I'm sure that's true with lots of people. I grew up with reading critics bemoaning the state of movies, right? Everything is a conglomerate, everything's a cookie-cutter, and blah blah blah, and in fact, doesn't the categorization and lumping people further support that? When I was working Disney, I got the same thing, and this is why I have such a twisted interpretation of it. People would come into my office and say, "Oh, your drawings look like Charlie Brown." And then somebody else would say they look like something completely different. What's the point? The point is people are trying to categorize. Is it positive or is it negative?

It depends which side of the binoculars you're looking through. If you're looking through the wrong end of the binoculars, it makes everything smaller. If you're looking through the right end of the binoculars, by comparing and contrasting two bodies of work, it enlightens: it makes both richer, deeper.

But *you* know that, and I know that, but I guess my point is that in the context of the culture, a context of where things are headed in terms of the arts, you know, it's *scary*. It's bad news. It's headed in a negative direction. And my point being (and I know what you're saying and there probably are a small group of people that would look at it in the positive way that you might look at it but) I'm afraid it does everybody a disservice. I was like tortured at Disney. I was treated like a king and tortured at the same time. It was like a farce. You are allowed to be in a room and do your own stuff, but then someone would go, "Oh, that looks like such and such." It's the way I took it. It was like Chinese water torture. Jesus Christ!

On the day of our first session, you changed agents. You left William Morris and joined CAA. How come?

Things happen. I guess it has its evil connotations. Everybody has a perception of CAA, and I'm not sure it's altogether untrue. But on a very personal level, things made sense. I've been very lucky, dealing with Hollywood, but nobody really knows . . . I just am very moody and I have my own agenda, and I don't even know what that is. But I know it's to fight a certain thing; it doesn't have to do with money, it doesn't have to do with position in the industry. Except that, in America, the better position you have, the more freedom you have—which I know now is not true completely. So that's why I'm always one hundred percent interested in finding out how to deal with this system. I don't want to get *hot* scripts. I don't like meeting actors. I'm not interested in any of that stuff. That's what Hollywood is all about, and I guess you could look at CAA and say they're the pinnacle of all that. But that's not the conversations with them I had. I had conversations where nothing was said literally, like "We're going to get you this, Tim"—I was just spoken to in a way I'd never been spoken to: as a person.

Not as an "artist"?

As a *person*. I wasn't out to change agencies, I love my agent. What mattered was, things were presented to me and I was spoken to in a way, it was almost uncanny. I've been trying to figure out how to deal with all this stuff, and to be in this industry. All I'm interested in is in punching through and trying to do interesting things. That's all.

You are interested in doing some theme-park attractions.

This is what I'm interested in: I'm not interested in anything literal. I'm interested in, if an idea comes up—and it could be painting a mural on a building, it could be doing an underwater Bob Hope special, it could be *anything*. See, what I'm tired of, to give you the clearest example, is that whole idea of marketing. Things are changing, and these people are not interesting thinkers, for the most part. They are not going to look at me and they are not going to look at you, and say, "Wouldn't you like to do interesting things? Wouldn't you like to *try* something?" See, I don't consider myself like a film director. I'm interested in openness, I'm interested in trying to create an environment for myself. I mean, I've gotten offers for things that are more money than anything. But I won't do it. No one understands. They think once you're hooked into the movie industry that you'll kind of do *whatever*.

"We've already established what you are, now we're just negotiating price." The famous punchline to the joke about the prostitute.

[Laughs.] It's that whole thing about what project is next. You know when you get there. And that's the only thing that will allow you to do it. You've got to have one hundred percent passion for it. See, part of my problem is, I'm a guy who is very discombobulated. I cannot, I realized fairly recently, deal with things the way other people do. Especially when people perceive you as something. For instance, I hate talking on the phone. You spend all day on the phone, and all that bullshit. People get upset with you if you don't return calls. In one week, you could end up having most of Hollywood angry at you, if you didn't return their calls. Now, I never returned my calls two, three years ago, but all of a sudden, it's a problem. I will *destroy* myself if I get into it.

What do you do when you're not working?

I'm never bored but I can't account for my time. What do I like to do? Fuck knows. I'm not a loiterer necessarily. I don't go down to 7-Eleven and hang out in the parking lot. I do my drawing and fool around with painting, I do enjoy that. But, I don't know. I'm not sitting there drooling and staring out of a window. I can't account for my time. Maybe that's why I was audited by the IRS. [Pause, laughs.] Maybe I *do* hang out at 7-Eleven parking lots.

You're not preparing for fatherhood, are you, Tim?

No, not yet. You can't prepare for that sort of thing.

Well, you can take steps to prevent it.

Well, those steps are being taken. We sleep in separate bedrooms, much like the Hayes Code. When we kiss, we both have one foot on the ground at all times.

You wear full-body condoms?

Yes, we wear full protective gear. And one foot on the floor at all times.

Because I know at one point you said that the idea of family for you was an impossibility.

Well, you know, it's a problem when you see too much. It usually happens with the firstborn. It's like a fucking lab experiment.

The first waffle gets burned, and tossed.

Exactly! How many firstborns do you know that are completely fucked up? And once the parents get through that, it's better. I'm just too *sensitive* for it, right now. I'm overly sensitive about it. I think I'd end up throwing little lizards on the child's bed to see what he'd do. Treating it much like the experiment that it is. It's an *experiment*. Let's throw water on it and see what it does!

Why bother making another movie, Tim? You hate putting them out.

It's like some sort of drug or virus, that takes over your body. The desire to do it is there.

What terrifies you so much about putting them out?

It's funny, I question it. It's a split. Obviously, I do this stuff. I'm talking to you. I'm not holing up in my castle in Switzerland, away from anybody, but I have a strong fear of letting this stuff out, for some reason.

What do you think you're afraid of?

I think because I don't know who I am. I think I haven't figured myself out. It's personal. The movie is my *baby*, and I'm putting it out there into the cruel world. It's scary, that's all. Just really scary.

What's the worst thing that could happen to it?

See, the worst thing that could happen, would be something you could understand. I wish they would tear down the screen, if they didn't like it. That would be the worst "good" thing that could happen. The worst "bad" thing would be . . . I don't know. It's fear of the unknown. Is anybody going to like this? It's judgment. Being categorized, and judged. I have a very strong aversion to that. I don't know where that comes from, but there it is. I'm in my little world, trying to do this film, then boom, it's out there. The film may have its unreality but the people that watch it are one hundred percent real people. And they always look angry. Everytime I go to these fucking screenings, the audience always looks angry to me. They look very scary. Its just fear.

You're not afraid of failing, are you?

It's funny, in some ways I'm not, and in some ways I guess I am. I will not base my decisions on what to do based on the thought of "success." So in some ways, I'm not afraid of that—I'll do what I want to do, and hope for the best. The fear just has to do with that aspect of *showing* it to people. I don't know if that's failure, or just the fear of coming out into the open.

You really kind of want to be in a cave, hanging upside down, with your drawing.

Yeah, but then again, I've been through that. At Disney, I was in my own little cave, and I was not getting out, and that's no good. Definitely, you want to get out and you want feedback. I think I am just afraid of it. I think that my impulse is to hide in the cave. Again, it's the split, it's Batman. It's classic, really, it's classic.

8
CLINT EASTWOOD

CLINT EASTWOOD FILMOGRAPHY

1971	Play Misty for Me
1973	High Plains Drifter
1973	Breezy
1975	The Eiger Sanction
1976	The Outlaw Josey Wales
1977	The Gauntlet
1980	Bronco Billy
1982	Firefox
1982	Honkytonk Man
1983	Sudden Impact
1985	Pale Rider
1986	Heartbreak Ridge
1988	Bird
1990	White Hunter, Black Heart
1990	The Rookie
1992	Unforgiven
1993	A Perfect World
1995	The Bridges of Madison County
1997	Absolute Power
1998	Midnight in the Garden of Good and Evil

for television

1985	Vanessa in the Garden

as actor only (selected)

1955	Francis in the Navy
1955	Revenge of the Creature
1964	A Fistful of Dollars
1965	For a Few Dollars More
1966	The Good, the Bad and the Ugly
1968	Hang 'Em High
1968	Where Eagles Dare
1969	Paint Your Wagon
1971	The Beguiled
1971	Dirty Harry
1973	Magnum Force
1978	Every Which Way But Loose
1979	Escape From Alcatraz
1984	Tightrope
1988	The Dead Pool
1993	In the Line of Fire

as executive producer only

1988	Thelonius Monk: Straight No Chaser

Clint Eastwood

At Euro Disney, outside Paris, high-profile architects have built five hotels celebrating various aspects of the American landscape: the Hotel
New York, the Sequoia Lodge, the Cheyenne, the Newport Bay Club
and the Hotel Santa Fe. This last inn, a Southwestern tongue-in-chic
extravaganza, is punctuated with rusting vintage cars, a saguaro cactus
in a glass cage and a parking lot that evokes a drive-in movie theatre—
the guests have to walk under the screen to enter the hotel's front door.
The architect, Antoine Predock, wanted to leave this giant movie screen
provocatively blank. (The Europeans would simply raid their memories
for images to project.) But Disney said *No*. A blank screen would not
do. Well then: what do you paint permanently onto a movie screen outside Paris to conjure the myth of the West?

Clint Eastwood, of course. "There is no one more American than
he" is what Norman Mailer said, hitting the nail squarely on the hard
head, steely gaze, and tight jaw. The Eastwood Hero is nothing if not
prototypically Western and tragically American to the core: always a
bullet in his gun, pain in his heart, a cold gray rain of rage in his eyes.
For years the biggest international movie star on the planet—turf that
he ceded in the last half of the '80s to actors with bigger biceps (in
Hollywood) and bigger guns (in Washington)—Eastwood has meta-
morphosed not into the dusty legend we might expect but rather into
an ambitious filmmaker. In 1988, *Bird*, his downwardly spiraling riff on
Charlie Parker, was avant-garde in its methods and its madness, and,
while saluted by the critics, left most of the audience behind. Two
years later, Eastwood stretched again with *White Hunter, Black Heart*, a
dryly comic take on John Huston's whimsical, obsessive attempt to
shoot an elephant before he'd shoot *The African Queen*. Without question, over these last twenty years—despite the mediocrities that pock-
mark his output—Eastwood has ridden a long way from his first film
as a director, *Play Misty for Me*.

Born on May 31, 1930, in San Francisco, Eastwood was a lonely, shy kid, attending eight different grammar schools as his family moved from town to town, with trailer in tow, in search of Depression-era jobs. In high school he concentrated on swimming, basketball, and jazz, playing piano for free meals in an Oakland club. After leaving home, he "beat around"—he was a firefighter and lumberjack in Oregon, a steelworker in Seattle—until the Army got him in 1951. (His heroic Army exploits: teaching swimming at Fort Ord.) After his 1953 discharge he wandered to Hollywood, where Universal signed him as a two-bit contract player, using him in the "Francis the Talking Mule" movies and other such stellar attractions. Dropped eighteen months later, he dug swimming pools and pumped gas until a chance meeting with a producer for *Rawhide*—the 1959-to-1966 TV series about Great Plains cattle drives—led to a screen test for the part of Rowdy Yates.

That role opened the door for The Man With No Name to sidle in, the gunslinging loner of Sergio Leone's *A Fistful of Dollars*, and two other spaghetti westerns in its wake, *For a Few Dollars More* and *The Good, the Bad, and the Ugly*. The pictures made Eastwood a star, though hardly a critical favorite. "Eastwood doesn't act in motion pictures," Vincent Canby famously wrote in *The New York Times* in 1968, "he is framed in them." By the late '80s, given the long shelf-life of his iconic portrayals and his own increasingly diverse work as a director, many of his earlier critics were whistling a different tune: Eastwood was now provocative, deep, a feminist not a fascist; at the very least, *interesting*.

With *Unforgiven*, his sixteenth feature as director and thirty-sixth as star, the reappraisal continues. *High Plains Drifter*, *The Outlaw Josey Wales*, and *Pale Rider* are Eastwood's grand triptych of Westerns: *Unforgiven* is the coda that changes how we view them. A polished piece of rawhide revisionism, it's anti-romantic, anti-heroic, and anti-violent. It's Eastwood's first dance with myth where the music's not cartoonish: it's mature, and at sixty-two, so is he. If *Unforgiven* is not his last western, it should be; if it's not recognized right away as a classic, it will be.

I met with Eastwood just before the release of that movie, in the late summer of 1992. We talked in a guest room at Mission Ranch, an inn he owns near his home in Carmel, California. As we spoke, sheep grazed in a meadow just out the window, bahhing and frisking about, providing a surreal commentary on the conversation. I half expected Clint to pull out a rifle and blow one of the noisy critters away, but that was the *old*, filmic Clint of my fantasy, and not the new-and-improved real guy lazing on the couch in front of me. Cordial but distant at first, Eastwood was quite friendly by the end of the night, though he keeps self-analysis a stranger in town.

SESSION ONE

What's the most vital thing to you about the work you do?

At this point in my career, it's the constant reaching, the constant stretching for new ideas, or, even in the current project, variations on a theme. It's very hard to find things that haven't been done. But I'm always looking for that excitement. Sometimes it doesn't happen.

Is it an emotional satisfaction or an intellectual one?

I think it's more emotional. Intellectual? I suppose that's when you're being analytical. I respond to material on an emotional level, and I like to respond to movies—as a member of the audience—at an emotional level. I don't always: sometimes I find myself getting carried away with how it's done, and that's a sign usually that it wasn't done so well. It's an emotional thing: would I like to see this? would I like to be in it? would I like to direct it? I ask myself a lot of questions, but I usually don't spend a long time answering them. I make a decision rather fast.

On intuition?

Yeah. More intuition. Sometimes I jokingly use the word "whimsical." But it's really intuition. I read something that sparks me. *Unforgiven* I read as a sample of the author's [David Webb Peoples] work, figuring it wasn't available. Coppola had it at the time, and he couldn't get it going. So I called up to ask about the writer's availability for something else, and he told me it was available. That was a surprise. It seemed to me very timely.

How long have you owned it?

Since 1983. By and large when I look back over the years, I've kind of spun off of instinct—and *luck*. *Outlaw Josey Wales* came to me as a blind submission. I read it and liked it.

Have you ever done anything counter-intuitive? Something that didn't feel right, but you felt you "should" do it, or it might be an interesting challenge.

Against my instinct? I've never done that. [Pause.] I may have done it, but I wasn't conscious of it at the time. Maybe something to keep the company going, keep my co-dependents going. [Laughs.] But I didn't consciously do it.

Is the kicking back at the end of a film—looking back at the accomplishment—is that the most satisfying thing to you, or is the process of doing it the satisfaction?

Some people are let down by finishing a project. I'm always *elated* to finish.

Some directors are very attached to process, a director like Altman in the extreme—where he feels almost all the value is in the doing of it.

Hitchcock always felt it was all in the planning of it. The execution was boring to him.

Because he had the whole film in his head.

Right, he was a sketch artist, so he'd sketch it out. Once he planned it, he could have an assistant director go out and shoot it, he didn't care. Everybody has their pet part of it. I enjoy shooting a film, but I really enjoy when it's all shot, and everyone has been excused, and I go to edit it, with maybe one or two people. Then, there is so much less pressure. There are not the thousands of questions. Shooting is an absolutely nerve-wracking process.

Editing is your time of maximum control and yet maximum flexibility.

Absolutely. That's where you can make or break it. That's when you breathe all the last life into it. And you have to have all the pieces—the pieces have to be there.

Do you discover the film in the editing?

No. I discover it in the shooting. I know what's there when I go to the editing. I may be surprised—it may play better or worse than I expected—but I pretty well remember everything I've done.

Can you recall significantly changing a film in tone or theme in the editing?

No. I've changed the tempo of things; especially in the early days, I jockeyed the balance a lot more. I'm more positive now about what I have. I'm careful now to put it together the way I originally conceived it, the first time around.

It's anathema to you to go out and shoot a film and not be sure what you want to get, the way some directors do.

I . . . I just can't conceive it.

Supposedly, one of the reasons you turned down Coppola on Apocalypse Now *when you were offered the role of Willard, is because there was no ending to the film and you didn't see much point in going all the way over there without knowing which way it was going to turn. The ending to* Heart of Darkness *is obviously quite important.*

Well, I read *Heart of Darkness* in school, and I didn't understand the ending of the film, the way it was. And also, there were several other problems. Francis had been talking to Steve McQueen and Steve had then recommended me. Steve wanted *me* to play Willard, so he could play Kurtz. I said, "Steve, I thought they wanted you for Willard?" And he said, "Well, I want to play Kurtz." I said, "Why?" He said, "Because I can do it in two weeks!" I said that's great but what makes you think I want to work for all this time? Then, later, Francis called—and I had just bought a house and my children were very young—and he said they were going to go to the Philippines for sixteen weeks. It was just too long. If it were eight weeks, I would have done it. And I said I didn't understand the ending. He said they were going to work on that. But anyway, *two years later* they were still shooting and Martin Sheen had had a heart attack, and I thought, God damn! That could be all of us! I saw the documentary [*Hearts of Darkness*] and I must say it was terribly amusing. Francis is a nice guy and everything—but two years—I would have gone insane! Absolutely insane!

I bring this up because you're a guy who knows what he's fishing for, known for coming in under budget with very rigorous shooting schedules and wanting first takes.

Well, I don't get first takes all the time, but I want it, yes. Once in a while you get great "start-up" actors, I call them—Gene Hackman and Morgan Freeman are great examples. They're the kind of guys where you start rehearsal and it looks so good, you say, "Wait a second, stop, roll this thing," because there's no reason to be wasting it. Guys like Hackman are ready to pull the trigger right away.

You distrust rehearsal anyway, don't you?

Well, I don't like people to get stale. I like people to do things naturally. I like things that come accidentally. I guess it comes from years of seeing something nice happen in a scene and then not ever being able to see it come up again. Usually a good performer can drag it up again, but it may never have that spontaneity. So I do make an attempt to always get that first take—there may be lighting problems, technical problems—but you've got to be like stepping up to bat. You're not stepping up to *bunt*. You're stepping up to hit the damn thing.

Once you said, "The more time you have to think, the more time you have to screw up."

Exactly! The more time you have to kill things with improvements. [Laughs.] You see movies where you get the feeling that the movie is *wrung out*. That it's been all squeezed-out before they ever printed the take. I like the inspiration of the first take. We used to do it, over on the Sergio Leone pictures, he'd print several things because he was always afraid the lab was going to screw up, he'd do protection takes. Nowadays, technically, it's good. When a guys says, "That's good, let's do one more." I think, Wait a second, that's contradictory. If it's good, do one more—why? Because it took forty-five minutes to set the lighting for this room? You mean you're going to print that one take and walk away?

We've made an investment in time here!

[Laughing] I mean, forty-five minutes, at least shoot it twice. But some actors are best on their third or fourth take; and there are others you've heard about, that love to do it twenty or thirty or forty times. But if you have really great players, great things happen by accident.

What's jazz taught you about film?

That improvisation can work well as long as you have the structure, as long as the tune is playing. As long as you know what the tune is, everyone can reach out. Actors who are acting *generously* are very much like jazz musicians: they are within the scene, but they are doing things that aren't exactly written. The unspoken word, the notes they are throwing in.

Unlike jazz, which needs to be in the moment, you may be in the moment with film but it's deferred like crazy—the process is almost diametrically opposed.

It's like saying, "Do this tune, we're going to do a few bars." And then to cut after those bars and say, "Day after tomorrow we're going to pick up from there and move into the bridge." In movies, how do you get all the high points so that it comes out as a nice tune?

Do you ever feel ambivalent about your work, once it's over and done with, and out there as a part of our culture?

Yeah. Sometimes. I don't think about it that much. I don't know whether it's callousness, or whether it's a . . . [Pause.] I just don't think about it. I don't think back on my work very much. I don't dwell on it.

What about when the work talks back to you—through the culture? Witness the endless celebration of the "Make my day" line or "A man's gotta know his limitations." Etcetera, etcetera. Now it's not yours anymore, it's the culture's, and I wonder if these ever come back to you in a way you're not comfortable with.

I must say, I knew when I did *Sudden Impact* that "Go ahead, make my day" would be the key line to the whole picture, just when I read it on the page. Now, I didn't know it would go like it did. People flew banners with it here above the golf course. After a while, I must say, I got sick of it. I guess it's a compliment, that you've said something that's lasted that long—but whether Colorado having a "Make my day" law is any satisfaction to me, I don't know.

Do you care if you feel your work is misinterpreted?

You know it's going to be misinterpreted in some way. Sometimes you try things that people don't get, other times they get it just fine. You take a chance. I enjoy chances. I guess I'm an excitement addict, or just crazy enough that I feel if the audience doesn't like it that's too bad.

Not just the question of them not liking it. One of the curious things about your work is that perhaps more than a lot of filmmakers, and this may have to do with Clint Eastwood as star as opposed to as a director, is that people impose agendas on you. In the '70s you were a fascist, and in the '80s you became a feminist—

And just what anybody wants to put in there! I was probably more a feminist in the '70s, certainly more than I was a fascist, that's for sure. I remember when *Dirty Harry* was offered to me. It was offered by an executive who said that Paul Newman had told him about it, and had said it's a great script, but he couldn't do it, because of political implications. It disagreed with certain feelings of his. Well, I read it, and I said, "I'll do it." What works for me is I don't give a damn if I disagree with the character or not—it's a lot more challenging for me to play the guy if I don't agree with him. It's much more challenging to put myself in a place to act out and be someone who I really have nothing in common with. That, to me, is acting. And the fact that people think you really *are* that guy is really not an uncomplimentary thing. Because, if you've affected them that much that they think you are this guy, and that you have this guy's *philosophy*, then you have done your job.

Well indeed, you, more than most actors, are assumed to inhabit the role to the point where you and the role are considered a kind of "unit of meaning."

That's the way it should be. That, to me, is the fun of acting. That's the way I've always thought. Both Don Siegel and I had a great time doing *Dirty Harry* in 1971—we were both pro-victim's rights, but we weren't anti-accused rights. We just thought, Here's a story that talks about the victim's rights. Okay, we'll do this story. Now, if there was a great story about the rights of the accused—who had been railroaded into prison—I would have been just as excited to play that.

Are you telling me, Clint, that all this time you have actually been playing against type? In the westerns? In the cop pictures?

[Laughs.] It's disappointing. I've run into young people along the way and they are disappointed if I don't pull out a gun. I used to have guys, after *Dirty Harry*, pull up next to me and say, "Hey, call me an asshole! Call me an asshole like you did in the picture." People ask me to say, "Do you feel lucky?" I can't. I played it at the time. But now I couldn't say it without laughing.

Do all the political interpretations of your work make you uneasy? I get a sense that they do.

Not really. [Pause.] You play a piece of music or paint a painting and put it up on the wall, it's up to people to interpret it. It may not be the right way or your way of interpreting it, but at least they are participating. But if a person thinks that I *am* the person that I played, then that's *terrific*. That's every actor's dream! That's every actor's accomplishment: you are the person, you're it, you're not even acting. That's what actors sit around at actor's workshops for year after year hoping to achieve.

Let me quote to you something Sergio Leone said about your relationship to acting, and here he's comparing you to De Niro, with whom he had recently worked. I know you are dedicating Unforgiven *to Leone, and to Siegel. Leone said, "They don't even belong to the same profession. Robert De Niro throws himself into this or that role, putting on a personality the way someone else might put on his coat, naturally and with elegance, while Clint Eastwood throws himself into a suit of armor and lowers the visor with a rusty clang. [Eastwood laughs.] It's exactly that lowered visor which composes his character. And that creaky clang it makes as it snaps down, dry as a Martini in Harry's Bar in Venice, is also his character. Look at him carefully. Eastwood moves like a sleepwalker between explosions and hails of bullets, and he is always the same—a block of marble. Bobby, first of all, is an actor. Clint, first of all, is a star. Bobby suffers, Clint yawns."*

[Laughs.] I think Sergio was being profound at the time. There may have been a tinge of envy at the time: I went off and directed pictures and ended up directing a lot more films than he did in his career. But I can give you quotes from Sergio during *Fistful of Dollars* that said I moved like a cat, and he was very impressed with the way I moved. But at this point he was working with another actor and another style.

What happened with Sergio is that we got along great on those three films, and he offered me *Once Upon a Time in the West*. At the time, when we did *The Good, The Bad, and The Ugly*, he was talking about *Once Upon a Time in America*, and he wanted me to play an Irish gangster—and I went off and came back here and did other films. And we kind of lost touch with each other. And he changed his interpretation of me, and he's probably changed it many times. But a few years ago, I went back to Rome, and I hadn't seen him in many years—and I had done *Bird* and the Italian critics were very favorable. And he called me up, and asked me if I wanted to get together and have lunch. I was surprised. And we went out and had a great time, a time like we'd never had before—and we got together another time for dinner. He didn't want anything from me, he just wanted to hang out. It was almost like he was taking a little trip of nostalgia, because he died right after that. He seemed genuinely happy about *Bird* and joked about its length [141 minutes], because I was always accusing him of leaving things too long. And we kidded each other and left on the best terms we had ever been on. And then he died.

And so the two guys who probably had the most influence on me, in terms of getting started in motion pictures, were now both dead. Because Don Siegel had also died, he'd had several bouts with cancer. So I dedicated *Unforgiven* to them.

What was Siegel talking about when he mentioned your violent temper? He said, "You can't push Clint. It's very dangerous. For a guy who's as cool as he is, there are times when he has a violent temper."

Well, that was the old days.

You're mellowed now.

I hope so. He knew I could kick off. But we were young guys, hanging out. I could channel my temper into being in touch with my anger for the role. Channel it into another energy, for the most part.

You were able to subvert all that free-flowing hostility into your roles?

Maybe. Maybe. It's like Lena Horne—you've got to have that sort of love/hate thing with your audience. If you love 'em, they won't respond to you. [Pause.] I never hated them, but I made them reach forward to me. I feel like if they lean forward and they see that they're interested in what I'm doing, fine, but if you get placating to the audience it becomes condescending to them, and then they'll feel that. They're very sensitive. Very sensitive. Maybe they won't seem sensitive at times and they may ignore you when you do your best work, but by in large they are cut in to the whole thing. And that's how they pick the people who they want to embrace, and put the people into certain roles that they like best.

You're thought of as being quite close to your audience, and never being condescending to the characters you play, and yet I'm wondering if there have ever been times—perhaps at the height of your commercial success—if it didn't bug you that the audience was just wanting the same thing, over and over, or if it didn't just start to feel a little moronic to you—all the people who wanted you to keep saying "Make my day." I mean, even the most sensitive, saintly, patient artist would be driven to—

Driven mad, yeah. A lot of the films I've done, let's say a film like *Bronco Billy*—which is a film that did modest business, not great, not bad, but wasn't in the same league as the films that immediately preceded it, like *Every Which Way But Loose*—and yet you think it's one of your better things, you're reaching out and trying something different, and the audience doesn't go for it. It makes you wonder what the hell is the matter? Or I'll do something like *The Beguiled* in the late '60s and they don't go for it at all. You've got to be philosophical about that. You can't think: well, I'll just do genre flicks now. If they want killing, I'll just kill. If they want mayhem, I'll out-mayhem myself. If you succumb to that, you become a self-parody. And I'm not interested in that. One good thing about having a certain amount of commercial success is you can afford to take a time out. If you don't, it's kind of crazy—because you have only one career and one lifetime. If you look back on it and you've made sixty Westerns and forty cop pictures, it's sort of empty. Now a lot of guys may be happy with that: hey, it's great, I can go out and golf and hit the ball on the weekends and I really don't give a crap about anything. But I like films and I like making them and I like seeing them and I grew up watching a lot of different kinds of films and different kinds of actors, and I think it's spread over into my life.

Do you consider yourself an auteur?

I hate the word. Always hated the word. It's loaded. It makes it seem like it's one guy, rather than the whole ensemble. I've always considered myself a platoon leader. An auteur? Anyone who sits and thinks of himself as an auteur has got to be kind of narrow.

How about the other label we touched on: feminist? It was just after Tightrope *that you got designated by the* Los Angeles Times *as the leading feminist filmmaker in the country.*

Yeah, when I did *Play Misty For Me* in 1970, after I had done *The Beguiled*, I remember feminists standing up at the San Francisco Film Festival and saying, Why are you so oppressive to women? I said I didn't feel like I was oppressive. In the two last films I'd done, the best roles in the pictures had been played by women. What's oppressive about that? But that argument didn't go down well.

Let's cut to the chase, Clint. Do you consider yourself a feminist?

No, I never thought of myself one way or the other. I grew up in films with Claudia Colbert, Betty Davis, and Joan Crawford were playing fantastic roles, and I enjoyed those movies as much as the ones with Cagney and Gary Cooper. So I never consider myself as pro- or con-.

And what about how you consider yourself now?

Well, I consider myself a pro-feminist, but at the same time, I've always been, in a lot of my thoughts. I could sit and intellectualize about it for days, and make it sound like I'm the most noble guy on the planet, but that just ain't the case. I love women. Maybe that's being a pro-feminist. I loved them, starting with my mother. That's how far back it goes.

I must say that in the '50s, when I was around playing bit parts, it was a pretty *dumb* time for women in films. It was after the age of elegant women; it was the time of the ponytailed gal in jeans running around acting kind of dopey. I think the era of real female participation in films got lost there for quite a while. I think it has changed now.

You mentioned Misty. *When I watched it again the other day, I was shocked that what I was watching was* Fatal Attraction—*it's the same picture.*

Everybody asked me about it at the time. More power to them. Plagiarism is the surest form of flattery. It's Universal's problem. I kiddingly told Sherry Lansing, "You owe me a beer, you stole our story." And she said, "Yeah, I always loved that picture, I always loved that picture." So more power to them. I don't know how many stories there are out in the world. They took it and they put a spin on it, a spin that we even considered. When I was preparing for it, somebody suggested: what happens if the guy is married? I felt that was a manipulation I didn't want to get into.

Let's talk about the Eastwood hero. I'm sure there are a hundred different things to say about this character, and as many exceptions as rules, but one thing that does strike me is that if there is an Eastwood hero, it is a guy who is deeply damaged, who has been profoundly hurt, and is acting out of that hurt.

I think so. I think the heroes all have something that is nagging at them. Dating back to *A Fistful of Dollars* and those stylized things. You never knew what his past was, but at the end of the screenplay you did know what his past was, there was a big expository scene that was boring, and Sergio and I had some contention about this. It's better for people to have the mystery, rather than to unload, to dump all this stuff on them. But most of the heroes I've played have definitely had something in their background—something painful. Up through the present film, where he's really got damage. Through some pain, through some trial and error, through some suffering in life, you come to what you are. And guys of great strength who get things done—whether escapist heroes or not—would have to have something in their lives to bring them to that point. They couldn't be guys who just went on and had a normal life—had a normal job, and this fell into place—it just can't happen that way.

Would you say that you're one of those sorts of guys?

Are you looking for a parallel in my life? [Long pause.] I don't know. I don't get into a self-analytical position very often, and I try to avoid it. I could say that I have the ability to take the things in my life—the hurts and disappointments, whatever—and channel them into moving forward, channel them into positive force.

Did you feel in the roles you created that you were tapping into something that was not *a stretch for you? Obviously, you didn't grow up as a gunslinger, but you were a lumberjack and a gas pumper and . . .*

I beat around. I had my beat-around years, and my years of being lost. Lost in that I didn't know what I wanted to do, or what I thought I could do. But I've never sat and analyzed how they fit in. I think it's strictly an imaginative thing. Just as you can imagine something positive in someone's life—a force going forward—so can you imagine a background that's slightly damaged. It's just the imagination of the actor. You have to give yourself that obstacle to make the character interesting, to give it some depth. And you can take it to extremes—like in *Tightrope*, where the guy really has doubts about himself, or it can be somebody who has really had some *pain* in his life, like the outlaw Josey Wales or William Munny in *Unforgiven*.

The wounds those characters carry are profound.

It just takes a little imagination to do that. They are all suffering through a lot more than I've suffered in real life.

I'm not going to ask you for more self-analysis than we were traipsing by there, but I'd like to ask you, parenthetically, as to why you don't want to get into a self-analytical mode?

I just . . . I just . . . [Pause.] It's not out of fear or anything, it's kind of like if I know too much about it I'll wreck the ability to do it. Really, you're taking an art that is not an intellectual art form, it's more an emotional art form—so you approach it on more of a gut level, and you're bound to have better luck with it. At least I've found that avenue. The analytical stage only becomes how we're going to do it, how we're going to present it. I don't want to take the spontaneity out of developing the character. It's nice to find things out as you go. I've been lucky that way a lot of times. I start out with a character, with certain goals and certain things in mind, and then I find out things as I go. Part way through a film I'll come to a complete understanding.

Is the process of discovering character fundamentally different in films you're directing as opposed to films you're not directing?

Not really. There's a different switch for the directing part than the acting part. The directing part you might approach emotionally also, but you have a technical aspect you have to deal with.

Another aspect of the Eastwood hero—which we can send out here riding along the horizon to riddle with verbal bullets—is his sort of fundamental and over-riding decency to others, but, when riled, a sort of termination with extreme prejudice.

Yeah. Yeah, that's true.

They are not characters that bend. They snap.

Yeah, they don't just bend. They are loyal characters, but when they've been wronged, yeah, they snap. I agree with that. That's something I'm attracted to. I guess I find that appealing.

Is the fascination for you in what makes him snap?

That's always the drama, the apex of the drama. What makes him snap is always interesting. What was so fun in playing this current character [William Munny] is that he's sort of forced by lack of prosperity into doing the only thing he really knows how to do well. And he has bad feelings about that, and he keeps bringing up his own demons—people he has killed. There's a morality. It's not like doing penance for the mayhem I've created on the screen over the prior years, but in a way, it's the first time I've read it in a way, have been able to interpret it in a way, that death is not a fun thing. Somebody, somebody is in deep pain afterward—the loss of a friend, or even the person who perpetrates it.

There are consequences to the violence.

There are consequences, all the way down the line. Whether an audience will like that, I don't know.

The scene where The Kid is crying about the killing he's committed and is drinking the whiskey, that's a beautiful scene. There's an emotional honesty to it. Now, one of the things you've been slammed with over the years is that your pictures don't show the consequences of violence. They show the bottled rage, the explosion, the physicalization of the rage—which is very cinematic, which makes sense visually and dramatically—but they are weak on the consequences of violence, emotionally and otherwise. This picture really changes that formula.

Yeah, it does. And I think that was the big appeal to me when I bought it in '83. I sort of nurtured it. I put it away, like a little tiny gem that you put on the shelf and go look at it and polish it, and think, I'll do this. Age is good for the character, so I'll mature a little bit. Three years ago I decided, I've got to do this. And today, you see things put in motion, a lot of the stuff that has gone on this last year and a half, where, a *decision* is made that is maybe not the right decision—where force was used to the extreme. Like the Rodney King incident. Where force was used, beyond reason, maybe. It's like Hackman in *Unforgiven*.

He's like a Daryl Gates character.

Yeah. How to handle this situation? [A prostitute is cut up by her client.] Well, women weren't well thought of in those days, especially prostitutes—so give their employer a few ponies and call it a day. And I can get back to my house and get to sleep. And he triggers off, by lack of action, a whole set of circumstances where a lot of innocent people fall by the wayside. It's hard to find screenwriters who would write that.

Why do the repercussions of violence matter to you now when they didn't matter to you so much before?

I think just generally changing in life. We're all constantly changing, for better or for worse. Hopefully, we're gaining more knowledge as the years go by. And just all of a sudden, it comes there. I'm not smart enough to have written it down, so all of a sudden I see it, and say, "That's it, that's the element I've wanted that's been missing for me." This is an element that I haven't been able to deal with properly. Maybe skirt here and there, deal with in pictures, but not really explore. It's something that's attractive. There were a lot of ways to change this script, and soften it, and conclude it differently, or conclude it happier, to give a resolution to the cut whore . . .

Where she would ride off with Munny, and you'd restore domesticity.

And you tie them all together. And all of these things pass over to your mind as you're thinking about it, but you think: that's wrong, we can't compromise this. That's not what this is about. It's not about tying up domesticity.

The world of Unforgiven *is a complicated world. It's an adult world: it's a world where violence doesn't solve any problems, it just changes the problems. That's a sea change for you.*

Exactly. And that was very appealing, very appealing to play and to explore. We're talking about people purging themselves and changing attitudes. I remember when I first spoke to Gene Hackman about it, and I asked him if he'd be interested in playing his role, he said, "Well, I don't want to do anything with any violence in it." I said, "Really?" He's had his share of violent films, too. I said, "Gene, I know exactly where you're coming from. I've been involved in a lot of violent films and action dramas and what have you, but I would love to have you look at this, because I think there's a spin on this that's different. I don't think this is a tribute to violence, and if we do it right, it's not exploiting it, in fact, it's kind of stating that it doesn't solve anything." So when he read it, he could see where it was headed, and he decided to do it.

Did you relish demythologizing your persona?

Yeah. It was nice. It was fun. And you've got to be uncompromising there too; there's nothing glamorous about it. He's a guy who's pretty much on the bottom.

He's nose-deep in pig shit.

Literally. He's deep in it.

What about demythologizing the West, the "Wild West"?

I didn't mind that either. Because it's been demythologized along the way. It's great to do it, because I didn't have to work at it, it was there to do as part of the nature of the story. It was in the structure and the honesty of it. It was odd to start out with a guy who's quite inept. He's having trouble getting on his horse. [Laughs.] He's rusty. It's different than the characters I've played, where of course he couldn't miss with the gun.

This is more interesting, and I think the West is more interesting, not less interesting, as a place where people don't just get plugged up on the horizon, riding twenty miles an hour, but get shot three times in the chest while taking a shit. That's one of the oddest murder scenes in memory.

It is odd.

And there's no build-up to it; you've made it anti-romantic. There's no joy in the killing in this movie.

Yeah. The Kid thinks he's going to have joy, when he kills the guy in the shithouse. He thinks this is his moment. He's going to become the killer he's always dreamed of. But all of a sudden afterwards, he thinks, What have I done?

I don't think there's ever been a Western where the fear of death is discussed so openly. Munny sees the maggots at the door, so to speak. Tell me about your attraction to this idea.

This first philosophizing about death is when he's reminiscing about killing this guy—the guy whose teeth he shot through the back of his head, he's kind of morose about it. He's haunted by the memory of this guy who didn't do anything to deserve to get shot. And then when he has fever, he starts hallucinating and he sees a guy with maggots crawling out of his head. He's constantly pursued by the visual image of what he's done in the past. Or images he's seen. Like for a guy who's been to war. Like for a guy who's seen the Lt. Calley [My Lai] massacre in Vietnam. There are certain things you'd like to put out of your mind.

Like for the guy who's made a lot of violent movies and carries around a lot of visual images from those movies in his head?

[Smiling] Well, I don't know if that's analogous ... it could be. It could be that the guy has all those violent images portrayed on the screen, and here comes along a piece of material that allows him to do something that he's never been able to do in the past—which is to show where it all leads to. To philosophize about what is the value of it all.

Did the Rodney King tape get to you?

[Pause.] First time you see it, you're overwhelmed. You're overwhelmed—boy, seems like a little much to me! 'Course you don't hear anything so you don't hear the dialogue, or what went on, the prelude to it all. But anyway, under any circumstances, that seemed excessive. But then I get mad at the media after a while for running it—'cause they're exploiting it. The exact same people that are critical of the exploitation of the violence are exploiting it every time they can, running it back and forth. I got tired of it. It's like now on TV news with accidents—they dolly in on the parts of a person. The media has gotten so calloused about it. It's all one-upmanship for ratings, so that's kind of annoying. But without knowing it, there are certainly parallels to what goes on in *Unforgiven*. What's so astute about the writing is that it is something that's gone on forever.

Beyond the preacher riding in, in Pale Rider, *and saying, "If there were more love in the world, there'd be less dying," do you have any thoughts on what perpetuates that cycle of violence?*

No. It just seems like part of history, from the Old Testament on, and sometimes it's done in the name of God and sometimes in the name of whatever. There's no shortage of rationalizations. Everything fits if you want it to. The whole Cold War was based on each side thinking it was right. And that's what's fun about a screenplay like this: Gene Hackman's character is right, that's the only way he knows how to do it—he knows all those tough towns, he knows if he sets up a good bunch of fear and kicks ass right away, that everyone is going to go away. He's a nice guy, he's building a house, he wants to see the sun set from his porch, he wants a peaceful life, he's not a bad guy.

And he doesn't "deserve" to die like he does. Your response is, "Deserve's got nothing to do with it." That's the Eastwood hero confronting the absurd, the irrational world in an emotionally unsatisfying but truthful way.

That's it. That's an "Eastwood hero" line in a very honest situation. It doesn't have *dick* to do with it.

The other "Eastwood hero" line in the movie is, when he's told the dead men had it coming, Munny says, "We've all got it coming." The interesting thing is that, while I think those lines will resonate for people, they are not like cartoon lines like "Make my day." If they punctuate the scene, they don't do it as exclamation marks, but more as question marks.

Yeah, they don't conclude the sequence. I never had the answers, but at sixty-two you realize you have fewer answers than you thought you had at thirty-two. At thirty-two you had them all.

In this film the punishment never fits the crime. It's never about justice, but about vengeance-meets-commerce, which I guess is what a bounty really is.

Justice never becomes part of it.

Justice is never even on the horizon.

Yeah, I don't think so. Justice doesn't have anything to do with it. It's about conscience more than justice. [Long pause.]

Leaving this movie, I couldn't imagine you ever again playing a comic-strip action character.

Yeah, I probably *can't*. I might inadvertently get involved in something like that, but I think the days of me doing what I have done in the past are gone. This film is my work of the present. And hopefully the work of tomorrow is an expansion of that. To be saying smart lines and wiping out tons of people—I'll leave that for others to do, for the newer guys on the scene. And that's just part of my growing process. I wouldn't know what to do with such a thing now; I'd have a hard time concentrating on it. At one point, I could throw myself into that; now, I need more of a demand. I don't know how to equivocate it: it's like you need more foreplay or something. [Laughs.] You need something better. You could knock out genre pieces all your life and you could do them like they did in the old days—start Monday. You could do four, five of them a year, and you'd have to luck into something good, like *Treasure of Sierra Madre*. They lucked into that.

Let me ask you about what I would call gun-control and penis-control in Unforgiven. *Ned asks Munny if he does it with his hand?*

Talking 'bout it like they're a bunch of kids! He's got a basic curiosity about it. You're out there by yourself a long time. It's not those hogs, is it? [Laughing]

And Munny says, "I don't miss it much." Which I take to mean the shooting and killing as well as the sex. The fact that you can't bring your gun into town. And twice we have the subject of bent guns: English Bob gets his gun back and it's comically bent, and when The Kid is spraying the field with gunfire, Ned rather demurely questions him as to whether his rifle might be bent. You don't have to be Sigmund Freud [Eastwood laughs] to understand that they're not just talking 'bout the guns here. And given that the whole narrative starts, the whole thing unwinds, because of a guy's insecurity about the size of his pecker. And that guy's name is Quick Mike: so he's quick as well as small, which I'm sure makes him a little sensitive.

Right. And there's also some lines Richard Harris is throwing out there. And there's also the Gene Hackman story about "Two-Gun" Corky Corcoran, whose dick was as long as the Walker Colt that he carried. Gene's story demythologizes the Western myth, right there, talking about what a chickenshit killing it was. And in a subsequent scene he talks about, it ain't so easy to shoot a guy, whereas in most Westerns it's pretty easy, rather effortless. [Long pause.]

The writer, as in White Hunter, Black Heart, *is the one who watches, who doesn't know, and who fabulates. "The desirability to take a liberty when depict-*

ing the cover scene" is the subject here, how you change reality to fit the demands of the marketplace. Well, that's also what a film has to do.

Exactly. It's just bringing that thing up: it's probably how history got so distorted to begin with. Everyone telling something in a bigger way. Like in this film, the story of the cut whore gets bigger and bigger every time it's told. Beauchamp, who's going to chronicle it, can't wait to distort it. And finally he gets to witness his big shootout.

And they start to recount the narrative before Munny is even out of the saloon.

It's an unusual approach. A very unusual approach. But one of my favorite films was *The Oxbow Incident*. You can see it today and it still holds up. The whole thing about mob violence. And it got a bad release because of only one person. The studio head's wife hated it. Zanuck's wife thought it was the worst piece of shit.

When you were finished shooting the shootout in the saloon, were you conscious of the fact that it may be the last time you do something like that?

Uh-huh. [Pause.]

How did that feel?

It felt okay. It felt good. I must say I was even conscious throughout the film that this might be my last Western. I felt that this was the perfect story to be my last Western. I also thought that this might be the last time I do both jobs—acting and directing—on a picture. Maybe it's time to do one or the other. It's funny, you're the first person who's kind of picked up on that, but I did have a feeling when I was doing that sequence that it would probably be the last time.

That's what's great about how you warn everyone when you come out of the saloon. Not only are you going to kill them, but you're going to kill their families, their friends, you're going to burn down their houses if they threaten you. [Eastwood laughs.] So I thought in terms of the directorial writing there, it felt like William Munny and Clint Eastwood saying—if you threaten me again, I'm going to kill everybody, so this is it!

So this is the end of it! And there's also a slight fear in that. Instead of walking out like a bold Western hero, he's aware he can't let his guard down—don't shoot me now, I'm coming out—you come near me, here's how bad I am: I'll kill your friends, your girlfriend, your boyfriend, your sister, your brother, your mother, and right on down the line.

And then there's the matter of the postscript. He fled probably to San Francisco with the kids and prospered in dry goods.

Well, some say he might have prospered. No one really knows. I think it's ambiguous. It's up to the audience. We know he's got two kids and we may wish him a good life.

Although it's not in the film, did you imagine what his homecoming to those kids must have been like? Emotionally, for that character?

Yeah. Actually, I played it out. There was a homecoming scene.

That was the only thing I left the movie feeling a lack of. I wanted to see how he'd face the kids, which is really how he would face himself.

It was a good scene. I could show it to you and you'd be the only person in the world to see it. It was a good scene but the movie was over. It seemed like it broke a mood.

Did he reconnect to the kids?

Yes, he comes back and the son tells him The Kid's come by and left them his share of the money, and then the son asks him if he's killed anyone. William sort of lies to him. It was good, but it opened up something, and I felt it was best to end it where it was. Whether it was right or wrong, I don't know, but it seemed like the right thing to do. So it ends with that last look at Ned, lying there dead, propped up like a showpiece, like they used to do in those days, and those women looking at him, and their inner feelings—it's just enough. Then the visit to the grave and the scroll, as an epilogue.

I love endings that let people put what they want into them. They can add whatever they want. I had an argument years before with an editor. In *The Outlaw Josey Wales*, when Josey Wales rides back out of town in the end, the editor said, "Why don't we put a superimposition of the girl there, so we know he rides back to the girl." And I said, "There is no need to do that, because the audience is willing that, anyway." Even if he rides out north and the girl and the family that he left are east, we know that he's going to circle back around and come back to the east. Because that's where they want him to go; that's what they're willing to happen. So to put a superimposition would be really corny.

But the editor wanted that closure.

Yes. He wanted the wrap-up. You can't do that. It's not necessary. The audience is willing this reunion to happen: he goes back and stays with that family and his life is great. In the audience's mind. But some audiences might say, Well, it's not that easy. The woman died in childbirth two years later, and he goes off to camp with the Indians. Who knows? There are dozens of ways to go.

SESSION TWO

Let's stick with Unforgiven. *In the scene with the whore, Delilah, Munny admits that he's scarred. Now, in your oeuvre, as we discussed, there are many protagonists who are scarred, who are badly wounded—in an emotional sense—but who wouldn't talk about it. They'd act out of the feeling, but they wouldn't verbalize it. So perhaps now you're giving sanction to the idea that it's okay to talk about these things.*

He's obviously beat up. He's saying, You're a beautiful woman, you're not ugly like me. This man carries so many demons, he feels like a very unworthy person. When Ned says, "Do you ever go to town to find a woman?" he replies, "What would a woman want with a man like me?" I think he has very low self-worth.

But the fact that he verbalizes *that seems different, seems like something new for your persona. Instead of just acting out of the feeling—whether a lack of self-worth, or a bitterness, or a rage—rather than just acting out of it in an explosive way, he verbalizes it. That seems like something new.*

Yeah. I think it's new in the context that everything else is new in the piece, too. The whole character is different, if you're relating it to my other characters, who, if they had demons, they suppressed them, or else they dealt with them, and they're gone. They're not haunting.

Earlier you said, unprovoked by me I might add, that you are "not doing penance" for all the other characters you've played. Obviously, that concept is something that's on your mind.

I said that unprovoked, but I said that in such a way that *maybe it is*. I'm not *consciously* doing penance for the mayhem I have created on the screen in the past, but in a way, it fits in. That's why it's perfect for it to be the last Western. Because he is a man that is haunted by this experience. And he's driven back into doing what he thinks he does best. It's not a conscious thing to do penance—if I hadn't done those other pictures nobody would even think about it. But like you were mentioning, a lot of those people had things in their backgrounds that were kind of painful. This is the first one where you know all about it. He's been involved with some pretty bad mayhem in his day.

And yet the interesting thing about the end of the picture is that it eats its cake and has it too. In the end, he still is the killer that he was—it's there at a moment's reach, when it needs to be.

He goes on a suicide mission, and gets away with it. Because he doesn't have that fear of shooting a man, that thing that Gene Hackman talks about earlier.

Another theme that comes up in your work a lot is regeneration through violence. That violence is not simply an end, but a means to something else happening: it's cleansing. Something good comes out of it, even if it's off screen, at the end of the movie. Those people in Lago are going to know something different than they did before, in High Plains Drifter. *And rain is usually a good metaphor to wash things clean. In this film, everyone knows they need a good rain, but we feel at the end of the movie that what the rain will bring is mud. There is no regeneration through the violence that's occurred.*

Yeah. He's pretty well wiped out the whole law enforcement faction of the community. [Laughs, pauses.] I don't know what to tell you on that one. The rain has a washing effect, but maybe it is turning to mud. The meaning of the symbol for each person may be different.

Do you feel the lack of regeneration is pessimistic, here?

A little, yeah. What's going to happen to the girls? Are they going to run the whorehouse by themselves now, without this guy lording over them? What are they going to do? What is Delilah going to do, after she sees him ride off? He's probably the only man she's opened the door with, had a discussion with about her feelings about being scarred up. Where it all goes from there is in the eye of the beholder.

Another thing that shows up in your work, again and again, is a kind of attachment to the dispossessed, which the protagonist usually shows. There's an affinity for the downtrodden and the dispossessed. Now I can't believe that you've blundered into these characters accidentally; there's obviously a self-selection process here, so I assume that you share this same affinity. Am I correct?

I probably have an affinity for the underdog, the downtrodden, the depressed. Who knows why? Either it's dramatically, or being raised during the Depression. I don't know. Seeing a lot of that growing up in the '30s. I've never analyzed it. I never had the ambition to. I occasionally think about why do I like this? Why do I like that? Somewhere along the line there's some inkling of something, that makes you gravitate towards a certain type of thing.

Like in *Heartbreak Ridge*, I was always wondering what it's like to be a military guy—what happens when you're a warrior and there's no war. You're an outcast. I remember being in the military during the Korean War, everybody stopped on the highway to pick up soldiers. You could stick your thumb out and you wouldn't wait two seconds. And then, right after the war, it all died out: you were just dogfaces walking down the highway. Who could care less? And several moods passed during the Vietnam escapade. But what happens to somebody who doesn't know anything but one thing? To the point where it has disturbed his whole life, his relationship with women, his former wife. 'Cause he only knows one thing, and how do you do a cram course in life when you're at the end of your military career? There's no answer to it. I don't have an answer to any of my characters, really. Its fun to open them up and explore them, but I don't come up with any great conclusions.

The dispossessed, downtrodden underdog which your film persona is so attached to seems quite different than your public persona away from the screen as a card-carrying Republican. Society tends not to view Republicans as critters who have that sort of affinity. That tends to fall to the Jesse Jackson Rainbow Coalition.

Well, I'm not in any of those camps. I'm not in the Jesse Jackson's Rainbow Coalition and I'm not in the Republicans' camp. I became a Republican only because when I turned twenty-one, Eisenhower was running and I wanted to vote for him, as opposed to Stevenson. So I did that. And also, the Republicans were a minority and it's fun to be part of a minority. At that time, they were outnumbered three-to-one in California. So I just became that. But actually, I would say that my views are probably leaning towards sort of a libertarian point of view.

You're a bloody anarchist!!

Not liberal. Liberal always has the connotation of somebody that wants to spend somebody else's money. And conservatives don't want to spend any of their own money. But libertarians love independence and I like everyone leaving everyone else alone. I've never approved of government meddling in just about anything. Whatever people want to do is fine, as long as you're not bothering anybody else.

So you're looking for a fusion of Milton Friedman and Noam Chomsky.

Yeah, exactly!

You get those two guys together, you've got a ticket.

You could. You've got a much better chance of getting those two guys together than some of these guys we've got now.

Let's look at your two stretch-mark movies: Bird *and* White Hunter, Black Heart.

Left stretch-marks inside my brain, just over the cranium.

Spike Lee was quite upset with Bird. *He told me, How is it when Clint Eastwood does a movie about Charlie Parker, that the two other most important people in the movie, Chan Parker and Red Rodney, are white? How can it be that Red Rodney gets more screen time in the movie, is more important, than Dizzy Gillespie? And why is it we only see Chan, and not Bird's two black wives? Spike felt the movie was racist in that regard, in that it presents Bird surrounded by white people.*

You know, it's a shame to take—and I think it's reverse racism, although I'm sure he doesn't quite know what he speaks of, I think he's a clever kid—but it's ironic to take jazz, which is at the forefront of all integration in this country, or anywhere in the world for that matter, and in the early days in New Orleans, where people were judged just by what they did, and not by their color, and even though bands were segregated, by necessity sometimes in the '30s and '40s due to where they were playing in the country—Stan Kenton had a white band and Count Basie had a black band cause you could only do it that way, and we touched on that in *Bird*—but in the early days of jazz, the creoles and blacks and whites, everybody respected everybody for what they were doing.

Well, the music simply would not have existed as a form without black and white coming together.

Exactly. And they were the predecessors of all integration, in this country, and is the truest American art form. And for some guy to come along, *now*, in the '90s, and try to segregate it in his mind, is . . . [Pause, frustrated.] Chan existed, and it is Chan's book that most of the material was taken from. She was with Bird during his most productive years. I met his first wife, she came to see me. She was with him when he was seventeen, and she was like sixteen. And they were married for a very few years. He didn't become a star until way after he'd left her. But Chan was with him on 52nd Street in the heyday years. Red Rodney was with him a lot of times, too. So was Dizzy. They were all participating in the film. The Red Rodney incident, of him travelling through the South with them, happened to be rather humorous, and it was true. But that didn't diminish all the black actors who were in that film. Forrest Whitaker certainly had the best part in the movie. So I don't know what Spike Lee is talking about. I think he was just shooting from the lip a little bit. I'm sure if he stopped and thought about it, he wouldn't worry about it. I wouldn't be prejudiced if he wanted to do a thing on Mozart or Beethoven. That would be great, more power to him. From a film director's point of view, being a black man doesn't preclude you from doing a white story. Women could do that: how dare a male director do the story of Madame Curie?

Well, this was the argument I had with him about Malcolm X. *Not that I don't think he should be the one to direct it, but I differ with his concept that "only a black person should be allowed to direct* Malcolm X.*" You're on a slippery slope with that rationale.*

It takes all black directors and says, Okay, all white directors will lay off black subjects. Speilberg won't do *The Color Purple*, and blacks can only do stories about blacks. That's pretty limited, I would say. Spike Lee, I'm sure he has ambitions to do a wide array of work sometime within the next twenty years.

Bird *was almost but not quite a non-narrative film. It certainly was, for a major motion picture release by a big studio with a name director, as far out, in terms of linearity, as I've seen in many, many years. And from an unlikely source. What were you thinking, Clint?*

I was just out there soloing, along with everybody else. To me *Bird*, the flashbacks within flashbacks, the doublebacking into flashbacks, is very complicated; but I think if a person paid attention, they could gather it all and still come back to ground zero, back to square one, and still be intact with the film. And I hope I accomplished that. But the nature of the film, the nature of Parker's life, the nature of an addict, of a jazzman, all those things sort of lend themselves to that sort of narrative structure.

Were you basing the concept on the nature of a Parker solo—off certain sets of chord changes—which overlaps, and goes back, and reinterprets, and leaps forward, and so on?

Yeah, I guess so. He would sometimes find a figure and work his away around it until he could exhaust it. But I can't consciously say. I could make up something that would sound really cineaste and intellectual—

We won't blow your cover, here—

—but I'd just be bullshitting the hell out of you, because it's just the nature of the way it unravelled. It seemed logical for it to unravel that way. The script was generally leaning towards that. I did a lot of changing in that particular one, as opposed to *Unforgiven*, where I stayed very close to the writer's concept. That's just the way I saw it. If I was an alto player, that's the way I'd play it.

What were you hoping the audience would take away from that film?

Just an atmosphere, an atmosphere of a brilliant person who was obviously very disturbed, but he was a *brilliant* person. And also an era of American music, where probably the last great harmonic frontier was crossed, in the bop generation. When the last great leap in music was made. People didn't used to play like that. It was a shock. I can only tell you from being there, it was something else. Musicians thought, God damn, those guys are playing some wild stuff and the general public thought, What the hell is that? And eventually, the musicians picked up on it and the public thought it was interesting. And certain groups came in and made it more commercial. I saw Dizzy's big band when I was sixteen. It was exciting, exciting stuff.

What did you learn doing Bird?

It was a great enjoyment for me. What I learned I'd have to work backwards to, because I don't know. I learn something from every project. Delving into jazz, delving into the bop generation, visualizing seeing Charlie Parker for the first time, which was quite an experience and no record quite captures it. Wow! He was the most confident artist I had ever seen. Self-confidence, without twitching a muscle. It was pin-stripe suits and ties. Charlie Parker just stood there and played. The combination of sound and effortlessness. And you listen to tapes of him speaking: he was very lucid and glib, very well-spoken and well-thinking, but obviously there was a crazy side to him.

Did you figure out anything about the crazy side, the madness, in doing the project?

No, but I've delved into that in other films: the self-destructiveness. He was one of those guys who was going to soar for a short period of time. There's an irony at the end of the picture, where the doctor who finds him thinks he's an old man. There's something about a guy who's rushing through it like that: does he know something? Does he know it's going to end early? Is he afraid of something? It's kind of like, would James Dean be as popular today, and as mysterious a figure, if he'd lived on and made ten or fifteen more films, and eight of them not so good. Maybe a couple pretty good, and maybe a couple of great ones. There's something about dying at your peak. And although Charlie Parker didn't die at his peak, there was a lot of mystery about him. Buddy Jones, a friend of mine, used to play bass for him, and he told me, all the musicians would jump in cars and drive all night just to see him play, to hear what he was doing. It's interesting to wonder what makes a guy like that tick. The story doesn't really say what makes him tick.

You don't explain his genius at all in the picture.

Never did. The only thing I would do is to tell Forrest Whitaker all the time not to be scattered, to keep his line, to remember he's the best alto saxophone player in the world, to stay his line, not to be afraid when he wanted something—don't be looking all over—get onto it: what you do, you do the very best, and you know that.

Why does the film not provide more about what and where he came from, in a psychological and emotional way?

It just wasn't written that way. It was taken from Chan's book, *My Life in E Flat*. It was taken from her point of view, and Red Rodney chipped in a lot, too. But getting back to what you were talking about, somebody trying to make it prejudiced—a white and black thing. There were just a lot of mixed players around. Bird hung out with a lot of black people and a lot of white people. People didn't care. Bop musicians were radicals. They could care less.

Why did you never show Bird practicing? One of the criticisms of the film is that it made Bird out to be a natural genius, as if it all came to him on the bandstand, and there wasn't the blood, sweat, and tears of woodshedding. Much as some people look at Michael Jordan as if he came out of the womb a brilliant basketball player, and there wasn't an awful lot of hard work involved.

Obviously, they practiced incessantly. There was a point in Bird's life where the drummer did throw a cymbal at Bird because he was so bad—he left and never played publicly for a year. He just practiced around the clock.

So why didn't the film show that?

That's another story. There's another story with Dizzy. There's another story with Miles. They never got on that well, but the fact is they worked together. If someone was doing my life, there's a lot of sections to it, but in a movie maybe they could only do one. Bird practicing? Well, we showed him practicing as a kid.

Speaking of your life, and you mentioned Miles conveniently enough, I'd like to bring up the epigraph of the film, which is Fitzgerald's "There are no second acts in American lives." Your life has obviously had more than a second act. I know the quote was fitting for Bird's life, but do you believe in the concept?

It seemed fitting for him, because he was only going to live the one act. For me, no, it's a three-act play. I hope. [Laughs.] Hopefully the play pyramids, and doesn't falter in the end.

Miles, of course, had about five acts in his.

Yeah, he had a lot of different facets to his career. And then after he had that wreck in the Lamborghini and broke his hip, he retired and had all his drug and booze problems, but he came back. I first met him in Seattle. I was doing *Rawhide* at the time, it was quite a few years ago, in the late '50s or early '60s. He wasn't with Coltrane yet. And he came over at intermission and asked me, [imitating Miles' hoarse rasp] "Will you send a picture to Miles Jr.? Miles Jr. is a fan of yours." I said, "Sure, Miles. I'll send one out." Then he told me to hang out and I said I would. So after the set he came over and said, "Let's go out and get some *bitches*." So we went out to some after-hours joint, Seattle was kind of a closed town, but these clubs would last till way in the morning. So we went out, and screwed off, and went down to this joint on First Avenue. Man, he was a character! And I'd see him after that, and we always had kind of a pretty decent relationship, but I never did talk to him about Bird, only because the story never did include that part of Bird's life, and I thought I had all the impressions I needed.

A last question about Bird: *I never saw a color film that felt and looked to me so much like a black-and-white film.*

Yeah, that was purposeful. And so was *Unforgiven*, too, in a way, in that I approached the art direction, costuming, and the cinematography—the whole film—like it was black-and-white. There is something about black-and-white films that have great drama to them. But you can't just photograph them that way, you have to do it from the art direction, the costuming, and so on, everything has to fit.

I mean, Bird *was a dark movie. It was dark in every way: in tone, in feeling, in spirit, in execution.*

In spirit, yeah.

It was so dark that I know some people who care about Bird, who know he had demons, wished it showed a bit more of his joy.

Well, there was joy there. I think there are happy moments in the picture. But it's a tragedy that someone that brilliant dies at such a young age. What makes him destruct like that? Why the destruction? It's so unnecessary. What a waste. Maybe that's the way it was meant to be.

Speaking of another guy who may have squandered talent, but who didn't go out quickly: John Huston. Is your doing White Hunter, Black Heart *a little bit like Huston going after the big bull elephant?*

No, not really. Some of his movies left big impressions on me. *Treasure of Sierra Madre* remains one of my favorites. The fascinating thing about Huston is that he was a real crazy character—he lived a very hard life, he smoked and drank and never took good care of himself—but he lived quite long and unlike a lot of directors he directed up to the very end, in a wheelchair and with an oxygen tank on *The Dead.* It's kind of a strange thing, when a guy can just wreck himself like that. He did some crap—there was a period of years where I don't think he did anything good, and then all of a sudden he does *The Man Who Would Be King.* Just when you thought he didn't have it, he'd surprise you, and give it to you.

Why did you make that picture? Your personal affection for him?

I just liked the story a lot. I agree with a lot of his philosophy, even though I'm not a total dissipate like he was. Even though we're at opposite ends of the poles as far as feelings of responsibility to the financiers, his ideas of how he approached the film—how he would do the best he could, and move forward, and never worry about who was going to see it, and to be true to what you believed in—there's a lot to be said for that.

The wonderful tyranny of whimsy.

Yes. He needed a lot of outside activities: whether it was some gal he was chasing or a racehorse he was running or betting on, he needed a lot of distractions to keep him going.

Are you that way?

Not necessarily. But I can work on several things at one time.

Your reputation is being quite disciplined and organized in making a film, of coming in under budget and early, so I wonder if for you there was a little perverse satisfaction in exploring a director who ignored the clock?

Well, maybe. On another note, he kind of knew what he wanted, and only shot what he wanted. He was a very lean director. He didn't shoot a ton of stuff. He wasn't like George Stevens, who was at the opposite end of the spectrum and would cover everything. Huston was of the school of Howard Hawks and John Ford. They knew what they wanted to put down. Maybe he was a little looser than they were. He came up in that era, but he did some crazy things—went off to Europe, to Africa. He did a couple of interesting pictures back to back: he did *African Queen*, then went straight up to Paris and did *Moulin Rouge*. Totally different kinds of films. With little preparation, he did some amazing things.

Both White Hunter *and* Bird *have to do with the demands of art and how we harness or don't harness the irrational. Now, it may have been a stretch you playing Huston, but of course it would have been more of a stretch you playing Bird. [Eastwood laughs.]*

I liked playing Huston. There's a certain way about him. When I was in the military, in 1951, I subbed as a projectionist. And over the couple years I was doing this I must have run *The Battle of San Pietro* I don't know how many times—so many times I could tell you every shot in it. It was done by Huston, and narrated by Huston. And there was something about his approach. I think I learned more about him from that than actually watching him with his face on camera. I saw all the footage of Orson Welles' last picture, where Huston plays a director, much like himself, which was never released. Welles' widow wanted me to complete the film. And I saw that two-hour documentary on Huston which came out a few years ago. And you talk to people. And Peter Viertel was a close friend of John's. They had a big falling out and that's why Viertel wrote the book. Everyone thought he had zapped his friend, but when he wrote the book he was actually on good terms with Huston and John had given the book his blessing.

It's quite a curious film. What do you think it's about?

It's about obsession, about obsessive personality. On the one hand you're showing a man with a macabre sense of humor, who will take people to the most uncomfortable place in the world to film. He and Bogart are the only ones who didn't get sick down there, because they drank so much. They drank so much whiskey that their systems couldn't be penetrated by the bugs. [Laughs.] These guys had about eight percent alcohol in their systems. To go down there, and then to wander off and want to go off hunting. Everything in the picture is true, except that Kivu didn't die.

Why couldn't he pull the trigger?

In the book he pulls the trigger, and the elephant charges and kills Kivu and wreaks mayhem all over the place. I didn't think it was necessary to pull the trigger. I felt if Kivu got killed, that's the whole lesson: he doesn't have to kill the elephant. It tells the same thing, without putting down the animal, which I certainly wouldn't do for the film. To me, I would never shoot an animal for a film.

Well, Industrial Light and Magic could have rigged up a Babar for you to shoot between the eyes—

Oh I could have done it, it can be tricked up. But I just didn't think it was necessary. I think it shows: we shouldn't have been here in the first place. What are we doing out here?

Is the trauma going to make him a better artist?

I think so. When he starts the film, which will be *The African Queen*, he makes a film that's a very popular film.

Of course we're to think that he doesn't give a damn whether it's popular or not; he's just out to make what he thinks is a good film.

Yeah. Viertel wrote the dialogue, "You can't let six million popcorn eaters push you this way or that way." It doesn't matter. Do the film the way you believe it, and if they want to come to it, that's fine. And that whole cynicism of it: that he was going to die flat-broke in a Los Angeles flophouse, and they're going to name a special Academy Award after him and all the wrong guys will win it. [Laughs.] It's cynical, but it's so true. How many times has Irving Thalberg rolled over in his grave when they give out his award?

There's a line of dialogue from the film, which impressed me, vis a vis your work, your career, your filmmaking, and I'd like you to react to it: "We're lousy little gods who control the lives of the people we create."

Yeah, he definitely believed that.

I'm not so much interested in Huston's attitude as much as how you apply these things to your own work.

I don't think in those terms. That's a very flamboyant person, who goes on about being "lousy little gods." I would never wax that poetic.

You'd say something more like, "We're lousy little shits—"

I'd say, Hey, we're leading the audience on a tour, and it's up to them to follow. We're leading the tour. We're the tour guide. This is the way we're going. If you think defensively, and you worry—why would they think this? or what if they think that? or why would anybody want to come and see this film? Why does anybody want to get up in the morning?—it's not necessary to ask those questions.

Do you think about the audience at all when you're making a film?

I think about it when I first read the material, when I get involved in the decision to make the film. I think, Would the audience like to see this? And would I like to see this film? Would I like to play in this film? Would I like to direct this film? Now, I've gotten that far. Then there's a time when you have to shut all that off, and say, Now we make the film, we never look back at the audience. Sometimes it's tempting to say, Hey we can wrap this up, and make a real happy Hollywood ending, but you're worrying too much about the audience then. You've got to trust it. In golf they use the expression, "Trust your swing." It's a narrow fairway out there, and you've got to trust that you can hit the ball down that line. You've got to trust that the audience is going to come with you. You're entering the tunnel, and they will follow you. And if they don't, they weren't going to in the first place.

Were you frustrated that not as many people followed you into the tunnel on Bird *and* White Hunter *as you might have liked?*

No. Nobody makes a film for an empty house, or purposely drives people out of the house. It's just that you make a film, and if it falls between the cracks and doesn't have the broad appeal, that isn't what you make it for. I would still make them the same way. You can't second guess that. The average moviegoing audience of twenty-five-to-thirty-year-olds is probably not interested in John Huston or Charlie Parker. Maybe that kind of character is too far removed. There are not that many kind of one-of-a-kind people, and not many people are exposed to that kind of persona.

Do you feel yourself working against the clock, now?

No. No, in fact, I'm working more relaxed now. Like I mentioned earlier, I'd had *Unforgiven* for quite a while, and could have done it before. I don't know what little voice in me says the time is right for something.

What's given you the feeling of relaxation you have now about your own work?

[Long pause.] I have no secret key. I've just been taking a longer look at the material. I've done a few things along the way that have kind of been thrown together, and sometimes you do that. How was it for John Ford in those days of six, seven movies a year? And for the actors, how did they do it? Get down to wardrobe and learn these lines, boom. Directors didn't sit there and say, I need fourteen weeks of editing.

They didn't do it like Warren Beatty does it now.

Jesus, how did *The Grapes of Wrath* come out so good when they didn't do all that? When they didn't take all that time. They were real craftsmen and had real confidence. Either that, or they had nothing to lose. There was a different mindset in those times.

Why have you not written a film?

I've written sequences and scenes, and reworked scripts, but I've never done one from scratch. I've never come up with one. I'm not sure I'd be any good at it. A man's gotta know his limitations.

Okay, you've made your quota of one Eastwood line per interview.

I mean: what kind of a mind would you have to have to come up with a story like Huston does to tell off that anti-Semitic woman in *White Hunter*? Most people would say, "You're full of shit. You're a bigot, you're an asshole." But to lure somebody in, and sucker her around, and throw this zap story at her. You'd have to be a real perverse bastard, to enjoy it so much. Maybe it's that Irish storytelling tradition. The set-up is half the fun.

He builds a great scaffold and then he drops her from it.

And building the scaffold is the fun part.

Exactly. The hanging is a foregone conclusion. Which is itself a metaphor for what you guys do: you build elaborate scaffolds from which to drop stories.

Yeah. That's probably why Huston's mind was good for filmmaking.

Are you going to write an autobiography?

Not for a while. I've been approached a lot. I always say there's no way to write an autobiography when I'm in the middle of it.

Well, when you're done with it, it's too late. Do you see this decade as a time when you'll be able to take some acting roles for some of the directors you highly esteem?

When I first came up in the '50s, I never had a chance to work for any of the great directors. I never had the chance to work for Ford or Hawks or Hitchcock or Zinnemann or Stevens or Wilder. I didn't have a chance to work for any of those guys. I was a bit player, and then when I became well known, they were either dead or retired. I knew Frank Capra, and got to spend time with him over the years, but never worked for him.

Are you thinking more now about the possibilities of forgiveness and redemption than you did as a younger man? This is something I talked to Francis about, as he was doing Godfather III, *since those were the themes of that film, as they are in* Unforgiven.

If I have, I haven't thought about it. Maybe by getting the property at an early age and setting it aside until now, I was preparing for a certain time. I thought the subject was interesting then, and thought it would become more interesting as time went on. It just seemed like the perfect last western. And it delves into things I wanted to delve into. As we as a society grow more tolerant of violence, of accepting life and death in the streets, and we don't seem to put our foot down. It seemed to be a much more serious thing for generations past. It seems we get hardened.

We accept a higher and higher level of despicable behavior on a daily basis.

I know it. Like for judges: well, the victim wasn't my daughter or my son or my family, we can tolerate it and move on. As our society drifts that way, maybe from my point of view, it was time to analyze it from how it affects people. The perpetrator and the perpetratee.

Outside the golden rectangle of Hollywood projection, are things in our society not going the way you thought they were going to go ten, twelve years ago? Were you more hopeful then?

Maybe. Sometimes you just wonder. It seems like the entertainment and communications industries have become so big, and they are so competitive, that it seems like as far as violence and mayhem go, there's a great competition to get it meaner and deeper on the front page of every paper. You got to beat the guy across the street. We see a lot more than we did years ago. Vietnam brought war into the living room. And now the Rodney King beating runs 57,000 times on television.

But Clint, I'm not sure which is better, because now we've had a war that rehabilitated the whole idea of an old-fashioned war, where you don't see anybody die on the battlefield. In the Gulf, we didn't seen any real human cost to that war, because we didn't see the pictures of the charred Iraqi bodies.

I'm just using this as a tolerance level. Now, when a child has been run over by a car, there are microphones stuck into faces of the parents, and guys asking, What are your feelings at this moment?

It's the decline of civility.

Yes, absolutely. Where does it end? That's the commerce, that's the capitalism of the electronic media: how do you cut to the most blood? Maybe there is a penance there. Maybe that's why Gene Hackman didn't want to be involved in violence.

Well, the action pictures now make Dirty Harry *seem like* Oklahoma.

Oh yeah, like nothing. You look at pictures where people are dismembering people, and saying, "Here, let me give you a hand." Dirty Harry would never do that. Dirty Harry just wanted to rid the streets of the anti-social, people working against society. But now, it's like everything is mobs of mayhem out there: cut 'em up, kill 'em up, dismember 'em, cut their heads off. I don't know what effect this has on society. Maybe none. I grew up with Jimmy Cagney blowing guys away and Humphrey Bogart blowing guys away and John Wayne, but everybody knew the difference between a movie and reality.

There wasn't even a ratings system during the Crusades, and there was still plenty of violence.

Yeah, there was more mayhem created in the name of God—my God is more right than yours; but in the '60s and '70s we were entering into the fall-guy generation and we're at the peak of it now, where nobody is responsible for their own actions. It's like: I can't help the way I am, my mother accidentally backhanded me when I was a kid, and she had PMS. There's all kinds of reasons for things, instead of people grabbing themselves by the gut and saying, This is what I have to atone to. But that's the era we're living in now, and it's being bred into us. It's always somebody else's fault. Right now, politically we get that, is it the Congress's fault or the President's fault? Get with it, it's everybody's fault. But nobody wants to take responsibility. Congress is sitting there worried about their perks and President Bush is worried about being re-elected. Aw shit!

And no one will make a courageous decision. Not even old H. Ross Perot.

I think the only reason his popularity is as high as it is, is that people are thinking, Maybe there's a guy who *could* make possibly make a courageous decision. And they're figuring that neither the Republicans nor the Democrats have the balls to do it. [Nine hours after this interview ended, Perot announced he would not run.] If he came out and said, I only want to be there one term. Instead of spending three-quarters of the first terms setting yourself up for the second.

Ol' George has said he will "do anything he has to do" to get re-elected. As if that were the objective for all government, simply to stay in power. Which is a horrible idea.

Yeah, it's horrible. I mean, Nixon went out in disgrace, but at least his first term was somewhat presentable. He opened up a lot of dialogue. Now, it's pathetic.

But you're happy just being the ex-mayor of Carmel!

I was so happy. It was a two-year term, and council members are four years. About one year into it, I thought, You know something, Eastwood, it's really nice this is only a two-year term, because that's exactly what it's going to be for you.

Did it teach you anything about government in America?

[Pause.] It's *fucked*. [Much laughter.] Whether it's a small town or a big city, whatever the size of the playing board is, it's the same problems. It seems like my best move as a politician is that I got in by a great majority, so I just made all my moves in the first six months. I fired the planning commission, I dumped, I changed everything—things that normally would be quite shocking, I did quickly.

Seize the day.

I seized it, grabbed it, ran with it, and I got things done, like a library annex, that had been pending for twenty-five years. I could have hung around for another term and done a few more things, but it would have been half of what I did that first term. Plus the fact that you can't have a career. I did two films while I was mayor—*Heartbreak Ridge* and *Bird*.

No wonder Bird *was so dark, it was actually about the city council!*

[Laughing] It was my city council meeting! And in *Heartbreak Ridge* I was playing a character who I'd really like to have been as mayor. Stand tall and take names!

David Breskin was born in Chicago in 1958. In New York City, from 1980 through the early 1990s, he wrote on cultural and socio-political subjects for *Esquire*, *Gentlemen's Quarterly*, *LIFE*, *The Village Voice*, *Musician*, and most prominently, *Rolling Stone*, where he was a contributing editor. He is the author of a novel, *The Real Life Diary of a Boomtown Girl* (Viking, 1989), and a book of poems, *Fresh Kills* (Cleveland State University, 1997). His poetry has appeared in many periodicals, including *The New Yorker*, *The Paris Review*, *DoubleTake*, *TriQuarterly*, *New American Writing*, *Salmagundi*, and *Boulevard*. In addition, he's produced records for jazz artists Bill Frisell, John Zorn, Joey Baron, Ronald Shannon Jackson, Vernon Reid, and Tim Berne. He lives on Russian Hill in San Francisco.

Other titles of interest

**AN ILLUSTRATED
HISTORY OF HORROR
AND SCIENCE-FICTION
FILMS**
The Classic Era, 1895–1967
Carlos Clarens
New introd. by J. Hoberman
328 pp., 135 illus.
80800-5 $14.95

ELIA KAZAN
A Life
Elia Kazan
864 pp., 130 photos
80804-8 $19.95

**BUSTER KEATON:
CUT TO THE CHASE**
A Biography
by Marion Meade
464 pp., 51 photos
80802-1 $16.95

A TALENT FOR TROUBLE
**The Life of Hollywood's
Most Acclaimed Director,
William Wyler**
Jan Herman
544 pp., 33 photos
80798-X $16.95

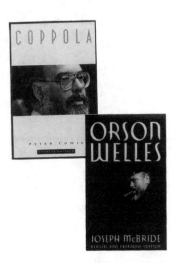

THE AMERICAN CINEMA
**Directors and Directions,
1929–1968**
Andrew Sarris
393 pp.
80728-9 $14.95

BILLY WILDER
Updated Edition
Bernard F. Dick
192 pp., 25 photos, film stills, and
frame enlargements
80729-7 $13.95

CHAPLIN
His Life and Art
David Robinson
896 pp., 185 illus.
80600-2 $21.95

**THE CINEMA OF
ORSON WELLES**
Peter Cowie
262 pp., 131 photos
80201-5 $14.95

COPPOLA
A Biography
Updated Edition
Peter Cowie
352 pp., 89 photos
80598-7 $14.95

CRIME MOVIES
Carlos Clarens
Updated by Foster Hirsch
376 pp., 212 illus.
80768-8 $15.95

THE DARK SIDE OF THE SCREEN
Film Noir
Foster Hirsch
229 pp., 188 photos
80203-1 $17.95

GROUCHO AND ME
Groucho Marx
Foreword by James Thurber
390 pp., 22 photos
80666-5 $14.95

THE GROUCHO LETTERS
Letters from and to Groucho Marx
319 pp.
80607-X $13.95

HITCH
The Life and Times of
Alfred Hitchcock
John Russell Taylor
336 pp., 31 photos
80677-0 $14.95

JOHN FORD
Joseph McBride and
Michael Wilmington
234 pp., 104 photos
80016-0 $11.95

MEMOIRS OF A
MANGY LOVER
Groucho Marx
224 pp., 45 illus.
80769-6 $13.95

MIDNIGHT MOVIES
J. Hoberman and
Jonathan Rosenbaum
360 pp., 81 illus.
80433-6 $14.95

MY WONDERFUL WORLD
OF SLAPSTICK
Buster Keaton and
Charles Samuels
282 pp.
80178-7 $13.95